MW01640116

North Korea in Transition

North Korea in Transition

Prospects for Economic and Social Reform

Edited by

Chang-Ho Yoon
Korea University, South Korea

and

Lawrence J. Lau
Stanford University, USA

Edward Elgar
Cheltenham, UK • Northampton, MA, USA

Published by
Edward Elgar Publishing Limited
Glensanda House
Montpellier Parade
Cheltenham
Glos GL50 1UA
UK

Edward Elgar Publishing, Inc.
136 West Street
Suite 202
Northampton
Massachusetts 01060
USA

A catalogue record for this book
is available from the British Library

Library of Congress Cataloguing in Publication Data

North Korea in transition : prospects for economic and social reform / edited by Chang-Ho Yoon and Lawrence J. Lau.
p. cm.
Based on papers from the conference, Developing social infrastructure in North Korea for economic cooperation between the South and the North, held at Korea University, Seoul, Nov. 1998.
1. Korea (North)—Economic conditions. 2. Korea (North)—Economic policy. 3. Korea (North)—Social conditions. I. Yoon, Chang-Ho, 1949– II. Lau, Lawrence J., 1944–

HC470.2 .N67 2001
338.95193—dc21

00–066240

ISBN 1 84064 623 3

Printed and bound in Great Britain by MPG Books Ltd, Bodmin, Cornwall

Contents

List of Figures vii
List of Tables ix
List of Contributors xiii
Preface xv
Acknowledgement xvii

PART ONE Introduction

1. Overview 3
Lawrence J. Lau and Chang-Ho Yoon

PART TWO The Political Economy of North Korea

2. North Korean Economy Today 19
Bradley O. Babson
3. Development, Structure and Performance of the DPRK Economy: Empirical Hints 29
Nicholas Eberstadt

PART THREE Development Potential under Reform

4. North Korea in Global Perspective 69
Marcus Noland
5. Policy Reforms and the Prospects of Economic Growth in North Korea 94
Jong-Wha Lee

PART FOUR The Experience of Other Transition Economies

6. Reform without Losers: a Pareto-improving Transition from a Centrally Planned to a Market Economy 119
Lawrence J. Lau
7. Privatization and Restructuring in East Germany: How the Treuhand Dealt with Privatization and Corporate Governance in a Radically Changed Environment 142
Jürgen Müller

PART FIVE The Availability of Social Infrastructure

8. Transformation of the Telecommunications Infrastructure in North Korea 183
Chang-Ho Yoon and Young Soo Lee
9. Strategies for Developing Transport Infrastructure in North Korea 215
Jae-Hak Oh
10. Practical Approaches for Energy Sector Cooperation between South and North Korea 237
Jeong-In Kim and Seung-Jun Kwak

PART SIX The Importance of Industrial Location

11. Industrial Location Planning in North Korea 269
Duk Hee Lee
12. The Rajin–Sonbong Economic and Trade Zone (RSETZ): the Sources of Difficulties and Lessons for the Future 301
Icksoo Kim

Index 335

List of Figures

3.1	Urbanization in the DPRK and ROK, 1955–95	37
3.2	Inferred and Reported Military Manpower in the DPRK and ROK, 1975–95	39
3.3	DPRK Imports of SITC 9 Items from USSR/Russia, 1972–95	41
3.4	Reported Percentage of Labor Force in Primary Sector DPRK versus ROK, ca. 1986–95	45
3.5	Comparative Export Earnings: World, Asia, Africa, DPRK 1970–95 (1970 = 1)	49
3.6	Relative Trade Performance: DPRK and USSR/Russia 1987–97 (1987 = 100) Export	50
3.7	Relative Trade Performance: DPRK and USSR/Russia 1987–97 (1987 = 100) Import	51
3.8	Capital Goods as a Percentage of Total DPRK Merchandise Imports, 1972–97	53
3.9	DPRK Export Performance: Steel, 1984–95	56
3.10	DPRK Export Performance: Cement, 1982–95	56
3.11	DPRK Export Performance: Textiles, 1980–95	57
3.12	DPRK Export Performance: Magnesite, 1980–95	57
3.13	DPRK Export Performance: Gold, 1978–95	58
3.14	DPRK Imports of Oil and Oil Products, 1986–95	58
3.15	DPRK Imports of Coking Coal, 1986–95	59
3.16	Capital Goods Imports during (8-year) Periods of Economic Crises: Estimated Absolute Value for China, Cuba, DPRK	59
3.17	DPRK Balance of Trade, Food versus Non-food, 1972–95	60
4.1	North Korean GDP Growth	72
4.2	North Korean Trade	75
4.3	North Korean Arms Trade	75
4.4	Model Simulation Results	80
6.1	The Distribution of Value of Industrial Production by Ownership (China)	125
6.2	The Growth of Industrial Output by Sector of Ownership (China)	125

6.3 The Distribution of Retail Sales by Ownership (China) 126
6.4 The Distribution of Retail Sales by Ownership (Guizhou Province) 126
7.1 THA Companies' Status in Early 1993 159
7.2 Progress in Privatization until June 1993 Weighted by the Number of Employees of the Second Quarter of 1991 160
7.3 Progress in Privatization Weighted by the Number of Firms, as of June 1993 161
8.1 The Relationship between GDP per Capita and Tele-density 187
8.2 Per Capita Income, Tele-density and International Outgoing Traffic in Transitional Economies (1990–95 Annual Growth Rate) 188
8.3 Fiber-optical Trunk Lines in North Korea 191
8.4 Cost of WLL per Subscriber 197
8.5 Changes in Tele-density (Economies in Transition) 200
8.6 Revenue per Mainline ($), 1996 203
8.7 Revenue per Mainline (Economies in Transition) 204
8.8 Time Profile of Cost, Revenue and Profit (Residential Revenue per Line = US$300, Business Revenue per Line = US$700) 204
8.9 Decomposition of Time Profile of Cumulative Profits (Residential Revenue per Line = US$300, Business Revenue per Line = US$700) 205
8.10 Time Profile of Cumulative Net Profits (Business Revenue per Line = US$700, Residential Revenue per Line = US$300 (A), Residential Revenue per Line = US$200 (B), Residential Revenue per Line = US$100 (C)) 205
8.11 Decomposition of Time Profile of Cumulative Profits (A) (First Stage Investment Only: Residential Revenue per Line = US$300, Business Revenue per Line = US$700) 206
8.12 Decomposition of Time Profile of Cumulative Profits (B) (First and Second Stage Investment Only: Residential Revenue per Line = US$300, Business Revenue per Line = US$700) 206
9.1 Trends in North Korea's Vehicle Ownership and Road Length 217
9.2 Trends in North Korea's Rail and Electrified Rail Length 217
9.3 Motorization Projections for North Korea 225
9.4 Share of South Korea's Transport Investment, by Mode, from 1975 to 1996 228
11.1 East Asia Economic Zone Plan 280
11.2 Eight Candidates for Industrial Zones 287
12.1 Fork-type Transport Network Linkage in TREDA and the Competitive Positions of North Korean Ports 322

List of Tables

3.1 Comparative Demographic Indicators from Official Data: DPRK and ROK, 1993 34
3.2 Estimated Life Expectancy at Birth for DPRK and ROK 1955–85 36
3.3 Estimated Armed Forces as a Percentage of Total Population and Estimated Defense Budget as a Percentage of GNP: North Korea and Other Highly Mobilized Countries, 1986 40
3.4 Reported Distinction of DPRK Population by Employment Category, 1946–93 43
3.5 Distribution of Labor Force: DPRK 1993 versus ROK 1995 44
3.6 Distribution of Labor Force: DPRK and Selected Other Socialist States 46
3.7 Labor Force Participation Rates for North and South Korea and Selected Other Countries, Recent Years (Percentage) 47
3.8 Reported Labor Force Participation Rates by Age and Sex, 1993 (Percentage) 48
3.9 DPRK Capital Goods Trade in International Perspective 52
3.10 Indicators of Malnutrition Among Children under 5 Years: Anthropometric Survey Data for DPRK and Other Asian Countries 62
4.1 Composition of Output, 1992–96 (Millions of US Dollars at US$1 = Won 2.15) 73
4.2 Government Budget Balance, 1994–96 (Billions of Won) 73
4.3 General Government Revenues, 1996 (Millions of Won) 74
4.4 Trading Partners, 1997 (Millions of US Dollars) 76
4.5 North Korean Trade by Largest Commodity Groups, 1996 77
4.6 Distribution of Labor Force at Time of Reform 86
5.1 Recent Trend of Macroeconomics Indicator for North Korea 95
5.2 Estimates of GNP Per Capita and Growth Rate for North Korea and Selected Other Countries, 1995 96
5.3 Comparison of South and North Korean Economies (1997) 98
5.4 Cross-country Growth Regression (Dependent Variable: Growth

of Real per Capita GDP, 1965–90, 74 Countries) 102
5.5 Educational Attainment of Population Aged 15 and Above for North Korea and Selected Other Countries, 1990 106
5.6 North Korea, Estimated and Projected Demographic Indicators, 1960–2020 107
5.7 Comparative Demographic Indicators: Estimates for North and South Korea, 1995 108
5.8 North Korea, Estimated and Projected Population, 1960–2020 109
5.9 North Korea Growth Prospects under Alternative Reform Scenarios, 1995–2020 111
6.1 Comparisons of the Average Annual Rates of Growth of Selected Economic Indicators 127
6.2 Phasing Out the Plan-track: Agricultural Products (Percentage of Output Value) 138
6.3 Phasing Out the Plan-track: Industrial Goods (Percentage of Output value) 138
6.4 Phasing Out the Plan-track: Total Retail Sales (Percentage of Sales) 138
7.1 Sectoral Employment Structure in East and West Germany, 1989/90 149
7.2 Extent of Management Transfer to the THA 153
7.3 Distribution of Mergers by Sectors 162
8.1 Tele-density as a Function of GDP per Capita 187
8.2 Telecommunication in North Korea 189
8.3 Basic Indicators of North Korea's Population and Households 193
8.4 Urban and Rural Mainlines and Tele-density 194
8.5 Demand Projection 194
8.6 Residential, Largest City and Rest of Country Tele-density, 1996 195
8.7 Urban and Rural Mainlines and Tele-density in the Transition Economies 196
8.8 Required Level of Investment 198
8.9 Time to Attain Different Tele-density (by Years) 199
8.10 Number of Lines and Additional Investment Required for North Korea 202
9.1 North Korea's Transport Infrastructure 218
9.2 Existing Trade Ports in North Korea 221
9.3 Stock of Transport Infrastructure in South Korea and North Korea 227
9.4 Trends in Transport Investment of South Korea from 1975 to 1996 (Billions of US Dollars) 228
9.5 Projected Stock of Transport Infrastructure in North Korea

	(High Economic Growth)	229
9.6	Projected Stock of Transport Infrastructure in North Korea (Low Economic Growth)	230
9.7	Overseas Loans to South Korea from 1962 to 1992 (Millions of US Dollars, Percentage)	232
9.8	Feasibility of Private Sector Delivery of Infrastructure Components	234
10.1	Trends of Primary Energy Sources in both North and South Korea (Million TOE)	240
10.2	Trends of Coal Production in DPRK (Million Ton)	241
10.3	Imports of Coal (Bituminous, Cokes) in DPRK (Thousand Ton)	242
10.4	Operation Rate for Crude Oil Refining Facilities (Thousand Ton, Percentage)	243
10.5	Electric Power Generation in DPRK (Billion KWh)	243
10.6	Future Estimation of the Electric Power Demand	244
10.7	Summary of Quantitative Evaluation of Energy Efficiency and Renewable Energy Options for DPRK (1999–2000)	246
10.8	Country-to-country Source Receptor Relationship (Percentage)	248
10.9	A Case of Interregional Electric Power System Connection	249
10.10	Comparison of Future Energy Demand between North and South Korea in Year 2000 (Thousand TOE)	251
10.11	Small-scale Electric Power Connection between North and South Korea	252
10.12	Large-scale Electric Power Connection between North and South Korea	253
10.13	Status of Russian Gas Export (m^3, Percentage)	256
10.14	Future Gas Export in Far Eastern Region (BCM)	257
10.15	Different Routes and Final Gas Prices with and without Passing Fee ($/MMBTU)	258
10.16	Summary of PNG Projects in Asia-Pacific Region	258
10.A.1	Fixed Cost for A, B Line (Millions of US Dollars)	262
10.A.2	Interest Rate	262
10.A.3	Fixed Cost for C Line (Millions of US Dollars)	262
10.A.4	Fixed Cost for D Line (Millions of US Dollars)	263
10.A.5	Fixed Cost for E line (Millions of US Dollars)	263
11.1	Industrial Location Pattern by Production Characteristics	272
11.2	Transportation-oriented versus Production Factor-oriented Industries	273
11.3	Locational Factors by Industry	281
11.4	Synthetic Assessment of Locational Factors by Zone	289
11.5	Locational Factors of Eight Candidates of Industrial Clusters	290

11.6 Candidate Industries by Zone 291
11.7 Industrial Location Plan by Stages 296
12.1 Cross-border Trade between Jilin and Hamkyongbuk-do (Millions of US Dollars, Percentage) 307
12.2 The Amount of FDI Attracted into the RSETZ in Comparative Perspective (1991–97, Millions of US Dollars, Percentage Share) 310
12.3 FDI into the RSETZ by Investing Country (as of the 1997 Year-end) 311
12.4 FDI into the RSETZ by Industry (as of the 1997 Year-end) 312
12.5 Comparison between Shinuijoo and the RSETZ 317

List of Contributors

Bradley O. Babson
Senior Advisor, World Bank

Nicholas Eberstadt
Research Associate, National Bureau of Soviet and Asian Research and American Enterprise Institute

Icksoo Kim
Professor of International Business, Korea University

Seung-Jun Kwak
Associate Professor of Economics, Korea University

Jeong-In Kim
Associate Professor of Industrial Economics, Chung-Ang University

Lawrence J. Lau
Kwoh-Ting Li Professor of Economic Development, Stanford University

Duk Hee Lee
Research Fellow, Korea Institute for Economics and Trade

Jong-Wha Lee
Professor of Economics, Korea University

Young Soo Lee
Associate Professor of Business Administration, Hankuk Aviation Univerisity

Jürgen Müller
Professor of Economics, FHW Berlin

Marcus Noland
Senior Fellow, Institute for International Economics

Jae-Hak Oh
Head, Division of ITS Research, The Korea Transport Institute

Chang-Ho Yoon
Professor of Economics, Korea University

Preface

Recent political developments in Northeast Asia after the historical summit talks suggest both the possibility and desirability for both Koreas and the neighboring powers to establish a new framework for regional peace on the Korean peninsula, replacing the structure inherited from the cold war days. The United States and North Korea have also managed to reach an agreement to reduce mutually hostile threats on a reciprocal basis, and to normalize diplomatic relationship by removing economic sanctions, thus creating conditions potentially favorable for the expansion of trade and the inflow of economic assistance and foreign direct investment to North Korea.

However, one cannot take for granted that North Korea will choose to transform its internal system and adopt an open-door policy in an effort to revive its stagnant economy. The decision depends on the assessment by the North Korean Government of whether North Korea will be able to survive economically (and eventually politically because of the internal instability that a collapsed economy may cause) in the absence of economic reform and whether it will be able to retain its political control in the event that it undertakes economic reform. Here the contrasting experiences of China and Russia will weigh heavily on the North Korean decision makers.

One of the central issues that need to be examined in this context is the extent of the development potential of the North Korean economy. Another central issue is the potential compatibility of economic reform with the maintenance of internal political stability. This volume attempts to address some of these questions. The current North Korean gross domestic product (GDP) is between 3 and 5 per cent of the South Korean GDP and the gap is likely to be widened over time unless North Korea undertakes substantive economic reform. Most of the contributors to this volume concur that the development potential of North Korea, like its other East Asian neighbors, is large and can be best realized through economic reform, including the development of tangible and intangible social infrastructure and the adoption of an open-door policy. The importance of social infrastructure is also recognized by President Kim Dae Jung of South Korea in his recent speech, in which he expressed his strong support for commitments by his government and by multilateral institutions to finance infrastructural development in North Korea. Moreover, economic reform, especially the kind that takes care to avoid the creation of net losers, can in fact enhance the stability of the incumbent regime. China and Vietnam provide successful examples of such reform. Long-term peace and prosperity on the Korean peninsula depend on whether North Korea finds that it is in its best interests to join the family of nations and that in turn depends in part on the degree to which its development potential can be realized through economic reform.

Lawrence J. Lau and Chang-Ho Yoon

August 2000

Acknowledgement

The volume is drawn from the proceedings of the papers presented at the Conference on 'Developing Social Infrastructure in North Korea for Economic Cooperation between the South and the North', held at Korea University, Seoul in November of 1998. The editors would like to express their gratitude to the Korea Research Foundation for its sponsorship of the Conference and the entire project.

Editors would also like to express their indebtedness to all the participants in the conference who contributed greatly to the creation of the volume through open and stimulating discussions. Special thanks go to Professors Sung-Joo Han, Eui-Gak Hwang, Jooyeon Jeong, Seungkuk Cho, Choong-Yong Ahn, Suck-kyo Ahn, Kap-Young Jeong, Keun Lee, Dr Seok Hyun Hong, Il-Dong Koh, Hong-Tack Chun, Won-Bae Kim, Soon-Won Chung, Hansuk Kim, Sangwhan Lho, and Jung-Hee Lee who provided valuable critical comments and encouraging remarks. Professor Chang-Jin Kim at Korea University offered useful guidelines for collecting and processing data on North Korea's traffic infrastructure. Most of them are now well reflected in the current volume.

Mr Young-Woong Song and Seung Hoon Lee at Korea University completed the complex final editorial stages and were helpful in updating the portions of the volume.

PART ONE

Introduction

1. Overview

Lawrence J. Lau and Chang-Ho Yoon

1.1 INTRODUCTION

More than half a century has passed since Korea was divided into the South and the North. Although the population is highly homogeneous ethnically, the military confrontation and ideological antagonism have made the two Korean economies totally dissimilar. In fact, while many of the East Asian economies, including China, recorded remarkably high growth rates in the last two decades, North Korea alone confronted the inevitable slowdown of Stalinist quantitative growth.[1]

There was, according to most observers, little or no significant difference between the levels of per capita gross domestic product (GDP), estimated to be approximately US$70, of North Korea and South Korea in the immediate aftermath of the Korean War (1950–53). During the initial phase of extensive development, from the mid-1950s to the mid-1970s, the rate of growth of the North Korean economy had on occasions exceeded that of South Korea. Between 1957 and 1961, North Korea achieved an average annual growth rate in excess of 20 per cent. In the 1960s, the average annual rate of growth of the North Korean economy was estimated to be 7.8 per cent, and during the period 1971–75, 10.4 per cent, compared to 7.6 per cent and 7.8 per cent respectively for South Korea.[2] It then fell to 2.6 per cent for the period 1981–90 and plunged into the negative region in the 1990s, accompanied by poor harvests, resulting in a continual decline in real income per capita and mass starvation. The annual rate of growth at one point declined to as low as −15 per cent in the 1990s, according to some observers.[3] The Bank of Korea has estimated the average annual rate of growth for the decade (up to 1998) to be approximately −4.5 per cent.

Half-hearted Reform

Since the 1980s, North Korea has encountered significant difficulties in managing the transition from extensive development to intensive development. The ideological emphasis on virtual self-sufficiency posed a major barrier to institutional reforms necessary for North Korea to benefit from the international division of labor. The incumbent regime has never yet articulated a long-term vision for its open-door policy, and attempted only a series of half-hearted, piecemeal reform measures that were inconsistent with one another and often followed by erratic reversal.

The piecemeal reform started with the hope of muddling through by balancing the conflicting preferences of the hard-liners and the reformers. In the early 1980s, North Korea first extended the scope of managerial responsibility for the local government in agricultural production. In 1984, it opened the economy to foreign investors in a limited way by adopting a new law permitting foreign direct investment in North Korea through joint ventures. Although the new law, which was modeled after China's successful joint venture law of 1979, signaled that North Korea had begun to acknowledge the importance of foreign trade and investment, it failed to attain sufficient credibility to attract foreign strategic investors from the West and its effects were quite disappointing. Much of the inefficiencies that resulted from systemic problems of the centrally planned economy remained intact.

Even then, the half-hearted open-door policy turned out to have increased the trade volume of North Korea from less than US$3 billion in 1985 to more than US$5 billion in 1988. Since then, for better or worse, North Korea has become much more dependent on foreign trade and aid. If this trend continues, the virtue of self-reliance will become increasingly difficult to defend.

The Collapse of the Soviet Bloc

The optimism with regard to the initial success of the open-door policy did not last long. North Korea was hit by a fatal blow when Soviet aid and trade evaporated overnight in 1991. Until 1991, the Soviet Union accounted for almost 60 per cent of North Korea's total international trade and provided two-thirds of its imported oil at subsidized prices. Right after the collapse of the Soviet bloc, North Korea's trade volume decreased by almost 50 per cent and has never recovered to its previous level. International trade contracted sharply from US$4.71 billion in 1990 to US$2.18 billion in 1997. North Korea lacked the institutional flexibility to cope with such external shocks. The order of magnitude of these shocks was too great for the North Korean economy to adjust within a short period of time. In addition, any drastic measure for internal structural reform threatened to undermine the power base of the incumbent regime. Unable to attract foreign capital and technology and to find new export markets, the country suffered from an unprecedented shortage of foreign exchange and was plunged into a prolonged economic recession with significant risks of economic collapse.

Although ensuing floods and droughts in the mid-1990s added calamity to the agricultural sector, the manufacturing sector has remained as the most seriously damaged. Structurally, North Korea cannot achieve self-sufficiency in food by pursuing an agriculture-led growth policy alone. Agriculture has become a part of the industrial economy, relying heavily on industrial inputs such as chemical fertilizers, tractors, fuels and spare parts, and tends to decline *pari passu* with the manufacturing sector.

Prolonged Economic Recession

Since the early 1990s, the industrial sector of North Korea has been suffering from a vicious circle of working capital shortage. As the country could not import sufficient amounts of oil, raw materials and intermediate inputs, the capacity utilization rate of the manufacturing sector plummeted to approximately 20 per cent and capital stocks continued to deplete. In fact, both industrial output and the scale of construction activity declined by more than 60 per cent. According to statistics recently submitted by North Korea to the International Monetary Fund, during the four-year period from 1992 to 1996, GDP declined by 50 per cent to US$10 billion, which turned out to be less than 3 per cent of South Korea's GDP in 1996.[4] North Korean foreign debt surged to US$12 billion, reaching a debt to GDP ratio of 120 per cent.

The tragic decline of the North Korean economy brought about almost insurmountable hardship for its people and widespread social distress. Since the mid-1990s, North Korea has suffered from chronic shortages of food, energy and medicine. The public distribution system often fails to function, and a large segment of the population has been living on stalks, roots and leaves. At the time North Korea asked for humanitarian aid from the international community, at least a few hundred thousand, out of a population of 23 million, reportedly starved to death. According to a recent UNICEF report, close to 60 per cent of North Korean children are stunted and 14 per cent wasted. Public facilities lack heating and running water. Hospitals and health care systems are nearly depleted. Immunization coverage levels have fallen below 50 per cent from one of the highest ratings in the world in the 1980s. A large number of families have been broken apart, and tens of thousands of abandoned children had to beg for food around the farmers' markets and in the border areas. The previously enviable achievements in higher education are now faltering, and deterioration of human resources threatens the growth potential of the economy.

The North Korean government is desperate to take the country out of the crisis. To revive agriculture, irrigation infrastructure and small hydroelectric generation plants have been and continue to be constructed. Agricultural production decisions are now more decentralized than before. The government has legalized private ownership by individual households of small plots of arable land in the rural areas and extended freedom of travel for ordinary citizens. The government has also allowed market transactions of daily necessities such as food and clothing. Ordinary urban households now purchase approximately two-thirds of their food either from farmers' markets or from relatives in the rural areas. The government continues to send delegates to international fora to plead for humanitarian aid. In order to coordinate economic activities in a more efficient way, the government has since 1995 established fiber-optic telecommunication links that connect major industrial and urban areas. Technical education for the intelligent use of personal computers is encouraged with the hope of building a software industry, aimed possibly at the export market. Given the severity of the structural imbalance in North Korea's economic system, however, these efforts alone are not likely to reduce significantly the crushing burden of the crisis.

Despite the prolonged economic distress, there are no reports as yet of mass outbreaks of violence, thefts and other crimes. The armed forces are still under strict control and they monitor and uphold the powerful socialist state in their own way. Among the ordinary citizenry, however, latent dissatisfaction is likely to have grown over time.

Prospects for Economic Reform

Thus far, North Korea has not undertaken visible reform measures that have the potential of attracting large-scale foreign investments. North Korea's recent strategy to survive the external shocks reflects its strategic intransigence as well as genuine ambivalence, generating mixed signals to the international community. On the one hand, North Korea has sent more than a hundred government bureaucrats abroad to study the basic concepts of modern accounting and international economics, and continued its efforts to broaden economic ties to non-communist countries. On the other hand, North Korea took a militant approach to the rebuilding of its nearly collapsed economy. Instead of demonstrating cooperative spirits to the USA, North Korea directly confronted the superpower by creating crises for the purpose of gaining leverage in negotiations.

The first nuclear crisis of 1994 led to the nuclear accord called 'Agreed Framework' between the USA and North Korea. It was a political bargain under which North Korea would ultimately dismantle its nuclear facilities and commit itself with the USA to peace and security in a nuclear-free

Korean Peninsula. In return for this agreement, the USA organized a multilateral effort to provide two light-water reactors with a total power-generating capacity of 200 megawatts by the year 2003. This huge energy project is worth US$4.6 billion, more than four times the current annual volume of North Korean exports. As the economy has shown no sign of recovery, North Korea has continued to adopt a brinkmanship strategy deploying its militant bargaining assets. Recently, North Korea successfully negotiated for a significant amount of food aid (approximately 500 000 tons of food) by allowing the USA to inspect and verify whether certain suspicious-looking holes in the ground were nuclear-related. North Korea has also been preparing to launch tests of long-range intercontinental ballistic missiles in the hope that it can extract better terms from the USA in the forthcoming package deal. The USA may be willing to lift economic sanctions and normalize diplomatic relations if North Korea stops developing weapons of mass destruction such as nuclear and chemical weapons and ballistic missiles.

The prospects for North Korean economic reform revolve around North Korea's perception of the basis for the survival of the regime. Suppose North Korea learns that it will never be allowed to have both a nuclear program and a package consisting of foreign economic aid, investment and security guarantees, will it then choose to undertake fundamental internal reforms to prepare for shared prosperity and peaceful coexistence in Northeast Asia? The answer depends on the availability of international humanitarian aid and China's support, the combination of which has sustained North Korea at subsistence level so far. If the economy can be maintained at the subsistence level without reform, then there is significant probability for North Korea to continue to choose a strategy of muddling through by international blackmail through provocative military threats.

However, the strategy of feeding its people through foreign aid while making trouble for the donor countries is certainly not sustainable over the longer time horizon. The international community will find it increasingly difficult to manage tension reduction by a policy of engagement alone. The relatively young ruling circle of North Korea is likely to opt for an alternative policy if it perceives that the North Korean economy will eventually collapse in the absence of reform. If diplomatic efforts by the neighboring countries can reduce or eliminate any inclination towards miscalculation, the remaining rational answer is very straightforward. If the economic gains from reform prove to be sufficiently large over an extended period of time to enable any losers to be adequately compensated during the transition process so that the survival of the incumbent regime need not be threatened, North Korea will take steps towards that direction. If agreements could be reached for security guarantees from both the USA and China, the lifting of economic sanctions, and systematic development assistance from the international community, North Korea might be more likely to choose to transform its economy in a sustainable manner by gradually integrating into the global economy, including South Korea.

The Main Theme of the Volume

This volume deals with the development potential of North Korea under reform. It is intended to provide insights into both the present and the future of the North Korean economy through rigorous economic analyses. One conclusion that emerges is that, based on the historical experience of other East Asian economies, the growth potential for the North Korea economy under reform can be significant and realizable in the forthcoming decades, provided appropriate policies are adopted. The volume is divided into six main parts, including the introduction. In Part Two, the current economic and political situations in North Korea are assessed. Part Three examines the development and growth potential of North Korea under reform from a macroeconomic perspective. In Part Four, some possible lessons for North Korea from the experiences of China's economic reform since 1979 and German reunification are drawn. Since the realization of the development potential under reform depends critically on the availability of social infrastructure, Part Five examines rigorously the possibilities for North Korea to provide modern infrastructure in telecommunications, transportation and energy, the lack of which may constitute major bottlenecks to economic development. In Part Six, the industrial location policy of North Korea is evaluated and a basic policy framework for efficient industrial location is presented. There is also a critical review of the case of a thus far unsuccessful locational policy decision in the past.

1.2 THE POLITICAL ECONOMY OF NORTH KOREA

This part addresses broadly the overall structure and performance of the North Korean economy, and assesses the effects of the recent engagement policies of the USA and South Korea.

Bradley Babson offers a comprehensive treatment of North Korea's response to its economic crises in the 1990s. He points out that North Korea's brinkmanship strategy of using crises to secure concessions from the international community has been largely accompanied by a policy of avoiding the fundamental reform that would be required to remedy structural deficiencies. The author explains that since the 'Agreed Framework' in 1994, the engagement policy has been based on a two-pronged approach. One is a complex set of bilateral and multilateral political processes that attempts to prevent the development of weapons of mass destruction and normalize diplomatic relations of North Korea with its neighboring countries and the USA. The other is the humanitarian effort that addresses North Korea's food and health crises. This two-pronged approach, however, has so far not been sufficient to induce North Korea to reduce its military threat and open its economy to the rest of the world. Babson emphasizes the need for a more comprehensive strategy of engagement that defines a set of processes for interaction, with explicit linkages between international economic assistance and progress in economic and political reform.

Nicholas Eberstadt presents an overall view on the current status of the North Korean economy and explains its steady decline during the recent period. Eberstadt provides a comprehensive treatment of official statistics on foreign trade, population, health and urbanization trends of North Korea, and makes useful suggestions on how one may draw inferences from inconsistent and inaccurate data that have often been manipulated by the government. Using the concept of 'mirror statistics', the author investigates the relationship between the economic decline and the changes in the pattern and magnitude of foreign trade. Eberstadt presents evidence on the stagnation of the export industries, the very low import content of capital goods, and institutional constraints created by the ideological emphasis on food self-sufficiency that distort the efficient pattern of trade. He blames institutional rigidity and lack of accommodating policy tools for the sustained economic crises and expresses concern for the possible deterioration of human resources.

1.3 DEVELOPMENT POTENTIAL UNDER REFORM

This part deals with one of the fundamental questions in regard to the potential effects of economic reform in North Korea. North Korea will embrace reform policies only if the envisioned economic gains are large enough to finance the social costs of structural adjustment and compensation of potential losers.

Marcus Noland uses a dynamic general equilibrium model to assess the resource reallocation effects of radical reforms such as economic opening and military demobilization in North Korea. The author stresses that although there are potentially huge economic benefits from reforming the distorted North Korean economy, there are also considerable economic and political obstacles to successful rehabilitation of the North Korean economy. He concludes that the policy options in the Korean Peninsula depend crucially on North Korea's decision regarding what kind of society it wishes to have in the future.

Jong-Wha Lee examines the long-run growth potential of North Korea under various reform scenarios. Reforms are classified by their speed and scope into three types: piecemeal reform (muddling-through strategy), gradual reform, and rapid reform. Using the reduced form version of an extended neoclassical growth model, the author shows that more extensive and rapid reform is likely to produce higher growth in the next couple of decades. He also points out that in the absence of rapid reform, the educational system may eventually break down and the quality of human resources may deteriorate. Lee also presents a comprehensive comparison of the two Korean economies in the recent period and projects that the income gap between North and South Korea is likely to be substantially reduced along the reform path after a couple of decades.

Both authors suggest that in order to realize the potential gains from reform, the engagement policies of the USA, China, Japan and most importantly South Korea, coupled with security guarantees, must be effective enough to persuade North Korea to want to integrate into the global economy.

1.4 THE EXPERIENCE OF OTHER TRANSITION ECONOMIES

This part is devoted to drawing lessons from the experiences of other transition economies. Lawrence Lau examines the 'dual-track' approach adopted by China in its transition from a centrally planned to a market economy. The approach, based on the continued enforcement of the existing central plan while simultaneously liberalizing the market, can be understood as a method for making implicit lump-sum transfers to compensate potential losers of the reform. The author highlights the critical role of enforcement of the plan by the state and full liberalization of the market track. He examines how the dual-track approach has worked in practice in product and labor markets in China's economic reform and suggests that it acted as a mechanism for implementing simultaneously efficient and Pareto-improving economic reform. No one, including the government, is made worse off as a result of the reform. From the point of view of political economy, the dual-track approach minimizes opposition to reform ex ante and maximizes support for reform ex post. Thus, it may have wide implications in an initially distorted economy like North Korea where the regime has to walk a tightrope balancing the conflicting preferences of both hard-liners and reformers.

Jürgen Müller explains the transformation process of the economy of the former German Democratic Republic (GDR) after its reunification with the

Federal Republic of Germany. He first examines differences in the economic structures, institutions and especially governance structures of enterprises between the East and West, and then identifies the essential tasks in moving from a communist economy to a market economy. The central question addressed by Müller is the comparative ability of public and private owners to select and introduce high-quality managers into enterprises in the East. The theoretical argument is that uninformed owners, such as government and citizens of the East, are likely to hire managers of below-average ability. In fact, the more firms there are to be restructured, the more likely that weaknesses in the managerial labor market will bind and constrain the ability of the government to restructure firms. In this context, the policy of allocating Eastern firms to experienced and informed Western firms avoids the failure in the labor market.

This chapter has very interesting implications for the transition of the North Korean economy. South Korean firms are not only more experienced in the international business environment but also possess knowledge of the more idiosyncratic features of North Korea, including societal norms and language. They can thus be relatively more informed in the selection of high-quality managers to assist in the restructuring of the North Korean enterprises than other foreign investors and the North Koreans themselves. It is therefore in the interest of North Korea to give top priority to cooperation with South Korean entrepreneurs in any reform effort.

1.5 THE AVAILABILITY OF SOCIAL INFRASTRUCTURE

This part investigates the availability of social infrastructure in North Korea. Building infrastructure in North Korea is a formidable task. It requires tens of billions of dollars to establish modern transportation and communication networks that connect the major industrial and urban areas. Such a huge amount of capital is difficult to mobilize domestically in a poverty-stricken and starving economy and must come from outside.

Chang-Ho Yoon and Young Soo Lee examine the current status of telecommunication development in North Korea and evaluate the potential of transforming the telecommunication structure in a market-friendly way. They point out that North Korea has already recognized the importance of the information infrastructure in the middle of its economic crisis in 1995, and began to install fiber-optic trunk lines connecting its major cities. Since there appears to be initial signs that North Korea has begun to permit individual initiatives in the rebuilding of the collapsed economy, the societal demand for telecommunication infrastructure is likely to grow rapidly in the future. The experiences of many economies in transition indicate that successful development of the telecommunication infrastructure requires an above-nomal return from business users and relatively well-to-do residential users. The government can use such profits to subsidize universal connectivity in the later stage of development. The authors emphasize that the potential growth in the demand for telecommunication services in North Korea is also large enough to attract foreign strategic investors, especially if both Koreas allow their peoples to communicate freely, since demand growth will then be astronomical. The authors then examine various paths for transforming the inefficient public telecommunication sector into dynamically efficient enterprises by drawing lessons from the experiences of the former socialist Central and East European countries and China.

Jae-Hak Oh examines the present state of the transport infrastructure in North Korea and recommends appropriate development strategies and directions for institutional reform. The author summarizes the major problems confronted by North Korea as deficiency of transport infrastructure, poor maintenance, unbalanced modal shares and inefficiency of the supporting institutional structure. In terms of transport capacity and motorization, North Korea's transport infrastructure is at a similar stage as South Korea in 1975, and will require tens of billions of US dollars if North Korea is to follow the growth path of South Korea and reaches the current level of per capita income in the South by the year 2020. The author points out that considering the present financial situation of North Korea, it will be almost impossible to finance such a huge long-term project without foreign (including South Korean) investment, cost-based pricing and private sector participation. The author also suggests that North Korea has to make the best use of its strategically advantageous position to operate international transport services commercially in Northeast Asia. For example, since 98 per cent of the railway network is still single-track and remains very inefficient in terms of operating speed, double-tracking for the major routes must be given top priority in the near future. Advanced transport technologies such as the Intelligent Transport System that improves operational capacities of existing facilities are now available and should be fully utilized. Also, to support the open-door policy in the short run, immediate construction of access links to existing ports and large-scale sharing of ports in South Korea are recommended.

Jeong-In Kim and Seung-Jun Kwak examine the problems of energy shortage in North Korea and suggest possible solutions. The authors point out that even after the completion of the light-water nuclear reactor power plant by KEDO (Korean Peninsula Energy Development Organization), the energy shortage in North Korea will not be totally solved. North Korea needs continual access to foreign technology and financial sources and has to re-engineer existing power systems to improve efficiency. The authors also emphasize that as a part of a short-run strategy, it is desirable for the North to cooperate with the South by connecting the electricity transmission networks of the two Koreas.

They suggest that a long-run solution for the energy shortage lies in the use of Russian natural gas. The natural gas industry in Russia has remained one of its most successful sectors and has the potential to meet the needs of Far Eastern countries. With low fossil fuel prices, and low environmental pollution emissions, natural gas plants are economically feasible and efficient for the North Korean economy. To participate in the multilateral economic cooperation for the gas pipeline project, North Korea has to maintain close contacts with South Korea and Japan so as to establish mutually beneficial arrangements.

1.6 THE IMPORTANCE OF INDUSTRIAL LOCATION

This part presents two studies on policy issues related to industrial location in North Korea. Duk Hee Lee examines both industrial location factors and situational factors specific to the Korean Peninsula. He emphasizes that any industrial development and restructuring policy must take into account the complementarities of the two Koreas: combining the cheap labor cost and relatively abundant natural resources of the North with the advanced technology, capital and marketing capacity of the South. The author suggests both a long-term locational plan by zones and a short-term development strategy that gives priority to Kaesung–Haejoo and Pyungyang–Nampo zones in the western area. These zones are not only suitable for the labor-intensive and light industries, but are also strategically positioned to take advantage of the existing infrastructure and the geographical proximity to China.

Icksoo Kim examines the effectiveness of the open-door policy of North Korea by carefully tracing the policy formation process in the case of the Rajin–Sonbong Economic and Trade Zone (RSETZ). The zone was established as a future center for trade and finance in Northeast Asia. The author analyzes major contributing factors for its disappointing economic performance, such as the political nature of the location decision, the lack of investment incentives to build sufficient transportation infrastructure, and government's overambitious plans without realistic financing. These factors act as supply constraints in the economy and further depress the demand for transportation and telecommunication services through bottleneck multipliers. The author claims that the vicious circle will continue unless the North Korean government shows credible commitment to the open-door policy through institutional reforms similar to what China has done.

1.7 CONCLUDING REMARKS AND SUGGESTIONS FOR FURTHER RESEARCH

The central theme that runs through this volume is that like any other East Asian economy, North Korea has a great development potential and can make considerable progress in catching up to the level of South Korean per capita GDP in a couple of decades. However, given the magnitude of the economic crisis and the distortions caused in part by the political ideology in the past, a half-hearted piecemeal approach to economic reform is not likely to succeed. Credible and committed economic reform in a sustained manner is needed to attract foreign capital and technology that are necessary for North Korea to build its social infrastructure and to manage its industrial transition to become part of the global market economy. The relatively young ruling circle of the incumbent regime is less likely to risk its future by directly confronting the superpower and is more likely to undertake reforms if it can find a way to realize its development potential without losing its political power. In this respect North Korea may well benefit from the lesson of the Chinese experience of dual-track economic reform examined in this volume.

One of the basic assumptions supporting the above argument is that despite prolonged economic distress, the quality of the human resources in North Korea is, at least at the high end, still well maintained and preserved. Of course, there is concern that given the mass starvation and the malfunctioning public health system, human capital in North Korea may have undergone depletion similar to physical capital during the recent period. Further empirical research has to be done in this area to determine how much damage has been done and what kind of development assistance is required to help recover the quality of human resources.

Most of the chapters of this volume are written from the viewpoint of how economic progress can be maximized by reforming the North Korean economy. This volume does not directly deal with the cultural, political and sociological aspects of the Korean nation being separated into two states over an extended period of time. Neither does this volume treat the international diplomacy surrounding the Korean Peninsula, nor the normative aspects of the kind of society North Korea should be in the future. This volume, however, is intended to provide some insights into the economic forces that will play a major role in shaping the future course of North Korea.

NOTES

1. See, for example, Paul Krugman (1994) for a discussion of the limits to Stalinist quantitative growth.
2. The data on the growth rates of the North Korean economy are originally from the Research Institute for National Unification, Seoul, Republic of Korea and cited by the Economist Intelligence Unit (1998). For 1965, per capita GDP was estimated to be US$162 in North Korea and US$105 in South Korea. The North led the South in per capita GDP and the degree of industrialization until the late 1960s. The data on per capita GDP of South Korea are taken from the National Statistical Office of the Republic of Korea (1997).
3. Based on data submitted by North Korea to the International Monetary Fund, reported in Noland, this volume.
4. According to the Bank of Korea, the GDP of the North Korean economy in 1996 may be estimated to be US$21.4 billion, which is 4.4 per cent of the South Korean GDP in the same year.

BIBLIOGRAPHY

Economist Intelligence Unit (1998), *Country Profile: North Korea*, London.

Krugman, Paul (1994), 'The Myth of Asia's Miracle', *Foreign Affairs*, **73** (6): 62–78.

National Statistical Office of the Republic of Korea (1997), *A Comparison of the Socio-Economic Situation of South and North Korea*, Seoul (in Korean).

PART TWO

The Political Economy of North Korea

2. North Korean Economy Today

Bradley O. Babson

Since the early 1990s the North Korean economy has undergone steady decline, leading to widespread social distress and fears of an imminent collapse that could plunge Northeast Asia into instability with uncertain consequences. The principle cause of this decline was the loss of Soviet aid and trade, which also revealed deep and longstanding structural flaws in the North Korean economy. In its initial response to these developments, North Korea has acquired a reputation as a masterful employer of crisis and brinkmanship to secure concessions from the international community that advance its welfare. There is evidence, however, that North Korea's response to its ongoing economic distress has evolved, and that North Korea may now be at the brink of a new phase of policy that could lead to more effective efforts to modernize the economy. If so, this would have significant implications for relations with the international community.

2.1 RESPONSE TO CRISES OF EARLY AND MID-1990s

The nuclear crisis of 1994 led to the Agreed Framework and the creation of the Korea Energy Development Organization (KEDO). With this came a commitment to a steady supply of oil financed by the USA and other KEDO members, together with the financing and construction of two light-water nuclear reactors, in return for North Korea's agreement to suspend development of nuclear facilities that could produce weapons grade plutonium. While this agreement brought North Korea and the USA back from the brink of a major confrontation over North Korea's nuclear program, in economic terms, North Korea succeeded in effectively substituting a new international oil subsidy for a Russian oil subsidy that was lost when the Soviet Union collapsed in 1992, and securing financing for the completion of operational nuclear power plants at a time when North Korea's economy was deteriorating sharply. Also, in view of the fact that North Korea lost its primary export markets with the Soviet collapse, the Agreed Framework provided a commitment to removing economic sanctions imposed by the USA that would open the way to creation of new export markets. While the effective substitution of external subsidies was only partial, and the hoped for relaxation of USA trade sanctions has not yet been achieved, this strategy yielded sufficient economic and psychological benefits to North Korea to enable the regime to cope with continuing losses of output in the mid-1990s.

North Korea has also used its food crisis to obtain large commitments of international food and humanitarian assistance since 1995, significantly broadening the stake of the international community in sustaining the North Korean people in the face of economic deterioration and natural disasters. While North Korea has never been self-sufficient in food and requires either international subsidies or international trade to import food, the loss of trade markets following the Russian collapse of 1992 and the subsequent hardening of terms of agricultural trade with China reduced the external support for North Korea's food supply on which it had been dependent for many years. The natural disasters that followed together with breakdowns in the public distribution system exacerbated the impact on the Korean people of reduced domestic food production, leading the North Korean Government to make unprecedented appeals for international humanitarian assistance. The economic effect of this policy was to shift the source of external support for North Korean food supply from China and Russia, to the USA, European Union, South Korea and Japan, who have been the principal sources of the international humanitarian response. As this response was limited in relation to the needs, in part because of fears of diversion to military personnel, and the danger of total collapse of the North Korean economy became a distinct possibility, China modified its policy and has provided both agricultural and fuel oil assistance to keep North Korea from a total breakdown. In effect, Chinese assistance is acting as a regulator, meeting the difference between aid from other sources and the minimum requirements for regime survival.

Between 1994 and 1997, North Korea's use of crisis to bargain for new forms of international economic support was accompanied by a policy of avoiding reforms that would be required to respond to both longstanding structural deficiencies in economic policy and management and the impact of the change in economic relations with Russia and China of 1992–93. If Kim Il Sung had not died in 1994, the story may well have been different. He had perceived the essential weaknesses of the North Korean economy and had called in early 1994 for a shift away from a policy that emphasized heavy industry to one that would emphasize agriculture, light industry and expanded foreign trade. If they had been implemented, his new policy directions might have resulted in a significant opening up of North Korea's economic relations with the market economies and accompanied a thawing of political relations with South Korea that also looked promising in the early part of 1994. However, Kim Il Sung's death in June 1994 was a major setback to the realization of these potentials. With primary importance given to the political transition of the North Korean regime, economic liberalization was relegated to the back burner. Even so, the economic problems facing the country during this transition could not be ignored, and the North Korean response was to seek limited and controlled economic engagement with the international community through the implementation of the Agreed Framework, especially cooperation on the KEDO project to construct two light-water nuclear reactors; expanded international humanitarian support to ameliorate the food crisis; and proceeding with an experimental policy of attracting foreign investment through the establishment of the Rajin–Sonbong Economic and Trade Zone (RSETZ). The policy during the three years following Kim Il Sung's death could be summarized as bargaining for foreign resources, while minimizing potential risk to the fragile regime in transition, and avoiding adopting economic reforms that might lead to social or political instability.

In view of the structural deficiencies of the North Korean economy, these responses were inadequate to stem continuing decline of GDP. While estimates of North Korea's GDP vary widely, there is a general consensus that total output declined by something in the order of 50 per cent between 1992 and 1997. Both industrial and agricultural production suffered a sharp decline, leading both to an increasingly idle work force and a breakdown in the system of State Enterprise surpluses financing State socialism. The decline in turnover and profit taxes from the enterprises in turn led to erosion of food subsidies to the urban population and a deterioration in social services, especially for health, increasing the vulnerability of the North Korean population. These developments were accompanied by the rise of an illegal but increasingly visible 'second economy' where market forces are replacing the failures of the State distribution system, especially for food. In view of the paucity of hard information about the state of the North Korean economy, it has been difficult to assess the true dimensions of the decline or reach consensus on the actual extent of starvation and social distress.

Outsiders have watched these developments with growing apprehension that the economic decline in North Korea might be leading towards a total collapse that would further destabilize an already highly tension-filled security situation in the region. The combination of nuclear confrontation with economic collapse raised fears of irrational responses with potentially catastrophic consequences. A great deal of attention was given to monitoring indicators of North Korea's economic decline and exploring the potential dynamics of a collapse, especially the impact on the regime's political options and potential economic and cost implications of reunification between the two Koreas under these conditions.

2.2 EXTERNAL DEVELOPMENTS IN 1997–98

Since the summer of 1997, there has been a kaleidoscope of events and acceleration of engagements between North Korea and the international community on both political and economic fronts. While these have not yielded consistent signals of North Korean policy intent, they do demonstrate an evolving dynamic of interaction between developments within North Korea and developments in South Korea and more widely in the international community.

The most important of these developments has been the initiation of the Four Party Peace Talks, involving North and South Korea, the USA and China, to seek a formal end to the Korean War and the establishment of a foundation for durable peace. Preparatory talks began in August 1997, and through a succession of meetings have advanced trust building and agreement on mechanisms to address the various issues involved. While some may argue that progress has been slower than desirable, the commitment to the talks and process appears genuine for all parties.

The election of Kim Dae Jung as President of South Korea in December 1997 together with the South Korean economic crisis have transformed South Korean policy towards North Korea. Under President Kim's 'Sunshine' policy, South Korea is seeking to broaden both political and economic relations with the North, without the intention of seeking early reunification of the two States. Under this policy, private businessmen are encouraged to advance economic relations with the North, and rules governing commercial relations have been relaxed. North Korea, on its part, has received business delegations and has agreed to proceed with a variety of commercial relationships, most of which are located outside the RSETZ area. This reveals a pragmatic willingness to consider workable projects in various areas of the country, an apparent relaxation of the earlier policy of seeking to contain foreign investment in a geographically remote and controlled zone. The acceptance by both Koreas of the idea of not seeking early reunification, and working towards a gradual broadening of relations while protecting their security interests, also exerts an important influence on the policies the international community more generally.

North Korea has made overtures to the International Financial Institutions (IFIs), including signaling its interest in joining the Asian Development Bank, and hosting a fact-finding mission from the International Monetary Fund in September 1997 and an introductory mission from the World Bank in February 1998. Membership in the IFIs is not expected to occur soon, both because of North Korea's reluctance to report the detailed information on its economy that would be required to meet obligations of membership, and because a number of major shareholders of the IFIs (particularly the USA and Japan) will not be supportive of any application for membership until major security and political issues affecting their relations with North Korea have been resolved. Even so, North Korea's overtures did lead to a sharing of some macroeconomic information not previously disclosed to the international community, and reveal a new willingness to learn more about the workings of the international economic system, which is a precursor to any future policy shift towards more openness and engagement with the market economies. This development is complemented by the fact that beginning in 1997, North Korea started sending officials abroad for training in market economics, with the support and assistance of the United Nations Development Program (UNDP). By mid-1998, the number exceeded 30.

Perhaps the most dramatic example of North Korea's willingness to engage the international community in new ways was the Roundtable on Agricultural Recovery and Environmental Protection that was hosted by UNDP in Geneva in May 1998. For this meeting the Government prepared a report with UNDP assistance that provided both a detailed account of the problems that have beset North Korean agricultural production in recent years and a strategy and proposal for rebuilding production capability with international assistance. Attending the meeting were officials from 25 countries, the European Union, various UN organizations active in North Korea, the IMF and World Bank, and a broad representation of NGOs who have been providing humanitarian food assistance. The meeting was the first time that North Korean authorities engaged in a formal dialogue with donor countries and organizations to discuss their economic problems and seek support for ways to respond to them. The meeting also led to a clearer understanding that to improve North Korea's agricultural production would require a gradual shift from humanitarian food aid to development assistance on the part of the international community, and a need for willingness to address policy issues and wider problems in the economy beyond agriculture on the part of North Korea.

Another significant development was the successful conduct of a statistically valid nutrition survey of 3600 households in September and October 1998. The survey was important not only because it provided compelling documentation for the first time of the extent of child malnutrition on a national level as the worst in East Asia, but also because it represented the result of a close collaborative effort of UNICEF, World Food Program and European Union to insist that adequate information about the health status of the population was necessary to ensure continuing support for humanitarian relief efforts supported by the international community. The survey also demonstrated that foreign and local teams could cooperate without undue interference to produce reliable information. In addition to information on age, weight and height used to estimate prevalence of wasting and stunting for the children measured by the nutrition survey teams, UNICEF was able to collect information on a wider number of health status indicators at the household level from participating families. This broader perspective is important in understanding that wasting and stunting are actually measurements of 'growth failure' in children that result not only from inadequate food intake, but also other factors, such as anemia, lack of clean water and sanitation, chronic diarrhea and ineffective treatments. This implies that addressing North Korea's malnutrition problems will require much more than simply providing food aid, and a number of international humanitarian relief efforts are increasingly turning to general problems in the public health system.

Despite these encouraging signs of increased willingness to engage the international community in new ways on economic and social matters, North Korea continued to demonstrate military belligerence and unpredictability throughout 1997 and 1998. The submarine incursion into South Korean waters in June 1998, and the launching of a missile over Japan in August, reminded the international community in highly visible ways that North Korea represents a highly credible threat not only to the security of South Korea, but also other nations in Northeast Asia. Suspicions of construction of an underground nuclear facility further augmented suspicions of North Korean intentions and threatened the continued viability of the Agreed Framework during the second half of 1998, despite progress in bilateral talks between the USA and North Korea, the resumption of the Four Party Peace Talks process and signs of improving bilateral relations between the two Koreas, notably the reception by Kim Jong Il of the elderly Chairman of Hyundai and historic tourism agreement. These mixed messages of North Korean policy and intentions fostered uncertainty about the future path of North Korea's relations with the international community and internal political and economic reform.

2.3 CONSOLIDATION OF THE KIM JONG IL REGIME

Internally, North Korea also has undertaken a series of changes that send signals about the consolidation of power under Kim Jung Il and the potential directions of future economic policy and relations with the international community. In October 1997, Kim Jong Il was named Chairman of the Workers Party, and began to exercise expanded influence over the political and administrative organs of the North Korean Government. This was further extended in September 1998 when the Supreme People's Assembly modified the Constitution and gave him the equivalent of Head of State powers through his appointment to the position of Chief of the National Defense Commission and the bolstering of the powers of the Commission. He now exercises effective control over the military, Party and Government. The role of the military in the new arrangements appears to be dominant, meaning that the regime is now guided more by interests within the military establishment than the interests of other élites. As a result, preservation of the regime and advances in security and welfare are likely to be more central to formulation of policy than is ideology in the future. The initial characterization of the Kim Jong Il regime could be 'conservatively pragmatic'.

Another significant result of the meeting of the Supreme People's Assembly was the restructuring of the Government apparatus and relationship of the Party to the Government. A Cabinet system was adopted, with the Prime Minister assuming the powers of Head of Government, and the Cabinet given responsibilities for State management. The State management powers of the former President and Central People's Committee were abolished, and other functions transferred to a new Supreme People's assembly Presidium, with the Chairman of the Presidium empowered to represent the State in international relations, including diplomatic and international legal functions. At the same time, most policy-making Commissions were abolished and policy as well as administrative responsibilities assigned to line ministers, who are also members of the Cabinet. The number of Cabinet officials holding high posts within the Worker's Party has dropped from six to two, representing a further separation of functions of the Party and Government. In addition to these changes, a number of economic ministries and organs were consolidated and local administration simplified, with Local Economic Committees abolished and Local People's Committees empowered to execute Cabinet decisions. Taken together, these changes suggest that the North Korean government is being streamlined and will be more effective in managing change, coordinating implementation of policy and dealing with foreigners, than the previous system. This would be consistent not only with a consolidation of power and control over the Government apparatus by Kim Jung Il, but also with a policy of progressively adopting new policies and opening up to expanded interactions with the international community.

Particularly meaningful aspects of the Constitutional amendments adopted in September 1998 are changes in the legal basis for economic management. Significant changes include relaxation of restrictions on entities permitted to possess means of production, relaxation of limits on private property, and introduction of cost accounting and concepts of cost, price and profit in economic management. The new Constitution also contains language that can be construed as guiding the country from an isolationist towards a more pragmatic path, especially in including as a goal of the economy 'growth and prosperity of the Fatherland' instead of the 'country's independent development'. These changes imply a direction of policy that may be more market-friendly and more outward-oriented than previously permitted under the former Constitution.

Following the adoption of the Constitutional changes by the Supreme People's Assembly, Kim Jong Il has also consolidated the bureaucracy. The personnel make-up of the new Cabinet and subsequent cascading of personnel changes at the vice minister level and below reveal a shift to a younger more technically oriented bureaucracy. Of 31 ministers, 24 were newly appointed (16 of 23 economy-related ministers). This restructuring of the bureaucracy is also consistent with the changes in organization and responsibilities of the Cabinet, and reinforces the view that North Korea is preparing itself to usher in a new era of policy and management of change.

Finally, the 1999 New Year's editorial published by the North Korean newspapers, entitled 'Let this year mark the turning point in the building of powerful nation', suggests that Kim Jong Il has consolidated his regime and is ready to proceed on both domestic and external agendas. It talks about a 'second grand march' and in the economic area says that 'to put production on a steady footing in all domains of the national economy, put the economy as a whole on the right track and provide the people with stable and better living conditions is the cardinal task facing us in economic construction this year'.

2.4 IMPLICATIONS FOR THE INTERNATIONAL COMMUNITY

It is fair to ask whether these developments are indicators of the likely directions of change in North Korea, or merely a consolidation of power and strengthening of the ability of the Kim Jong Il regime to retain legitimacy in the face of continuing economic decline. While it is impossible at this juncture to say with certainty that North Korea is on the verge of a new approach to managing its domestic economic recovery and international relations, there are sufficient signs that this possibility should be taken seriously. For this reason, it is also necessary to ask the question whether enough is known about the North Korean economy to discern the elements of a strategy of economic recovery that would be in the realm of the feasible. Because of deficiencies in information about the North Korean economy and absence of mechanisms to engage North Korean officials in dialogue on economic policy and management issues, it is impossible for outsiders to evaluate with certainty the course of future policy and reform. Nevertheless, a start needs to be made, using whatever information and analytical tools are available to sketch out potentials for restoring growth and addressing the microeconomic problems that are presently strangling the country. This is an important direction for future research on the North Korean economy.

A major constraint that North Korea faces, if in fact it is indeed ready to embark on a shift in economic policy and relations with the market economies, is the extreme low level of knowledge within North Korea of even the most basic precepts of market economics and international standards in commercial practices. Very few North Koreans have received formal education or training in economics and finance, and this limits their capacity to formulate more efficient economic policies, negotiate with foreign investors, design good projects or understand the functioning of foreign markets. A major multidimensional training effort will be needed to equip North Korea with the knowledge and skills to become a genuine participant in the international economic system. This also presents an opportunity to the international community to build new relationships through support and involvement in training and educational activities.

Another important question is how to respond to the possibility that North Korea may put itself on an economic recovery path while maintaining a threatening posture for regional security. Since 1994, the framework for engaging North Korea by the international community has been based on a two-pronged approach. One is a complex set of bilateral and multilateral political processes that address the nuclear program, missile development, peace accords, bilateral relations between the two Koreas, normalization of relations between North Korea and Japan, and so on. The other is the humanitarian effort supported by international organizations, donor countries and NGOs to address North Korea's food deficit and health problems. This two-pronged framework does not include the necessary third leg of the stool that would be needed for a comprehensive framework for engaging North Korea, which is a defined set of processes to help North Korea overcome its economic difficulties. It can be argued that without this third leg in place, with articulated linkages both to the political processes and the humanitarian processes, the current framework provides inadequate incentives and controls to both encourage North Korea to make concessions to reduce its threat to the security of neighboring countries and constrain economic progress to be in step with advances in other areas of concern to the international community. It can be further argued that the present system of oil subsidies provided through KEDO and food subsidies provided through humanitarian aid programs is proving to be unsustainable and will be of limited future utility as incentives to gain North Korean concessions. The US Congress has placed increasingly tough conditions on appropriation of funds for KEDO oil deliveries under the Agreed Framework, and aid fatigue has set in among humanitarian donors who argue that North Korea needs to make more aggressive efforts to improve its domestic production rather than settling into a pattern of depending on international food subsidies indefinitely.

Also, responding meaningfully to North Korea's human crisis will require more than mobilizing and distributing food and health supplies. Improving agricultural productivity, expanding access to safe water and sanitation, and upgrading health practices, will require the international community to be willing to provide development assistance over and above humanitarian aid. This involves very different ways of working and commitments on the part of both donors and North Korean counterparts, and cannot be effective without a more general effort to address North Korea's economic problems.

A piecemeal approach to economic engagement with North Korea is already beginning to emerge, stimulated in part by the 'sunshine' policy of South Korean President Kim Dae Jung. This will likely lead to less than optimal results, as there could be a temptation to rely primarily on ad hoc private sector deals with the North Korean Government and State Enterprises, without adequate attention to policies and public infrastructure bottlenecks in transport, power and communications that would increase efficiency of private investment. Institutional weaknesses if not addressed will also constrain economic potential. Considerable technical assistance from the international community will be needed to help create capacities that will enable North Korea to manage economic and social development in transition to more market-based organization, and to participate more effectively in the global economy.

In light of these factors, a more comprehensive strategy for engagement by the international community is needed that defines a set of processes for interacting on economic recovery and development, with explicit linkages between support for advances in international economic assistance with progress on the political agendas accompanied by a gradual shift from humanitarian to development assistance. Potential elements of such a framework would include relaxation of economic sanctions, advances in trade and investment relations, blending development and humanitarian assistance provided by governments and step-by-step advances in relations with the International Financial Institutions, culminating in support for membership and access to their resources.

BIBLIOGRAPHY

Babson, Bradley O. (2000), 'Social Policy Issues in North Korea's Transition', North Korea Workshop II, Rice University

3. Development, Structure and Performance of the DPRK Economy: Empirical Hints

Nicholas Eberstadt

3.1 DPRK STATISTICS: PROBLEMS AND POTENTIAL

Quantitative economic analysis requires quantitative economic data. Quantitative economic data on the DPRK, unfortunately, remain extremely limited, and are also rather problematic. For reasons very much of its own, the Pyongyang has striven for decades to enforce a stringent embargo on all manner of domestic information – political, cultural, social, economic – that might permit outside observers to arrive at an independent assessment of the condition of that country or the performance of that regime. While that embargo has not been absolutely watertight – tidbits have continued to trickle out over the years, and their flow may even have been increasing lately – the contrast between the DPRK and almost the entire rest of the world is glaring, and has grown more ever extreme over the tenure of the regime. If we live in the age of the 'information revolution', the North Korean Government is directed by the world's most dogged counter-revolutionaries.

For lack of hard data, students of the North Korean economy are sometimes reduced to describing that country's economic situation in terms of what Nicholas Kaldor once referred to as 'stylized facts' (Kaldor 1961). Yet rigorous examination of development patterns and patterns of economic performance in the DPRK simply cannot rest upon any set of 'stylized facts'. As Lord Kaldor himself argued, such 'facts' are actually models that simplify a complex reality – and any operative model of the North Korean economy begs the question of empirical substantiation.[1]

In its early years – say, the decade following the Korean War armistice – the DPRK made a practice of regularly releasing some information on the country's major social and economic trends (Chung, 1974). By the early

1960s, though, Pyongyang had begun to impose a 'statistical blackout' over the economy and society under its sway. That blackout continues to this very day, three and a half decades later.

The particulars of this prolonged campaign of secrecy are striking. Unlike any other established Marxist–Leninist state, the DPRK has never, in its 50-plus-year history, published a statistical yearbook. The DPRK has not published a won-denominated national accounts series for any period of its history[2]; in fact, it has never even published a won-denominated estimate of the country's total output. It has never published a detailed price index, and since the mid-1960s has published no price indices at all. It has published almost no information on banking or the monetary situation since the early 1960s. And it has not released even a summary review of its international trade and finance trends for nearly four decades.

Over the years, of course, the DPRK has released some figures bearing upon its economic performance and development: reports on physical output for diverse commodities; levels of dollar-denominated 'national income'; indices of intertemporal changes in production; and other seemingly randomly announced soundings. These data, reports and claims provide some basis for analyzing DPRK economic performance. If the objective of our analysis is to offer a quantitative economic assessment that is inherently plausible, internally consistent, and internationally comparable, we must recognize that existing DPRK data pose at least four distinct types of potential problems to those who would utilize them.

The first potential problem concerns the risk of deliberate exaggeration, misrepresentation or falsification of statistical information. Under Communist systems, according to some Western scholars, sensitive or inconvenient data are typically suppressed rather than doctored: authorities attempt to maintain the integrity of numbers, the argument goes, even if these are only circulated internally (cf. Bkum, 1994). Circumstantial evidence suggests, however, that the DPRK's officially released statistics may be characteristically subject to more political revision than statistics from other communist countries – and that the pressures for political alteration of officially released North Korean statistics may have been mounting over time.

Like most other Marxist–Leninist governments' statistical organs, the DPRK Central Bureau of Statistics (CBS) is organizationally part of the State's planning apparatus: the CBS reports directly to the DPRK Administrative Council's State Planning Commission (Chung, 1974, Appendix B). North Korea watchers from the Soviet bloc, however, warn that the alteration of official data to concord with plan and policy occurs with an altogether different frequency, and on an altogether different magnitude, in the DPRK than in other Soviet-type economies (STEs).

One economist from the former Soviet Union with long experience in

Pyongyang flatly states that 'official [DPRK] reports falsify the real state of affairs' in North Korea (Trigubenko, 1991, p. 2). Another Soviet bloc 'North Korea hand' – a former East German ambassador to the DPRK – illustrates what he views as the evermore surreal nature of the DPRK's economic claims by contrasting its official production targets for various commodities with Soviet bloc estimates of North Korea's actual production levels at the time (Maretzki, 1991). According to his numbers, North Korean economic planners failed to achieve most of the key production targets in the country's second Seven Year Plan (1978–84) – often by large margins – but then set even more lofty targets for the third Seven Year Plan (1987–93), even in areas where actual output was stagnating or declining!

If official DPRK data are vulnerable to deliberate misrepresentation for reasons of state, outside observers may be confronted by an observational paradox: that is to say, the very numbers North Korean authorities see fit to release may also be the figures most prone to official falsification.

A second potential problem with DPRK statistics – related to the first – concerns completeness of coverage. If the coverage of any given economic activity is largely incomplete, or if completeness of coverage varies substantially over time, the reliability of statistical returns with respect to both levels and trends will be seriously compromised.

As it happens, the CBS' coverage practices have changed consequentially in some areas in recent decades. An unannounced move in the early 1970s, for example, summarily excluded the country's military ('non-civilian') population from the demographic figures collected through the DPRK's household registration system (Eberstadt and Banister, 1992). Given North Korea's extremely high degree of military mobilization, this made for a sudden, major incompleteness of coverage in unadjusted population totals. It is not clear whether the CBS was denied information on the country's military economy as well as its military population; any such restrictions, however, could clearly have an impact on calculated macroeconomic results.

A third potential problem relates to the professional competence of North Korea's statistical authorities. The DPRK has no indigenous tradition of statistical expertise to draw upon; it had no established community of statistical specialists at the time of the State's establishment; and as a practical matter the State's posture of extreme isolation and secretiveness has for many decades forestalled the sorts of international exchange and assistance that might help to develop statistical capability. Under those circumstances, it would not seem particularly difficult for unintentional errors and biases –including possibly major ones – to creep into official North Korean statistical series.

A fourth problem with DPRK economic data could not be resolved even if the three previously mentioned problems somehow were. For even if a wealth of accurate figures on production, wages, prices and the like were somehow at hand for the DPRK economy, it would still be extraordinarily difficult to present a meaningful and internationally comparable picture of North Korea's quantitative economic performance.

The general problem here is the dilemma of valuing output produced by a Soviet-type economy (STE) in market terms. Although Western economists have developed a variety of techniques and devices for representing the results from centrally planned economies in a market-style framework[3], none of those attempts could solve the conundrum of how to offer a common unit of measurement for systems with such fundamentally different approaches to pricing and resource allocation (Rosefielde and Pfouts, 1995). This basic methodological predicament has consistently hampered attempts to place the performance of communist economies in a comparative international perspective.

Given these practical and methodological problems, analysts assessing the quantitative performance of the DPRK economy confront a truly daunting task. Intrepid scholars have attempted to deflate North Korean industrial output series (Goto, 1982), and to use econometric techniques to divine a point estimates for DPRK per capita GNP (Chun, 1992; Noland, 1995); researchers in Western governments and universities have offered limited time series for DPRK aggregate product (Hwang, 1993; ROK Bank of Korea various years; USCIA, 1978); and a detailed depiction of national accounts for North Korea for the late 1950s (a period of maximum statistical openness for Pyongyang) has even been attempted (Goto, 1990). Interesting as all these efforts may be, however, the reliability of assessments resting upon official DPRK economic data are necessarily limited for the very reasons we have already enumerated.

Indeed, when one only considers that North Korean authorities have released without explanation two radically different estimates of the country's per capita GNP for the year 1989 – one of $2580, the other of $917, or barely a third the former – one may begin to appreciate the challenges that consumers of official DPRK economic data face. And while other data derived from external, 'classified' sources are additionally available for analysis of the DPRK's long-term economic performance, the limitations of those numbers are also readily apparent.[4]

Facing such imposing constraints, how can we hope to measure the development of the North Korean economic system? In this chapter, we will attempt to do so on the basis of data that may cast light on economic trends, but which are not commonly used to do so. The two sources of data we shall draw upon most heavily will be official North Korean demographic statistics, and overseas reports on North Korea's patterns of merchandise trade (numbers known in the vernacular as 'mirror statistics').

Within broad limits, demographic data may be seen to reflect a country's patterns of economic development and economic performance. In the case of North Korea, demographic data have the virtue of being not only relatively abundant (cf. Eberstadt and Banister, 1992; DPRK CBS 1995), but also of being apparently relatively uninteresting to DPRK policy makers – and thus less susceptible to official, politically motivated alteration. Demographic accounts are far easier to check for internal inconsistencies than are national accounts – and by their very nature, demographic indicators tend to be meaningfully comparable between countries.

'Mirror statistics' have limitations long recognized (cf. Morgenstern, 1963). Nevertheless, they offer a glimpse of a consequential component of the DPRK economy – its external sector.[5] They also permit us to peer, to a degree, into the workings of the DPRK domestic economy and thus to draw some inferences into its long-term performance.

In the following sections, we will attempt to illuminate trends in the structure, performance, and development of the North Korean economy. Most of this discussion will examine the period before North Korea's most recent economic emergency.[6] We will conclude by reviewing the quantitative evidence on the dimensions of the DPRK's current economic crisis.

3.2 POPULATION

Over the past decade, DPRK authorities have been relatively forthcoming with demographic information. In 1989, the DPRK transmitted some demographic data – much of it drawn from the country's household registration system – to the United Nations Population Fund (UNFPA) to meet conditions for possible UNFPA technical assistance with an upcoming population census. Pyongyang eventually did conduct a population census – evidently, its first ever in the history of the regime – in January 1994, but decreed that the count be tallied for the situation as of year-end 1993 (DPRK CBS, 1995).

A number of unanswered questions still attend those data (suffice it to say that it is highly unusual to use a census to collect information about conditions in the previous year, rather about the actual day of the census itself). A number of inconsistencies – some of them non-trivial – between the census data and the earlier registration system reports can be identified. Even so: available DPRK population data permit a reasonably confident reconstruction of the country's basic population trends over the past several decades.

Table 3.1 presents some basic official figures on the DPRK population situation at the end of 1993, and places them in international perspective through comparison with the ROK. By year-end 1993, DPRK's population was reportedly about 21 million – slightly less than half of the ROK's estimated 44 million population in mid-year 1993. The DPRK is much less densely populated than the ROK and also reportedly has a significantly lower ratio of males to females in its population. Part of that discrepancy may be due to an official undercount of Pyongyang's military manpower. But this discrepancy also reflects in some measure the lingering effects of the Korean War, in which the North suffered even more severely than the South.

Table 3.1 Comparative Demographic Indicators from Official Data: DPRK and ROK, 1993

	DPRK	ROK
Population (millions)	21.2	44.2
Area (thousands sq. km)	122.8	99.3
Population density (persons per sq. km)	173	445
Sex ratio (males per 100 females)	94.9	101.3
Median age (years)	27	31*
Population aged 0–14 (per cent)	27.9	23.2*
Population aged 15–64 (per cent)	66.6	70.7*
Population aged 65 and older (per cent)	5.5	6.1*
Crude birth rate (births per 1000 pop.)	19.9	16.5
Crude death rate (deaths per 1000 pop.)	4.9	5.5
Rate of natural increase (per 1000 pop.)	13.9	11.1
Average household size (persons)	4.7	3.3

Notes: DPRK census data are for year-end 1993; ROK census data are for mid-year; * = 1995.

Source: Derived from DPRK Central Bureau of Statistics, Tabulation of the Population Census of the Democratic People's Republic of Korea (31 December 1993); and ROK, National Statistics Office, *Social Indicators*, 1995; and *Korea Statistical Yearbook*, 1996.

Between 1953 and 1993, North Korea's population reportedly grew by nearly 150 per cent, at a pace averaging about 2.3 per cent a year (South Korea's population, for its part, grew by about 110 per cent between the mid-1950s and the mid-1990s, or by a little less than 1.9 per cent a year). In the late 1960s and very early 1970s, North Korea's rate of natural increase is estimated to have exceeded 3 per cent a year (Eberstadt and Banister, 1992, p. 104), but had reportedly dropped to about 1.4 per cent a year by 1993. That slowdown was mainly due to a sharp drop in fertility levels within North Korea. In the late 1960s and very early 1970s, North Korea's 'total fertility rate' (TFR) – a snapshot measure of average births per woman per lifetime –

was well above six, and may have approached seven. By the late 1980s, North Korea's TFR was down to about 2.5 – a decline of over three-fifths in just 20 years. DPRK census results suggest that North Korea's TFR continued to drop thereafter, to about 2.2 by 1993 – a level just barely higher than that required for long-term population replacement.

North Korea's dramatic and sustained fertility decline is consonant with, and suggestive of, 'development' – if that term is broadly construed. Over the past century and a half, secular fertility decline seems to be a handmaiden of socioeconomic modernization; certainly it has been characteristic of every country that has risen to affluence through the process of modern economic growth. Unfortunately, there is no fixed, mechanistic relationship between fertility levels or fertility decline on the one hand and levels of income or productivity on the other. To the great frustration of demographers, the relationship between economic change and fertility decline looks tremendously diverse, both today and in the historical past. So while North Korea's fertility patterns confirm that the country has been undergoing far-reaching socioeconomic transformation, they are of little service in attempting to specify the precise dimensions of its economic transformation.

3.3 HEALTH AND LONGEVITY

Health levels reflect upon living standards, and may also provide clues about a population's potential for productive economic activity. Perhaps the single best summary measure for a population's health is its expectation of life at birth. Estimates for life expectancy for North and South Korea are presented in Table 3.2. Note that these estimates are based upon reconstruction of population data from the respective countries, rather than simply upon the claims of their governments.

According to these estimates, both North and South Korea enjoyed rapid health progress over the decades between the end of the Korean War and the mid-1980s. No less striking, perhaps, is the similarity of both levels and paces of increase in life expectancy in the two Koreas: over this long period, male and female life expectancy at birth in North and South Korea remained essentially indistinguishable from one another. When one considers the very different development paths embraced by the two contending regimes, and the fact that contact between the two populations was virtually nonexistent over those years, the result looks even more remarkable.

Preliminary analysis of the North Korean '1993' census suggests a life expectancy at birth for males of about 68 years, and for females of about 74 years. This would have been just below South Korea's levels, where the respective figures were estimated at 68 and 76 in the year 1991 (United

Nations, 1997). By implication, life expectancy in North Korea would have risen by over two decades between the early 1960s and the early 1990s. In international perspective, that would qualify as a relatively rapid pace of improvement. Interestingly enough, DPRK data provide no evidence of a slowdown in the tempo of life expectancy improvement during the 1980s or very early 1990s.

Table 3.2 Estimated Life Expectancy at Birth for DPRK and ROK, 1955–85

	North Korea			South Korea		
	Both sexes	Male	Female	Both sexes	Male	Female
1955–60	–	–	–	49.2	46.9	52.5
1960	49.0	46.0	52.1	–	–	–
1960–65	51.9	48.9	55.0	50.7	48.1	53.5
1970–75	61.3	58.2	64.6	–	–	–
1978–79	65.2	62.1	68.4	–	62.7	69.1
1980	65.7	62.7	69.0	64.9	63.2	68.8
1985	67.2	70.4	70.4	–	64.9	71.3

Notes: For North Korea, the life expectancy estimates given for 1960–65 are 1963 estimates; for 1970–75, 1973 estimates, and for 1978–79, 1979 estimates.

Source: Eberstadt and Banister (1992), *The Population of North Korea*, p. 48.

If North Korea's life expectancy at birth were in the low 70s in the early 1990s, it would have been about nine years higher than the average for the 'less developed regions' as a whole at that time (United Nations, 1998). Internationally, there is a strong correlation at any given point in time between a country's expectation of life at birth and its level of per capita output (cf. Pritchett and Summers, 1996). That is to say: within the constellation of possible development indicators, life expectancy ordinarily proves to be a reasonably powerful predictor of per capita productivity and income differences among countries.

But there is also enough unexplained variance in the simple correlation between life expectancy and per capita output in international cross-sectional data. The confidence interval for a longevity-based prediction of any given country's output level must be quite broad – and even then there will be countries whose actual performance falls outside of those predicted bounds.

As a practical matter, advances in hygiene, public health practices and state capabilities now make it possible to attain relatively low levels of mortality on very low levels of income. Sri Lanka offers a case in point: the

World Bank places its 1995 life expectancy at 72, and its unadjusted per capita GNP at $700 (World Bank, 1997, p. 214) – $3250 with PPP adjustments. With a stricter regimen of social control than Sri Lanka's it might be possible to elicit similar longevity results on even lower incomes.

3.4 URBANIZATION

Data on long-term urbanization trends in North Korea are presented in Figure 3.1. According to these data, North Korea has made the transition from a predominantly rural to a predominantly urban society. North Korea's level of urbanization appears to have been higher than South Korea's for some time after the Korean War, but the DPRK seems to have been overtaken by the ROK during the 1970s. Since then the pace of urbanization has continued to be brisk in South Korea, whereas it appears to have stagnated in the North.

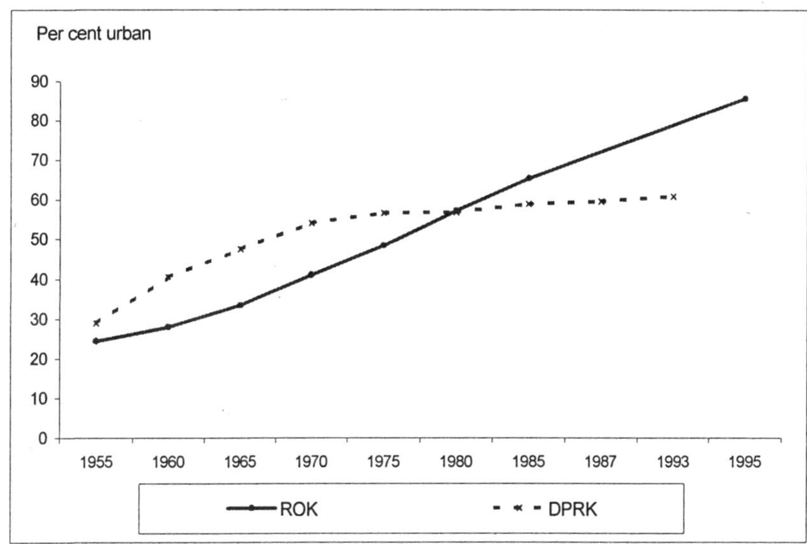

Notes: For South Korea, urban areas are defined as administrative cities with an urban population of 50 000 or more. The definition of the urban population in North Korea has not been published.

Source: For ROK, see Social Indicators in Korea, various editions; *Korea Statistical Yearbook*, various editions. For DPRK, see Eberstadt and Banister, *The Population of North Korea*, 1992.

Figure 3.1 Urbanization in the DPRK and ROK, 1955–95

The level and pace of urbanization provides some indications of a country's economic development. Classic quantitative studies of the process of modern economic growth remarked upon the positive association between economic development and urbanization (Kuznets, 1966; Chenery and Syrquin, 1975). As Kuznets noted, some of that association was conjunctural, rather than causal (Kuznets, 1966, p. 270). But urbanization also presupposes an indispensable measure of productivity enhancement, and structural transformation, within an economy. At a minimum, a populace must be able to afford and maintain this increasingly urbanized existence – and that alone requires shifts in output structure, investment patterns, occupational distribution, intersectoral resource flows. That presupposes, among other things, improvements in per capita output within the agricultural sector.

It is tempting to read North Korea's rapid urbanization in the 1950s and 1960s, the sudden slowdown of urbanization in the 1970s, and the virtual stagnation of urbanization thereafter, as a verdict on overall development trends in the DPRK since the end of the Korean War. Such a reading may well be correct. But the slow pace of urbanization in North Korea over the past two decades could also have been shaped by non-economic factors (for example, possible policies to prevent population concentration for security or military reasons).

Actually, Figure 3.1 probably exaggerates North Korea's level of urbanization in comparison with that of South Korea. Unlike the ROK, the DPRK's definition of 'urban area' appears to be quite elastic; the DPRK's formal delineation between urban and rural districts, moreover, appears to employ a distinctly lower threshold of urban activity. Thus, areas that might not qualify as urban in the ROK may often be counted as urban in the DPRK. In 1987, for example, two out of every five 'urban' residents in the DPRK lived in centers with fewer than 100 000 inhabitants. In the ROK in 1985, by contrast, only about one out of five people then considered 'urban' lived in a place with fewer than 100 000 residents. To the extent that urbanization ratios are taken to betoken productivity improvement and structural transformation within a modern economy, North Korea's figures on urbanization consequently tend to provide an 'optimistic' impression of such developments.

3.5 MILITARIZATION

Although Pyongyang has long cloaked its defense efforts under a special blanket of secrecy, it is nevertheless widely understood that the DPRK is exceptionally – indeed extraordinarily – militarized. North Korea's prolonged and far-reaching military mobilization fundamentally affects its overall economic structure and its patterns of economic performance.

North Korean demographic data and externally collected 'mirror statistics' provide some insight into the magnitude of the North Korean military effort. In data North Korea transmitted to UNFPA in 1989, population totals were provided for the entire country through 1970 – but only for the 'civilian' population thereafter. Thanks to that quirk, it was possible to estimate the size of the DPRK's 'non-civilian' male population – a group that arguably proxies North Korean military manpower for the years 1975–87. Those estimates are presented in Figure 3.2, which contrasts them with official data on the size of the ROK's armed forces.

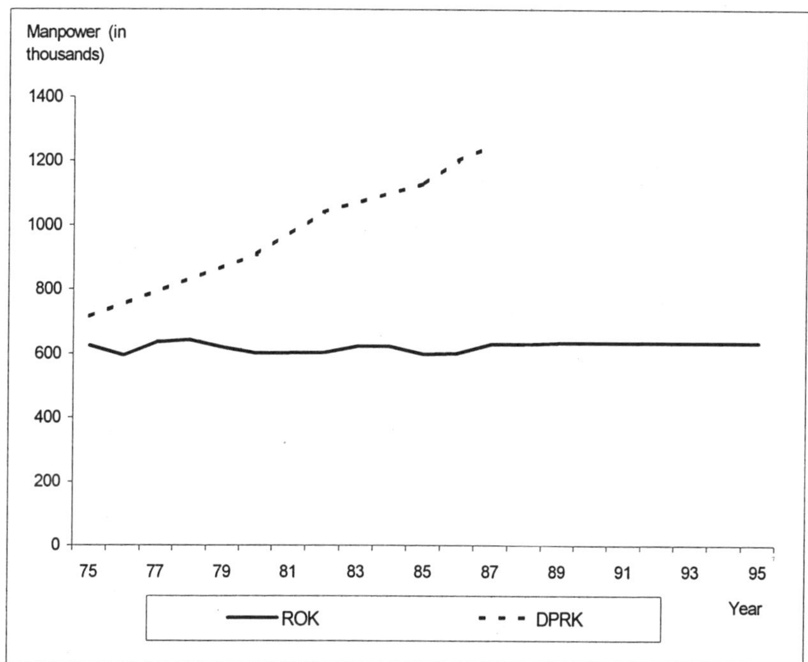

Notes: Military manpower for ROK as reported. Military manpower for DPRK inferred from estimates of non-civilian male population based on demographic reconstructions.

Source: For ROK, IISS The Military Balance, various editions; for DPRK, see Eberstadt and Banister (1992), *The Population of North Korea.*

Figure 3.2 Inferred and Reported Military Manpower in the DPRK and ROK, 1975–95

In the 1970s and 1980s, North Korea apparently effected an absolutely massive buildup of its military manpower. By 1986, those numbers suggest, the DPRK was billeting over 1.2 million soldiers. By the criterion of manpower mobilization, North Korea would have been the most militarized country in the world in the late 1980s, with over 6 per cent of its total population in the armed forces (a fraction similar to that of the USA in 1943), and fully a fifth of the country's men between the ages of 16 and 55 in the barracks.

Table 3.3 Estimated Armed Forces as a Percentage of Total Population and Estimated Defense Budget as a Percentage of GNP: North Korea and Other Highly Mobilized Countries, 1986

	Military manpower/population	Defense budget/GDP
DPRK	6.0	–
Iraq	5.5	57 %[a]
Syria	3.5	18 %[b]
Israel	3.4	19 %[c]
United Arab Emirates	3.1	8 %[b]
Jordan	2.6	12 %[a]
Nicaragua	2.2	11 %[d]
Singapore	2.1	6 %[b]
Taiwan	2.1	7 %[c]
Greece	2.0	6 %[a]
Qatar	2.0	5 %[d]

Notes: Estimates for North Korea refer to year-end 1986. Estimates for other countries refer to mid-year 1986. IISS estimates refer to active duty military manpower. a = 1985, b = 1984/85, c = 1985/86, d = 1984.

Source: Eberstadt and Banister (1992) *The Population of North Korea*, p. 94; International Institute of Strategic Studies, *Military Balance 1987*.

Table 3.3 places this military disposition in international perspective, using estimates for other countries from the London International Institute of Strategic Studies (IISS). As of 1986, the only country on earth even approaching North Korea's ratio of military manpower to total population would have been Iraq – locked at that time in what had escalated into a desperate total war against Iran.

No reliable official data are available on North Korean military expenditures.[7] But comparisons with other highly militarized economies can still be instructive. In the mid-to-late 1980s, Syria and Israel may have been deploying just over half as much manpower for their militaries as North

Korea; in both cases, their military budgets amounted to nearly a fifth of total national output. In Iraq, whose manpower mobilization ratio most nearly approximated North Korea's, the defense budget may have equaled almost three-fifths of GDP (Iraq, though, was in the midst of a 'hot' war at that time).

In a market-economy framework, North Korea's actual ratio of military expenditures to national output would be determined not only by its ratio of military to total manpower, but also by the pattern of output consumption by its defense force, the capital–output ratios of its military industries, and marginal rates of transformation (price relations) between military and civilian sectors.[8] None of that information, of course, is available today. Nevertheless, it is safe to assert that North Korea's ratio of military expenditure to national output was one of the world's very highest as of the late 1980s, and had been so by then for many years.

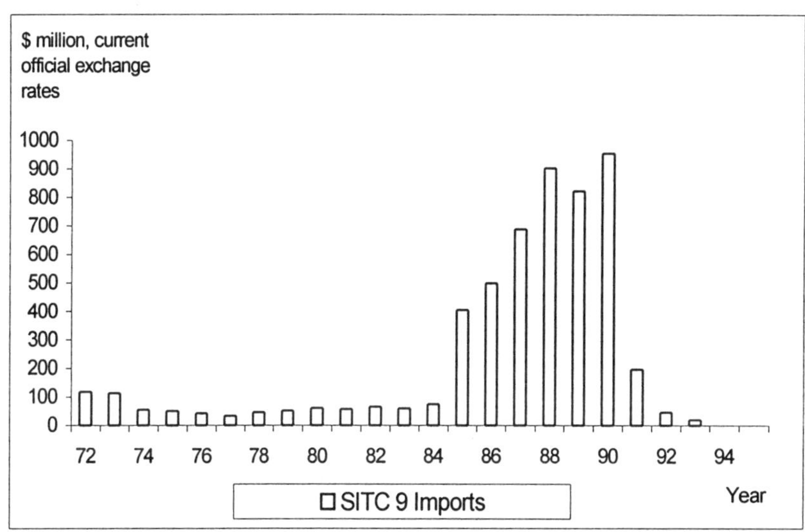

Figure 3.3 DPRK Imports of SITC 9 Items from USSR/Russia, 1972–95

North Korea's 'military burden' is determined not only by government priorites, but by the specifics of the contest into which it has entered. In all likelihood, North Korea's defense industries have been locked into a competition on highly disadvantageous terms. Confronting the US–ROK alliance in a high-tech (and rapidly innovating) military adversary, North Korean defense industries presumably have embarked upon projects where their rates of return upon capital expenditures were extremely low; if so, it is possible that the resource requirements of the North Korean defense effort could have escalated suddenly and steeply, even after manpower buildup had been long under way.

There is some evidence from 'mirror statistics' that the DPRK may have attempted to relieve the strain on its military industries (and thus on its entire national economy) in the late 1980s through a closer security relationship with the USSR. Soviet trade statistics, when translated into the Western 'SITC' schema, reveal an abrupt and dramatic rise in shipments to the DPRK of merchndise in the grouping that would include weaponry and munitions (SITC Category '9'). One may reasonably infer that Figure 3.3 traces the volume of Soviet arms shipments to North Korea over the years (after converting rubles into dollars at current official rates of exchange).[9]

Between 1985 and 1990, the value of the Soviet merchandise shipments detailed in Figure 3.3 would have exceeded $5 billion (at current official dollar–ruble exchange rates). In 1991, of course, this commerce collapsed; by 1993 it had all but ceased. It is widely recognized that the dissolution of the Soviet Union brought a shock upon the DPRK economy. What is less widely appreciated is that the USSR's final crisis may have brought special stresses for North Korea's defense sector and military industries.

Official data offer only the most obscure glimpse of the DPRK's military sector in the 1990s. However one interprets those official data, it is apparent that North Korea continues to be one of the most highly militarized societies on earth, at least by the yardstick of manpower mobilization. The empirical data do not, further, provide any reliable indications of the recent trend for the DPRK's ratio of defense allocations to overall national output. One may observe, however, attempts at military modernization may be especially costly in an economy where technological innovation lags and international avenues of technology transfer are marginal. Thus, even if the ratio of armed forces to total population had declined somewhat in recent years, it would not necessarily follow that the country's 'military burden' had abated as well.

3.6 LABOR FORCE

With the release of the DPRK '1993' census, more information than ever before is available on the North Korean work force. These data, to be sure, are not bereft of ambiguity.[10] Such ambiguities notwithstanding, these numbers, in conjunction with earlier DPRK data on manpower disposition, provide insight into the country's economic structure and its development.

According to DPRK statistics, North Korea's labor force has been transformed over the over the past half-century overwhelmingly agrarian to overwhelmingly industrial (see Table 3.4). By those numbers, almost three-fourths of the country's manpower qualified as 'farmers' in 1946, whereas only an eighth were then considered to be 'laborers'. By 1993, on the other hand, 'farmers' or 'agricultural cooperative members' had dropped to under a fourth of the country's workforce, and 'laborers' made up over three-fifth of the identified total. 'Office workers', for their part, had risen from about 6 per cent in 1946 to about 13 per cent in 1993. If we could rely upon these numbers, they would indicate that the DPRK had released fully half its manpower over the past 50 years from farm into industrial activities.

Table 3.4 Reported Distinction of DPRK Population by Employment Category, 1946–93

	Farmer/agricultural cooperative member	Worker	Office worker	Other
1946	74.1	12.5	6.2	7.2
1949	69.6	19.0	7.0	4.4
1953	66.9	21.2	8.5	3.9
1956	56.6	27.3	13.6	2.5
1960	44.4	38.3	13.7	3.6
1963	42.8	40.1	15.1	1.9
1986	25.9	56.3	17.0	0.9
1987	25.3	57.0	16.8	0.9
1993	23.5	63.1	13.4	–

Source: For 1946–63, Joseph S. Chung (1974), *The North Korean Economy*, 146–7; for 1986–87, Eberstadt and Bannister (1992), p. 83; for 1993, DPRK, p. 508.

Those sectoral aggregates, unfortunately, dissect the North Korean labor force by class-based criteria, rather than according to occupational differentiations. By that somewhat tortured taxonomy, a worker who services tractors in a repair shop in an agricultural cooperative counts as a 'farmer', whereas an employee raising crops for an enormous, largely self-sustaining, state factory counts as a 'worker'.

Fortunately, the DPRK '1993' census for the first time provides a breakdown of the industrial distribution of the identified North Korean labor force. These provide a rather different impression of the country's employment structure.

In 1993, for example, occupation-based employment statistics indicate that North Korea's 'secondary sector' absorbed twenty-five percentage points less of the country's overall workforce than would be suggested in Table 3.4 – and that the 'tertiary sector' absorbed almost seventeen percentage points more. The figures in Table 3.5, in short, depict a DPRK employment structure distinctly less 'industrialized' than had been implied heretofore by official data – but by the same measure, an employment structure seemingly that much less distorted.

Table 3.5 Distribution of Labor Force: DPRK 1993 versus ROK 1995

	DPRK		ROK	
	Total (1000s)	%	Total (1000s)	%
Overall labor force	11 004	100	20 377	100
Manufacturing	4 118	37.4	4 773	23.4
Farming	3 381	30.7	2 551	12.5
Construction	464	4.2	1 896	9.3
Transport and communication	402	3.7	1 068	5.2
State farms	251	2.3	–	–
Commerce	509	4.6	3 763	18.4
Education, culture, health	844	7.7	1 312	6.4
Others	1 305	9.4	5 014	24.8

Source: Derived from DPRK Central Bureau of Statistics, *Tabulation of the Population Census of the Democratic People's Republic of Korea* (December 31, 1993); and ROK, National Statistics Office, *Korea Statistical Yearbook 1996.*

It may be instructive to contrast the new data on North Korea's labor force distribution with the opposite figures for South Korea, as we do in Table 3.5. Some results from this comparison seem entirely unsurprising. In keeping with its traditional emphasis on development of industry (especially heavy industry), 'manufacturing' absorbs a much larger share of North Korean than South Korean manpower (37 per cent versus 23 per cent). By the same token, 'commerce' reportedly occupies much less of the North Korean than the South Korean work force (5 per cent versus 18 per cent). More unexpected is the reported result that North Korea devotes a distinctly smaller share of its manpower to construction than does South Korea (4 per cent versus 9 per cent) – a reflection, perhaps, of the possibility that by the early 1990s the troubled DPRK economy was simply not undertaking many new building projects.

But the most arresting difference between the two Korea's employment structures relates to their 'primary sectors'. The new North Korean labor force data reveals the number of people actually engaged in agriculture by nearly a third the number classified as 'farmers'. Together, 'farming' and 'state farms' reportedly accounted for 33 per cent of the DPRK's workforce in its '1993' census – over twenty percentage points more than the corresponding figure for South Korea's primary sector for 1995.

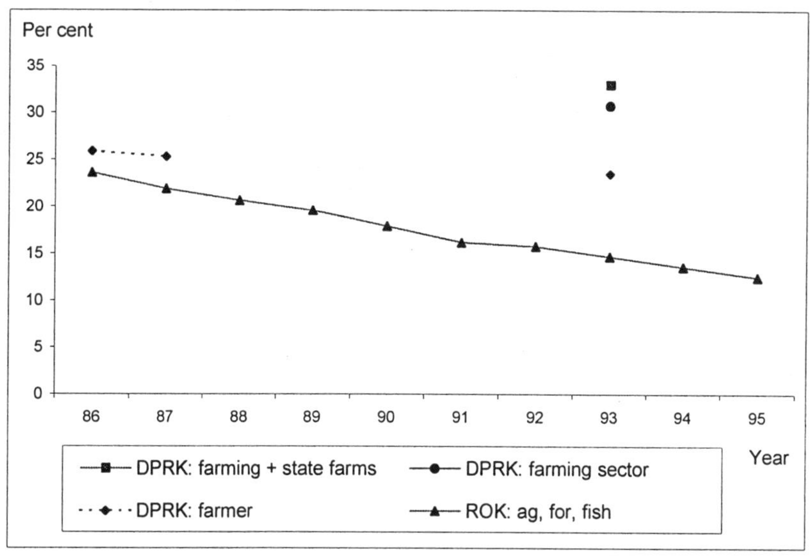

Figure 3.4 Reported Percentage of Labor Force in Primary Sector, DPRK versus ROK, ca. 1986–95

Although information on the potential productivity of North Korea's workers is all but nonexistent, the DPRK's labor force distribution patterns provide hints about overall productivity levels, and trends, in that economy. Figure 3.3, for example, contrasts trends in employment in the 'primary sector' in North and South Korea in the 1980s and 1990s (see Figure 3.4). While a mechanistic comparison between sectoral employment patterns and per capita output is obviously unwarranted, we may note that the last time 'primary sector' activities occupied 35 per cent or more of South Korea's work force was in the late 1970s – when ROK per capita output was roughly only a quarter as high as it is today.

We should further note that the displacement of manpower out of agriculture appears to have been much more rapid in South Korea than in North Korea during the 1980s and 1990s – implying a much slower pace of structural transformation for the North during those decades.

Comparisons of output or productivity between market-oriented and centrally planned systems are, as already noted, fraught with irresolvable difficulties. It may therefore be more appropriate to divine indications of North Korea's level of development by comparing the distribution of the DPRK's labor force with those from other socialist countries (see Table 3.6). If the proportion of the work force absorbed in agriculture can be regarded as a rough proxy for the level of per capita output, North Korea's level of per capita output in the early 1990s would have ranked distinctly below those of the Soviet bloc countries at the end of their socialist era – but at the same time, disctinctly above those of contemporary China and Vietnam, Asian socialist states that seemed to have devised a formula for marring continued Communist rule with rapid material advance.

Table 3.6 Distribution of Labor Force: DPRK and Selected Other Socialist States

Countries	Year	Sector (%)		
		Agriculture	Industry	Service
Poland	1989	7[a]	37	56
Czech Republic	1989	11[a]	39	51
Slovakia	1989	15[a]	34	51
Hungary	1989	15[a]	36	49
Bulgaria	1989	19[a]	47	34
USSR	1987	19	38[b]	43
Belarus	1990	20	42	38
Ukraine	1990	20	40	40
Romania	1990	28[a]	38	34
DPRK	1993	33	37	30
China	1993	54	23	23
Vietnam	1989	71	12	17

Notes: a = agriculture and forestry, b = industry and construction.

Source: Noland, Marcus (1995), 'North Korea in Global Perspective', in this volume; China State Statistical Bureau, *China Statistical Yearbook 1995* (Beijing: China Statistical Publishing House).

The '1993' DPRK census casts light not only upon work force distribution, but on labor force participation rates (see Table 3.7). Even for a Communist society, North Korea's degree of labor force mobilization is remarkably high – almost 85 per cent for males 16 and older, and fully 76 per cent for the entire adult population.[11] Note further that these North Korean rates ostensibly pertain to the civilian population only: if military manpower were taken into account, the rate for 'mobilized adult manpower' would be still higher.

The DPRK constitution defines the 'working ages' to be 16 to 60 for men, and 16 to 55 for women. According to the '1993' DPRK census, work force participation for North Korean citizens within those age groupings is astonishingly total – as near to universal, one may venture, as could occur in a society inhabited by human beings (see Table 3.8). One wonders, indeed, how all of those represented as engaging in economic activity could actually be capable of productive work.

Table 3.7 Labor Force Participation Rates for North and South Korea and Selected Other Countries, Recent Years (Percentage)

Country (year, age group)	Total	Male	Female
North Korea, excluding army (1993, 16+)	76.0	84.6	68.9
South Korea (1995, 15+)	62.0	76.5	48.3
Communist States			
Czechoslovakia (1980, 15+)	67.8	75.5	60.8
East Germany (1981, 15+)	67.5	76.2	60.0
Hungary (1980, 15+)	60.5	71.9	50.2
Cuba (1981, 15+)	53.4	72.8	33.8
China (1982, 15+)	78.7	86.5	75.0
Vietnam (1989, 15+)	77.3	81.6	73.6
Asian NICs			
Hong Kong (1995, 15+)	62.8	77.3	48.0
Taiwan (1989, 15+)	60.4	74.8	45.4
Singapore (1995, 15+)	64.3	78.4	50.0
Developed Market Economies			
Germany (1995, 15+)	58.5	69.7	48.2
Japan (1995, 15+)	63.4	77.6	50.0
Switzerland (1995, 15+)	55	64	46.4
USA (1995, 16+)	66.6	75	58.0

Source: Derived from DPRK Central Bureau of Statistics, *Tabulation of the Population Census of the Democratic People's Republic of Korea* (31 December 1993); ROK, *Social Indicators in Korea, 1995 and Korea Statistical Yearbook*, 1996; ROC, *Republic of China Statistical Yearbook* 1990; all others, ILO, *Yearbook of Labor Statistics*, various editions.

North Korea's extraordinary current labor force participation rates are suggestive of an especially relentlessly executed 'extensive development' strategy. The course of that strategy is partly revealed by estimated labor force participation rates for earlier years – although those calculations are necessarily more tentative than the 1993 figure. In 1963, estimated labor force participation rates for North Koreans 15 years of age and older may have been about 55 per cent: 75 per cent for men, 40 per cent for women (Eberstadt and Banister, 1992, p. 82). By 1986, the DPRK's overall labor force participation rate for persons 16 and older had risen to an estimated 74 per cent (no breakdown by gender is available) – almost twenty percentage points higher than in the early 1960s (Eberstadt and Banister, 1992, pp. 83–4). North Korea's estimated labor force participation rate for 1993, however, is only slightly higher than for 1986. Evidently, the limits of extensive mobilization had been reached.

Table 3.8 Reported Labor Force Participation Rates by Age and Sex, 1993 (Percentage)

Age	Male	Female	Total
16–19	62.5	66.3	64.6
20–24	90.9	92.7	91.8
25–29	89.0	86.8	87.8
30–34	95.9	87.0	91.4
35–39	98.5	89.4	93.9
40–44	98.8	91.1	94.9
45–49	98.6	91.1	94.7
50–54	97.8	86.5	93.6
55–59	95.9	16.3	52.8
60+	16.5	4.1	8.4

Source: Derived from DPRK Central Bureau of Statistics, *Tabulation of the Population Census of the Democratic People's Republic of Korea* (December 31, 1993), pp. 505 and 517.

3.7 FOREIGN TRADE AND DOMESTIC ECONOMIC INFRASTRUCTURE

The volume and composition of North Korea's international trade over the past generation can be reconstructed on the basis of 'mirror statistics'. Under ordinary circumstances, 'mirror statistics' are by no means free from error. An additional complication in North Korea's case is the presumably unusual share of DPRK international commerce in illicit goods (weaponry, narcotics, and the like) that ordinarily do not show up in trade partners' official export or import accounts. Despite these limitations, North Korea's 'mirror statistics' may nevertheless depict levels and trends in Pyongyang's international commerce tolerably well.[12]

The most striking aspect of the DPRK's trade patterns is the extreme weakness of its long-term performance – a corollary to what Chun and Park describe as the regime's 'inward looking development strategy emphasizing heavy industry first' (Chun and Park, 1997, p. 681). That weakness is highlighted in Figure 3.6, which compares the DPRK's estimated nominal export earnings for the 1970–95 period with the performance of other regions (see Figure 3.5).

Even in nominal US dollars, North Korea's 1995 export volume was scarcely higher than it had been 20 years earlier. On a nominal per capita basis, it was actually lower in 1995 than it had been in 1975; on a real per capita basis – if such a deflator could be devised – it would probably look lower still.

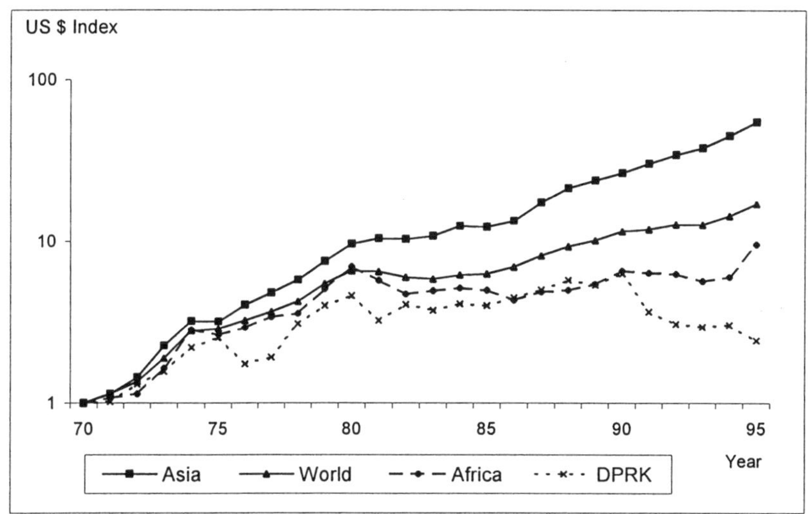

Figure 3.5 Comparative Export Earnings: World, Asia, Africa, DPRK, 1970–95 (1970 = 1)

Admittedly, 1995 was an annus horribilis for the DPRK – a time of severe economic troubles, empirical indicators of which we will review in a moment. But even before the crisis that commenced with the USSR's collapse, North Korean trade performance was dismal. Between 1970 and 1990, North Korea's nominal increases in export earnings lagged far behind the world average (to say nothing about the rest of Asia); its aggregate export performance over those decades, in fact, could best be likened to that of the troubled African continent. And even that comparison casts DPRK trade performance in an unduly favorable light, for North Korea's overall trade volume only rose at all in the 1980s thanks to an upsurge of Soviet–DPRK commerce – a commerce willed into existence by political decisions in Moscow. Excluding its Soviet trade, the estimated nominal dollar value of

DPRK trade turnover declined by almost a quarter between 1980 and 1990; non-Soviet exports are estimated to have fallen by almost 30 per cent over that same decade.

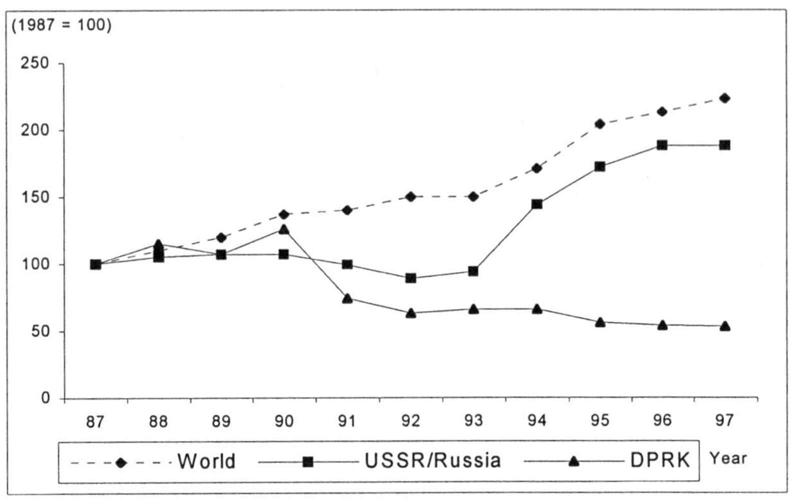

Figure 3.6 Relative Trade Performance: DPRK and USSR/Russia, 1987–97 (1987 = 100) Export

North Korea's economic downturn in the 1990s is ascribed – not least by Pyongyang – to the dissolution of the economic bonds that connected the USSR and the DPRK. Yet the end of the Soviet Union can only explain a fraction of North Korea's subsequent macroeconomic travails: for North Korea's adjustments to the end of the Soviet empire was distinctly different from Russia's own (see Figures 3.6 and 3.7). For the Russian Federation, the end of Soviet Communism presaged an initial trade shock – but then a gradual recovery of both imports and exports, and thereafter an impulse for an expansion of trade toward volumes that might be more ordinarily expected from a country of Russia's population and income level (Russia's import trends appear in this series to the less vigorous than its export growth – but in part this may reflect contemporary Russia's notoriously enterprising, and custom duties-averse, approach to transnational commerce).[13] Indeed: despite Russia's domestic economic turmoil during the 1990s, the country's international trade turnover expanded substantially – albeit not as briskly as the tempo of overall global trade during those same years. North Korea was an entirely different story. There, 'mirror statistics', indicate a collapse of trade turnover after the exit of the USSR from the international stage – and in a world economy characterized by continually expanding trade turnover, an inability to even maintain previous normal volumes of exports and imports.

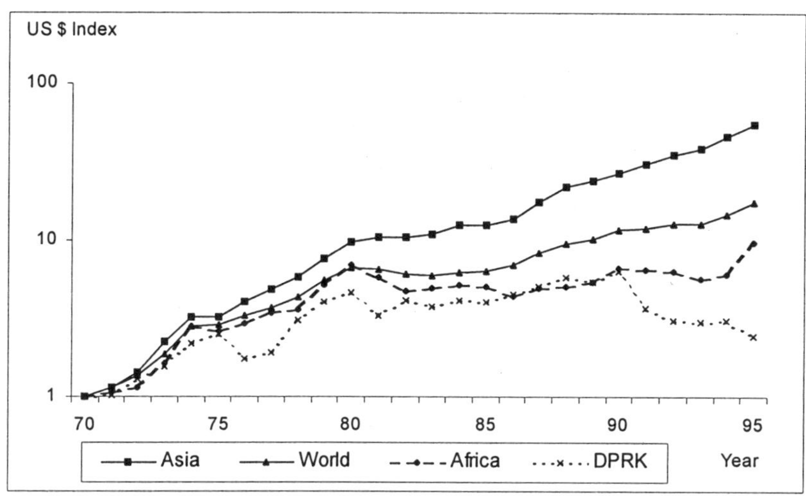

Figure 3.7 Relative Trade Performance: DPRK and USSR/Russia, 1987–97 (1987 = 100) Import

It belabors the obvious to observe that North Korea's approach to economic development is one that has limited interaction with, and integration into, the world economy over the past generation. What may not be quite so obvious, however, is that the same policies that led to stagnation (or worse) in North Korea's trade volume also resulted in stagnation in the DPRK's trade composition. Between the early 1970s and the early 1990s, the merchandise structure of global trade evolved markedly – automobiles, office equipment, and other machinery and equipment, for example, came to account for a much larger fraction of overall exports. In North Korea, on the other hand, export patterns (as reflected by mirror statistics) were basically stuck in the same structure between the late 1970s and the mid-1990s: throughout that period, the DPRK's major reported exports consisted of foodstuffs (first rice, later marine products); minerals (gold, magnesite), and relatively simple manufactured goods (steel, cement and starting in the mid-1980s, textiles). None of those products today would be described as particularly knowledge-intensive or skills-sensitive. Those data appear to square broadly with the proposition that the North Korean economy has been beset by economic and technological stagnation (or worse) for the better part of a generation.

Trade data and mirror statistics can provide some insight into the state of the DPRK's economic infrastructure. Table 3.9, for example, 'traces and contrasts trends in the import and export of machinery and equipment' – broadly speaking, of 'capital goods' – into North Korea and other countries or regions over the past generation.

Table 3.9 DPRK Capital Goods Trade in International Perspective

Country/region	Capital goods as a proportion of trade (%)			Capital goods trade per person (current $ value)		
	Import					
	1970s	1980s	1990s	1970s	1980s	1990s
USSR	35.9	37.1	–	45	18	–
CMEA Europe	35.7[a]	31.7[b]	–	175[a]	303[b]	–
Cuba	26.6	31.7	21.0	97	237	77
China	21.8[c]	28.6	37.8	2[c]	10	28
DPRK	27.7[d]	19.8	16.4	14[d]	17	9
ROK	28.8	30.2	35.1	68	238	774
Developing Economies	27.4	32.1	46.5[e]	27	57	114[e]
	Export					
	1970s	1980s	1990s	1970s	1980s	1990s
USSR	18.4	14.6	–	24	49	–
CMEA Europe	42.3[a]	46.7[b]	–	192[a]	455[b]	–
Cuba	negl.	negl.	negl.	negl.	negl.	negl.
China	3.7[c]	3.3	13.9	negl[c].	2	11
DPRK	3.8[d]	6.9	10.4	1[d]	6	6
ROK	14.8	32.3	45.0	32	294	922
ROK	4.8	12.8	27.4[d]	4	23	67[e]

Notes: Trade volumes estimated in current $ at official exchange rates, imports c.i.f. (except developing economies), exports f.o.b. 'Developing Economies' defined per UN taxonomy (less China); per capita trade volumes calculated according to 1975, 1985, 1990/95 pop. a = 1970, 1973–79; b = 1980–88; c = 1980, 1975–79; d = 1972–79; e = 1990–94.

Source: Eberstadt (1999).

During the past decade, a number of quantitative studies have pointed to the importance of investments in machinery and equipment to the process of modern economic growth (cf. De Long and Summers, 1991). Further research has indicated that imports of capital goods in particular can play an instrumental role in economic development, not only by augmenting a country's capital stock with productivity-enhancing machinery, but also by lowering the relative price of domestic investment in fixed reproducible capital (cf. Lee, 1995). In the developing economies as a whole, as Table 3.9 attests, both the absolute per capita value of capital goods imports and the share of capital goods within total imports have risen substantially over the past generation. Import-facilitated modernization of industrial infrastructure, in turn, appears to have led to secular increases in both the absolute per capita value of capital goods exports, and their share within exports overall for the countries in question.

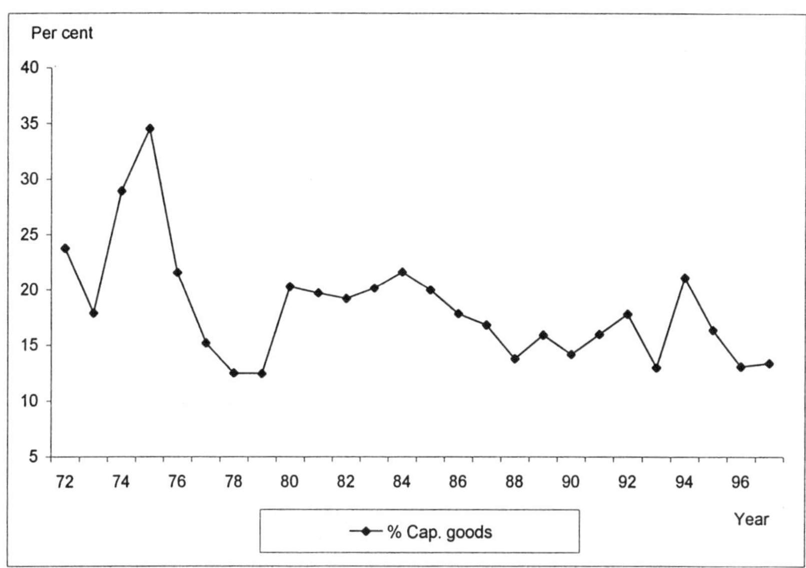

Figure 3.8 Capital Goods as a Percentage of Total DPRK Merchandise Imports, 1972–97

The situation appears to have been entirely different in North Korea. For the DPRK, 1975 appears to have been the high-water mark for capital goods imports, even in nominal terms; in real terms, if we could determine those capital equipment imports it might very well have tended downward through the 1970s, 1980s, and 1990s (and as Table 3.9 emphasizes, North Korea's allergy to capital investment on the basis of imported foreign machinery seems to have been unique among the Communist economies). No less significant, the share of capital goods within DPRK imports appears to have declined progressively over these same decades (see Figure 3.8).

The low priority accorded to capital goods imports in the DPRK economy over the past generation may be illustrated by a single comparison: at official exchange rates and in current dollars, the total volume of North Korea's capital goods imports for the period 1972–95 only slightly exceeded the estimated value of its Soviet weapons imports over the years 1985–90, as represented in Figure 3.3.

As a result of longstanding patterns, North Korea today surely has one of the very lowest proportions of foreign machinery in its overall capital stock of any contemporary economy – possibly even the very lowest. Thus, despite the DPRK's seeming fetish for 'investment', industrial production has been severely constrained. By insisting upon the use of domestically produced machinery and equipment, the DPRK has opted for a high-cost, low-productivity industrial base. Irrespective of the actual age of North Korea's capital stock, one may guess that the technology embodied in it is unusually antiquated and limited. One hint to this effect is North Korea's continuing inability to generate exports of machinery or equipment (at least: machinery and equipment of a civilian nature). Indeed, on a per capita basis, North Korea's level of such exports is probably lower today than it had been a decade earlier – possibly even two decades earlier.

Noteworthy also is the conspicuous lack of investment in 'transport equipment' revealed by DPRK mirror statistics. By those numbers, it would appear that the DPRK has been seriously underinvesting in means of transport for the better part of the past generation (Eberstadt, 1998). To go by those figures, the revolution in transportation that has swept up the rest of the world has swept the DPRK by.

3.8 THE CURRENT DPRK ECONOMIC CRISIS

The North Korean economic slump during the present decade is corroborated by available empirical data – but illuminated by them only to a degree. Available statistics, in fact, cast far less light on the country's current economic troubles than would satisfy the curiosity of international scholars, policy makers, or humanitarian activists. Drawing upon 'mirror statistics', though, it is possible to make a number of points about the DPRK's current economic straits.

First, the Soviet Union's collapse proved to be a serious stress upon an already frail DPRK external sector, and only further underscored North Korea's limited ability to compete in the international marketplace. Between 1989 and 1992, estimated DPRK trade turnover (in current dollars at official exchange rates) dropped by 45 per cent. Over the following three years, far from beginning a recovery, estimated North Korean trade turnover declined still further. By 1995, North Korea's estimated per capita export earnings amounted to less than $50 – an amazingly low level for a predominantly urban, non-agricultural country with only a limited domestic division of labor.

The DPRK's difficulties in adjusting to the rigors of an international marketplace in which its purchase orders for its wares were not preordained may be discerned in Figures 3.9–3.13, which trace the value of the DPRK's five main Soviet-era civilian commodity exports (steel, cement, textiles, magnesite and gold) into the early post-Cold War epoch. On the whole, the exports in question would seem to qualify as 'homogenous' rather than highly specialized products; and since the volumes sold in the late 1980s were marginal from the standpoint of overall international purchases, placing them would not seem to pose any prima facie issues with respect to market stability. Other things being equal, one might have imagined that export capacity freed up by lapsed Moscow contracts could be redirected toward other international markets; to judge by 'mirror statistics', though, the DPRK has not generally managed to do so, at least to date.

A second point – related to the first – is that, since the Soviet break-up, North Korea has proved incapable of securing supplies of the intermediate products that might help it return to status quo ante economic performance (never mind development). Energy imports provide a case in point. According to 'mirror statistics', imports of both oil and oil products and coking coal have dropped precipitously since the Soviet era (see Figures 3.14 and 3.15). In a flexible economy with high elasticities of substitution, the constraints on production posed by such disruptions might not be dramatic. Alas, the DPRK does not today appear to be such an economic system.

Thirdly whereas other economic systems, including Communist systems, typically slash capital goods imports during periods of economic dislocation and emergency, the DPRK's pattern of capital imports looks to have been largely unaffected by its post-Soviet travails. The point can be made by contrasting recent DPRK capital goods import patterns with those of China before and immediately after the 'Great Leap Forward' on the one hand, and those of Cuba since 1987 on the other (see Figure 3.16). In both the Chinese and the Cuban cases, the share of imports devoted to capital goods plummeted after the onset of crisis, but then gradually recovered; in North Korea, by contrast, the share of capital goods within imports has remained rather steady – albeit at levels as low as for China or Cuba's 'emergency' years. One can interpret this incongruity diversely – but one possible inference to draw from it is that the DPRK's economic decision makers have been less willing than other Communist planners to reconsider their predetermined designs even under the sudden weight of crushing exigence.

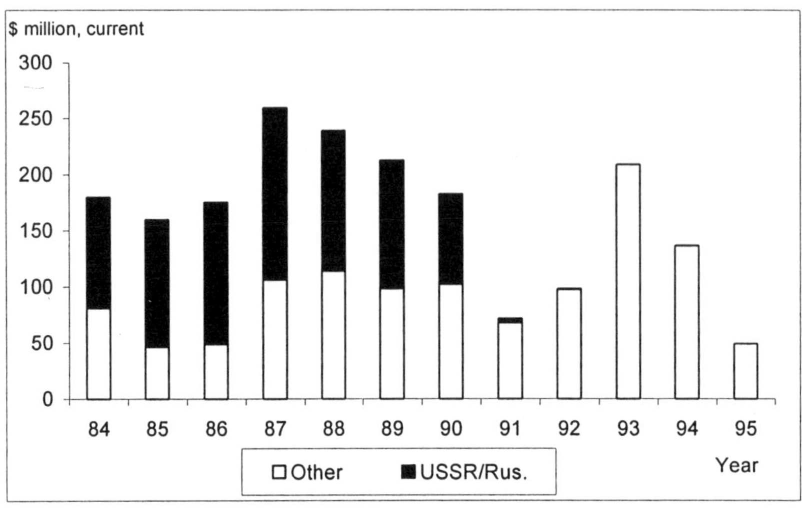

Figure 3.9 DPRK Export Performance: Steel, 1984–95

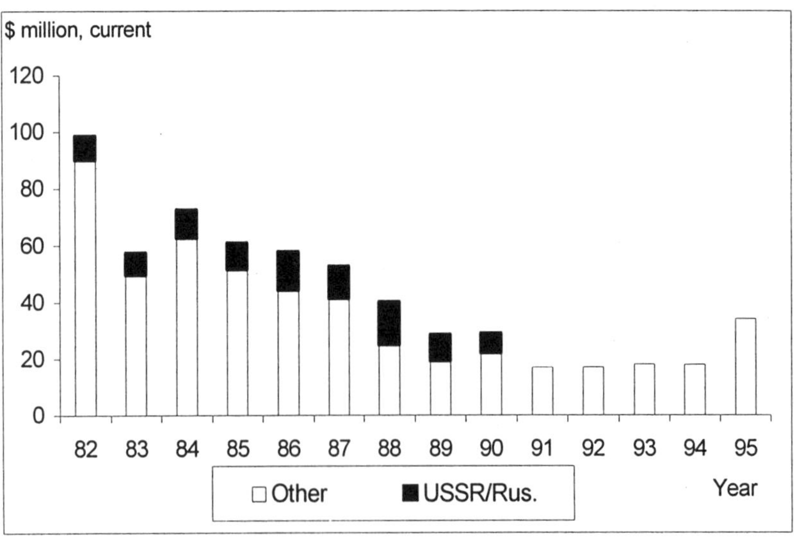

Figure 3.10 DPRK Export Performance: Cement, 1982–95

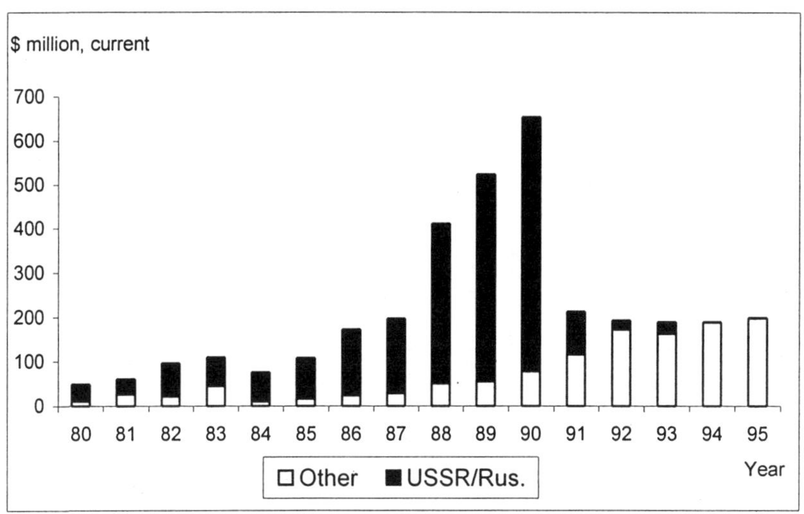

Figure 3.11 DPRK Export Performance: Textiles, 1980–95

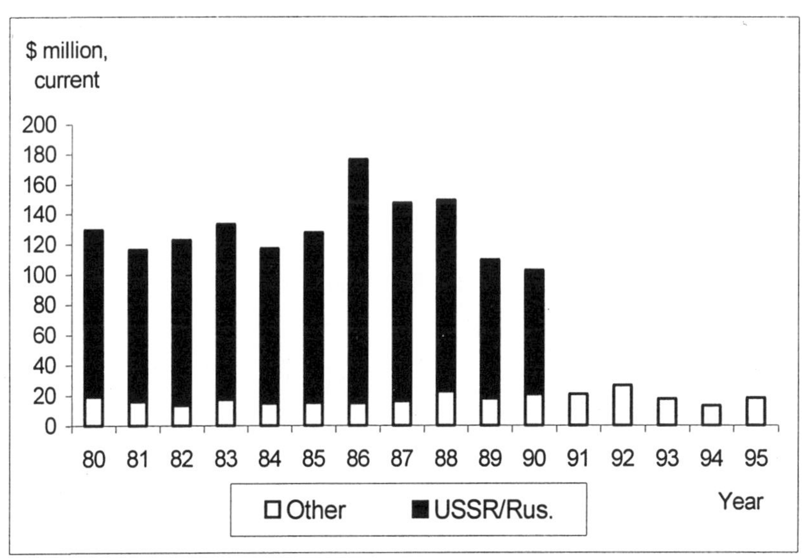

Figure 3.12 DPRK Export Performance: Magnesite, 1980–95

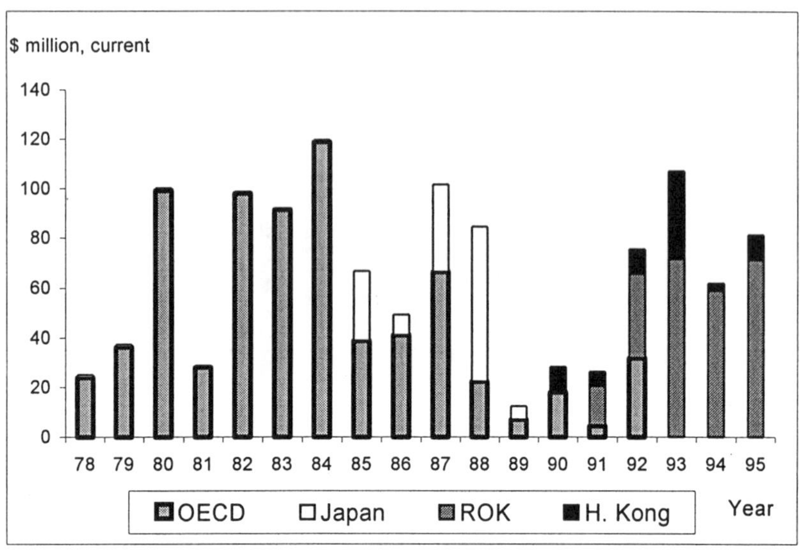

Figure 3.13 DPRK Export Performance: Gold, 1978–95

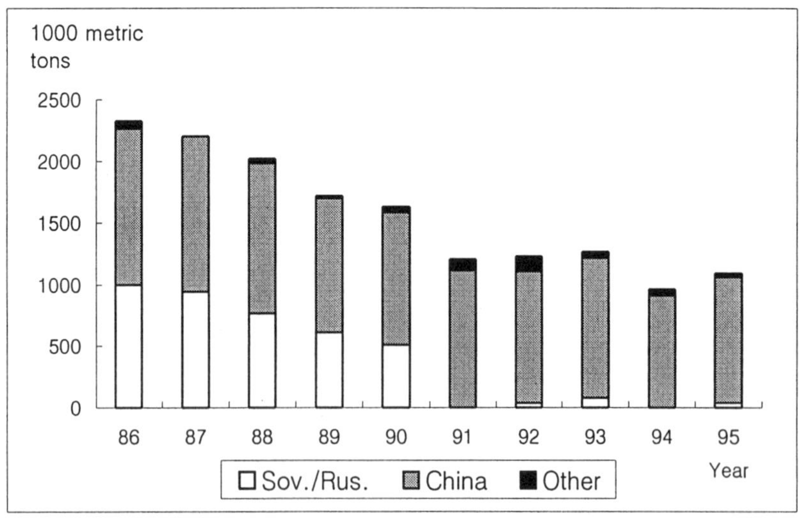

Figure 3.14 DPRK Imports of Oil and Oil Products, 1986–95

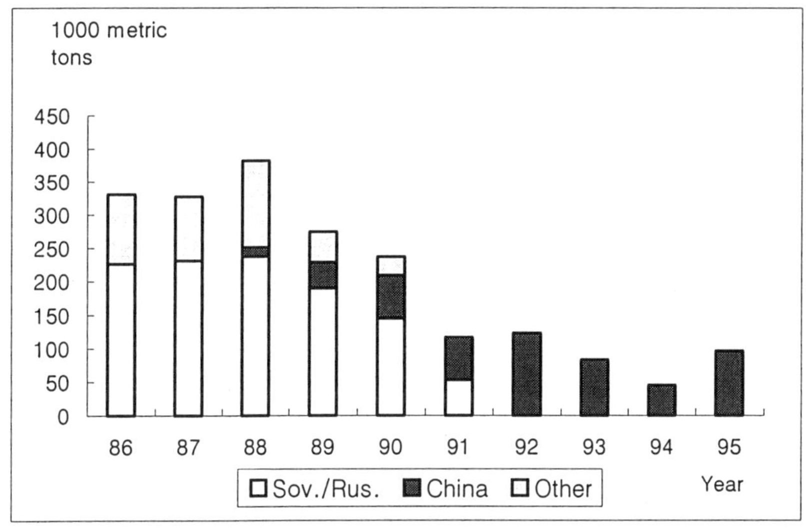

Figure 3.15 DPRK Imports of Coking Coal, 1986–95

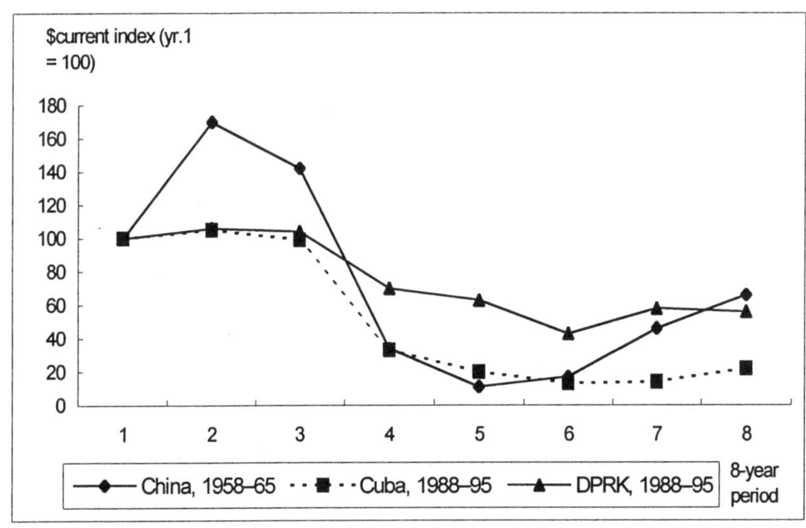

Figure 3.16 Capital Goods Imports during (8-year) Periods of Economic Crises: Estimated Absolute Value for China, Cuba, DPRK

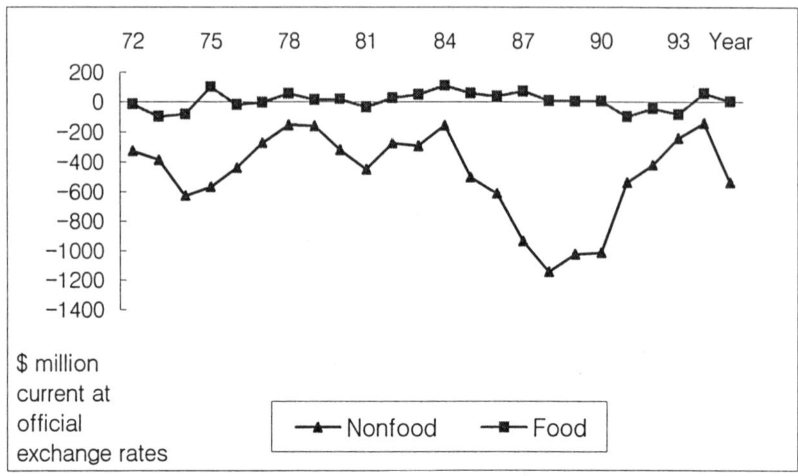

Figure 3.17 DPRK Balance of Trade, Food versus Non-food, 1972–95

Finally, 'mirror statistics' hint that the DPRK has stubbornly pursued for decades a variant of 'food self-sufficiency' policy much more likely to heighten than mitigate the risk of nutritional distress. For while North Korea's estimated balance of trade for non-food products has been allowed to run steadily negative throughout the 1970s, 1980s, and 1990s, its exports and imports food have been held to rough parity over those same years. Figure 3.17 strongly suggests that North Korean policy has stipulated that the government should purchase no more foodstuffs from abroad than foreigners buy from the DPRK. Such a policy might help to explain why a third or more of North Korea's work force is deployed in the 'primary sector'. But it could neither capitalize upon the country's 'comparative advantages' (insofar as the DPRK is a largely urbanized Northeast Asian country with limited arable land and a relatively short growing season), nor cope expeditiously with agricultural shortfalls if and when they occurred. North Korea's apparent 'food self-sufficiency' policy, in short, stands as an open invitation to nutritional hardship; the only question (one may argue) was when nutritional hardship would take up the offer.

At this juncture, given the DPRK's official appeal for emergency international food aid and foreign relief workers' reports of widespread starvation with North Korea, there is pressing demand for accurate information on the magnitude of the humanitarian crisis within that country. Outside surveys of 'border crossers', of the sort conducted along the China–DPRK border by some humanitarian groups maybe compelling and informative and compelling, but they are not to date adequate for estimating either countrywide losses or countrywide need. And while the DPRK may collect and process data that would help outsiders understand more precisely the dimensions of the country's ongoing hunger problem, Pyongyang has to date been loath to divulge any of this.

One possibly pregnant tidbit, however, was released during the recent SPA gathering that ratified Kim Jong Il's ascendance within the state hierarchy. According to official reports, 687 delegates were impaneled for the 10, September 1998, SPA – exactly the same number as for the 9, April 1990, SPA.

According to the DPRK constitution, one SPA delegate is required for every 30 000 people in the country. And until now, every SPA session has, by its number of delegates, implied a greater countrywide population than for the session before it. Projections from the early 1990s had suggested that the North Korean population would increase by over three million persons between mid-year 1990 and mid-year 1998 (Eberstadt and Banister, 1992). Under formal constitutional rules, population growth of that rough magnitude would have called for an increase of roughly 100 delegates between the 9th and 10th SPAs, rather than a fixed total from one session to the next.

Naturally, one must caution against overinterpretation of this single datum. Strict constitutional observance is not the long suit of DPRK governance. At the same time, it is worth remembering that outside observers have typically underestimated not overestimated the human losses caused by famine under Communism in other locations, under other highly secretive regimes.

3.9 CONCLUDING OBSERVATIONS

The DPRK is, manifestly, a system charcterized today by economic failure. To outside eyes, that failure may today appear to be 'overdetermined' – yet it is important to ascertain, as best we can, the factors that contributed to it.

The DPRK, for many decades, appeared to be a rapidly modernizing state. Structurally, it witnessed a redeployment of population form rural to urban life, and from agricultural to non-agricultural work; in more human terms, it recorded rapid and sustained improvement in national life expectancy. Yet by the 1980s, North Korea's economic progress would look to have ground towards stagnation – and in the 1990s, catastrophic reversals were apparently being suffered. How is this bizarre 'development path' to be explained?

Empirical data available to date can only offer some clues. But it is apparent that the failure of the North Korean economic experiment speaks of the failure of the extensive, total mobilization strategy for sustained economic growth. The DPRK pursued that model more faithfully than any other centrally planned state – and the results do not inspire enthusiasm.

Table 3.10 Indicators of Malnutrition Among Children under 5 Years: Anthropometric Survey Data for DPRK and Other Asian Countries

Countries	Year	Nutritional measure (%)		
		Severe	Moderate /severe	Moderate /severe
		Underweight	Wasting	Stunting
Cambodia	1990–95	7	8	38
China	1990–95	3	4	32
Indonesia	1990–95	8	13	42
Laos	1990–95	12	11	42
Malaysia	1990–95	1	–	–
Mongolia	1990–95	–	2	26
Myanmar	1990–95	16	8	45
Philippine	1990–95	5	8	33
Thailand	1990–95	4	6	22
Vietnam	1990–95	11	12	47
Bangladesh	1990–95	21	18	55
India	1990–95	21	19	52
Nepal	1990–95	16	11	48
Pakistan	1990–95	13	9	50
Sri Lanka	1990–95	7	16	67
DPRK	1998	32*	19	57

Notes: * under 7 years of age.

Source: UNICEF, 1999, electronic database; World Food Program, 1999.

The particulars of North Korea's total mobilization strategy, of course, compounded the likelihood of economic catastrophe. North Korea's military posture, for example, created an extraordinary burden upon the country's productive base – a burden increasingly difficult to meet, for reasons alluded to above. Deeply seated policy hostility to international trade, for its part, cut off oportunities for productivity improvement that other modern countries naturally enjoy. The DPRK's perverse stance toward machinery and capital equipment from other countries essentially doomed North Korea to a high-cost, low-productivity industrial infrastructure – hardly auspicious attributes in a state that aspires to have an economy in which heavy industry is the leading sector.

In all, the DPRK's political economy at the start of the 1990s was astonishingly fragile – as subsequent events would cruelly demonstrate. Where other economies heavily dependent upon the USSR would quickly recover from the trade shock precipitated by the Soviet collapse (for example, Vietnam), North Korea did not. And whereas other modern, non-agricultural, urbanized economies typically managed to protect their people from nutritional distress, North Korea's economic shocks seems to have translated directly into monstrous hardship for the ordinary populace.

The extremities of those hardships are suggested by survey data on the prevalence of malnutrition among children. There are, to be sure, reasons to question specific observations – especially for survey data for North Korea. Even so, as Table 3.10 indicates, the children in the DPRK would appear to endure more physically unfavorable circumstances today than children in other Asian regions – Bangladesh, Indian, and Myanmar included. These data, in fact, seem to suggest that North Korea's socioeconomic retrogression has been long in train – not sudden.

In the past, national populations have recovered from hunger emergencies with a speed that has sometimes surprised outside observers. Even so, if we believe that economic performance depends not only upon physical infrastructure but upon human resources, these numbers would seem offer a grim prognosis for the years immediately ahead.

NOTES

1. Indeed, in representing 'the characteristic features of the economic process as we find them in reality' (Kaldor, 1961, p. 177), 'stylized facts' necessarily constitute a distillation of experience. For the DPRK, it is not always clear what we are supposed to be distilling – or what he possess to distill.
2. The DPRK, however, did recently (September 1997) provide a delegation from the International Monetary Fund (IMF) some summary, dollar-denominated numbers purportedly representing sectoral output for the years 1992–96 (International Monetary Fund, 1997). Earlier in 1997, it also provided a few macroeconomic time-series estimates on per capita GNP for the years 1989–1995 to the United Nations (Kim, 1997, p. 575). We will discuss those numbers momentarily.
3. The most important of these efforts arguably being Bergson's (Bergson, 1961).
4. The primary tasks of the longstanding US intelligence focus on North Korea, for example, has been to gather information on the military threat poised by a DPRK Korean People's Army (KPA) arrayed for possible operations against the South. In unclassified Congressional hearings 20 years ago, however, it was revealed that this surveillance project had been misestimating that potential threat rather badly. Whereas intelligence analysts had concluded the KPA possessed a standing armed force of some 400 000 in the mid-1970s, and that those numbers were fairly stable, re-analysis of existing information suggested that North Korean armed forces actually exceeded 700 000, and that the KPA was in the midst of a tremendous buildup (US House of Representatives, 1979). A detected error of this magnitude on a matter of such consequence and priority naturally raises questions about undetected errors in other, less carefully scrutinized areas of the Western intelligence

agencies' research program on North Korea.

5. The most important study to date of North Korea's foreign trade patterns is perhaps Choi (1991). In the following pages, we will draw upon a North Korea trade database that the author has been assembling, rather than upon Choi's estimates. There are some discrepancies between our results, but for the most part those are minor.
6. Dating the advent of that emergency is of course somewhat arbitrary. Two milestones for that gathering crisis, however, might be the December 1993 communique officially acknowledging the failure of the third Seven Year Plan and the 'grave condition' of the local economy, and the March 1995 diplomatic appeal for international humanitarian food aid.
7. Although Pyongyang did regularly report a figure for 'defense' within its annual budget, that series has lacked credibility since at least the early 1970s.
8. For reasons already alluded to, accurate calculations of such quantities are vastly more difficult for a centrally planned economy.
9. Sure enough, reports by independent groups such as the Stockholm International Peace Research Institute (SIPRI) point to an upsurge of weapons shipments from Moscow to Pyongyang in the late 1980s; much of the materiel identified was reportedly 'high tech' equipment – avionics systems, high-precision fighter aircraft, and so on – that the DPRK presumably could not produce itself, or could only produce at a crushing domestic resource cost.
10. By implication, for example, the DPRK's armed forces are entirely excluded from these data; and while one may assume the new labor force figures include workers in the country's extensive military–industrial sector, no official clarifications have been volunteered on this matter.
11. China's and Vietnam's rates of labor force participation may look comparable to the DPRK's, but in predominantly agrarian societies active labor force participation is often overestimated.
12. Estimates on trade turnover for North Korea are presented here in current US dollars – not real, inflation – adjusted dollars – for a variety of technical reasons, the most important being the absence of any reliable index for converting current Soviet rubles, in which much on North Korea's trade was denominated, into constant US dollars.
13. Comparing Soviet and Russian Federation trade trends, as many readers will appreciate, should be highly problematic for reasons reaching beyond the Russian 'transition' process itself. For one thing, the Russian Federation only accounted for about 60 per cent of the USSR's external trade in 1990 – therefore any USSR/Russia data series will be seriously biased down. On the other hand, much of Russia's pre-1992 trade was conducted with other Soviet republics – all of which by definition skirted market rules and logic. If included at official exchnge rates, this commerce with the 'near abroad' would seem to mark out a great drop in Russian international trade between 1988 and 1993. It is not clear that these two countervailing trends offset each other – but from our perspective, it is probably reassuring that the biases upon the USSR/Russia trade series push in opposite directions.

BIBLIOGRAPHY

Bergson, Abram (1961), *The Real National Income of Soviet Russia Since 1928*, Cambridge, MA: Harvard University Press.

Blum, Alain. Naitre, vivre et mourir en URSS, 1917–91, Paris: M.Plon.

Chenery, Hollis and Moises Syrquin (1975), *Patterns of Development*, 1950–70, New York: Oxford University Press.

China State Statistics Bureau (1995), *China Statistical Yearbook 1995*, Beijing: China Statistical Publishing House.

Choi, Soo-young (1991), 'Foreign Trade of North Korea, 1946–88: Structure and Performance', Unpublished Ph.D. dissertation, Northeastern University,

September 1991.

Chun, Hong-tack (1992), 'Estimating North Korea's GNP by Physical Indicators Approach', *Korea Development Review*, **14** (1), 167–225 (in Korean).

Chun, Hong-tack and Jin Park (1997), 'North Korean Economy: A Historical Assessment', in Dong-se Cha, Kwang-suk Kim and Dwight H. Perkins (eds), *The Korean Economy 1945–95: Performance And Vision For The 21st Century* Seoul: Korea Development Institute, 665–730.

Chung, Joseph Sang-hoon (1974), *The North Korean Economy: Structure And Development*, Stanford, CA: Hoover Institution Press.

De Long, J. Bradford and Lawrence H. Summers (1991), 'Equipment Investment And Economic Growth', *Quarterly Journal of Economics*, **106** (2), 445-502.

DPRK Central Bureau of Statistics (1995), *Tabulation of the Population Census of the Democratic Peoples Republic of Korea* (31 December 1993), Pyongyang: DPRK Central Statistics Bureau.

Eberstadt, Nicholas (1995a), *Korea Approaches Reunification. Armonk*, NY: M.E. Sharpe & Co.

Eberstadt, Nicholas (1995b), 'The CIA's Assessment of the Soviet Economy', in idem, *The Tyranny of Numbers: Mismeasurement and Misrule*. Washington, DC: AEI Press, 136–49.

Eberstadt, Nicholas (1997), 'Prospects For US–DPRK Economic Cooperation: Indications From Past North Korean Trade Performance' *Korea and World Affairs*, **21** (4).

Eberstadt, Nicholas (1998), 'North Korea's Interlocked Economic Crises: Some Indications from Mirror Statistics', *Asian Survey*, **38** (3), 516–35.

Eberstadt, Nicholas, 'Self Reliance and Economic Decline: DPRK's Trade in Capital Goods, 1970–95', *Problems of Post-Communism*, forthcoming.

Eberstadt, Nicholas and Judith Banister (1992), *The Population of North Korea, Berkeley*, CA: University of California Institute of East Asian Studies.

Eberstadt, Nicholas and Jonathan Tombes (eds), *Comparing the Soviet and American Economies*. Washington, DC: AEI Press, forthcoming.

Goto, Fujio (1982), 'Indexes of North Korean Industrial Output, 1944–75', *KSU Economic And Business Review*, (9), Kyoto Sangyo University.

Goto, Fujio (1990), *Estimates of the North Korean Gross Domestic Product, 1956–59*, Kyoto: Kyoto Sangyo University Press, 1–34.

Hwang, Eui-gak (1993), *The Korean Economies*, New York: Clarendon Press.

International Institute of Strategic Studies, *Military Balance*, London: IISS, various editions.

International Labor Office, *Yearbook of Labor Statistics*, Geneva: ILO, various editions.

International Monetary Fund (1997), *Democratic People's Republic of Korea: Fact-Finding Report*, Washington, DC: IMF Asian and Pacific Department, 12 November.

Kaldor, Nicholas (1961), 'Capital Accumulation and Economic Growth', in F. A. Lutz (ed.), *The Theory of Capital*, London: Macmillan and Co. Ltd., 177–222.

Kim, Philip Wonhyuk (1997), 'North Korea's Food Crisis', *Korea and World Affairs*, **21** (4).

Kornai, Janos (1992), *The Socialist System: The Political Economy of Communism*, Princeton, NJ: Princeton University Press.

Kuznets, Simon (1996), *Modern Economic Growth: Rate, Structure and Spread*, New Haven, CT: Yale University Press.

Lee, Jong-Wha (1995), 'Capital Goods Imports and Long-run Growth', *Journal of*

Development Economics, **48** (1), 91–110.
Maretzki, Hans (1991), *Kim-ismus in Nordkorea: Analyse des lezten DDR-Botschafters in Pjyoengyang*, Boeblingen, Germany: Anita Tykve Verlag.
Morgenstern, Oskar (1963), *On the Accuracy of Economic Observations*, Princeton, NJ: Princeton University Press.
Noland, Marcus (1995), 'The North Korean Economy', *Joint USA–Korea Academic Studies*, **6**, 127–78.
Pritchett, Lant and Lawrence H. Summers (1996), 'Wealthier Is Healthier' *Journal Of Human Resources*, **31** (4), 841–68.
Republic of China, Directorate of Budget, *Accounting and Statistics*.
Republic of China (1990), *Statistical Yearbook 1990*, Taipei: ROC Executive Yuan.
ROK Bank of Korea, *Estimate Of North Korea's GNP*, Seoul: BOK, various editions, (in Korean).
ROK Bank of Korea (1996), *Economic Statistics Yearbook 1996*, Seoul: BOK.
ROK National Statistics Office, *Korea Statistical Yearbook*, Seoul: NSO, various editions.
ROK National Statistics Office, *Social Indicators in Korea*, Seoul: NSO, various editions.
Rosefielde Stephen and Ralph W. Pfouts (1995), 'Neoclassical Norms and the Valuation of National Product in the Soviet Union and its Postcommunist Successor States', *Journal of Comparative Economics*, **21** (3), 375–89.
Rubin, Marc (1996), *North Korea's Trade with the USSR and Russia*, Washington, DC: U.S. Bureau of the Census, International Programs Center, November, unpublished.
Stockholm International Peace Research Institute, *World Armaments and Disarmaments: SIPRI Yearbook*, Stockholm: Almqvist and Wicksell, various editions.
Trigubenko, Marina Ye (1991), 'Industry of the DPRK: Specific Features of the Industrial Policy, Sectoral Structure and Prospects Report' at the International Symposium Economy of North Korea:Its Present State and Prospects, Korea Development Institute and Korean Economic Daily, Seoul, ROK, September 30–October, 1991.
UNICEF (1999), 'UNICEF Statistical Database on Child Malnutrition', accessed electroniclly at URL; http://www.unicef.org/statis.
United Nations (1997), *Demographic Yearbook 1995* New York: UN.
United Nations (1998), *World Population Prospects: The 1996 Revisions*, New York: UN.
US Central Intelligence Agency (1978), 'Korea, the Economic Race Between the North and the South: a Research Paper', ER 78-10008 Washington, DC: National Foreign Assessment Center.
US House of Representatives, Committee on Armed Services (1979), *Impact of Intelligence Reassessment on the Withdrawal of Troops from Korea*, Washington, DC: Government Printing Office.
Winiecki, Jan (1998), *The Distorted World of Soviet-type Economies*, Pittsburgh, PA: University of Pittsburgh Press.
World Bank (1997), *World Development Report 1997*, New York: Oxford University Press.
World Food Program (1999), Nutritional Survey of the Democratic People's Republic of Korea. Rome: WFP.

PART THREE

Development Potential under Reform

4. North Korea in Global Perspective

Marcus Noland

4.1 INTRODUCTION

North Korea today faces a famine of unknown magnitude. Despite the protestations of the North Korean government, this tragic state of affairs is less the result of natural disasters than the accumulated effects of decades of economic mismanagement. North Korea is the world's most autarkic economy and there is no economically rational reason why any country, much less one with North Korea's economic characteristics, should pursue a policy of agricultural self-sufficiency as a means to food security. Rather, the DPRK ought to be exporting goods in which it has a comparative advantage (such as light manufactures and some natural resource products), and importing products such as food in which it has a comparative disadvantage. In terms of domestic food availability, the pay-offs to reform would dwarf more narrowly targeted efforts to improve agricultural productivity.

But reforming the North Korean economy could prove both economically and politically difficult. Economic revitalization will require considerable institutional change, and experience has shown that it has been more difficult to reform relatively industrialized economies such as North Korea than it is relatively agrarian economies such as China and Vietnam. Moreover, given the degree of implicit distortion in the DPRK economy, liberalization would result in enormous shifts in the composition of output. International trade exposure would increase dramatically with much of this involving trade with South Korea and Japan, North Korea's natural trading partners, with which it maintains problematic relations. Internally, millions of workers might shift jobs as a result of changes in the composition of output. The incumbent regime could regard these changes as potentially destabilizing.

In short, there are considerable economic, political, and diplomatic obstacles to successful rehabilitation of the North Korean economy. The prudent response is to consider alternative scenarios, which do not assume successful reform.

4.2 HISTORICAL BACKGROUND

Historically the North Korean economy has been distinctive in the degree to which the mechanism of central planning was used to frustrate the development of market transactions both internally and externally. The other notable characteristic of the North Korean economy has been the paucity of reliable statistical data. The state's penchant for secrecy has meant little data has been released and what has been made available is of dubious validity. At times the regime has released clearly bogus data for political reasons, and even if the data are not subject to intentional fabrication, they may be unreliable for reasons as prosaic as the difficulty of translating the schema of a centrally planned economy into market terms, and poor sampling methodologies. Economists have devoted considerable effort to sorting through these problems, but the data problems in and of themselves have tended to push the study of the North Korean economy away from rigorous analysis and towards compendia of anecdotes.[1]

With that *mea culpa* it is worth reviewing what we think that we know about North Korea. The conventional wisdom is that at the time of the division of the peninsula, North Korea had relatively more physical and human capital than South Korea, was relatively more industrialized than South Korea, and had higher per capita incomes. North Korean economic policy could be described as classically Stalinist: agriculture was collectivized, the central planning apparatus was developed, and resources were mobilized for industrialization. Policies were undertaken starting in 1966 to foster a domestic military–industrial sector. Although North Korea was probably more urbanized than South Korea at the time of the partition, the *juche* emphasis on virtual self-sufficiency must have slowed the rate of urbanization, as apparently confirmed by Eberstadt (1995). The conventional wisdom is that per capita income in North Korea exceeded that of South Korea well into the 1970s.[2]

In all likelihood, the North Korean economy was already encountering significant difficulties in making the transition from extensive to intensive development by this time. In the aftermath of the first oil crisis, North Korea, among others, borrowed significantly from foreign banks recycling their petrodollar receipts.[3] North Korea was unable (or unwilling) to pay off these loans and defaulted, effectively foreclosing its access to international capital markets.[4] Eberstadt (N.d.) points out that North Korean capital goods imports never reattained their mid-1970s values.

Kim Il-Sung's decision to default on his Western creditors left North

Korea highly reliant on the USSR as its sole significant source of economic support.[5] But by the mid-1980s the Soviets had become disenchanted and began pressuring the North Koreans to begin repaying their accumulated debts. In 1985 the USSR and North Korea agreed on a repayment schedule, and, according to the US Central Intelligence Agency, by 1987 net flows had turned negative – that is, North Korean repayments exceeded the value of new Soviet assistance.

This was followed in short order by the break-up of the Soviet Union and the collapse of the Eastern Bloc. In 1990, Russia announced that it would no longer supply North Korea with subsidized oil, and the North responded by suspending repayments. Eberstadt, Rubin, and Tretyakova (1995) estimate that in 1991 North Korea suffered a trade shock equivalent to 40 per cent of total imports due to disengagement with the newly independent states, and by 1993 Russian exports had fallen to less than a tenth of their earlier levels. By June 1995 North Korea had appealed for and had begun receiving international food assistance. In July and August 1995 the country was hit by devastating floods, which were repeated on a smaller scale the following year. In 1997 the country suffered from drought. These calamities exacerbated the pre-existing food problem.

4.3 STATISTICAL OVERVIEW

At the outset of a statistical review of the North Korean economy it is tempting to warn readers that they are about to enter Alice's Wonderland, or at least that taking the following material too seriously could be hazardous to one's sanity. Perhaps it suffices to say that the figures cited below should be viewed with a skeptical eye.

A typical overview begins with output or income figures. Output in North Korea is measured on a material product basis, which is basically incompatible with the system of national accounts used in market economies.[6] Moreover, North Korea has a huge military sector which is difficult to assess economically.[7] Hwang (1993) makes a valiant effort to transform North Korean figures into the standard system of national accounts, but the results are not fully convincing. Chun (1992), Jeong (1993) and Noland (1996) all estimate North Korean per capita incomes using the physical indicators approach, obtaining estimates of the ratio of South Korean to North Korean per capita incomes in 1990 in the range of 3.61:1–4.48:1. If one updates these ranges on the basis of the Bank of Korea (BOK) real GDP estimates, then the ratio of South to North per capita income in 1997 was between 8:1 and 11:1.[8] Recently, with the assistance of the UNDP, the North Korean authorities have attempted to make their own estimates of

GDP, calculating that in 1996 GDP was $10.6 billion and per capita GDP was $480, using the official exchange rate of 2.15 North Korean won per US dollar. These estimates imply that South Korean incomes were more than 20 times higher than those in the North.[9]

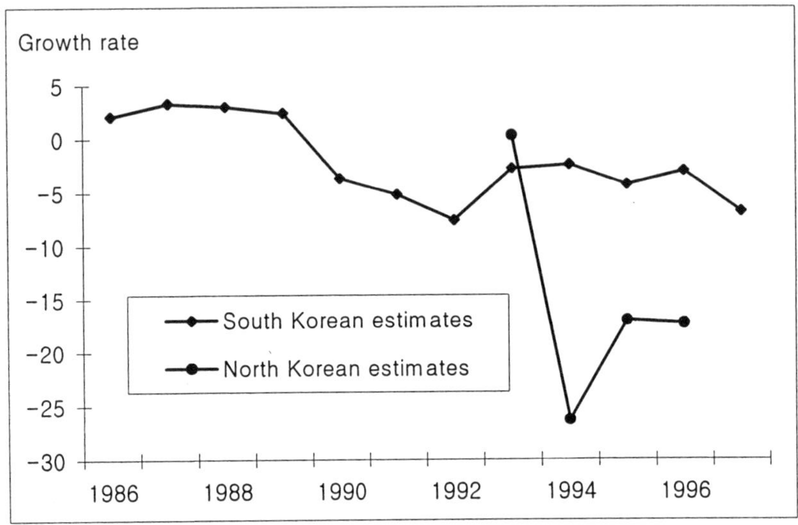

Figure 4.1 North Korean GDP Growth

Data compiled by the BOK and released by the National Unification Board (NUB) indicate that 1990 was the most recent year that the North Korean economy registered positive growth (Figure 4.1).[10] Data recently provided to the International Monetary Fund (IMF) by the North Korean government date the decline from 1994. Although the quantitative estimates contained in these two sets of figures differ significantly, qualitatively they are consistent – the North Korean economy is shrinking.

Some greater detail is provided in Tables 4.1, 4.2 and 4.3, which report figures the North Korean government provided to the IMF on the composition of output, government expenditures and government revenues. In certain respects this data is problematic as will be discussed below. Nonetheless, it is probably worth examining, if for no other reason than because it is the official representation of the condition of the economy.

Table 4.1 presents figures on the composition of output. What the data suggest is that the economy has collapsed around agriculture, that is, the fall in agricultural output is actually less dramatic than the decline in output in other sectors.[11] According to these figures, industrial output fell by nearly two-thirds between 1992 and 1996, and construction activity declined by almost as much. If construction is taken as a proxy for investment, investment may well have fallen below replacement level and the capital stock may be shrinking. This notion is reinforced by the government expenditure data reported in Table 4.2. If the economic development category is taken as a proxy for investment, then investment has fallen by more than half from values the North Korean government announced in the early 1990s. This point is further reinforced if one believes that certain military or military-related expenditures are hidden in the economic development budget. Estimates of North Korean military manpower and equipment do not show anything like this decline over the relevant period. Indeed, US and South Korean defense ministry figures show a slight increase in North Korean military deployment during this period. This suggests that the non-military part of the economy is being severely squeezed.

Table 4.1 Composition of Output, 1992–96 (Millions of US Dollars at US$1 = Won 2.15)

	1992	1993	1994	1995	1996
Total	20 875	20 935	15 421	12 802	10 588
Agriculture	7 807	8 227	6 431	5 223	4 775
Industry	4 551	4 689	3 223	2 228	1 556
Construction	1 315	1 256	910	819	508
Other	7 160	6 762	4 858	4 532	6 748

Source: North Korean submission to the IMF.

Table 4.2 Government Budget Balance, 1994–96 (Billions of Won)

	1994	1995	1996
Revenues	41.6	24.3	20.3
Expenditures	41.4	24.2	20.6
Economic development	–	–	12.4
Social and cultural	–	–	5.0
Defense	–	–	3.0
General administration	–	–	0.2
Balance	0.2	0.1	0.3
Memorandum item:			
GDP	33.2	27.4	22.7

Source: North Korean submission to the IMF.

Table 4.3 General Government Revenues, 1996 (Millions of Won)

Direct taxes	
Profits from state enterprises	6 290
User fees for working capital	2 250
Profits from cooperative farms	180
Indirect taxes	
Turnover taxes	8 080
Social insurance revenues	90
Other revenues	3 430
Total revenues	20 320

Source: North Korean submission to the IMF.

Two other things stand out in Table 4.2. First, for 1993, the government reports expenditures and receipts far larger than GDP. This would seem to violate the basic precepts of national income accounting. Second, it reports expenditures on defense that are far smaller than normally cited. Indeed, data on labor force participation provided by the North Korean authorities appear to omit the military entirely. All in all, these figures should probably be taken with very large grains of salt.

Data on government revenues are reported in Table 4.3. The largest single source of revenue is turnover taxes, which is typical of centrally planned economies (CPEs). These taxes present special problems for analysis because they are levied at differential rates depending on the legal status of the transacting parties (for example, the tax wedge imposed on an exchange between two state enterprises is different than the wedge imposed on a transaction between a state enterprise and a cooperative). Profits from state enterprises is the next largest source of government revenue. Excluding the problematic data for 1993, it would appear that the government sector accounts for roughly 90 per cent of national income.

The North Korean regime's obsession with secrecy ought to be less of a problem in analyzing the country's external economic relations – in principle mirror statistics reported by North Korea's trade and investment partners can be used to deduce North Korea's external transactions. Aggregate trade figures derived from the IMF's *Direction of Trade Statistics* and other sources are shown in Figure 4.2.[12] Two points stand out. First, reported trade volumes are not growing, reinforcing the impression of an economy in secular decline. Second, North Korea runs chronic trade deficits. These deficits must be financed in some way.

One possibility would be illicit commercial transactions. However, data reported by the ACDA does not support the idea that clandestine arms sales would be sufficient to cover the trade gap – indeed, the ACDA data, which are generally consistent with Eberstadt, Rubin, and Tretyakova's data on DPRK–Russia trade, indicate that North Korea is now a net importer of military hardware (Figure 4.3). Other possibilities in this realm would include drug trafficking and counterfeiting.

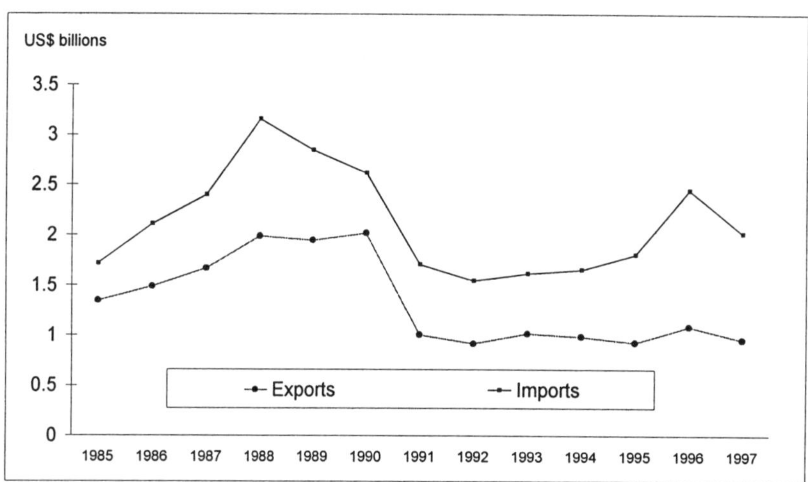

Figure 4.2 North Korean Trade

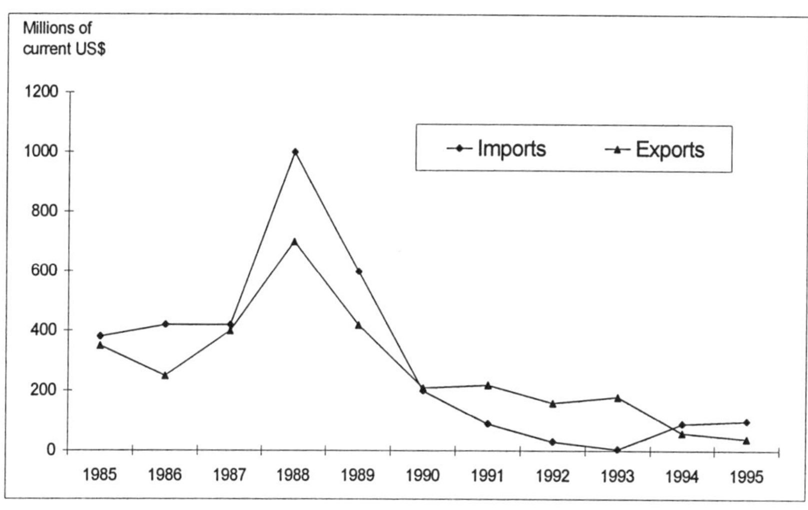

Figure 4.3 North Korean Arms Trade

Table 4.4 Trading Partners, 1997 (Millions of US Dollars)

		Exports	Imports	Net Exports
China (including Hong Kong)				
	Raw	131	627	
	Corrected	119	690	−571
Japan				
	Raw	269	197	
	Corrected	245	217	28
South Korea				
	Raw	0	0	
	Corrected	193	115	78
Russia				
	Raw	15	74	
	Corrected	14	81	−67
Germany				
	Raw	39	47	
	Corrected	36	52	−16
Global total				
	Raw	917	1727	
	Corrected	956	2018	−1062

Notes: DOTS import data (of partner country) adjusted for transportation and insurance charges. DOTS export data (of partner country) adjusted for 'missing' transportation and insurance costs. Since Intra-Korean trade data is not reported in DOTS, the numbers are taken from NUB. NK–Iran and NK–Libya trade data from KOTRA. KOTRA data also adjusted. 1996 NK-Lebanon trade data used instead of 1997 numbers. The raw values for global totals are written as reported by DOTS. The corrected totals reflect corrections in trade data concerning Iran, Libya, Lebanon and South Korea in addition to adjustments made for transportation and insurance charges.

Another possibility would be remittances from Japan, which are sometimes reported to be in billions of dollars. However, recent research (for example Eberstadt, 1996; Noland, 1996, 1998) has concluded that these private aid flows are probably considerably smaller than claimed. A final possible explanation is that the trade deficits are implicitly financed by China, which has permitted North Korea to accumulate large arrears in its trade account. In reality, the North Korean deficit is probably financed by a combination of unrecorded transactions, private aid flows, and Chinese munificence.

As shown in Table 4.4, China is by far and away North Korea's main trade partner, permitting the North Koreans to run annual bilateral deficits of approximately half a billion dollars. Indeed, China's prominence in North Korea's trade would be even larger if barter transactions and aid were counted in these figures. Following China, North Korea's largest trade partners are Japan, South Korea, Russia and Germany. If North Korea's trade with China and South Korea are regarded as politically determined, these two countries are financing nearly two-thirds of the North Korean deficit.

Table 4.5 North Korean Trade by Largest Commodity Groups, 1996

Industry	Exports (US$1000)	Share (%)
Non-identified products	582 290	48
Articles of apparel and clothing accessories	155 884	13
Fish, crustaceans, molluscs, Preparations thereof	64 526	5
Gold, non-monetary	34 469	3
Footwear	31 765	3
Feeding stuff for animals, not including unmilled cereal	27 373	2
Crude fertilizers and crude materials (excluding coal)	26 864	2
Electrical machinery, apparatus and appliances, N.E.S.	25 466	2
Non-ferrous metals	23 905	2
Iron and steel	21 544	2
Total – all commodities	1 214 574	100
	Memorandum item:	
Adjusted total – all commodities	1 104 158	
Industry	Imports (US$1000)	Share (%)
Petroleum, petroleum products and related materials	183 638	16
Cereals and cereal preparations	135 208	12
Textile yarn, fabrics, made-up articles, related products	114 628	10
Road vehicles (including air cushion vehicles)	84 279	7
Miscellaneous manufactured articles, N.E.S.	32 475	3
Artificial resins, plastic materials, cellulose esters/ethers	32 026	3
Machinery specialized for particular industries	31 845	3
Electrical machinery, apparatus and appliances, N.E.S.	30 896	3
Iron and steel	29 997	3
General industrial machinery and equipment, and parts	26 727	2
Total – all commodities	1 161 213	100
Adjusted total – all commodities	1 277 334	

Source: Statistics Canada, *World Trade Analysis 1980–96*.

The commodity composition of trade for 1996 is reported in Table 4.5. Again, interpretation is difficult for several reasons. First, the data reported in Table 4.5 by commodity does not match the data reported in Table 4.4 by partner. There are at least two sources of discrepancy. Some countries may report overall trade with the DPRK but not its commodity composition, so that the parts of the sample underlying the Table 4.1 figures are omitted from Table 4.5. Second, some countries may report trade with regions or the world as a whole that the UN data collectors then allocate to individual countries. This practice may help explain the large non-identified products category in the North Korean data. Indeed, the non-identified products classification has grown in the 1990s into the largest export category, perhaps indicating the rising importance of what is possibly a pure statistical artifact in the context of declining trade volumes. Thirdly, these data ignore barter transactions. Finally, it is unclear how the aforementioned arms trade is counted (if at all) in these figures.[13]

With these caveats in mind, the data in Table 4.5 indicate that apart from the non-identified products category the largest export sectors are apparel and marine products. Crude fertilizers, electrical machinery, non-ferrous metals, and iron and steel made the list of top ten export categories in 1994, 1995 and 1996. Exports tend to be concentrated in light manufacturing, some natural resources, and iron and steel.

The largest import categories are petroleum, cereals, and textile yarn. Road vehicles, electrical machinery, and machinery specialized for particular industries made the top ten import category list in 1994, 1995 and 1996. Broadly speaking, it appears that North Korea imports energy, food and capital goods, though Eberstadt (1998a) argues that the value of capital goods imports have been declining since the mid-1970s.

Most recently, North Korea have obtained significant international assistance to deal with its food shortage from China bilaterally, and through the World Food Program for other countries.[14] The quantity, value and concessional component of food coming from China is unclear.[15] Donations from the USA have often been associated with various diplomatic initiates giving rise to the praise food for meetings, or, in the case of the 1999 US inspection of a suspected nuclear site, food for access (Noland et al., 1999b). Similarly, North Korea has been receiving energy assistance in the form of oil and nuclear reactor construction through the Korea Energy Development Organization (KEDO), a multinational consort-ium established as part of a 1994 nuclear agreement with the USA. However the test firing by North Korea of the Taepo Dong 1 missile over Japan in August 1998 put the future of KEDO in jeopardy. More generally, the political basis in the USA, Japan, Europe and South Korea for continuing largesse may be unsustainable absent some breakthrough in political relations between North Korea and its non-

Chinese grantors.

4.4 RIGOROUS SPECULATION

Noland et al. (2000a, 2000b) constructed a static computable general equilibrium model of the North Korean economy calibrated to 1996. Noland et al. (2000c) extended this by including South Korea in the model and recasting it in a simple dynamic framework. This section briefly sketches the specifications of the models and the results from this work. Readers interested in a more detailed and technical account are referred to the original sources.

The model has 11 sectors (rice, corn, other agriculture, mining, light manufacturing, industrial intermediates, capital goods, services, construction, public administration and the military). The first eight are internationally traded, differentiated products and the latter three are not traded internationally. These 11 activities are produced using seven primary factors of production (high, medium and low quality land; agricultural, urban low-skilled and urban high-skilled labor and physical capital) and intermediate inputs. Production is constant returns to scale, constant elasticity of substitution in primary factors, and Leontief fixed factors in intermediates. Domestic and imported products are imperfect substitutes in demand.

Quantity rationing of external trade is the major source of distortion incorporated in the model. The trade distortions are calibrated on the basis of an analysis of latent comparative advantage and trade repression in Noland (1996). Domestic distortions are surely present, but are quite difficult to model. As indicated in Table 4.3, indirect taxes are non-trivial, but the sectoral distribution of these taxes is impossible to calculate since the tax depends on the legal status of the transacting parties. In the social accounting matrix (SAM) underlying the model, these taxes are assumed to be more or less uniform with some escalation with degree of processing. Other forms of distortion in North Korea are ignored in this model, though issues relating to factor usage and technological choice are analyzed in Noland et al. (1999) (the South Korean block of the model is conventional incorporating distortions in the form of direct and indirect internal taxes, and tariffs on external trade).[16]

In Noland et al. (2000a), the model was used to run five basic scenarios. In the first, North Korea costlessly recovers land damaged in the 1996–97 floods. In the second, quantity rationing of international trade is removed. The next three scenarios are in some sense extensions of the second. In the third, the North Korean economy experiences an 18 per cent sectorally uniform increase in total factor productivity (TFP) as a result of its economic opening and importation of capital equipment embodying new technologies from abroad.[17] The fourth scenario subjects the North Korean economy to an obsolescence shock to its capital stock as a result of economic opening, exposure to new technologies, and changes in relative prices of inputs and outputs. In Noland et al. (1997), this shock was calibrated as a half to two-thirds of the value of the 1990 pre-opening capital stock on the basis of the East German experience. In the current model, calibrated to 1996, the capital stock has already shrunk, and the assumed obsolescence shock is smaller at 25 per cent. Finally, Noland et al. (2000a) examined the issue of military demobilization and the peace dividend. In this scenario, the North Korean military is demobilized by 70 per cent, until the share of the military in national income approximates the 3 per cent exhibited in South Korea.[18] Each of these scenarios was implemented in ten steps or experiments.

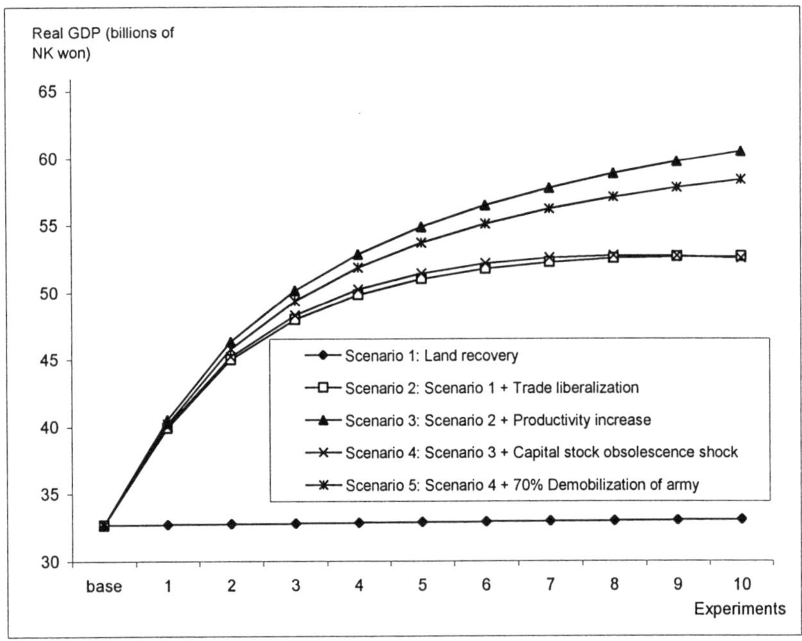

Figure 4.4 Model Simulation Results

In addition to scenario 1 (land recovery) and scenario 4 (systemic reform), Noland et al. (2000b) reported additional scenarios involving the provision of international food aid and more limited reforms in the agricultural sector. Noland et al. (2000c), which focuses on North–South integration issues, reported results from scenarios involving the formation of a customs union and a monetary union, as well as exploring the issue of cross-border factor flows.

Results for GDP from Noland et al. (2000a) are shown in Figure 4.4. Base GDP is calculated to be roughly 32 billion won, higher than the officially reported 23 billion won figure shown in Table 4.2. The reason is twofold. First, the officially reported figure appears to exclude the military. Second, the officially reported data do not appear to be internally consistent when entered into a consistent social accounting matrix (SAM). Even if one were to assume that little investment has occurred and that the capital stock has actually shrunk, the 1996 figures would imply a tremendous decline in output relative to the 1990 SAM constructed by Noland et al. (1997), suggesting that there were very big reductions in factor supplies or that much of the economy was operating at 10 to 15 per cent of capacity. The simplest way to generate a consistent SAM was to raise output. While it may well be the case that floods, famine, and the practice of scrapping capital and bartering it for food have reduced factor supplies and that utilization of remaining capacity has been low, there are also reasons to believe that the actual output is higher than reported by the authorities.[19]

In scenario 1, North Korea costlessly rehabilitates flood-affected lands in ten successive steps. As can be seen in Figure 4.4, the impact on GDP would be minimal, increasing it by less than 2 per cent. Domestic production of rice and other agricultural commodities would increase by around 4 per cent and corn production would rise by 12 per cent, but domestic food availability would remain below the quantitative target established by the United Nations Development Program (UNDP), the Food and Agricultural Organization (FAO), and the World Food Program (WFP).[20] At first glance this might seem odd – that increasing the arable land endowment of a famine-afflicted country would not have a bigger macroeconomic impact. Two things should be kept in mind though. First, North Korea already had been experiencing a famine prior to the floods that commenced in July 1995. Second, only around 15 per cent of the arable land was affected by the floods. So while natural disasters may have exacerbated the food availability problem, the famine is not a product of bad weather. Rather systemic mismanagement and a lack of intermediate inputs such as fuel and fertilizer are its proximate cause. The latter, in turn, is due to severe balance of payments constraints and policy decisions about the use of foreign exchange, which are fundamentally outside the agricultural sector. Nevertheless, this result underlines a critical issue: if only a relatively modest component of the decline in output can be attributed to flood-related declines in agriculture, then what explains the rest?

Scenario 2 addresses the main distortion in the model, the severe repression of international trade. The gravity model results reported in

Noland (1996) suggest that in 1990 the total share of imports and exports in North Korean GDP would have been roughly 70 per cent if North Korea had exhibited the economic behavior of a normal country. With the economy now smaller, the expected trade share should be even higher. In scenario 2 the quantitative restrictions on trade are relaxed in ten steps, and the impact on GDP is shown in Figure 4.4 (qualitatively similar results are obtained in Noland et al. (2000c) when North Korea and South Korea form a customs union). As shown in Figure 4.4, the impact of the relaxation of the constraint would be greatest at the beginning and would decline thereafter, as could be expected on the basis of microeconomic theory. A complete freeing of this constraint would increase GDP by 40–60 per cent, depending on the precise specification, due to static reallocation of factors alone. Domestic availability of rice and corn on commercial terms would increase by 80–90 per cent.

This static reallocation effect would not be the only impact of liberalizing trade. Results derived from Coe et al. (1996) indicate that TFP might increase by 18 per cent (results reported in Noland et al., 1999 suggest that this is probably a conservative estimate). As shown in Figure 4.4, these gains would be almost exactly offset by the negative impact of an assumed obsolescence shock to the capital stock of 25 per cent. Obviously one should not attach too much weight to the exact figures derived from this modeling exercise. Rather, these results are probably best interpreted as indicating that, in an economy as distorted as North Korea's, even a relatively simple move such as increasing the economy's openness to international trade could have enormous macroeconomic effects, dwarfing the impact of a flood. The final scenario is a 70 per cent military demobilization in which North Korea's expenditure on the military is reduced to a share of GDP similar to the South's. Obviously there would have to be major diplomatic breakthroughs for this to occur, but the experiment is presented as a heuristic exercise to illustrate how large the potential pay-offs might be. In some sense this experiment too is dependent on the trade liberalization experiment: without liberalization it is unclear where the demobilized resources would be redeployed, however, with liberalization they can be redeployed to their highest efficiency uses.

Figure 4.4 illustrates that redeployment of resources on this scale at the margin could add another 8 to 10 per cent to GDP, with the five scenarios undertaken together increasing real GDP by 40–80 per cent from the base depending on specification. Domestic food availability would exceed the UNDP/FAO/WFP target for normal total demand in the unilateral liberalization scenario and the normal human demand in the customs union scenario. With non-defense government spending held constant in nominal terms, the other components of GDP would rise. Real consumption would nearly triple, while investment would nearly double. International trade would expand enormously. With the trade balance held constant, the real exchange rate would experience a modest appreciation; if the real exchange rate is held constant the trade deficit expands somewhat.

The composition of output would change enormously as light manufacturing, mining, construction and services expanded, while industrial intermediates, capital goods and the army contracted. Light manufacturing would experience an export explosion with exports increasing fortyfold, and mining exports more than triple. Imports would rise in all traded goods categories, led by a fifteenfold growth in capital goods imports. These qualitative results hold whether liberalization is on a most-favored-nation basis or on a preferential basis with South Korea. Even in the case of large financial inflows from abroad that drive up the real exchange rate, the traded-goods sector of North Korea expands relative to the base (Noland et al., 2000c).

These changes in composition have profound effects on factor usage and returns. In scenario 5, 2.5 million workers would leave the agricultural sector and another 350 000 would leave the army, with the bulk re-employed in the light manufacturing sector (even in the agricultural sector, the employment and wage changes would be greater under economic reform than through land recovery). Employment also would increase in the mining, construction and service sectors. The real wages of all three classes of labor would more than triple, with the largest increases experienced by the high skilled. The rate of return on capital also would more than triples. The rate of return on land would fall, however, as the increased availability of imported agricultural goods reduced domestic scarcity, and with it the implicit returns to land. There would be some shift in the distribution of income away from land and toward urban high-skilled labor.

Noland et al. (2000b) reported one additional scenario of interest, under which, in the absence of reform, North Korea is provided food aid until the UNDP/FAO/WFP normal human demand target is reached. The result would be to crowd out both domestic production and imports on commercial terms. The aid in effect acts as implicit balance of payments support, and import demands for all traded-goods increase. Public administration and military expenditures are held constant by construction. If this modeling assumption was relaxed, presumably these activities, too, would expand in response to the provision of aid.

These results are speculative and subject to a certain degree of spurious precision. Nevertheless, the modeling work conveys a number of important points. First, even when defined narrowly in terms of domestic food availability, the pay-offs to reform dwarf the impact of more narrow efforts to raise productivity in agriculture. In addition, the provision of aid may have unintended consequences. Second, there would be massive shifts in the composition of output under reform. Millions of workers would switch jobs, for example. Third, with reform the importance of international trade would increase tremendously. Fourth, the military acts as a significant drag on the North Korean economy, and demobilization could have significant economic benefits.

These results are useful in that they identify important channels through which reform could affect the North Korean economy. They are limited in that they are derived from static models. In particular, it is hard to imagine that the restructuring of the North Korean economy described in the previous section could occur without a significant infusion of foreign investment and management. This would take time, and probably have a significant impact on South Korea, which presumably would be the primary source of foreign investment for North Korea. Noland et al. (1998) and Noland et al. (2000c) have examined these issues using simple dynamic models focusing on the issue of economic integration between North and South Korea. Their results indicate that the formation of a customs union would have a significant impact on the North Korean economy as discussed above, but would have little impact on the South Korean economy because North Korea is simply very small in economic terms relative to the South.

From the Southern perspective, the story would change dramatically if the two countries were to form a monetary union and factor markets were to begin to integrate. This could have significant macroeconomic implications for South Korea. Noland et al. (1998), working from the 1990 North Korean SAM, report one scenario in which the South actually gains through economic integration in that the discounted value of the Southern income stream with integration actually exceeds that without integration. This result depends on two crucial assumptions, however. First, it depends on the assumption that Southern investment in the North takes the form of profit-making investment (not grants or transfers) and second, that the rate of technological convergence between the North and South is very rapid.

Noland et al. (2000c) re-examined these issues using the 1996 SAM, calibrating the rate of technological convergence on the basis of the German experience. The results make sobering reading. They find that under plausible assumptions about cross-border factor mobility and the rate of technological convergence, that after a decade of integration, Northern incomes would still be less than 60 per cent of those in the South. On this basis they conclude that some kind of population influx control probably would be required on a semi-permanent basis to prevent mass migration from the North to the South. While the potential gains to reform are enormous, capturing these gains is likely to be a wrenching, decades-long process.

4.5 POLITICAL ECONOMY

Both the significant increase in exposure to international trade (much of this with South Korea and Japan, two countries with which North Korea maintains problematic relations) and the large changes in the composition of output could have profound political implications, or alternatively, these implications could be thought to present significant, perhaps insurmountable, obstacles to reform under the current regime.[21]

The course of reform in North Korea would be more difficult than the one faced by China and Vietnam, Asia's two other major transitional economies, for two reasons. The first is structural. As indicated in Table 4.6, China and Vietnam were far more agrarian at the time they initiated reforms than North Korea appears today. Indeed, North Korea appears to be more like some of the economies of Eastern Europe or the former Soviet republics than China or Vietnam.[22] The reform path adopted by China and Vietnam was in essence the Lewis model in action: agriculture was liberalized, generating a rapid supply response and facilitating the large-scale movement of labor out of extremely low productivity activities in the agricultural sector and into the emerging, non-state-owned, light manufacturing sector. In theory, this nascent light-manufacturing sector could be taxed to create a safety net to ease restructuring of the old state-owned enterprises (SOEs), but neither China nor Vietnam has made much progress in this regard. Moreover, within agriculture, China and Vietnam could be distinguished from other CPEs (including North Korea) in that the collectivization of agriculture (or at least the adoption of collectivist production technology) did not progress as far. As the experience of Eastern Europe demonstrates reforming industrialized CPEs is more difficult than reforming agrarian CPEs, and decollectivizing agriculture is more difficult, the deeper the adoption of large-scale collectivist production techniques has proceeded.

The second hurdle that North Korea faces is ideological. The North Vietnamese government and their Vietcong allies defeated the South Vietnamese government in a civil war and could lay claim to ideological monopoly in the united Vietnam. Likewise, while China has the rump of Taiwan to contend with, no one seriously claims that the Taiwanese historically represented an ideological threat to the Chinese government. Reformers in both China and Vietnam were relatively free to construct tortured rationalizations about how their market-oriented reforms were really what Marx, Mao or Ho had in mind.

The ideological terrain faced by the current North Korean regime is very different. Rather than monopolist purveyors or dominant definers of the national ideology, they are clearly junior partners, in both size and achievement. Moreover, the dynastic aspects of the Kim regime make it even more difficult for the son to disavow the legacy of the father. And while the ideologues of Pyongyang can certainly try to reinterpret *juche* to mean market-oriented reform, the existence of a prosperous, democratic South Korea makes their task very difficult, indeed. After all, why be a second-rate imitation South Korean when one can head South and become the real thing?

Table 4.6 Distribution of Labor Force at Time of Reform

Country	Year	Sector		
		Agriculture	Industry	Service
Czech Republic(1)	1989	11[a]	39	50
Slovakia(1)	1989	15[a]	34	51
Poland(1)	1989	7[a]	37	56
Hungary(1)	1990	15[a]	36	49
Soviet Union(2)	1987	19[a]	38[b]	43
Ukraine(3)	1990	20	40	40
Belarus(3)	1990	20	42	38
Romania(1)	1990	28[a]	38	34
Bulgaria(1)	1989	19[a]	47	34
North Korea(4)	1993	33	37	30
China(5)	1978	71	15	14
Vietnam(2)	1989	71	12	17

Notes:
a. Agriculture and forestry.
b. Industry and construction.

Source: (1) Commander, Simon and Fabrizio Coricelli, 1995, *Unemployment, Restructuring, and the Labor Market in Eastern Europe and Russia*, Washington: World Bank, Tables 1.1, 2.2, 3.5, 5.1 and 6.11; (2) Eberstadt, Nicholas (1995), *Korea Approaches Unification*, Armonk: M.E. Sharpe, Table 6; (3) Bosworth, Barry P. and Gur Ofer (1995), *Reforming Planned Economies in an Integrating World Economy*. Washington: Brookings Institution, Table 3-1; (4) Eberstadt, Nicholas (1998), *Quantitative Comparison of Current Socio-economic Conditions in North and South Korea*, paper presented at the Second Conference of the International Interdisciplinary Project conference on Nation-Building for Korean Unification, Honolulu, Hawaii (21–25 January); (5) Sachs, Jeffrey and Wing Thye Woo (1994), 'Structural Factors in the Economic Reforms of China, Eastern Europe, and the Former Soviet Union', *Economic Policy*, vol. 18, 101–145, Table 2.

This, of course, raises the second point. Reform will mean vastly increased exposure to the outside world, in particular South Korea and Japan.[23] While today's North Korean economy has unexploited latent potential, its isolation means that there is no institutional mechanism to transform this latent potential into products that the rest of the world wants to buy. Even in the case of China, a significant part of the vitality of China's international trade sector can be attributed to foreign-invested enterprises which account for as much as 40 per cent of Chinese exports (Naughton, 1996, Table 3). In prosaic terms, North Korean enterprises need blueprints and worldwide distribution and marketing networks.

Foreign direct investment (and through it an infusion of new technology and management) would undoubtedly play a key role in creating this institutional linkage between potential output and world markets. However the most likely investors in North Korea are firms from South Korea and Japan, two countries with which North Korea has difficult relations. The US embargo is another disincentive for potential investors in the DPRK. It is unlikely that either Japan or the USA would normalize relations with North Korea without significant improvements in North–South relations. Normalization with Japan would permit the Japanese investment guarantee agency to insure Japanese investments in North Korea and pave the way for mainstream Japanese firms to make large-scale investments. Normalization with the US would permit the ending of the embargo and the disincentive to investment that it presents to potential investors of all nationalities. Even with the right policies a series of diplomatic tumblers will have to fall into place for such a reform strategy to work.

The signals with respect to North Korea's intentions are mixed. A Constitutional revision promulgated in August 1998 mentions private property (Article 24), material incentives (Article 32) cost, price and profit (Article 33) in an otherwise thoroughly orthodox elaboration of a planned, socialist, self-reliant, *juche* economy. However, shortly after the constitutional revision the *Rodong-Shinmoon*, the newspaper of the Central Committee of the Korean Workers Party, and *Kunloja*, the body's politico-theoretical magazine, published a joint article arguing that:

> If one wants the prosperity of the national economy, he should thoroughly reject the idea of dependence on outside forces, the idea that he cannot live without foreign capital. Ours is an independent economic structure equipped with all the economic sectors in good harmony and with its own strong heavy industry at the core. It is incomparably better than the export-oriented economic structure dependent on other countries. We must heighten vigilance against the imperialists moves to induce us to reform and opening to the outside world. Reform and opening on their lips are a honey-coated poison. Clear is our stand toward reform and opening. We now have nothing to reform and open. By reform and opening the imperialists mean a revival of capitalism. The best way of blocking the wind of reform and opening of the imperialists is to defend the socialist principle in all sectors of the economy. We will never abandon the principle, but will set ourselves against all attempts to induce us to join an integrated world.

Moreover, it appears that some prominent reformers (I use this term advisedly) have been purged, and the Committee for the Promotion of

External Economic Cooperation, the body tasked with encouraging international trade and investment has been dissolved in the recent governmental reorganization.

What if Pyongyang does not undertake the internal and external initiatives to achieve successful reform? North Korea's August 1998 public statement about its missile exports, its September 1998 test of the Taepo Dong 1 missile, and apparently renewed nuclear-related activities perhaps give some indication of the country's future course.[24] North Korea could continue to play a strategy of attempting to extort resources out of the rest of the world, offering to abandon weapons development and export while continuing to make clandestine sales.[25] The marriage of the rocket and nuclear programs would give the North Koreans impressive tools with which to intimidate their immediate neighbors and create proliferation nightmares for the USA. The truly frightening aspect of this reasoning is that this scenario would be a continuation of the status quo. Ironically, given the previously noted obstacles to reform, such an externally high-risk strategy might be the path of least resistance internally to a weak and risk-adverse regime. In large part this would amount to a continuation of the status quo, and it is hard to see how such a strategy could generate enough resources to pull North Korea out of its economic tailspin.

4.6 CONCLUSION

North Korea currently is experiencing a famine of unknown magnitude. Despite the pronouncements of Pyongyang and some in the aid community, this famine has less to do with weather-related reductions in food availability than the systemic collapse of the economy. The modeling work reviewed in this paper suggests that the payoffs to economy-wide reform (even when those payoffs are defined narrowly in terms of domestic food availability) greatly outweigh the pay-offs to agricultural rehabilitation more narrowly conceived. Yet it is far from certain that North Korea will adopt meaningful reform.

Economic reform could mean significant changes in the structure and organization of the North Korean economy. Millions of people could change jobs, for example, and the country's exposure to international trade and investment could dramatically increase. Much of the increase in international interdependence would occur with rival South Korea and former colonial master Japan. And even under relatively optimistic scenarios, the process of economic restructuring could take decades. The incumbent regime could well regard these developments as threatening to its survival.

Indeed, successful reform would be in significant part continent on improvements in North Korea's diplomatic environment. The most likely investors in North Korea are South Korean and Japanese. The US economic embargo is an impediment to potential investors of all nationalities. North Korea will not experience large-scale investment until it improves its relations with these three countries. The USA and Japan will not act until there is a significant improvement in North–South relations. This gives South Korea significant influence over the future course of developments on the peninsula. Yet in the end it is North Korea that will have to make fundamental decisions about what kind of society it wishes to be, both in respect to its internal organization and its external relations.

In this regard recent signals are at best mixed. While the August 1998 constitutional revision appears to legitimate certain market-oriented economic concepts, this was soon followed by a categorically anti-reform statement by the press organs of the KWP. The disturbing implication of the analysis of this paper is that in domestic political terms brinkmanship and extortion could be the path of least resistance. Revelations of missile sales, the August 1998 firing of a rocket over Japan, the subsequent threat to militarize the rocket program and possibly renewed nuclear activities all harken back to the brinkmanship strategies that brought the DPRK to the point of military conflict with the USA in 1994. Indeed, at the time of this writing, the USA has recently gained access to a single suspected nuclear site at the cost of 400 000 metric tons of grain. Absent some political breakthrough in North Korea's relations with the USA, Japan, Europe and South Korea, the political sustainability of this game in the democracies is doubtful.

NOTES

1. For introductions to the historical and institutional evolution of the North Korean economy and extensive citations to the analytical literature on North Korea see Hwang (1993), Eberstadt (1995), and Noland (1996) among others. Michell (1998) contains a nice summary of recent developments.
2. On the conventional wisdom see Eberstadt (1994) and S.K. Kim (1994). The conventional view would be consistent with the econometric evidence of Easterly and Fischer (1994) who found that CPEs typically exhibit stronger than average performance in the initial stages of industrialization, which deteriorates into weaker than average performance as allocative efficiencies become more and more costly. According to Hwang (1993) South Korean per capita income did not exceed the North's until 1986.
3. See Noland (1996) for quantitative material on the debt (non-) burden. In this and other regards comparisons between North Korea and Romania are striking (Noland, 1997).
4. This debt trades in a (admittedly thin) secondary market at a considerable discount, with recent quotes in the range of 12–15 cents on the dollar (*International Financing Review*, 29 August 1998). The discount narrowed in late 1996 reaching roughly 50 per cent and remained there through early 1998 when it began widening. Market participants indicate that the discount is an inverse indicator of regime viability: as conditions in North Korea worsen, the likelihood of collapse and absorption by the South increases and with it the prospect of debt holders being paid by the government of the unified peninsula. According

to this logic, the market has been signaling an enhanced expectation of regime survivability.

5. Soviet assistance took a variety of forms including provision of key commodities at friendship prices, technology transfer, and provision of significant trade credits and other forms of concessional economic exchange. See Noland (1996) for quantitative estimates and further discussion.
6. Net material product covers value-added in the material product sectors (manufacturing, agriculture, construction, commodity transportation, productive communication, productive commerce, and a few others). Material product multiplied by prices yields the gross output value of social production. There are three outstanding problems with this definition. First, produced intermediate products are doubled-counted. Second, non-material sectors (housing, health and welfare expenditures, education, science, art, personal services, state administration and so on) are ignored. Third, the prices, which are calculated to reflect the labor theory of value, do not reflect true scarcity values. As a consequence, even under the best of circumstances (such as having a cooperative government) concording material product accounts to a national accounts basis is difficult. Given the secrecy of the North Korean government, concordance is virtually impossible.
7. North Korea is the most militarized society on earth, with more than one million men (and increasingly, women) under arms out of a population of around 22 million. It is difficult to quantitatively assess the military's role in the economy. In general, militaries are difficult to evaluate economically, since many of their transactions occur on non-market terms. In the case of North Korea this general difficulty is compounded by the distorted nature of the non-military economy and the regime's secrecy. Moreover, the military is outside the control of the central planners, and appears to have been omitted from the figures provided to the IMF by the North Korean government. In addition it engages in activities that would be performed in the civilian sector elsewhere. The conventional wisdom (as represented by the US Arms Control and Disarmament Agency (ACDA)) is that the military accounts for roughly a quarter of national income, though the derivation and interpretation of this figure is problematic.
8. The prize for optimism, North Korean division, goes to Shishido and Hamada (1998), who, without revealing their methodology, report a PPP-adjusted estimate of North Korean per capita income in 1995 of $3596.9, which given the South Korean estimate of $11 172.1 would yield a ratio of 3.11.
9. These figures are subject to a variety of qualifications. If one is interested in making broad comparisons of welfare, the more relevant figures are purchasing power-adjusted comparisons. Presumably the price level (however distorted) in North Korea is relatively low compared to South Korea, so that a comparison of per capita incomes based on market exchange rates would exaggerate the differences in income levels. However, the official exchange rate is surely overvalued (and probably to a very large extent) which would tend to overstate North Korean incomes in a common currency, and push the bias in the opposite direction. One could argue that in an economy as distorted as North Korea's with a huge military sector and an ongoing famine, that income as a shorthand for household economic welfare is of questionable relevance. If one is using GDP per capita as a measure of technological prowess, then other, more direct, indicators are probably preferable.
10. These data are also of questionable accuracy. They are apparently calculated by taking measures of physical output and then calculating income using South Korean value-added weights, and then are subject to inter-agency bargaining within the South Korean government prior to public release. Given the collection methods, there is no way to verify the estimates of physical output. Furthermore, it is far from obvious that the South Korean value-added schema is the most appropriate. In other countries where such methods have been applied, the resulting estimates appear to overestimate the volatility of output, as industrial output exhibits greater variance than service activities.
11. The collapse of the industrial economy has adversely affected agriculture. The two primary fertilizers used in North Korea, urea and ammonium sulfate, are both petroleum-based, and shortages of petroleum feedstocks have adversely effected domestic production of fertilizer. Likewise, periodic blights have been worsened by a shortage of agricultural chemicals. Fuel shortages have impeded the use of agricultural machinery, and forced the reintroduction of

draught animals. Problems in production have been compounded by difficulties in distribution and the use of output. Fuel shortages have hampered distribution. At the same time some outside observers have questioned the uses to which output has been put: scarce cereals appear to continue to be used to produce luxury products such as noodles, urban areas with high concentrations of KWP members and government officials have received preferential allocations, and it has been claimed that military stockpiling continues. The end result of these difficulties has been a secular deterioration in food production, and in the absence of additional imports, in the food balance.

12. Even here one must be careful. Partner coverage may be incomplete. Additionally, there is a venerable history of trade ministry clerks around the world mistaking North and South Korea. Such errors have occurred in the past decade in Mexico, Austria, and most recently Lebanon. Moreover, the IMF reporting convention counts transport and insurance as part of imports; when one calculates the mirror statistics one has to adjust the constructed North Korean figures for this accounting convention. Lastly, these figures will ignore barter trade. Although the existence of barter transactions would presumably not bias trade balance estimates in any particular way, barter could significantly distort analysis of trade volumes and composition. See Noland (1998) for a more complete discussion of these issues.
13. That the military has its own trading channels is prospectively of enormous importance. They potentially could continue to engage in arms trade for pecuniary or strategic reasons, even if this were opposed by other parts of the state on diplomatic grounds.
14. See Smith (1998) for a highly informative discussion of famine-related issues.
15. See Snyder (1997) for a discussion of North Korea's food problem and the extent of Chinese assistance.
16. A comparison of the 1990 and 1996 North Korean SAMs indicates that the economy has experienced a tremendous fall in output. In the modeling that follows, this fall is explained partly by a decline of the North Korean capital stock. For modeling convenience, the remaining decline was handled as an exogenous fall in the level of total factor productivity (TFP). Alternatively, one could explicitly model the less than complete utilization of resources by introducing unemployed resources explicitly, but the gains associated with this strategy did not appear to warrant the great increase in model complexity. I am under no illusions that North Korea is a Walrasian economy.
17. This increase is calibrated based on the work of Coe et al. (1996). See Noland et al. (1999) and Noland et al. (2000c) for further discussion as well as an analysis of sectorally non-uniform changes in TFP.
18. In the model, we assumed that half of the army is engaged in activities (construction, manufacturing, and so on) that normally would be performed in the civilian sector of the economy, and that half of the army is engaged in war fighting activities. Demobilization is modeled as a reduction of resources devoted to strictly military activities.
19. First, they have an incentive to understate output to increase international aid flows. Second, as mentioned in the text, the official data appears to refer only to output or resources controlled by the central planners. Evidence indicates that military and economic activity outside the plan has increased, or at least has not decreased as rapidly as formal activity under the plan. Finally, aid flows, which account for a considerable share of food consumption, do not appear to be included in the official figures.
20. One can think of at least two possible channels by which the impact of the floods could be underestimated. First, if one assumes high substitutability among primary inputs, labor and capital could simply substitute for land. Second, some of the capital stock in the agricultural sector had been destroyed in the floods. As a mental experiment and check on robustness, we ran a variant of the first experiment in which the agricultural capital stock was augmented as land was recovered. The addition of capital along with land did indeed increase the output response, but the impact on GDP was still only around 2 per cent.
21. Even the increase in domestic food availability could have political implications – historically, political change has occurred in the wake of famines, not in the midst of them.
22. Some parallels with Romania are briefly discussed in Noland (1997).
23. Using a gravity model, Noland (1996) finds that nearly two-thirds of North Korean trade would be with South Korea and Japan if North Korea behaved as a normal country.

24. There is considerable confusion (much of it due to bureaucratic and domestic politics) over the missile North Korea launched in September 1998. Some have claimed that this was a test of the Taepo Dong 1 missile, while the North Koreans and some others have claimed that it was a satellite launch. Recently Robert D. Walpole, the US Central Intelligence Agency's senior intelligence officer for strategic programs, has stated that it was a three-stage rocket possibly capable of delivering a small payload across the Pacific (September 25, 1998, *Washington Post*). The North Korean government has threatened to use the rocket as a military delivery system.
25. Press reports beginning in August 1998 document a series of North Korean demands made to various US delegations demanding up to $1 billion for access to possible nuclear-related facilities and an end to missile exports. As of June 1999, the USA had gained access to one of these sites at the cost of 400 000 metric tons of grain.

BIBLIOGRAPHY

Chun, Hong-tack (1992), 'Estimating North Korea's GNP by Physical Indicators Approach', *Korea Development Review*, **14** (1), 167–225 (in Korean).

Coe, David T., Elhanan Helpman and Alexander Hoffmaister (1996), 'North-South R&D Spillovers', *Economic Journal* **107** (440), 134–49.

Easterly, William and Stanley Fischer (1994), 'The Soviet Economic Decline: Historical and Republican Data,' *NBER Working Paper* 4735, Cambridge, MA: National Bureau of Economic Research.

Eberstadt, Nicholas (1994), 'Reform, Muddling through, or Collapse?', in Thomas H. Henriksen and Kyongsoo Lho (eds), *One Korea?* Stanford, CA: Hoover Institution Press, 13–30.

Eberstadt, Nicholas (1995), *Korea Approaches Reunification*, Armonk, NY: ME Sharpe.

Eberstadt, Nicholas (1996), 'How Much Money Goes from Japan to the DPRK?', *Asian Survey*, **36** (5), 523–42.

Eberstadt, Nicholas (1998a), 'The DPRK's International Trade in Capital Goods, 1970–1995: Indications from Mirror Statistics', *Journal of East Asian Affairs*, **12** (1), 165–223.

Eberstadt, Nicholas (1998b), 'A Quantitative Comparison of Current Socio-economic Conditions in North and South Korea', paper presented to the Second Conference of the International Interdisciplinary Project on Nation-Building for Korean Unification, Honolulu, Hawaii, 21–25 January.

Eberstadt, Nicholas, N.d., 'The DPRK's International Trade in Capital Goods, 1970–1995', Washington: American Enterprise Institute, processed.

Eberstadt, Nicholas, Marc Rubin and Albina Tretyakova (1995), 'The Collapse of Soviet and Russian Trade with the DPRK, 1989–1993', *The Korean Journal of National Unification*, no. 4, 87–104.

Hwang, Eui-Gak (1993), *The Korean Economies*, Oxford: Clarendon Press.

Jeong, Kap-Yeong (1993), 'Comparing the North Korean Level of Economic Development by Principal Components Analysis', in Young Sun Lee (ed.), *North Korea's Reality and Unification*, Seoul: Center for East and West Studies, Yonsei University, 87–111 (in Korean).

Kim, Sang-Kyom (1994), 'Opening North Korea's Economy', in Jang-Hee Yoo and Chang-Jae Lee (eds), *Northeast Asian Economic Cooperation*, Policy Studies 94–08, Seoul: Korea Institute for International Economic Policy.

Michell, Anthony (1998), 'The Current North Korean Economy', in Marcus Noland (ed.), *Economic Integration of the Korean Peninsula*, Special Report 10, Washington: Institute for International Economics, 137–63.

Naughton, Barry (1996), 'China's Emergence and Prospects as a Trading Nation', *Brookings Papers on Economic Activity*, no. 2, 273–344.

Noland, Marcus (1996), 'The North Korean Economy', *Joint U.S.–Korea Academic Studies*, no. 6, 127–77.

Noland, Marcus (1997), 'Why North Korea Will Muddle Through', *Foreign Affairs* **76** (4), 105-18.

Noland, Marcus (1998), 'The External Economic Relations of the DPRK and Prospects for Reform', in Samuel S. Kim (ed.), *North Korean Foreign Relations*, Hong Kong: Oxford University Press, 187–211.

Noland, Marcus, Sherman Robinson and Ligang Liu (1998), 'The Costs and Benefits of Korean Unification', *Asian Survey*, **38** (8), 801–14.

Noland, Marcus, Sherman Robinson and Ligang Liu (1999), 'The Economics of Korean Unification' *Journal of Policy Reform*, **3** (3), 255–99.

Noland, Marcus, Sherman Robinson and Monica Scatasta (1997) 'Modeling North Korean Economic Reform', *Journal of Asian Economics*, **8** (1), 15–38.

Noland, Marcus, Sherman Robinson and Tao Wang (2000a), 'Rigorous Speculation: The Collapse and Revival of the North Korean Economy', *Working Paper Series*, 99-1 Washington: Institute for International Economics.

Noland, Marcus, Sherman Robinson and Tao Wang (2000b) 'Famine in North Korea: Causes and Cures', *Working Paper Series*, 99-2, Washington: Institute for International Economics.

Noland, Marcus, Sherman Robinson and Tao Wang (2000c), 'Modeling Korean Unification', Washington: Institute for International Economics, processed.

Shishido, Shuntaro, and Mitsuru Hamada (1998), 'Northeast Asia in the 21st Century – Per Capita Income and the Real Scale of the Economy in the Year 2025 as a Macro-economic Framework', *ERINA Report*, no. 24, 2–7.

Smith, Heather (1998), 'The Food Economy: Catalyst for Collapse?', in Marcus Noland (ed.), *Economic Integration of the Korean Peninsula*, Special Report 10, Washington: Institute for International Economics.

Snyder, Scott (1997), 'North Korea's Decline and China's Strategic Dilemmas', *Special Report*, Washington: United States Institute for Peace, October.

Yeon, Ha-Cheong (1993), 'Economic Consequences of German Unification and its Policy Implications for Korea', *KDI Working Paper 9303*, Seoul: Korea Development Institute, April.

5. Policy Reforms and the Prospects of Economic Growth in North Korea

Jong-Wha Lee

5.1 INTRODUCTION

The formidable economic challenge for North Korea is to surmount its present poverty trap and move towards a high growth path. Faced with a disastrous food shortage and continuous economic decline, the North Korean economy appears to be nearing a catastrophic situation.

Will North Korea survive its current hardship and achieve strong growth in the long run? It seems very unlikely that on current policies of central planning and self-sufficiency the DPRK economy will recover from its plight in the foreseeable future. Considerable reforms of its economic institutions and policies will be required for sustainable growth. In this paper, we explore the prospects of policy reforms North Korea could take to stimulate economic growth and then analyze the effects of the reforms on its future growth.

Recent cross-country evidence suggests that high growth performance requires greater openness to international trade, good quality of institutions, high government saving, and well-educated human resources. Since North Korea is equipped with relatively well-educated human resources, it has substantial potential for future growth. If North Korea adopts market-oriented reform and opening policies, it will have the opportunity to display the kind of dynamism the East Asian countries previously showed. We will make conditional projections of the future growth rates for the North Korean economy depending on the extent of hypothetical reforms it could take toward market-oriented and opening policies.

Whether North Korea can embrace fundamental reforms in an attempt to reverse its economic decline remains difficult to judge. At the present time, the probability that North Korea reforms itself into a complete market economy, either voluntarily or through a popular uprising, is considered to be very low. The North Korean party and military leaders may not adopt such reforms that they believe may threaten their hold on power and endanger the nation's security. However, the economic situation in North Korea is too urgent for Kim Jong Il and his advisors to ignore. At least for their own survival the North Korean leaders will attempt to implement economic reforms they consider to be necessary to overcome the current predicament. In this regard, we consider that the reform scenarios for the North Korean economy are not totally unrealistic. These conditional projections are also a useful experiment which illustrates North Korea's economic potential for growth over the next decades.

Table 5.1 Recent Trend of Macroeconomics Indicator for North Korea

Year	GND growth rate (%)	Per capita GNP (US$)	Foreign trade (US$ billion)			Foreign debt (US$ billion)	Foreign debt/ GNP (%)
			Total	Export	Import		
1990	−3.7	1064	4.72	1.96	2.76	7.86	34.0
1991	−5.1	1038	2.72	1.01	1.71	9.28	40.5
1992	−7.6	943	2.66	1.02	1.64	9.72	46.1
1993	−4.3	904	2.64	1.02	1.62	10.32	50.3
1994	−1.7	923	2.11	0.84	1.27	10.66	50.3
1995	−4.5	957	2.05	0.74	1.31	11.83	53.0
1996	−3.7	910	1.98	0.73	1.25	12.00	56.1
1997	−6.8	741	2.18	0.91	1.27	11.90	67.3

Source: Bank of Korea.

5.2 CURRENT SITUATIONS OF THE NORTH KOREAN ECONOMY

Failing Strategy of Autarkic Development

North Korea's economic situation continues to worsen. Although the lack of accurate statistics poses great difficulty in drawing a precise picture of North Korea's current economic status, it must be in crisis. Since 1990, North Korea's GDP has been continuously shrinking and its trade deficit and foreign debt rising (Table 5.1). Faced with a disastrous food shortage and severe energy constraints, North Korea appears to be plunging into a catastrophic collapse.

Although the North Korean government has blamed external factors such as the unfavorable weather and the collapse of the socialist bloc for its current difficulties, critics see the current crisis as an unavoidable consequence of its inefficient economic system. The North Korean economic system is known to be the most centralized and closed system in the world today.[1] Although many centrally planned economies have adopted market-oriented reforms since the1970s, North Korea has adhered to rigid central planning. Economic management has always been under the complete control of the party leadership. The North Korean economy has suffered from the common ailments of centrally planned economies. As observed in the former Soviet Union and the East-Central European socialist states, artificial controls of prices, inefficient allocations of resources across sectors and lack of competition all have contributed to the inefficiencies in command economic system.

Table 5.2 Estimates of GNP per Capita and Growth Rate for North Korea and Selected Other Countries, 1995

Country	GNP per capita, 1995		Average annual growth of GNP per capita 1985–95 (%)
	US$	PPP price	
North Korea	957	–	– 1.6*
Vietnam	240	–	–
Mongolia	310	1 950	– 3.8
China	620	2 920	8.3
Albania	670	–	–
Uzbekistan	970	2 370	– 3.9
Romania	1 480	4 360	– 3.8
Ukraine	1 630	2 400	– 9.2
Russian Federation	2 240	4 480	– 5.1
Poland	2 790	5 400	1.2
Slovak Republic	2 950	3 610	– 2.8
Czech Republic	3 870	9 770	– 1.8
Hungary	4 120	6 410	– 1.0
South Korea	9 700	11 450	7.7
Japan	39 640	22 110	2.9

Notes: * average growth rate over the period 1986–95.

Source: World Bank, *World Development Report*, 1997; North Korean data are based on the estimates by Bank of Korea.

The lack of North Korea's international trade and external cooperation with the international community has also seriously constrained its economic growth. Since 1956, its economic management has been based on the ideology of *juche,* which emphasizes self-sufficiency. This is in fact a development strategy with inward-oriented economic policies of an autarkic state. In this strategy the limited exposure of industries to foreign competition as well as the lack of importation and adoption of advanced foreign technologies have hindered the economy's sustained growth.

Initially, the North Korean economic policies – centrally planned and self-reliant – were very auspicious. Similar to other centrally planned economies that had stressed on the development of heavy industries, North Korea enjoyed high economic growth: an annual average growth rate was about 7.8 per cent in the 1960s and recorded 10.4 per cent during the period of 1971–75.[2] But the growth strategy based on the accumulation of capital forced on by the government were not able to sustain as inefficiencies of resource allocation eventually grew and as the rates of return to accumulated capital began to decline. Average growth rates fell to about 2.6 per cent between 1981–90 and further to a negative rate of −4.5 per cent between 1991–95. Due to its economic inefficiencies, North Korea has not only failed to catch up with South Korea but has also fallen behind other centrally planned economies (see Tables 5.2 and 5.3).

Recent Change in Economic Policies

In recognition of the steady deterioration of economic conditions, the North Korean regime has made some efforts to liberalize and to open up its economic system. Since the mid-1980s, there have been some signs of change in the economic policy: economic plans introducing limited local autonomy were introduced and a foreign investment law was adopted (see Kim, 1993 and Noland, 1995).

In 1984, as a partial remedy for the shortage of consumer goods, North Korea launched the so called 'August Third Consumer Goods Program' aimed at advocating the use of underutilized labor and unused industrial waste in the production of simple consumer goods. The program emphasized the role of local governments; it established direct sales stores where locally produced goods were sold directly to consumers, bypassing centrally planned production quotas and procurement. Considering that the North Korean economy had previously been under the complete control of the central government, the program allowing for local autonomy in the decision-making process was seen as a first step in the direction of decentralization. However, this limited effort in decentralizing the decision-making process does not mean that the North Korean economic system is in transition toward a market economy (Smith, 1997, p. 11). The state still owns all enterprises and the central planning authority artificially sets prices on all factors and goods.

Table 5.3 Comparison of South and North Korean Economies (1997)

	(Unit)	North (A)	South (B)	A/B × 100 (%)
Gross national product	($ billion)	17.7	437.4	4.1
Per capital GNP	($)	741	9 511	7.8
Total trade	($ billion)	2.2	280.8	0.8
Exports		0.9	136	0.7
Imports		1.3	144.6	0.9
Foreign debt	($ billion)	11.9	120.8	9.9
	(% of GNP)	67.3	27.6	243.8
Defense expenditure*	($ billion)	4.5	9.2	48.9
	(% of GNP)	21.3	4.4	484.1
Power generation	(billion kWh)	19.3	224.4	8.6
Crude oil imports	(million ton)	0.51	118.8	0.4
Grain production	(million ton)	3.49	6.14	56.8
Rice production	(million ton)	1.50	5.45	27.5
Iron ore	(million ton)	2.91	0.30	970.0
Lenghth of railway	(km)	5 214	6 580	79.2
Length of roads	(km)	23 377	84 968	27.5

Notes: * 1996 estimate.

Source: Bank of Korea.

Officially, North Korea opened its doors to foreign investment with the passage of the 1984 Foreign Joint Venture Law that was modeled after China's successful 1979 joint venture law. However, the new law failed to attract the much needed foreign investors: between 1984 and 1993 only 144 joint ventures were established by small North Korean companies in Japan (Oh, 1997, p. 31). Then, as a response to the contraction of North Korea's trade relations with the former Soviet Union, the DPRK regime changed its lukewarm stance and strongly endorsed joint ventures with industrial countries. In 1991–92 it enacted a flurry of new business laws with very generous provisions – nominally at least – for foreign investors and established the Rajin–Sonbong Economic and Trade Zone (RSETZ). In addition, North Korea actively participated in the UN-sponsored Tuman River Project, which intended to establish an international industrial complex at the juncture of North Korea, China and Russia. In spite of North Korea's efforts, the result so far has not been satisfactory. Even by 1997, the Rajin–

Sonbong Economic and Trade Zone was only able to induce less than $100 million in foreign investment. There are several reasons why the new joint venture laws have not been met by the universal acclaim of Western countries. First of all, the Rajin-Sonbong area is geographically isolated and it lacks the necessary infrastructure for large-scale projects. Second, foreign investors are very dubious about North Korea's economic policy, which they consider still advérse to opening the economy to the outside world. North Korea remains protectionist by international standards.

On the surface, the North Korean leadership appears to have implemented or tried to implement economic reforms. However, so far the reform policies were too limited to have an appreciable impact and there has yet to appear signs of Pyongyang embracing reform policies with enthusiasm. During the last decade, the lack of market mechanism and external cooperation has been the most salient reasons for North Korea's economic failure. In the absence of substantial reforms adopting market-oriented and opening policies, North Korea's current economic hardship will prolong endangering the survival of the economy.

5.3 SOURCES OF ECONOMIC GROWTH: A CROSS-COUNTRY ANALYSIS

The growth performances during the last three decades are very diverse among the countries in the world. The four East Asian tigers – Hong Kong SAR, Korea, Singapore, and Taiwan – grew extremely rapidly at an average of over 7 per cent per year in per capita terms between 1965 and 1995. On the other hand, many of the Sub-Saharan African countries recorded less than 1 per cent average per capita income growth during the same period.

In this section, we explore the main factors that influenced the growth rates of per capita income for the last three decades. The analysis is based on a general framework of cross-country regressions, which puts the experience of individual countries in a global context. This approach allows us to understand the specific factors associated with economic growth across countries and the key differences between fast and slow growing economies. This exercise will provide a basis for understanding the future growth prospects of North Korea and offers insights to the effects of the policy reforms that North Korea can implement to stimulate its economic growth.

Framework for the Empirical Analysis of Growth

The basic empirical framework is based on an extended version of the neoclassical growth model, as described by Barro (1991), Barro and Lee

(1994), and Barro and Sala-i-Martin (1995). This model predicts conditional convergence of income, implying that a country with a lower initial income relative to its own long-run (or steady-state) potential level of income grows faster than a higher-income country over time. The basic idea is that the farther an economy locates away from its steady-state level, the greater is the gap of reproducible (physical and human) capital stock and technical efficiency from their long-run potential levels. The gap of existing capital and technology from their steady-state levels provides the economy with the chance for rapid catching up, through the higher marginal productivity of capital accumulation and the diffusion of technology from the more technically advanced economies. Hence, this model predicts convergence of per capita income over time: the lower is the initial level of per capita income relative to steady state, the higher the subsequent growth is. In the cross-country context, it implies that poorer countries would grow faster than richer countries, if the variables influencing the steady-state level of per capita income are controlled. As a reduced form the model can be represented by

$$(1/T)\ \log(Y_T/Y_0) = a_0 + a_1 \log(Y_0) + a_2 Z + e \qquad (5.1)$$

where the dependent variable indicates growth rate of per capita income for the period T (in this paper, 25 years from 1965 to 1990), $\log(Y_0)$ is a log value of the initial level of per capita income and Z denotes an array of the variables that influence the steady-state level of per capita income. The conditional convergence implies a negative coefficient on the initial income.

A wide variety of external environment and policy variables will affect growth rates by changing the long-run potential income. Considering the results from previous empirical research, we classify the important determinants of long-run per capita income into three broad categories: (1) natural resources and geography (including natural resource intensity, access to sea and location in the tropics), (2) human resources (initial human capital stock, initial life expectancy and growth of working-age population), and (3) institutions and policy variables (quality of institutions, openness and government saving).

Natural resources and geography

We include three kinds of natural environment variables that represent the natural barriers to economic growth. The first variable is a measure of natural resource intensity, and is constructed by the logarithm of the land-population ratio in 1965. Sachs and Warner (1995b), and Gallup and Sachs (1998) observe that natural resource-abundant economies have tended to grow more slowly than resource-poor economies over the period 1970–90. The basic idea is that more plentiful primary resources tend to shrink the manufacturing sector and to expand the primary and the non-trade good sectors. Considered that the labor-intensive manufacturing export has worked as a crucial force for economic growth in the 1970s and 1980s, the contraction of manufacturing sector caused by resource abundance may lower growth. The abundance of natural resources also tends to force the economy to remain in primary production and thereby lower the ability to generate continuing technology improvements and thereby achieve sustained economic growth. In addition, natural resource-abundant economies may provide greater opportunities and incentives for rent-seeking and corruption. Particularly, when natural resources are commonly owned or taxed heavily by the government, unproductive activities to obtain a larger piece of profits from the common resources become more prevalent in the economy.

The second natural environment variable is access to sea, as indicated by whether a country is landlocked or not. Ocean shipping plays an overwhelming role in international merchandise trade. Landlocked countries must be placed in a disadvantaged position for the subsequent growth by paying a much higher transportation cost for all imported goods than coastal economies equipped with natural seaports.

A third natural environment variable is location in the tropics. Very few tropical economies have been able to achieve sustained growth. Hot and humid temperature and infectious diseases in tropical climates lower productivity of workers. Tropics that are associated with lower population density and abundant natural resources are likely to concentrate on agriculture production rather than on labor-intensive manufacturing.

Human resources

The various models of new growth theories emphasize human capital as a key factor to drive the long-term growth of income. In the framework of extended neoclassical growth model, for given values of the other explanatory variables, a higher human capital stock leads to a higher steady-state per capita income. In the endogenous growth model, human capital generates perpetual growth by either preventing returns to a broad capital from falling or by increasing capabilities for the innovation and adaptation of new technologies.

The human resource variables include a measure of human capital stock. We use the average years of secondary and higher schooling for the working-age population at the initial year of the period (that is, 1965), available from Barro and Lee (1996). The greater initial educational stock indicates that a more skilled work force can produce more output from a given natural and physical resource. Hence, the country with a greater education stock is located in a more favorable condition for future growth. In addition, life expectancy at birth, as a log value at the initial year of the period, is used to measure health attainment, which is considered as another important component of human capital stock. A higher life expectancy would tend to indicate a healthier, more productive worker.

A third human resource variable is net growth of the working-age population (aged 15–64), as measured by the growth rate of the working-age population subtracting the growth rate of the total population. For a given population growth rate, faster growth of the working-age population increases the size of work force, which contributes to output growth.

Table 5.4 Cross-country Growth Regression (Dependent Variable: Growth of Real per Capita GDP, 1965–90, 74 Countries)

Independent variable	Coefficients	
Initial income		
Initial GDP per capita (log)	−2.10 0 (−10.3)	−2.126 (−8.5)
Natural condition		
Natural resource abundance	−0.135 (−2.5)	−0.131 (−1.9)
Landlocked	−0.405 (−1.6)	−0.383 (−1.4)
Tropics	−1.227 (−5.1)	−1.168 (−3.9)
Human resources		
Schooling (log)	0.265 (2.1)	0.267 (1.9)
Life expectancy (log)	3.580 (4.0)	3.546 (3.8)
Growth of working-age pop.	1.626 (4.9)	1.576 (4.0)
Institutions and policy		
Openness	1.920 (6.6)	1.865 (5.6)
Quality of institutions	0.180 (2.8)	0.190 (2.2)
Government saving rate	0.101 (4.6)	0.106 (4.4)
Regional dummy		
Asia		−0.053 (−0.1)
Latin America		−0.083 (−0.2)
Sub-Saharan Africa		−0.196 (−0.4)
Adjusted R^2	0.87	0.86

Institutions and policy variables

We construct three institutions and policy variables. The first variable we consider is a measure of quality of institutions. It is a measure of quality of public institutions and their relationship to the functioning of market. The measure comes from Knack and Keefer (1996) which is based on surveys of international investors. The overall index, scaled between 0 and 10, is an average of five indicators including (a) quality of bureaucracy, (b) corruption in government, (c) rule of law, (d) expropriation risk and (e) risk of repudiation of contracts by government. The overall index therefore measures the security of property and contractual rights, and the efficiency of the government's intervention in market.

The second policy variable is a measure of openness. Open economies have greater access to cheap imported intermediate goods, larger markets, and advanced technologies. An economy's openness to international markets can be represented by various measures including tariff rate and black market premium of exchange rates, or indicators of trade policy regimes. We use the openness measurement constructed by Sachs and Warner (1995a). This index is calculated as the fraction of years between 1965 and 1990 that the country was considered to be open to trade and thus sufficiently integrated with the global economy. The evaluation of the country's openness is made on the basis of four dimensions of trade policy: average tariff rates, quotas and licensing, export taxes and black market exchange rate premium.[3]

A third policy variable is government saving (defined as the difference between current government revenues and current government expenditures). It is the average ratio of government saving to GDP over the period 1965–90. Higher government saving rate is considered to increase national saving rate and thereby raise the growth rate. In the Solow-type neoclassical growth model, higher saving rate raises the steady-state level of output per capita and thereby increases the growth rate for a given starting value of GDP. Higher government saving is also an important policy indicator of sounder overall macroeconomic management, such as more prudent monetary and exchange rate policies.

Regression Results

Table 5.4 presents the regression results using the basic framework of equation (1) and the explanatory variables just described. The dependent variable is the annual growth rate of real GDP per capita between 1965 and 1990, which is obtained from Summers and Heston (1991) version 5.6. The regressions apply to a data set for 74 countries – those with a complete data set for all variables. Column 1 of Table 5.4 shows the result of the basic regression. The result shows strong evidence for conditional convergence: the coefficient on the log value of initial GDP is highly significant, and the estimated coefficient is −2.10 (t = −10.3). Thus, a poor country with a lower initial income level grows faster, with the variables influencing the steady-state level of income controlled. Specifically, the coefficient implies that a country at half the income level of another country grows by 1.45 percentage points (= 2.1 × ln(2)) faster than the richer country.

The regression result confirms our hypotheses about natural resources and geography. The estimated coefficient on the natural resource intensity variable is −0.13 (t = −2.2), indicating that countries with abundant natural resources grew more slowly than other countries. The other geography variables show the coefficients with the expected signs: countries that were landlocked or located in the tropics all recorded significantly lower growth rates than others countries during the period from 1965 to 1990.

The human resource variables turn out to have a strong effect on economic growth. The educational attainment variable, as a form of log value of secondary and tertiary schooling years, has a positive and significant effect on the growth rate: the estimated coefficient on the schooling variable is 0.306 (t = 2.1). The mean of the schooling variable is −0.67 (s.d. = 1.16), corresponding to a mean secondary and higher schooling year of 0.86 (s.d. = 0.85). Therefore, one standard deviation increase in the secondary and schooling raises the growth rate of per capita income by 0.35 per cent per year. The logarithm of life expectancy at birth – a measure of health attainment – is highly significant in the regression: the estimated coefficient 3.58 (t = 4.0) implies that one standard deviation increase in life expectancy at birth at 1965 is estimated to raise the growth rate by 0.82 per cent per year (the mean of the log (life expectancy) is 4.0 (s.d. = 0.23), corresponding to a mean life expectancy of 56 years (s.d. = 12)). The net growth rate of working-age population also has a significantly positive effect on growth rate. The coefficient 1.63 (t = 4.9) implies that a one standard deviation increase of 0.32 in the net growth rate of working-age population is associated with an increase in the growth rate of 0.52 percentage points per year.

The regression result provides clear evidence that the institution and policy variables play a significant role in determining economic growth. The quality of institutions has a strong positive effect on growth, indicating that countries with more constructive interactions between the government and the market tended to have higher growth rates over the period, 1965–90. The estimated coefficient implies that each increment of 1 in this index (on a scale of 10) is associated with an increase in the growth rate of 0.18 percentage points. Thus, for instance, the difference between the Philippines' poor score on the institutional quality (2.97) and Singapore's high score (8.56) accounts for a 1 percentage point difference in their average annual growth rates.

The openness variable appears to be very strongly and positively associated with growth rate. The estimated coefficient 1.92 (t = 6.6) indicates that an economy open to trade during the entire period from 1965 to 1990 grew 1.92 percentage points faster per year than an economy, which was completely closed throughout the period.

The government saving variable has a significantly positive impact on growth: a 10 percentage point increase in government saving ratio raises the growth rate of per capita income by 1.1 per cent per year.

Table 5.4 shows the result of regression with the inclusion of regional dummies. Column 2 of Table 5.4 shows that Asia, Latin America, and Sub-Saharan African dummies have statistically insignificant coefficients. Even with the three regional dummies controlled, the regression shows that most of the explanatory variables are still significant and have the estimated coefficients of the same magnitude.

5.4 CONDITIONS FOR NORTH KOREA'S CATCHING UP

The empirical exercise on the sources of growth across countries shows that a strong convergence effect from lower per capita income, good natural and human environments, and market-based and open economic policies are the key factors in sustaining long-run economic growth.

With regard to per capita income, North Korea is placed in a favorable condition for the future economic growth. The lower per capita income level of North Korea could provide a strong starting point for its convergence effect if other conditions are satisfied.

North Korea also has some natural advantages that enable it to pursue export-led growth. It is a coastal economy with natural seaports. The relative abundance of labor implies low initial wages and the ability to compete internationally in labor-intensive manufactures such as footwear, apparel, textiles, and electronic assembly operations. These labor-intensive manufactures can provide the North Korean economy with a sound basis for export-led industrialization.

Given its relatively good conditions in terms of initial income level and natural resources, North Korea's growth potential can be said to be very positive. However, whether North Korea can actually achieve high growth and catch up with the industrialized countries, South Korea in particular, depends on other critical factors such as human resources, economic institutions and policies. In this section, we first examine the human resource variables that are inherited to North Korea in details. Then, we examine the prospects of North Korea's substantial reforms toward market-oriented and open economic policies.

Human Resources in North Korea

Educational attainment

Official North Korean data on school enrollment and educational attainment shows that North Korea has a substantial educational stock almost comparable to that of South Korea, at least in quantitative terms.

According to the official data reported by Eberstadt and Banister (1992) and Eberstadt (1995), North Korea had about 4.3 million pupils aged between

6 and 15 enrolled in primary and secondary schools in 1987. The enrollments implied a gross enrollment ratio of about 96 per cent, which was almost the same as South Korea's 95 per cent in that year. In the early 1960s, the enrollment ratios for North and South Korea were also very much the same, about 71 per cent in both countries. Hence, currently North Korea seems to have a substantial quantity of primary and secondary educational stock, matching up to that of South Korea. However, the quality of education in the North is lower because its education system is less efficient than that of the South in terms of the contents of curriculum, the quality of instruction, and the provision of educational resources.

Table 5.5 Educational Attainment of Population Aged 15 and Above for North Korea and Selected Other Countries, 1990

Country	Highest level attained (Percentage of the population over 15)				Average years of school
	No school	Primary	Secondary	Higher	
North Korea	–	–	–	13.7	–
South Korea	8.0	16.1	61.9	13.9	9.94
Japan	0.2	32.1	50.0	17.7	8.98
China	22.2	34.6	41.3	1.9	5.85
Bulgaria	4.2	44.7	38.1	12.9	9.18
Cuba	6.0	41.8	43.0	9.2	7.38
Czech.	0.3	34.2	58.3	7.1	10.10
Hungary	1.2	54.5	35.6	8.8	8.93
Poland	1.3	43.7	48.4	6.5	9.47
Romania	4.4	19.8	70.2	5.5	9.44
Russia	0.1	18.8	68.7	12.5	10.50

Notes: For North Korea, the figures indicate the educational attainment of population 16 and above at year-end 1987.

Source: Barro, Robert and Jong-Wha Lee (1996), 'International Measures of Schooling Quality', *American Economic Review*; North Korea data from Eberstadt and Banister (1992), *The Population of North Korea*, p. 77.

Eberstadt and Banister (1992) report that in 1987 over half a million (521 000) North Korean students were enrolled in tertiary schools, while the corresponding figure was about 1.3 millions in South Korea. It implies that the gross tertiary enrollment ratio of North Korea was not much lower than that of South Korea (34.2 per cent in 1985) given the difference in their population size. The official data on educational attainment of the population shows that North Korea has a substantial stock of college-educated human resources, comparable to that of South Korea. In 1987, 13.7 per cent of population aged 16 and above were college-educated adults, while in South Korea the corresponding figure was 13.9 per cent in 1990. Table 5.5 presents a comparison of educational attainment between North Korea and other selected economies. North Korea has a far greater post-secondary educational stock than China and East European transitional economies.

Table 5.6 North Korea, Estimated and Projected Demographic Indicators, 1960–2020

Year	Crude birth rate (per 1000 persons)	Crude death rate (per 1000 persons)	Infant mortality rate (per 1000 live birth)	Life expectancy at birth (years)
1960	40.5	12.5	70	55.2
1965	46.3	11.1	58	57.6
1970	35.8	8.3	47	61.5
1975	23.0	6.1	35	65.5
1980	22.0	5.6	30	67.7
1985	23.5	5.4	28	69.8
1990	24.1	5.3	24	71.1
1995	21.8	5.3	22	72.2
2000	17.9	5.3	20	73.1
2005	15.8	5.6	18	73.9
2010	15.4	6.0	16	74.6
2015	15.8	6.5	15	75.3
2020	15.7	7.0	13	76.1

Source: United Nations, World Population Prospects 1950–2050 (the 1994 revision), 1994.

Life expectancy

The available statistics shows that North Korea has a relatively high life expectancy at birth, given her low per capita income. North Korea's life expectancy at birth is 72.2 in 1995, which is about the same as that of South Korea (Tables 5.6 and 5.7). Perhaps it reflects the contribution made by the state health system, which provides universal health care to the majority of population. Nonetheless, the actual life expectancy can be considerably lower than the official statistics because of recent famine and natural disasters.

Working-age population

We expect that North Korea will expand its labor force over time. The share of working-age population has been increasing since 1970 and is estimated to continue the rising trend, reaching 70.2 per cent in 2020 from 66.3 per cent in 1995 (see Table 5.8). Over the 1995–2020 period, the average growth rate of working age population is estimated to grow by 1.39 per cent per year, surpassing the growth rate of total population of 1.16 per cent per year.

Table 5.7 Comparative Demographic Indicators: Estimates for North and South Korea, 1995

	North Korea	South Korea
Population (thousands)	23 917	44 851
Area (1000 sq. km)	122.8	99.4
Population density (persons/sq. km)	194.8	451.3
Sex ratio (males/100 females)	97	101.4
Annual population growth rate (%)	1.6	0.9
Population aged 0–14 (%)	29.1	23.6
Population aged 15–64 (%)	66.3	70.8
Population aged 65 and above (%)	4.6	5.6
Crude birth rate (per 1000 persons)	21.8	16.1
Crude death rate (per 1000 persons)	5.3	6.3
Infant mortality rate (per 1000 persons)	22	8.8
Total fertility rate (per woman)	2.2	1.8
Life expectancy at birth (years)	72.2	72.9

Source: North Korea data from United Nations (1994) and South Korea data from Korea Statistical Office.

Prospects for Economic Reform

Although there is no professional consensus on the future of North Korea, at least three broad scenarios are discussed.[4] The first scenario is that North Korea tries to ride out the current crisis without doing anything. This status quo policy promises at least short-run stability to its leadership but in the mid-run or long run the economy's continuing decline will increase economic distress on the majority of population leading to political and social explosion. In this case, North Korea will be subject to a sudden collapse and subsequent absorption by South Korea. In the second scenario, North Korea makes minimal economic adjustments to cope with current difficulties while still preserving the Leninist system. This *muddling through* strategy may not be viable in the longrun, given the severity of the DPRK's current economic difficulties. Nonetheless the North Korean government would prefer this over others in order to keep the population insulated from foreign influence and minimize its political instability (Noland, 1997). The third scenario is that North Korea embarks on *fundamental reforms* of its institutions and economic policies. Whether North Korea will adopt the reform strategy and to what extent its leadership will press the reforms is extremely difficult to predict. The North Korean leadership will not pursue this path, which undermines its power base. The military is very likely to oppose such reforms it believes to be dangerous to the national security.

Table 5.8 North Korea, Estimated and Projected Population, 1960–2020

Year	Total population (thousand)	Population by age (ratio to total pop.)			Annual population growth rate (%)
		0–14	15–64	65 +	
1960	10 789	0.428	0.536	0.036	2.8
1965	12 408	0.445	0.521	0.034	3.3
1970	14 619	0.470	0.499	0.031	2.5
1975	16 562	0.451	0.517	0.031	2.0
1980	18 260	0.405	0.561	0.034	1.7
1985	19 888	0.327	0.635	0.038	1.8
1990	21 774	0.286	0.673	0.041	1.9
1995	23 917	0.291	0.663	0.046	1.6
2000	25 979	0.296	0.654	0.050	1.3
2005	27 663	0.277	0.667	0.056	1.0
2010	29 112	0.247	0.690	0.063	0.9
2015	30 514	0.223	0.706	0.071	0.9
2020	31 969	0.215	0.702	0.083	0.9

Source: United Nations, *World Population Prospects 1950–2050* (the 1994 revision), 1994.

Although the probability that North Korea will reform itself into a complete market economy in the immediate future is not very high, we predict that at some stage the North Korean regime will embark on certain reforms toward market-oriented and opening policies regardless of the extent.[5] Considering that the current food crisis and economic difficulties are continuing to deepen and they cannot be alleviated with the present inefficiencies of the system, North Korean leadership will attempt to implement reforms they believe as necessary for its own survival. The increasing external relations that North Korea has with South Korea, the USA and the international community such as the United Nations will inevitably expose the country to the outside world, thereby helping to promote economic reforms.

5.5 POLICY REFORMS AND GROWTH PROSPECTS FOR NORTH KOREA

The results from cross-country regressions can be used to construct long-term forecasts of economic growth for individual countries.[6] We use the regression result of column 1 in Table 5.4 to predict growth rate of real income per capita for North Korea for the period from 1995 to 2020. These projections have been constructed by multiplying the assigned values for each of the explanatory variables by the estimated coefficients in the regression. The critical assumption is that North Korea will survive with the policy reforms and that its collapse or reunification with South Korea will not occur during that period.

The estimate of per capita GDP in 1995 (in terms of 1985 purchasing power parity (PPP) prices) is used for the initial income variable. Using the PPP-corrected data, Noland (1995) estimated North Korean GNP per capita for 1990 to be $2284, which was about 27.7 per cent of South Korean GNP per capita for 1990. By applying the same ratio to the South Korean GDP per capita for 1990 of $6665 (in terms of 1985 PPP price from Summers-Heston Penn World Data version 5.6), the North Korean GDP (or GNP) per capita in 1990 is estimated to be $1850 in 1985 PPP price. Then, by taking the annual growth rates of per capita GDP from 1990 to 1995, the estimated North Korean per capita GDP for 1995 is $1350 in 1985 PPP price.

The values for natural resources and geographical variables are easily constructed. We assume that in 1995 North Korea's educational stock is the same as that of South Korea in 1990. The other human resource variables are constructed from the United Nations population database projections as described in section 5.3.

For the institutions and policy variables, we assume three different reform scenarios – slow (piecemeal), moderate (gradual) and rapid (big-bang) reforms. For the projection of slow or piecemeal reform, we assume that North Korea adopts market-oriented and opening policies, however few, which will be implemented slowly for the next 25 years. This scenario is similar to the 'muddling through' scenario, in which the North Korean government makes minimum institutional changes only as a means to survive. Specifically in the projection, we have assumed that North Korea would maintain 0.1 for openness, 2 for institutional quality, and 0 per cent for government saving, as the average values for the next 25 years. With this projection, per capita income of North Korea will grow at an average of 3.6 per cent per year over the period from 1995 to 2020 and thereby reach $3270 in 2020 (Table 5.9). It is no surprise that North Korea is forecasted to grow relatively fast as it is located in favorable conditions for the future growth, with factors such as the strong convergence force from the very low initial income level and its relatively abundant human resources. However, its growth rate will not match the high rates achieved by the East Asian tigers and China – 6.6 per cent and 5.6 per cent respectively during the last three decades from 1965 to 1995 because the assumed institutions and policy conditions of North Korea are far less favorable than those of East Asia and China.

Table 5.9 North Korea Growth Prospects under Alternative Reform Scenarios, 1995–2020

	Reform scenarios		
	Slow reform[b]	Moderate reform[c]	Rapid reform[d]
Average growth rate, (1995–2020 %)	3.6 %	5.3 %	7.1 %
GDP per capita in 2020 (1985 PPP price)	3270	4930	7500
GDP per capita relative to South Korea In 2020 (%)[e]	18.7 %	28.1 %	42.9 %

Notes:

a. Per capita GDP levels and growth rates are based on 1985 international PPP (purchasing power parity) prices. North Korean per capita GDP for 1995 is estimated to be $1350, which is about 14.7 per cent of South Korean per capita GDP for 1995.

b. The slow reform projection assumes that North Korea will introduce minimal market reform and opening policies slowly. The projection is based on the cross-country regression result in column 1 of Table 5.4.

c. The moderate reform scenario assumes that North Korea adopts the policies similar to those of China in the 1970s and 1980s.

d. The rapid reform scenario assumes that North Korea adopts the policies which the fast growing East Asian four tigers maintained over the period, 1965–90.

e. The average per capita GDP growth rate for South Korea between 1995–2020 is estimated to be 2.6 per cent and the per capita GDP in 2020 is $17 480 (in 1985 price). This projection is also made based on the cross-country regression result in column 1 of Table 5.4, assuming that South Korea will keep the current economic institutions and policies.

By applying the same projection technique based on the regression result of Table 5.4, we estimate that South Korea is likely to grow at around 2.6 percent per year for the period 1995–2020. This average growth rate is substantially lower than the annual growth rate of 7.2 per cent achieved between 1965 and 1995. The decline of average growth rate is mainly due to the convergence effect from the rising per capita income level, which increased from $1040 in 1965 to $9200 in 1995 (in terms of 1985 PPP price), and the decrease in the net growth rate of the working-age population which is estimated to drop from 1.03 per cent per year over 1965–90 to −0.05 per cent per year over 1995–2020[7] Then, the projected per capita GDP for South Korea in 2020 is about $17 480. When we compare the projected level of per capita GDP of North Korea with that of South Korea, North Korean per capita GDP will be equivalent to about 18.7 per cent of South Korean per capita GDP in 2020, slightly increasing from 14.7 per cent in 1995.

The result of projection from the scenario of slow reform shows that North Korea will not achieve the high growth rate similar to that achieved by the fast growing East Asian economies between 1965 and 1995 and will still lag behind those countries in 2020. With substantial reforms of institutions and economic policies, however, North Korea will substantially catch up to South Korea and other East Asia economies.

Table 5.9 provides two other growth projections with different policy reforms. The moderate (gradual) reform scenario assumes that North Korea adopts policies such as improvement of institutional quality (5.6 in a 10 scale), increase in trade openness (0.5 in a 1 scale), and higher government saving (1 per cent in GDP) similar to those China maintained over the period 1965–90. The projection shows that in this scenario, North Korea will grow at the rate of 5.3 per cent per year, raising its real income to around 28 per cent of South Korean per capita GDP in 2020.

The rapid reform scenario assumes that North Korea adopts policies the fast growing East Asian countries maintained over the period 1965–90: 5.6 for institutional quality, 0.97 for trade openness, and 5.6 for government saving. This scenario of rapid reform is obviously very unrealistic, and thus it is only significant as a thought experiment to illustrate North Korea's maximum potential for growth. In this projection, North Korea is estimated to grow as fast as 7.2 per cent between 1995 and 2020, which will make its per capita GDP leap to about 43 per cent of South Korean per capita GDP in 2020.

5.6 CONCLUDING REMARKS

Owing to its relatively lower income level and relatively good natural and human resource conditions, North Korea has substantial potential for catching up to South Korea and other East Asian countries. Yet its current self-sufficient and closed system does not allow it to jump toward high potential growth path.

We have analyzed the effects of hypothetical policy reforms that North Korea could adopt to stimulate the economy. If North Korea embarks on market-oriented reforms and opened up its economy to foreign trade and investment, it will achieve very high growth in the next 25 years. The conditional projection shows that an even modest, gradual reform can make the North Korean economy grow at over 5 per cent per year for the next decades. At the present time, however, it is very difficult to predict when and to what extent the North Korean regime will embark on fundamental reforms toward a market-oriented and open economy. The projections provided in this paper are, therefore, obviously very hypothetical and must be considered to illustrate the upside potential of the North Korean economy which it can secure depending on the extent of the market reform and opening policies it adopts. Nevertheless, as North Korea's economic system is dysfunctional, the regime's only alternative is to adopt market economy and open trade with neighboring countries. Perhaps, the North Korean regime could well adopt a gradual approach toward economic reform following the Chinese or Vietnamese model.

The survival of North Korea and the long-term peace and prosperity of the Korean peninsula must be in the best interest of the surrounding countries and the international community. Either the sudden collapse of North Korea or a military conflict on the peninsula will cast a serious threat to regional security. In order to survive the current economic predicament, North Korea needs emergency food aid, financial and technical assistance from its neighboring countries and international institutions. Regional and international communities may need to recognize the substantial growth potential of North Korea and help its economy to survive from the present hardship so that it will embark on far-reaching reforms toward market economy and open trade. The economy's human resources have been deteriorating because of the recent natural disasters and the breakdown of the national education and health system. International assistance will help North Korea to keep its growth potential such as human resources that would produce the economic recovery and long-term growth in the future.

NOTES

1. See Hwang (1993) and Noland (1995) for detailed description of the economic system in North Korea.
2. The data are originally from Research Institute for National Unification (Seoul) and recited from the Economist Intelligence Unit (1997).
3. Sachs and Warner judge a country to be open if it satisfies minimum criteria on all four aspects of trade policy: average tariff rate must be lower than 40 per cent on average; quotas and licensing must cover less than 40 per cent of total imports; the black market premium must be less than 20 per cent; and export taxes should be moderate. See Sachs and Warner (1995a) for details.
4. See Smith (1997) and Noland (1995, 1997) for more details.
5. Noland (1997) reports an interesting result of a poll of 31 participants at the conference on Economic Integration of the Korean Peninsula, September 1997. When they were asked to

assess the likelihood of alternative scenarios for the North Korean economy for the next five years, they picked up reform as the most likely outcome.

6. It must be a strong assumption that all economies including socialist ones such as North Korea can be assessed by the reduced-form version of the extended neoclassical growth model. But, the hypothetical assumption of this growth forecasting exercise is that North Korea will be transformed into a neoclassical economy (at least partially) by adopting some policy reforms. EBRD (1995) and Sachs and Warner (1996) use the same approach to analyze the growth prospects of the transitional economies in Eastern and Central Europe. Radelet et al. (1997) apply the same methodology in order to forecast the growth rates for Asian countries for the period 1995–2020.
7. According to the estimates of the United Nations, the share of working-age population drops from 70.8 per cent in 1995 to 69.4 per cent in 2020, while the share of retirement-age population (age 65 and over) increases from 5.6 per cent to 11.5 per cent in 2020.

BIBLIOGRAPHY

Barro, Robert J. (1991), 'Economic Growth in a Cross-Section of Countries', *Quarterly Journal of Economics,* **106** (2), 407–443.

Barro, Robert J. and Jong-Wha Lee (1994), 'Sources of Economic Growth', *Carnegie-Rochester Conference Series on Public Policy*, vol. 40, June, 1–46.

Barro, Robert J. and Jong-Wha Lee (1996), 'International Measures of Schooling Years and Schooling Quality', *American Economic Review, Papers and Proceedings*, vol. 86, May, 218–23.

Barro, Robert J. and Xavier Sala-i-Martin, (1995), *Economic Growth*, NY: McGraw-Hill.

Eberstadt, Nicholas and Judith Banister (1992), *The Population of North Korea*, Berkeley, Center for Korean Studies, University of California.

Eberstadt, Nicholas (1995), *Korea Approaches Reunification*, Armonk, NY: M.E. Sharpe.

Economist Intelligence Unit (1997), *Country Report (1996–1997*).

European Bank for Reconstruction and Development (1995), *Transition Report 1995*, London.

Gallup, J.L. and J.D. Sachs (1998), 'Geography and Economic Development', mimeo, Harvard Institute for International Development.

Hwang, Eui-Gak (1993), *The Korean Economies: A Comparison of North and South*, Oxford University Press.

Kim, Sungwoo (1993), 'Recent Economic Policies of North Korea', *Asian Survey*, September, 864–78.

Knack, S. and P. Keefer (1995), 'Institutions and Economic Performance: Cross-Country Tests Using Alternative Institutional Measures', *Economics and Politics* 7(3), 207–227.

Noland, Marcus (1995), 'The North Korean Economy', Working Paper Series 95-5, Institute for International Economics, Washington, DC.

Noland, Marcus (1997), 'Why North Korea Will Muddle Through', *Foreign Affairs,* July/August, 105–118.

Noland, Marcus (ed.), (1998), *Economic Integration of the Korean Peninsula*, Institute for International Economics, Washington, DC.

Oh, Kongdan (1997), 'Inter-Korean Economic Cooperation', in David R. McCann, (ed.), *Korean Briefing*, NY: M.E. Sharpe, 25–48.

Radelet Steve, Jeffrey D. Sachs and Jong-Wha Lee (1997), 'Economic Growth in

Asia', *Development Discussion Paper* no. 609, HIID, November.

Sachs, Jeffrey D. and Andrew D. Warner (1995a), 'Economic Reform and the Process of Global Integration', *Brookings Papers on Economic Activity* 1 (August), 1–118.

Sachs, Jeffrey D. and Andrew D. Warner (1995b), 'Natural Resource Abundance and Economic Growth', *Development Discussion Paper* no. 517a, HIID.

Sachs, Jeffrey D. and Andrew D. Warner (1996), 'Achieving Rapid Growth in the Transitional Economies of Central Europe', *Development Discussion Paper* no. 544, HIID, July.

Smith, Heather (1997), 'North Korea: How Much Reform and Whose Characteristics?', Brookings Institution.

Summers, Robert and Alan Heston (1991), 'The Penn World Table (Mark 5): An Expanded Set of International Comparisons, 1950–88', *Quarterly Journal of Economics*, **196** (2), May, 327–68.

United Nations (1994), *World Population Prospects 1950–2050 (the 1994 revision)*.

World Bank (1997), *World Development Report*.

PART FOUR

The Experience of Other Transition Economies

6. Reform without Losers: a Pareto-improving Transition from a Centrally Planned to a Market Economy

Lawrence J. Lau

6.1 INTRODUCTION

Is it possible to carry out economic reform without creating losers? The 'dual-track' approach adopted by the People's Republic of China in its transition from a centrally planned to a market economy since 1979 is analyzed as a mechanism for implementing Pareto-improving economic reform, that is, reform that enhances economic efficiency but without creating losers. The approach, based on the parallel operation of both the existing planned sector and the emerging market sector, and thus continued enforcement of the existing central plan while simultaneously liberalizing the market, can be understood as a method for affording protection of the vested interests while providing autonomy and incentive for new activities. In order for this approach to succeed, the planned sector must be insulated from the effects of the operations of the emerging market sector. The 'dual-track' approach may also be viewed as a method for making implicit lump sum transfers to compensate potential losers of the reform.

The Problem of Compensating the Losers

When an economy starts from a state of inefficiency, any efficiency-enhancing economic reform will result in a net gain in real output in the aggregate. Thus, in principle, it should be possible to make everyone better off, or at least make nobody worse off, as a result of the reform, by suitably taxing or otherwise redistributing from the winners to compensate the losers.

If this can in fact be done, then 'reform without losers' is achieved. 'Reform without losers' or 'gain without pain' is the dream of all economic reformers (and politicians) because it minimizes political opposition to and maximizes political support for reforms ex ante as well as maximizes political opposition to reversal of reforms ex post (because of the new vested interests created).

In practice, potential losers are seldom compensated, and even if they are, they are seldom fully compensated, for several reasons. First, there is imperfect information – it is difficult to identify the potential winners and losers as well as to ascertain the magnitudes of their individual potential gains and losses. Second, it is difficult to devise implementable general taxation and subsidy schemes that target the potential winners and losers specifically, that is, to tax only the winners and to compensate only the losers. Third, the only way to tax the winners and compensate the losers without introducing distortions in the economy is to use a system of fixed lump sum taxes and subsidies, that is, taxes and subsidies whose values do not depend on and hence do not affect the actions of the economic agents. Unfortunately, explicit lump sum taxes and subsidies require such detailed information on the individual economic agents that they are virtually impossible and most general taxation schemes, based on either earnings, income, consumption or retail purchases, are distortionary, that is, they will affect the actions of the economic agents and thereby prevent full economic efficiency from being achieved. Fourth, there are costs of information and implementation, that is, in order to effect transfers from winners to losers, a system of taxation and subsidies with its necessary institutions, for example the Internal Revenue Service, may have to be devised and implemented. That is why in many reforming economies, there is frequently no attempt to compensate the losers, and state promises of compensation, when made, generally lack credibility because of the perceived difficulty of implementation. The type of economic reforms implemented in the former Soviet Union and Eastern Europe, sometimes described as 'Big-Bang' reforms, generally suffer from this inability to compensate the potential losers. Potential losers are therefore likely to oppose the economic reform, often causing the reform to fail before it is even begun, or at least drastically reducing its chance of success.

Unlike economic reforms elsewhere, Chinese economic reforms have not aroused significant political opposition and enjoyed widespread popular support. This is because the Chinese economic reforms have implicitly adhered to the principle that no one should be made worse off as a result. Thus, there are no losers from the economic reforms, only winners, even though the distribution of the gains from the economic reforms may be highly uneven.

The Broad and Narrow Definition of the 'Dual-track' Approach

There are two possible definitions of the 'dual-track' approach. The first, or narrow, definition of the 'dual-track' approach is with reference to the prices for transactions in goods and factors. Under this definition, there are two prices for every good and factor, a planned price and a market price. The transactions specified in the central plan are executed at the planned prices, fixed by the central plan; and transactions in the market are executed at the market prices determined by the market supply and demand. Thus, the plan and the market operate in parallel. The second, or broad, definition of the 'dual-track' approach includes the phenomena described under the narrow definition, and more generally, the creation of new economic activities that do not impact, directly or indirectly, the planned sector. Thus, the establishment of an export-processing zone that does not trade with the domestic economy except for the employment of its surplus labor is an example of this broad definition of the 'dual-track' approach.

China's 'dual-track' approach to the transition from a centrally planned to a market economy combines both the plan and the market by preserving the rights and obligations of all economic agents under the pre-existing plan but allowing autonomy and incentive outside the plan. It may be understood as a method for implementing implicit lump sum transfers to compensate potential losers of the economic reforms. Since there are only winners and no losers, political opposition to economic reforms is minimized ex ante and political opposition to the reversal of economic reforms is maximized ex post.

But can a 'dual-track' approach to economic reforms bring about an efficient economy? The answer is a qualified yes, at least for the 'dual-track' approach of the narrow kind.[1] It can be shown that, by using a 'dual-track' approach, market liberalization reforms in addition to being Pareto-improving, that is, having no losers, also simultaneously enable the economy to be fully efficient, in the sense that all resources have been put to their fullest and best use. Thus, not only can economic reforms achieve 'gain without pain', but also actually maximal 'gain without pain'.

The success of the 'dual-track' approach in simultaneously achieving Pareto-improvement and full efficiency requires: (1) the feasibility of the original plan; (2) the granting of autonomy and incentive to economic agents for their participation in the market on the margin; (3) the allowance of resales of plan-allocated inputs, purchases of outputs for redelivery and subcontracting (which is described as full market liberalization); and (4) the continued credible enforcement of the rights and obligations under the plan by the state. In the longer run, the phasing-out of the plan track depends on economic growth, which in turn depends on efficient and rapid capital accumulation, which in turn depends on a high saving rate to supply the new resources. China is fortunate in having a saving rate that approaches 40 per cent, which makes it possible to maintain the distribution of rents of the status quo ante and still have sufficient new resources left to support the growth. With a ready supply of new resources, the redeployment of old resources, for example, reform of the state-owned enterprises (SOEs), is neither as important nor urgent.

Empirical evidence is provided on how the 'dual-track' approach has worked in practice. By the late 1980s, the market track has become the dominant track in the economy. In the 1990s, the plan track is gradually phased out, with compensation, once again making sure that there are no losers. The Chinese economic reform experience demonstrates that, under certain conditions, a 'dual-track' approach to economic reforms can simultaneously achieve 'equity' and full efficiency without the use of new information or new institutions.

6.2 THE CHINESE ECONOMIC REFORMS (1979 – THE PRESENT)

Over the past two decades, East Asia has been the fastest growing region in the world, and China has been the fastest growing country in East Asia, with an average annual rate of growth of approximately 10 per cent since its economic reforms began in 1979. Between 1979 and 1997, Chinese real GDP has quintupled from US$150 billion to US$815 billion (all in 1990 prices).[2] During the same period, real GDP per capita has increased more than fourfold, from US$150 to US$650 (again, all in 1990 prices). China is one of the very few socialist countries that have made a successful transition from a centrally planned economy to a market economy.

Why has China been successful in its economic reforms while others, such as the former Soviet Union, appeared to have failed? Two principal reasons may be identified. First, China has implemented economic reforms in such a way that there are no losers. In other words, no Chinese citizen is made worse off as a result of the Chinese economic reforms. Second, through its high saving rate – approaching 40 per cent in some years – China has had an abundant supply of new resources, most of which it has invested efficiently. The resulting rapid economic growth also makes it much easier to assure that there are no losers.[3] The abundance of new resources also makes it far less urgent a matter to try to redeploy the old assets efficiently, which requires the painful reform and restructuring of the state-owned enterprises. Our estimates show that almost 80 per cent of the fixed capital stock in 1996 is due to gross fixed investments made since 1979. A 'reform without losers' strategy might not have been possible if the saving rates were not as high as they were.

The four essential elements of Chinese economic reforms since 1979 may be identified. They are: (1) the 'open door' – meaning opening the Chinese economy to international trade and foreign investment; (2) marketization – the introduction of markets in goods, factors and foreign exchange to initially supplement and eventually supplant the plan; (3) the devolution of decision-making power on the basis of the 'contract responsibility system' – the de-communization of agriculture, empowering provincial and local governments, professionalization of the management of enterprises, and the granting of autonomy and incentives to enterprises on the margin; (4) the creation of new, non-state-owned modes of organization for production. This includes, in agriculture, the return to a system of individual cultivators with fixed rents and taxes in 1979 and in industry, the emergence of 'township and village' enterprises (TVEs), (foreign) joint venture, wholly foreign and private enterprises since 1984. Some state-owned enterprises and/or their subsidiaries have become publicly traded joint stock companies since 1990, with many private citizens becoming shareholders and hence partial owners. The trend of corporatization of state-owned enterprises (SOEs) is poised to accelerate this year.

The results of the Chinese economic reforms must be characterized overall as very successful, with two exceptions. First, the average annual rate of inflation over the post-reform period is approximately 7 per cent, much higher than the pre-reform average of less than half a per cent per annum Second, the 'contract responsibility' system, so successful in agriculture, failed by and large to elicit the improvement in efficiency in the state-owned enterprises in the industrial sector. We discuss each element of the economic reforms in turn.

The Open Door

The open door policy has been extremely successful. Chinese international trade has increased by leaps and bounds. With the inclusion of Hong Kong, the People's Republic of China is now the world's fourth largest trading nation. It is also by far the largest recipient of foreign direct investment among developing countries.[4] The official foreign reserves of China now exceeds US$100 billion, far more than is necessary to support the requirements of itscurrent account transactions.

Marketization

Marketization has also been extremely successful. The prices of all consumer goods and more than 95 per cent of the producer goods are determined in the market. The price of low-grade grain is controlled (subsidized), only for social welfare purposes. The price of energy is at world market levels. The dual exchange rates were unified in January 1994. Current account convertibility was achieved in December 1996. The labor markets have also been liberalized. The state no longer has the responsibility of placing college and university graduates. In return, college and university graduates can work wherever they wish. Stock and bond markets were also established in the 1990s.

The Devolution of Economic Decision Power

A great deal of power has been devolved to the provincial and local government levels. For example, foreign direct investment projects of below US$30 million can be directly approved by the provincial authorities. The managers of enterprises have more autonomy and power than before.

The Growth of the Non-state Sector

The state-owned sector has continuously shrunk relative to the aggregate economy: it currently accounts for no more than 30 per cent of the aggregate output. The proportion of aggregate economy-wide gross fixed investments accounted for by state-owned enterprises was 72 per cent in 1979. It stood at just over 50 per cent in 1996. Because of the de-communization of the agricultural sector, the state-owned sector accounts for only a very insignificant proportion of aggregate agricultural output. In industry, the state-owned sector's share of gross value of production fell from almost 80 per cent in 1979 to just above 30 per cent in 1995 (see Figure 6.1). This decline was caused primarily because of the considerably faster growth of the non-state sector. In Figure 6.2, we present the annual growth rates of the aggregate industrial output as well as the state-owned and non-state-owned components. It is immediately evident that the growth of the non-state sector far outstripped the growth of the state sector.

The growth of industrial output of the non-state sector has been largely propelled by the growth of the output of the township and village enterprises (TVEs). As of 1994, TVEs accounted for almost half of the aggregate industrial output and almost two-thirds of the aggregate industrial employment of China.

The distribution of retail sales by ownership shows a similar picture (Figure 6.3). Here the rapid rise in prominence of the private sector in retail sales is clearly evident. From almost nothing in 1979, the private sector is now the largest sector in terms of retail sales.

These trends in the transformation of ownership are not confined to the coastal or the more prosperous provinces. They are indeed nationwide. Even in Guizhou, the poorest province in China in terms of gross provincial product per capita, the distribution of retail sales by ownership is broadly similar to the national pattern (see Figure 6.4).

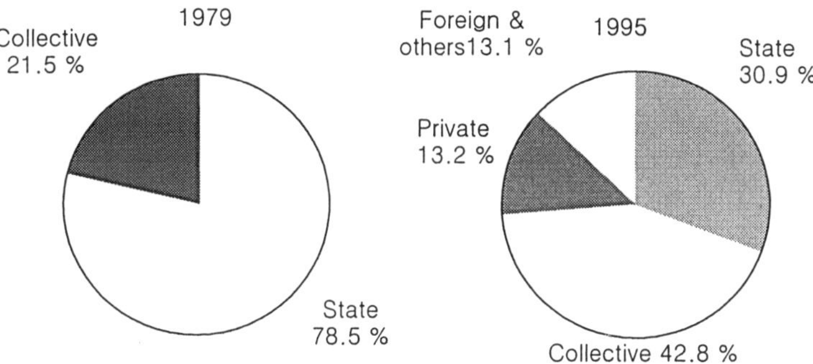

Figure 6.1 The Distribution of Value of Industrial Production by Ownership (China)

Figure 6.2 The Growth of Industrial Output by Sector of Ownership (China)

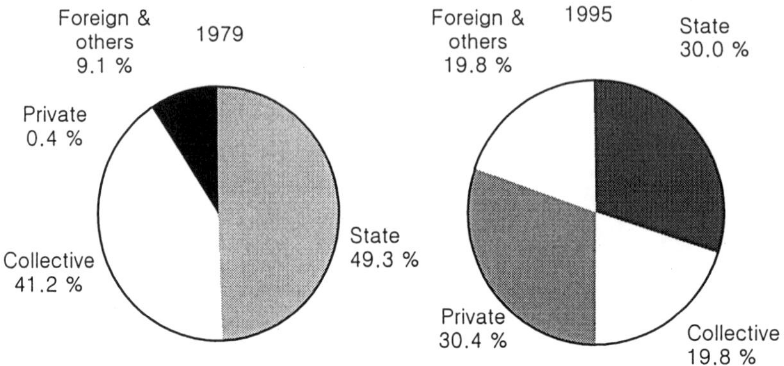

Figure 6.3 The Distribution of Retail Sales by Ownership (China)

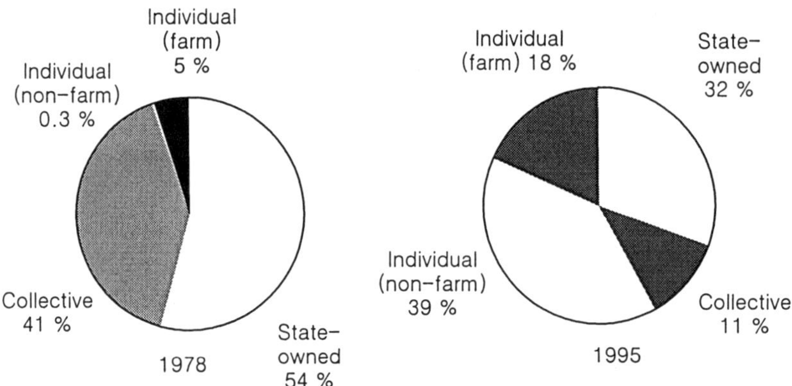

Figure 6.4 The Distribution of Retail Sales by Ownership (Guizhou Province)

In Table 6.1, we present selected indicators of the economic performance of China before and after the commencement of economic reforms in 1979. Table 6.1 shows that in every dimension except one – the rate of inflation – the economic performance post-reform has far much superior to that pre-reform. Of particular interest is the rate of growth of real personal consumption per capita – it went from 2 per cent per annum to over 7 per cent per annum – indicating a genuine and significant improvement in the standard of living. That is one of the fundamental reasons why a reversal of the economic reforms is most unlikely – everyone in China benefited significantly from the economic reforms.

6.3 ECONOMIC REFORM WITHOUT LOSERS

The principle of Chinese economic reform is that no one loses as a result. This implies the 'grandfathering' of the status quo ante, protection of 'vested interests' and 'discriminating' between the old and the new. For this reason, the availability of new resources and its efficient utilization takes on additional importance, because they determine the speed with which the transition from a centrally planned economy to a market economy can occur under a policy of economic reforms without losers. We have already seen that new enterprises and new activities have been primarily responsible for the phenomenal economic growth of China since 1979. The new resources come mostly from the high saving rates of between 35 per cent and 40 per cent. There has been little or no privatization of existing enterprises as well as little or no successful restructuring of existing enterprises until recently.

Table 6.1 Comparisons of the Average Annual Rates of Growth of Selected Economic Indicators

	1954–79 Pre-reform	1979–95 Reform
Real GDP	5.9	10.0
Real GDP/capita	3.8	8.5
Real gross value of		
Agricultural production	2.9	6.1
Light industry	8.7	16.5
Heavy industry	12.8	14.4
Real personal consumption	4.0	8.6
Real consumption/capita	2.0	7.1
Real gross fixed investment	7.7	11.9
Capital stock	5.3	9.1
Employment	2.5	2.6
GDP deflator	0.4	7.4
Retail price index	0.7	8.1
Exports (in current US$)	10.5	15.2
Imports (in current US$)	9.9	13.7

Economic Reforms without Losers: China's 'Dual-track' Approach

A dual-track strategy may be defined as follows: (1) in one track, the 'plan-track', the existing (often inefficient) central economic plan, and the distribution of rents under it, are left intact; and (2) in the other track, the 'market track', liberalization is carried out at the margin, that is, economic agents have both the right and the incentive to participate in the free market provided that the obligations under the original plan are fulfilled. In particular, market resales of plan-allocated inputs and consumption goods, and market purchases of outputs for re-delivery are allowed.

The 'dual-track' approach combines the pre-existing plan and at the same time introduces the market; it grandfathers the 'vested interests' through the enforcement of the rights and obligations under the pre-existing plan; it uses the 'contract responsibility' system to stimulate participation in the market on the margin; it creates new, reform-oriented 'vested interests'; it is easy to implement because it relies solely on existing information and institutions, including enforcement. There is no doubt that because it is Pareto-improving, it must be efficiency-enhancing. The question is: can the dual-track approach achieve full efficiency for the economy?

An Economist's Definition of Efficiency

An economy is said to be 'efficient' if and only if no one output can be increased without decreasing another output. In other words, all resources in the economy have been put to their fullest and best use.

Comparison of the Big-bang Strategy and the Dual-track Strategy to Market Liberalization

Under the big-bang strategy of market liberalization, the central plan is completely abolished. All markets are instantaneously open. Producers are completely free to plan their production. Consumers are completely free to plan their consumption. The quantities and prices of all goods are determined through the equilibration between supply and demand in the market. Under the dual-track strategy, the central plan remains (and is frozen except for new increments of state-financed production capacity) but the rights and obligations under the central plan continue to be enforced. All markets are instantaneously open. Producers are completely free to plan their production and sales provided output delivery obligations under the plan are fulfilled. Consumers are completely free to plan their consumption, given allocated consumption goods. Aggregate quantities and market prices of all goods are determined through the equilibration between supply and demand in the market with planned prices remaining fixed.

Making Economic Reforms Painless

The distinction between the big-bang and dual-track strategies lies in the role played by the pre-existing central plan. The sale and purchase obligations of the economic agents remain even after the economic reforms, but they are fixed at the pre-existing levels. In addition, all planned transactions take place at the pre-existing, fixed plan prices. Thus, planned profits and losses (taxes and subsidies) of economic agents remain precisely the same. If economic agents do not do anything outside the plan, they are precisely just as well off as before. If they choose to do anything outside the plan, after fulfilling their obligations under the plan, they must, by definition, expect that they will be better off. Moreover, since the economic agents are free to resell their plan-allocated goods and to purchase from the market goods for re-delivery under the plan, they face, at the margin, the market prices. Any differences between planned and market prices therefore represent implicit feasible lump sum transfers. The values of these transfers depend on the market prices and are thus not fixed. However, they cannot be affected by the actions of the individual economic agents and hence their existence also does not affect the actions of the economic agents. Planned consumer goods deliveries to the government enable the maintenance of the pre-reform standard of living as a floor (for example in the urban areas).

Feasibility of the Pre-existing Plan

It is reasonable to assume that the pre-existing central plan is feasible, that is, it can in fact be carried out. Otherwise, it may not be possible for all the obligations specified in the pre-existing central plan to be fulfilled and the central plan itself will fail to be a credible arrangement for the lump sum transfers discussed above. Feasibility of the central plan implies the following conditions: (1) the production plan for each producer is feasible; (2) the consumption plan for each consumer is feasible; (3) material balance holds in the aggregate; and (4) the consumption plan for each consumer is affordable at the plan prices.

The Openness of All Markets

Both the big-bang and the dual-track strategies require that all markets are open for economic efficiency. In particular, market resales of plan-allocated inputs and consumption goods, market purchases of outputs for re-delivery under the plan, as well as subcontracting, are allowed. Under the dual-track approach, there are two prices for each good, q, the plan price and p, the market price.

The Role of State Power

Under the dual-track approach, the state is required, even after market liberalization, to enforce the rights and obligations under the pre-existing central plan (as well as any new contracts entered into through the market).[5] However, as soon as economic agents are allowed to participate in the market, the enforcement of the plan by necessity must shift to the enforcement of specific sales to and purchases from other economic agents as mandated in the pre-existing plan. Simple enforcement of the planned aggregate production no longer suffices because an enterprise, for example, can fulfill its planned aggregate production target and yet at the same time fail to make any planned deliveries to other enterprises at the plan prices. Thus, even if the planned aggregate production target is fulfilled, the plan itself may not be fulfilled because the mandated sales and purchases are not made. But if enforcement is shifted to plan-mandated purchases and sales, it is most likely that enforcement actions are taken in response to complaints by other economic agents whose rights have not been honored by specific enterprises. The potential recipients of the planned output deliveries must complain before the state planning commission will begin enforcement actions. The enforcement is not on total production, but on the actual delivery of goods as provided for in the plan. This also makes it likely that absent specific complaints, no enforcement actions are likely to be taken.

Whether the 'dual-track approach' works depends on the credibility of state enforcement, and expectations thereof. If the state is not credible, then the economic agents will have no incentive to fulfil their obligations under the pre-existing plan. And if anyone thinks that the plan-mandated deliveries at planned prices are not going to be received by him or her, he or she will not make the plan-mandated sales at the fixed plan prices either. Thus, if the overall belief or expectation is that there will not be effective enforcement, no one will comply, and the 'dual-track' approach reduces to the 'big-bang' approach. Perceived credibility therefore affect enterprise (and household) behaviour, and hence compliance with the pre-existing plan (post-reform). If economic agents do not comply with the pre-existing plan, it is no longer possible to assure that there are no losers.

In general, multiple equilibria (outcomes) are possible under a dual-track approach, depending on expectations of the credibility of state enforcement. If everyone thinks that the state will be able to enforce effectively, everyone will comply, then 'gain without pain' can be achieved. If everyone does not expect that there will be credible state enforcement, the 'dual-track' approach will degenerate into the 'big-bang' approach. Thus, in technical terms, there are multiple 'rational expectations' (or self-fulfilling) equilibria (a typical example is a bank run).

We have already shown that a dual-track approach assures that there are no losers. In other words, there is Pareto improvement. In addition, under the above assumptions, a dual-track competitive equilibrium is efficient, that is, all resources are put to their fullest and best use. We note that the assumption on allowing resales and purchases for redelivery is essential. Otherwise, the resulting outcome is not necessarily efficient.

Is Chinese Economic Reform Gradualist?

The 'dual-track' approach of Chinese economic reform is not gradualist because efficiency is instantaneously achieved as if under a 'big-bang' reform. Efficiency is achieved because both the prices and quantities of goods allocated within the plan are fixed, and on the margin all economic agents face the market prices. Chinese economic reform appears gradualist because the population is protected from shock (pain). However, the pre-existing central plan is 'phased out' gradually.

6.4 EXAMPLES FROM THE CHINESE EXPERIENCE

We provide below eight examples of economic reforms implemented in China that utilize the dual-track approach of the narrow kind. Although different in each case, the economic reforms all share the common features described above. The examples are: (1) the agricultural reform (the introduction of the 'contract responsibility system' in agriculture); (2) the industrial reform; (3) the 'dual-track' price system in urban consumer goods and services; (4) the foreign exchange reform; (5) growth of economic activities outside the 'plan'; (6) the tax reforms; (7) the rate of interest on household bank deposits, and (8) the furloughing of the surplus labor of state-owned enterprises.

The Agricultural Reform

The agricultural reform undertaken in China in 1979 may be regarded as the first successful application of the dual-track approach. Under this reform, the contract responsibility system was introduced in agriculture. The commune is assigned the responsibility to (1) sell a fixed quantity of grain (or other) output to the state procurement agency as previously mandated under the plan at predetermined (plan) prices and (2) to pay a fixed amount of taxes to the state as well as the right to (3) receive a fixed quantity of inputs, principally chemical fertilizers, from state-owned suppliers, again at predetermined (plan) prices. Subject to fulfilling these conditions, the commune is free to do whatever it wishes, for example, it can produce whatever it considers more profitable, and sell any excess output on the free market, and retain any profit. In fact, under this system, the commune as well as its members is permitted to purchase grain or other output in the market to fulfill the delivery quota (an example of a 'wash sale') – it is not required to actually produce the grain or other output itself.

In the implementation of the contract responsibility system, both the mandatory delivery quota and the taxes for the commune are fixed at their original planned levels. The commune in turn reassigns the collective responsibilities (and rights) to the individual farm households, allocating to them their shares of the commune's land and capital (and chemical fertilizers), and making them individually and directly responsible for the fulfillment of their shares of the delivery quota and taxes.

Thus, there is both a plan track and a free market track, each with different prices; however, the quantities of outputs and inputs under the plan track are fixed. It is therefore clear that under this system, only the market prices, and not the plan prices, are relevant for the allocation of resources. Note that both the commune (and its individual members) and the state cannot be worse off than before under this new arrangement. Moreover, as long as the state is not worse off in terms of the quantities of grain and other outputs and taxes delivered to the state, it will continue to be able to supply the urban consumers with food grains and industries with agricultural raw materials (such as cotton) at plan prices, with the consequence that even the urban consumers and industrial enterprises are no worse off as a result of the agricultural reform. Thus, the impact of the liberalization at the margin must be Pareto-improving for all parties.

Since the agricultural reform is only partial, one cannot assert that the full efficiency of the entire economy is attained. However, since the agricultural reform is Pareto-improving for all parties, overall efficiency of the economy is unambiguously enhanced by the agricultural reform.

The dual-track price system has some historical antecedent. Even prior to the introduction of the contract responsibility system, there were two prices for grain – the plan price paid for mandated grain deliveries to the state and the negotiated (market) price for above-quota transactions.

The Industrial Reform

There have been many studies on the Chinese industrial reform and its associated dual-track price system, which was introduced in 1984 (see, for example, Byrd, 1987; Wu and Zhao, 1987; Naughton, 1995). The industrial reform represents, in part, an attempt to extend the contract responsibility system to the industrial sector, based on the successful experience of the agricultural reform. Under the reform, the mandatory delivery quotas as well as the quantities of plan-allocated inputs for each enterprise were frozen at their then existing levels, and the enterprises are free to produce whatever they deem profitable and sell their output on the free market and retain any profit as long as they fulfill their delivery quota. At the same time, parallel-free markets for the above-quota outputs of enterprises were introduced, while the within-quota outputs continued to be sold at the generally lower, plan prices to authorized purchasers. This example highlights the crucial elements in a dual-track approach. First, the market track must provide for full liberalization (that is, no intervention of any kind), albeit only at the margin (but as we know, liberalization at the margin is sufficient for efficiency); second, the enterprises must be allowed to reap the full marginal reward;[6] and third, input and output quotas on the plan track must be enforced as outputs of some enterprises are needed as inputs of other enterprises. The ability of enterprises to meet their planned output quota may depend crucially on their timely receipt of the planned input delivery quotas.

The Dual-track Price System in Urban Consumer Goods and Services

Prior to the economic reforms of 1979, many essential consumer goods and services, such as grain, cooking oil, meat, electricity, housing, and monthly pass for mass transit, are rationed in the urban areas at lower than what would have been free market prices. With the introduction of the free markets and the dual-track price system, urban residents continued to be able to purchase grain, meat, electricity (lifeline rates), and housing (for those who had it) at the same pre-reform prices within the limits of the pre-reform rationed quantities, at the same time that they were able to purchase freely any quantity of any good at free market prices. They were thus no worse off than before. The state was also no worse off because the quantities of goods that it would be obligated to supply at the plan prices remained the same.

The Foreign Exchange Reform

Dual markets were permitted to exist for foreign exchange in China from the mid-1980s to the end of 1993. Between 1985 and 1994, there was an official exchange rate, available only for certain limited approved transactions, as well as an officially sanctioned swap rate, that was determined in Foreign Exchange Adjustment Centers (more commonly referred to as 'swap markets') in major cities around the country, among exporters and importers qualified to trade in those markets. The supply of foreign exchange in the swap markets was provided by the exporters through the foreign exchange they were allowed to retain from net increases in their export earnings relative to the base period.[7] The government did not control the transactions in the swap market, and the swap market exchange rate was mostly determined by supply and demand (see Khor 1994 for a detailed description). The swap rate was, not surprisingly, significantly higher than the official rate during this period.

At the same time, foreign visitors to China were required to use 'foreign exchange certificates' (FECs), which were available at the official exchange rate, rather than the 'renminbi' the Chinese domestic currency, for their transactions.

The dual exchange rate system functioned until January 1, 1994, when the two exchange rates – the official rate and the swap rate – were merged into a single rate, with its level determined in a market consisting of exporters and importers, and the foreign exchange certificates were finally withdrawn from circulation. Under the new system, domestic exporters are required to sell all of their foreign exchange to the interbank market (thus, rights of retentions were abolished); in return, they are allowed to purchase foreign exchange as needed for legitimate business purposes.

At the time of this reform, the share of centrally allocated foreign exchange already fell to only 20 per cent of the total. In this last step of the foreign exchange reform, central allocation of foreign exchange was completely abolished, but for those organizations which used to receive cheap foreign exchange, annual lump sum subsidies in the domestic currency sufficient to enable the purchase of the pre-reform allocation of foreign exchange were offered for five years to assure a smooth transition (in other words, the state tried to maintain the same level of hithertofore implicit subsidies received by these organizations).

The exchange rate reform turned out to be a complete success: the exchange rate has remained stable and even appreciated slightly from 8.7 yuan per US dollar to 8.3 yuan per US dollar today. Since July 1 of this year, foreign and joint-venture enterprises, which hithertofore must use technically separate foreign exchange swap markets, have been permitted to use the same foreign exchange markets maintained by the banks for the domestic enterprises. The best way to characterize the current exchange rate system is that it is 'current-accounts convertible', but not 'capital-accounts convertible'.

Growth of Economic Activities outside the 'Plan'

A distinctive feature of Chinese economic reform is the growth of economic activities outside the state plan even before state-owned enterprises have begun to be privatized or shut down. These new economic activities are entirely market-oriented and are driven by new investments outside of the state plan (Qian and Xu, 1993; Naughton, 1995).[8] Two cases may be distinguished here. The first case is the entry and expansion of new unregulated enterprises, known collectively as 'non-state enterprises' in China, such as township and village enterprises, foreign-owned enterprises, joint-venture enterprises, and private enterprises, which face 'hard budget constraints.' The second is the parallel development of new unregulated and market-oriented activities of state-owned enterprises, commonly described as 'one-factory-two-system'. For example, state-owned enterprises may set up subsidiaries as collective enterprises, universities may establish high-tech firms, and military hospitals may use slack resources to provide medical services to the public to augment their revenues.

The first case has worked extremely well. A crucial condition for the second case to work is that the regulated activities of the state-owned enterprises must be left to function at its previous level without disruption.[9] Under this condition, new activities can only increase welfare. Sufficient enforcement power of government is an essential condition here to prevent disruptive diversion of resources from the regulated to the unregulated activities of the state sector.

The Tax Reforms

We first discuss the fiscal contracting system introduced in the 1980s (see Bahl and Wallich, 1992 for details). The experiment of the fiscal contracting system between the central and provincial governments started in 1980 and the system eventually covered all provinces by the mid-1980s. Under the fiscal contracting system, the province/municipality assumed the responsibility of collecting the taxes for the central government and committed to deliver to the central government a fixed amount of revenue per year and was allowed to retain any excess (thus, this is similar to a tax-farming system). Since the committed amount to be delivered to the central government would be based on the historical experience, neither the central government, nor the provinces/municipalities, would be worse off under this arrangement.

Of course, it is possible that the provinces/municipalities may fail, or claim to fail, to collect even the fixed amount due the central government. In practice, this applied mostly to the poorer provinces – 19 out of the 35 provinces/municipalities were able to retain 100 per cent of the revenues they collected at the margin.

The 1994 tax reform introduced a nationwide value added tax, abolished the fiscal contracting system and replaced it by a fiscal federalism providing for revenue-sharing as well as a separation of the national and local tax bases. Again, the reform ensured that all provinces were not made worse off. The provincial governments were guaranteed revenue no less than that of their

1993 actual expenditures for the three years between 1994 and 1996. As might be expected, the provinces/municipalities had a major spending spree in the last quarter of 1993, which also attested to their confidence that the central government would in fact be able to carry out their part of the commitment.

The Rate of Interest on Household Bank Deposits

The dual-track approach also applies to the setting of the rate of interest for household bank deposits. During the two high-inflation periods (1988–89 and 1993–95), the Chinese government promptly indexed the household bank savings deposit rates for new long-term time deposits to the consumer price index in order to protect depositors from inflation (Qian, 1994). Indexation of rate of interest on the savings deposit to the rate of inflation is part of the strategy of 'grandfathering' or 'not making people worse off'. This is in contrast to the rates for short-term deposits, which remained negative in real terms until very recently. Indexation of savings deposits was, however, once again abolished as of April 1, 1996, on the grounds that inflationary fears had abated.

A de facto dual-track credit market already exists in China although it is not officially sanctioned. The market rate of interest for loans has remained significantly above the official bank lending rate. The practice of 're-lending' by state-owned enterprises with preferential access to credit is widespread.[10] As China moves to develope its money and capital markets, it is inevitable that a dual-track price system for money will eventually develop as a transitional device. Already, an interbank call money market has been introduced in January 1996. There is a reasonably active secondary market for government bonds. More recently, an auction of ten-year government bonds in the style of the US Treasury Bond auction was successfully carried out in China. All of these developments suggest that in the not too distant future, on the margin, the rate of interest will be set in the market.

The Furloughing of the Surplus Labor of State-owned Enterprises

More recently, workers of state-owned enterprises have been furloughed at a percentage of their pre-existing wages and have been allowed to keep their enterprise-allocated housing. They are given the autonomy to seek alternative employment or to become self-employed. This has worked out quite well in Shanghai, where almost 900 000 of the 1 million workers furloughed have found alternative, gainful employment, possibly at lower marginal wages. The workers, who have been overpaid relative to the market, are no worse than before, taking into account the subsidies received. The enterprises and the state are also better off. In fact, efficiency in the labor market can actually be attained with this type of partial subsidies.

We give one example of Chinese economic reform that does not fit into the narrow definition of the 'dual-track' approach but does fit into the broad definition. And that is the establishment of special economic zones and foreign direct investment. This is not unlike the entry of new enterprises but takes place at the level of a country. The institution of special economic zones was chosen early as a reform measure in part to minimize its impact on and interaction with the rest of the economic system, which still operated under the state plan. Initially, special economic zones allowed only firms engaged in 'material reprocessing', that imported all of their inputs, except labor, and export all of their outputs – thus creating no disruption to the domestic aggregate supply and demand, labor being in surplus. The same rule applied to foreign and joint-venture firms operating in China but outside the special economic zones. The principal purpose of this approach is minimizing the impact of the new economic activities on the old-style domestic state-owned enterprises. Thus, once again, there were two tracks and the reform was Pareto-improving.

The initial success of the special economic zones and foreign direct investment was made possible through (1) the existence of overseas Chinese entrepreneurs willing to invest in China despite the uncertain economic, legal, political and social environment; and (2) the existence of slack and cheap labor in China. After a few years of experimentation, enterprises in the special economic zones as well as foreign and joint-venture enterprises were allowed to buy and sell on the domestic market at market prices.

6.5 MARKETIZATION UNDER THE DUAL-TRACK APPROACH

Under the dual-track approach, the central plan and the market coexisted at the commencement of economic reform. However, since the central plan has been essentially frozen at the original levels,[11] the output produced outside the plan has grown rapidly and the proportion of output that are sold and purchased at plan prices have declined continuously. In Tables 6.2, 6.3 and 6.4, we present the values of the transactions in each of the sectors of agriculture, industry and retail, which are conducted at plan, guide and market prices respectively. It is clear that by the early 1990s, most of the transactions are conducted at market prices. The plan has been phased out for many goods. These tables demonstrate the effectiveness of the dual-track approach as a strategy of transition from a centrally planned economy to a market economy. They also confirm the unmistakable importance of demand expansion due to the rapid economic growth, which takes place outside of the plan. The growth of the market (non-planned) portion of the output is largely due to the rise of new, non-state-owned enterprises established since 1984 whose sales and purchases are not included in the plan even though a part of it may also be attributed to the participation of the state-owned enterprises in the market.

Table 6.2 Phasing Out the Plan-track: Agricultural Products (Percentage of Output Value)

	1978	1985	1986	1987	1988	1989	1990	1991	1992	1993
Plan price	94.4	37.0	35.0	29.4	24.0	35.5	31.0	22.2	12.5	10.4
Guide price	0.0	23.0	21.0	16.8	19.0	24.3	27.0	20.0	5.7	2.1
Market price	5.6	40.0	43.7	53.8	57.0	40.4	42.0	57.8	81.8	87.5

Table 6.3 Phasing Out the Plan-track: Industrial Goods (Percentage of Output Value)

	1978	1985	1986	1987	1988	1989	1990	1991	1992	1993
Plan Price	100.0	64.0	–	–	–	60.0	44.6	36.0	18.7	13.8
Guide Price	0.0	23.0	–	–	–	–	19.0	18.3	7.5	5.1
Market price	0.0	13.0	–	–	–	40.0	36.4	45.7	73.8	81.1

Table 6.4 Phasing Out the Plan-track: Total Retail Sales (Percentage of Sales)

	1978	1985	1986	1987	1988	1989	1990	1991	1992	1993
Plan price	97.0	47.0	35.0	33.7	28.9	31.3	30.0	20.9	5.9	4.8
Guide price	0.0	19.0	25.0	28.0	21.8	23.2	25.0	10.3	1.1	1.4
Market price	3.0	34.0	40.0	38.3	49.3	45,5	45.0	68.8	93.0	93.8

6.6 CONCLUDING REMARKS

The Chinese experience shows that by using a broadly defined 'dual-track' approach to economic reforms, one can achieve gain without pain. Economic reforms without losers are possible. Equity does not necessarily have to be sacrificed in order to achieve efficiency. The market can be introduced without the dislocations. The necessary conditions for the success of the dual-track approach to the transition from a centrally planned economy to a market economy are: (1) feasibility of the original plan;[12] (2) autonomy and incentive for the economic agents to participate in the market on the margin, including, in particular, the freedom of resale of plan-allocated goods, purchase of goods for redelivery under the plan, and sub-contracting; and (3) credibility of state enforcement of the plan-mandated sales and purchases of goods and of state commitment against the 'ratcheting up' of planned output and delivery targets.

Thus, by adopting the principle of 'reform without losers', China has been able to maintain its political and social stability even as it undergoes a very rapid and successful transformation of its economy from a centrally planned one to a predominantly market one. Politically, the Chinese Communist Party is still firmly in control. Economically, the Chinese Government has gradually shifted form direct control to indirect control through macro-economic instruments. It appears that the 'dual-track' approach may also be suitable for reform of the North Korean economy because by assuring that no one loses, a gradual, smooth, and Pareto-improving transition to a market economy is possible. It also poses the least threat to political and social stability. The South Korean business community can provide significant assistance to the North in this economic reform effort – by providing capital, technology, and know-how – especially in the establishment of the special economic zones.

NOTES

1. See Lau et al. (1997).
2. To put these statistics in perspective, it is useful to remember that real GDP and real GDP per capita in the USA are approximately US$7 trillion and US$25 000 respectively. Thus despite its rapid growth, it will probably take another four decades to half a century before Chinese real GDP and real GDP per capita approach US levels.
3. With an economy growing at 10 per cent per annum there is no reason why anyone has to be worse off in absolute terms.
4. However, the inflow of foreign direct investment only began to be quantitatively significant after 1990s. Even then, at its peak, it accounted for less than 15 per cent of gross fixed investment in China.
5. It is important to point out that the enforcement required here is no different from the enforcement of contracts in a market economy.
6. This is for reasons of both incentive and the avoidance of distortions.
7. At the beginning, the enterprises were permitted to re-purchase part of their foreign exchange earnings at the official exchange rate.
8. The experience in Taiwan and South Korea showed a similar pattern (Lau and Song, 1992).
9. If entry of new firms reduces profits of SOEs through competition, why does the dual-track approach not hurt SOEs? As SOEs have plan-allocated inputs, they generally benefit from the lower plan prices; competition thus does not seem to be an important factor. The dual-

track system also protects producers of intermediate goods from competition because of the planned output deliveries. However, this may not be the case for the producers of final goods. Households are also not always protected by 'input quotas', that is by rationing at lower than market prices. Thus enterprises in the final goods sector may be hurt by competition from non-state enterprises. They may in the longer run lose their rents, if not fully compensated by the state. One has here an example in which reform does not necessarily leave every one at least as well off as before. However, only a minority of firms can be hurt through this type of competition.

10. But China has not officially adopted a dual-track approach to its lending activities in the banking sector. This would have guaranteed rollover of cheap old loans to SOEs while applying the free market rate to new loans. However, in reality, many credits were leaked from state banks to non-state enterprises at market rates.
11. This is not true of all industries, however. The planned output was increased in certain limited industries in which the state-owned enterprises had undergone state-financed expansion, for example, coal mining.
12. The prior existence of slack is helpful but not necessary.

BIBLIOGRAPHY

Arrow, Kenneth L, and Frank H. Hahn (1971), *General Competitive Analysis*, San Francisco: Holden-Day.

Bahl, Richard and Christine Wallich (1992), 'Intergovernmental Fiscal Relations in China', Working Papers, Country Economics Department, WPS 863, World Bank.

Blanchard, Olivier and Michael Kremer (1997), 'Disorganization', *Quarterly Journal of Economics*, vol. 112, 1091–126.

Boycko, Maxim, Andrei Shleifer and Robert Vishny (1995), *Privatizing Russia*, Cambridge, MA: MIT Press.

Byrd, William A. (1987), 'The Impact of the Two-Tier Plan/Market System in Chinese Industry', *Journal of Comparative Economics*, vol. 11, 295–308.

Byrd, William. A. (1989), 'Plan and Market in the Chinese Economy: A Simple General Equilibrium Model', *Journal of Comparative Economics*, vol.13, 177–204.

Byrd, William. A. (1991), *The Market Mechanism and Economic Reforms in China,* Armonk, NY: M.E. Sharpe, Inc.

Cao, Yuanzheng, Yingyi Qian and Barry Weingast (1999), 'From Federalism, Chinese Style, to Privatization, Chinese Style', *Economics of Transition,* **7** (1), 103–31.

Diamond, Douglas and Philip Dybvig (1983), 'Bank Runs, Deposit Insurance and Liquidity', *Journal of Political Economy,* vol. 93, 401–19.

Farmer, Roger (1993), *The Macroeconomics of Self-fulfilling Prophecies*, Cambridge, MA: MIT Press.

Hammond, Peter J. and Jaime Sempere (1995), 'Limits to the Potential Gains from Economic Integration and Other Supply Side Policies', *The Economic Journal*, vol. 105, 1180–204.

Khor, Hoe Ee (1994), 'China's Foreign Currency Swap Market', IMF Paper on Policy Analysis and Assessment, 94/1, International Monetary Fund.

Lau, Lawrence J. and Dae-Hee Song (1992), 'Growth versus Privatization – An Alternative Strategy to Reduce the Public Enterprise Sector: The Experience of Taiwan and South Korea', Working Paper, Stanford, CA: Department of Economics, Stanford University.

Lau, Lawrence L, Yingyi Qian and Gerard Roland (1996), 'Gain without Pain: An

Interpretation of China's Dual-track Approach to Transition', mimeo, Stanford University.
Lau, Lawrence J., Yingyi Qian and Gerard Roland (1997), 'Pareto-improving Economic Reforms through Dual-track Liberalization', *Economics Letters*, vol. 55, 285–92.
Lau, Lawrence J., Yingyi Qian and Gerard Roland (1998), 'Reform without Losers: An Interpretation of China's Dual-Track Approach to Transition', Working Paper, Stanford, CA: Department of Economics, Stanford University.
Lin, Justin Yifu (1992), 'Rural Reforms and Agricultural Growth in China', *American Economic Review*, vol. 82, 34–51.
Lin, Justin Yifu, Fang Cai, and Zhou Li (1996), 'The Lessons of China's Transition to a Market Economy', *Cato Journal*, vol. 16, fall, 201–31.
McMillan, John and Barry Naughton (1992), 'How to Reform a Planned Economy: Lessons from China', *Oxford Review of Economic Policy*, vol. 8, 130–43.
Murphy, Kevin, Andrei Shleifer, and Robert W. Vishny (1992), 'The Transition to a Market Economy: Pitfalls of Partial Reform', *Quarterly Journal of Economics*, vol. 107, August, 889–906.
Naughton, Barry (1995), *Growing Out of Plan*, Cambridge University Press.
Qian, Yingyi (1994), 'Financial System Reform in China: Lessons from Japan's Main Bank System', in M. Aoki and H. Patrick (eds), *The Japanese Main-Bank System: Its Relevancy for Developing and Transforming Economies*, Oxford University Press, 552–91.
Qian, Yingyi and Chenggang Xu (1993), 'Why China's Economic Reforms Differ: The M-form Hierarchy and Entry and Expansion of the Non-State Sector', *Economics of Transition*, vol. 1, 135–70.
Sachs, Jeffery, and Wing Thye Woò (1994), 'Structural Factors in the Economic Reforms of China, Eastern Europe, and the Former Soviet Union', *Economic Policy*, **9** (18), April, 101–45.
Sicular, Terry (1988), 'Plan and Market in Chinas Agricultural Commerce', *Journal of Political Economy*, vol. 96, 283–307.
Wu, Jinglian and Renwei Zhao (1987), 'The Dual Pricing System in China's Industry', *Journal of Comparative Economics*, vol. 11, 309–18.

7. Privatization and Restructuring in East Germany: How the Treuhand Dealt with Privatization and Corporate Governance in a Radically Changed Environment

Jürgen Müller

7.1 INTRODUCTION[1] – THE MOVE TO MARKET AS THE MAJOR OBJECTIVE

The reform of the once centrally planned economy of East Germany provides for some interesting lessons, also when discussing possible reforms in the North Korean economy. The major objective of the newly elected government of the German Democratic Republic (GDR) in April 1990 (after the fall of the Berlin Wall in November 1989) was a quick move to a type of social market economy that was present in West Germany. To restructure the state-owned enterprises, it created the Treuhandanstalt (THA) as a holding company of all state enterprises. After unification in October of 1990, the THA, now under the Ministry of Finance, became also the major vehicle for restructuring and privatization.[2] In this paper we will analyze the complex role the THA played in this process, compared to the privatization and restructuring strategies pursued in most post-socialist economies.[3] We show that while privatization is a crucial step, the whole restructuring process is much more complex than is often suggested.

Privatization has been isolated by many authors as the essential element to a successful transformation, because it insulates firms from noncommercial objectives of political overseers (Boycko et al., 1993). Privatization is nevertheless only one of the issues, because one can also have an increase in private ownership solely through the emergence of new firms, as the experience in Poland showed, that is, it is only one aspect of the transformation. Restructuring the economy at a sectoral and enterprise level was furthermore determined by the dramatic opening up of the economy to world trade.

For this reason, we first look at the structural difference between the East and the West and the different governance structures between the two economies to identify the resulting task in moving from one type of economy to another. Some theoretical considerations related to the principal–agent issues in this process help to steer the subsequent empirical analysis, before we evaluate the restructuring and privatization process, with lessons for other post-socialist countries at the end of the paper.

7.2 IDENTIFYING CONCEPTUAL DIFFERENCES

Differences in Economic Structures and Institutions between the Two Economies

When moving from a centrally planned to a market economy, one needs to worry not only about privatization, but must have all the major conceptual differences between the two systems in mind. These differences can be broken down into three interrelated categories:

1. The differing role of the state as an economic actor: we find an economic environment to facilitate exchange and specialization in the West, but little interaction in actual production decisions and control decisions. In the centrally planned economies of the East, we see a much more extensive role for the state, given its involvement in planning and allocation.
2. Ownership of assets: predominately private ownership in most industries in market economies, and partial ownership in industries faced with market failures versus little private ownership in the East.
3. Production and distribution of goods and services: state-run centrally organized command apparatus in the East as opposed to a market economy with a relatively small state sector, reflecting government priorities not consumer preferences. This implied a *central determination* of the vertical and horizontal structure of producers, with one *Kombinate* running each industry sector, and the elimination of small and medium-sized firms. Competitive elements were largely missing.
4. Different incentives: few direct financial incentives with central planning, since eastern managers are more influenced by political incentives within the firm, with control between firms (coordination)

highly centralized and determined by economic planners. In such a scheme prices have little use and do not reflect scarcity costs. On the other hand, coordination in the market economies of the West is highly decentralized with prices serving to disseminate information, and adjusting to equate supplies with demands.

The requirements of transformation are thus: to define a new role for the state; to change the level of government ownership through privatization; to allow the price mechanism and competitive markets to operate and; to allow for enterprise and sector restructuring after the liberalization of trade. In addition one needs to make changes in fiscal and monetary policy for macrostabilization.

Where is Government and Private Ownership Likely to Differ?

From this discussion we see privatization as a central, but not the only crucial issue of transformation. We therefore turn to the canonical principal–agent model[4] as an explanatory device to broaden our analysis beyond the issue of privatization, for example the principal is the owner–manager who has certain objectives such as profit maximization and determines the incentive schemes for his employees to attain his objectives. The presence of imperfect or asymmetric information and coordination costs requires incentive schemes to take into account opportunistic behavior of the agent.

If privatization is taken to mean a transfer of ownership from the public sector to a private non-government body, we need to consider on a broader basis why there should be a difference in performance:

1. With different degrees of bureaucratic and political interference, the objectives of the principal may differ. Additional layers of hierarchy – the public, the government, the bureaucracy, the management of the firm, the workers of the firms – lead to a distortion of objectives (for example through political interference with politicians changing the objectives to suit their needs, or through bureaucratic manipulation of stated objectives). In large private firms we get also an additional layer of shareholders, managers and workers. This also distorts objectives, but perhaps to a lesser degree.
2. The productive techniques employed may differ. With public ownership there might be a preference for a particular input mix (for example highly labor intensive) as opposed to a decision on purely technical grounds.
3. The control structure employed will differ, because with different ownership structures we have different information flows making for

different incentive structures (for example under private ownership we have information on stock prices which can be used to evaluate performance of managers).

4. The bindings of constraints may differ. With public ownership there is no need to have sector-specific regulation, but upon transferring firms to the private sector, regulation acts as another, often very different constraint.

Given these additional points, we need to evaluate ownership structures from the viewpoint of what combination of private–public ownership provides optimal societal benefit.[5]

The Crucial Differences of an Economy-wide Transition

However, the above evaluation is in the context of switching one firm's ownership structure where the background environment is that of a well-functioning market economy and there are enough people to introduce and staff a regulatory apparatus. This was not the case in East Germany, where a whole economy had to be transformed within a very short time. The argument for privatization in this case is not based on an assumption that privatization improves performance solely by insulating firms from noncommercial objectives of political overseers, as modeled by Boycko et al. (1993). This approach rationalizes rapid privatization but cannot explain the reliance on sales as opposed to giveaways or vouchers, which presumably would have provided a better and faster insulation from government objectives. Moreover, as noted by Sappington and Stiglitz (1987) and Shapiro and Willig (1990), a compelling theory of differences in efficiency between public and private ownership must explain why government intervention to advance its objectives is more difficult in privately owned firms. Suggestive of the government's influence over firm objectives is the fact that the THA not only employed noncommercial objectives in its firms, but was able to convey its noncommercial objectives to private owners through the sales mechanism that considered employment and incentive commitments in addition to sale price.

In discussions focused on the East German restructuring process, Demougin and Sinn (1992) suggest that the benefit of privatization through auction might be access to superior information of privately owned firms. They do not, however, specify access to managerial knowledge as an important information difference between public and private owners. Rather, they focus on different privatization schemes' impact on capital investment. Carlin and Mayer (1994) center attention on the need to restructure corporate governance relationships in Eastern Germany. But they do not recognize information-inspired imperfections in the managerial labor market as Dyck (1997) has. This leads them to infer that the state can restructure firms – without privatization in a fairly efficient manner – a finding in direct contrast to the experience of the THA.

We need to remember that the political and macroeconomic changes in East Germany implied that each firm, regardless of ownership structure, suddenly required fundamental changes in the mode and organization of production because of demand and supply shocks to the system and fiscal policy changes. For the old socialist firms to survive economic liberalization (and the globalized EU market) and to operate efficiently someone needed to restructure these firms. Restructuring is defined here not only as changes in the horizontal and vertical structure of the firm, but also changes in internal firm organization, employment policies, product market policies, and financial control that maximize the long-run profitability of the firm given existing stocks of labor and capital.

The probable lack of ownership concentration in many large Eastern European firms arising from most privatization programs pursued there suggests that the individual making restructuring decisions in these will not be an owner. Rather, managers at the business location assume the burden of reorganizing existing capital and labor stocks. The key to successful restructuring of large firms, therefore, is the ability of owners to select able managers to restructure their enterprises. But most of the existing Eastern managers were not capable of envisaging and implementing the required restructuring. Through no fault of their own, they simply lacked experience with a market economy and basic management principles. Consequently, what was often needed was a replacement of existing management with experienced Western management.

Viewed from this perspective, of first-order importance in determining the desirability of continued public ownership and various types of privatization is the comparative ability of public and private owners to select and introduce experienced Western managers into Eastern enterprises in a situation, where the whole economy is being restructured, that is when all of the firms in the economy have the same management gaps to fill.

The Institutional and Political Environment of Restructuring and Privatization

The law creating the Treuhand from March 1990 allowed for the conversion of state-owned enterprises into joint stock or limited liability companies and vested ownership of these firms in the Treuhand. The East German government thought that with this new organizational structure they could introduce elements of a market economy, such as limited private shareholding, without eliminating central control over the allocation resources. At the same time, the then opposition in parliament and on the streets, which supported this move, hoped to insulate these firms from the remaining administrative power of the still communist government.

With unification taking place only six months later, the tradition of predominant private ownership in West Germany demanded eventually a transfer of ownership of most East German enterprises from the Treuhand to the private sector or, for some public utilities, to the relevant cities or regional governments. In the short run, perhaps for the first five to ten years, there remained the possibility of government-led restructuring and a slower sale of these enterprises. Continued government ownership during such an intermediate period implied neither a lack of funds for investments, nor lack of decision making by incumbent management. Rather, the government of the Federal Republic would be able to use its significant financial resources to restructure these firms horizontally and vertically, to invest in support of new business plans, to introduce Western officials to supervise the transition, and hire new management.

The uncertainty of the speed of privatization was reflected in legislation passed by the East German parliament on June 17, 1990 that increased the Treuhand's market orientation but was ambiguous about the state role in restructuring. The legislation stated that the agency's purpose was to reduce the commercial activity of the state as rapidly and extensively as possible through privatization. However, the act also allowed room for an active role in restructuring East German firms, declaring that the Treuhand should promote the structural adjustment of the economy to meet market requirements by developing potentially viable firms into competitive enterprises and transferring them into private ownership.

The federal and state government's handling of state-owned enterprises in West Germany reinforced the uncertainty of the speed of privatization in the East. Despite the government's continued promise to rapidly privatize state assets, its privatization policy, for example of Veba, Lufthansa or Volkswagen had been only partially and slowly implemented. Only the increased budgetary pressures in the 1990, and more restrictions on state ownership by the EU, increased recently the pressure for privatization. Such a changed environment can now also be observed in South Korea.

7.3 ELEMENTS OF STRUCTURAL CHANGE

Differences in Economic Structures

The horizontal and vertical structure of the East German economy differed considerably from the West, with much more horizontal and vertical concentration in the East. The factor of outstanding significance was the presence of 152 *Kombinate,* very large both horizontally and vertically and often holding a monopoly position in their sector.[6] The importance of independent enterprises and cooperatives in the craft trades was far smaller than in West Germany. The East German agricultural sector too was dominated by large units, the *Landwirtschaftliche Produktionsgenossenschaften* or LPGs (Agricultural Productive Cooperatives) and *Volkseigene Güter* or VEGs (State Farms): they had vastly bigger areas of land to manage than typical West German farms. Retail trade was entirely in the hands of the centralized *Handelsorganisation* or HO (Trade Organization) and the *Konsumgenossenschqften* (retail cooperatives). For export trade, largely concerned with capital goods and imports, in which raw materials and fuel were the most important commodities, there were just a few special foreign trade companies.[7]

There were also substantial differences in the sectarian composition of the economy. Thus the East German economy had a relative preponderance of basic raw materials, manufactured goods and capital goods in comparison with consumer goods (Table 7.1). The proportion of employment accounted for by the manufacturing and construction industries, however, was similar to that in West Germany, due to lower labor productivity. The retail trades and other services were heavily under-represented, with the exception of the transport and communications sectors (meaning the railways and the post office). The relative proportions accounted for by wholesale and retail trade, financial and insurance services and hotels and restaurants were in some cases less than half West German levels. Even the public sector was proportionately slightly smaller than in West Germany. This was certainly also due to the fact that in West Germany many of the functions provided by the public sector were in East Germany supplied by the state-owned companies and *Kombinate*, for example children facilities, health or sports and arts centers.

This comparison in Table 7.1, based on the various proportions of sectoral employment,[8] shows the dominance of agriculture, energy and the production of basic raw materials and that of heavy industry in the East. These were exactly those sectors, which declined significantly in the last two decades in West Germany. The services sector, which in the West had provided the most powerful growth and employment impetus in the past decade, had taken a totally different line of development in East Germany. There was much more vertical integration of these activities, with a large part of the industrial services integrated into the *Kombinate* or the large production companies, such as construction and data processing. Because of the obsolete state of the plant and machinery, repair services as part of these activities were grossly inflated in size.

Table 7.1 Sectoral Employment Structure in East and West Germany, 1989/90

Elected branches of	East Germany (1989)		West Germany(1990)	
Trade and industry	in'000s	in %	in'000s	in %
Agriculture, forestry, fishing	920	9.9	961	3.4
Energy and mining	295	3.2	466	1.6
Energy and water supply	120	1.3	286	1.0
Mining	175	1.9	180	0.6
Manufacturing industry	3 168	34.1	8 941	31.4
Chemical industry	152	1.6	644	2.3
Metal production and processing	183	2.0	687	2.4
Engineering	548	5.9	1 216	4.3
Motor vehicle construction	208	2.4	1 148	4.0
Electrical engineering	398	4.3	1 247	4.4
Clothing industry	197	2.1	230	0.8
Textile industry	217	2.3	238	0.8
Food industry	336	3.6	743	2.6
Others	929	10.0	2 788	9.8
Construction industry	563	6.1	1 914	6.7
Wholesale and retail trade	721	7.8	3 728	13.1
Wholesaling	258	2.8	1 369	4.8
Retailing	463	5.0	2 359	8.3
Transport and communication	628	6.8	1 588	5.6
Railways	245	2.6	255	0.9
Shipping and harbours	33	0.4	44	0.15
Other means of transport	233	2.4	751	2.6
Telecommunications	127	1.4	538	1.9
Banking and insurance	63	0.7	891	3.1
Hotel and catering trades	180	1.9	913	3.2
Services, public sector, defence, etc	2 762	29.7	9 031	31.8
Total	9 300	100	28 433	99.9

Notes: Apprentices are not included; this would increase the numbers employed in East Germany by 353 000.

Source: Görzig and Goming (1991); Statistisches Jahrbuch der DDR 34 (1989).

Furthermore, the East German economy had only been integrated into the world economy to a very limited extent. Its one-sided integration into COMECON, which held less than 10 per cent of world trade, was unable to compensate for this, and for this reason the structural adaptation in the sectoral composition to Western trade patterns was, by the time unification took place, only very slight.

This short overview will serve as a description of the sectoral context surrounding the privatization strategy of the THA and within which its restructuring efforts need to be judged. A comparison of this kind ignores of course the fact that some of these structural differences between East and West Germany could have arisen simply on the basis of their different factor endowments and income, rather than as a result of state planning. But it does also clearly shows the structural shortcomings of the old East German economy when compared with a modern open economy capable of competing internationally.

Components of Horizontal Change in Market Structure

Three components are of significance for the adjustment of the horizontal company structures within each industry and the evolution of the future market structure:

- entry to and exit from the market;
- internal growth;
- mergers and demergers.[9]

Market entry arises on the one hand through the business start-up of self-employed people or those in the free professions and on the other hand by the 'green field' establishments of companies from other region or from abroad (like FDI). This can quickly lead to an increase of the private activities in a sector, even without privatization.[10] *Exit* relates to companies withdrawing from the market.

The role of *internal growth,* which is gaining a larger sectoral share for a leading company was not significant right after transformation. The number of previously independent companies was too small to result in any real internal growth and change in the sectoral composition. The huge *Kombinate* and large companies on the other hand lost initially much of their importance through rationalization and 'unbundling' and demerger, with the result that their internal growth was usually negative.

The greatest significance in the adaptation of industry structures to that in the West was therefore due to *mergers* and *demerger*, that is the sale of THA companies or their parts to other firms in the same line of business (or, in the case of vertical mergers, further up or down the same chain of production).

The old *Kombinate* or companies had been too large to be effectively reorganized. In many of the major industrial sectors there was often only one highly vertically integrated *Kombinate*. These *Kombinate* and their individual companies had to be unbundled both vertically and horizontally.

Horizontal unbundling of the *Kombinate* was often relatively easy as individual plants of the companies had been earlier nationalized and had just been added to the *Kombinate* of their sector for administrative purposes.[11] Breaking the *Kombinate* up horizontally into their individual plants, that is *demerger* was made easy by the *Treuhandgesetz (*or THG, the Act setting up the THA) which allowed for 'autonomous' horizontal (and vertical) unbundling.[12] Often some individual plants could then just decide on their own to leave through *spontaneos unbundling* the *Kombinate* in the hope to survive the transition better on their own.

The old *Kombinate* and their companies were generally very deeply vertically integrated. There were de facto no markets for intermediate inputs and none for the services associated with them: much had to be produced by in-house divisions and subsidiaries. Such companies could be quickly unbundled vertically, but a balance between the central 'core' activities of the *Kombinate* and those which could be hived off had to be maintained, requiring sometimes difficult negotiations between the *Kombinate*, their subsidiaries and the THA headquarters. Vertical disintegration was even more important, because this unbundling related not only to a large number of social services (health services, old people's homes, holiday cottages), but also to associated services such as transport, repair workshops, and so on.[13] 'Spontaneous' vertical unbundling therefore resulted in a far greater splitting up of companies, meaning it created far more independent companies than did the spontaneous horizontal unbundling.

Geographical or spatial unbundling of business locations was another element of structural change. It involves separating off the parts of the business sites not essential to its core operations. Vertical unbundling had of course already carved off many buildings and production locations from the former company sites. Geographical unbundling, often as a result of much smaller production volumes, continued this process by separating off the remaining buildings and the sites on which they stood until the minimum necessary for sustainable operations was achieved. The remaining land could then be made available to other companies.[14] This step also reduced the possibility of running assets down excessively during the restructuring process (as a result of insufficient supervision).[15]

7.4 THE THA AS A CENTRAL INSTRUMENT OF STRUCTURAL CHANGE

Taking Control

When the THA was founded in April 1990, it took over almost all the companies in East Germany.[16] On paper, at least, it was the world's largest industrial conglomerate.[17] Initially, however, the number of companies belonging to the THA had been far smaller, as many new companies only came into being as a result of the spontaneous unbundling of *Kombinate* and splitting off parts of companies. This resulted in an addition of about 3000 companies between March 1990 and March 1993.[18] Other companies were not identified as belonging to the THA until some time later.

The supervision problems, which this involved, were thus enormous. It was, however, for some time not clear in what way corporate governance was to be exercised. The originally planned holding company for the 152 centrally managed *Kombinate* – organized by four industrial sectors[19] – was abandoned in August 1990 by the THA President of the day, Mr Rohwedder. The matrix organization adopted later, with 15 regional branch offices and a certain number of Industry Directorates in the THA Central Office, however, could not be put into effect until early 1991. Even in this form, the task was enormous. On January 1, 1991, the 1231 THA employees had 3826 companies to *manage* from Central Office and 6718 from the 15 regional branches.[20] Therefore, the THA quickly added a dominant share of western German management personnel both at the Executive Board level and in the Industry Directorates and the 15 branches (see Table 7.2).[21] This enabled it to rapidly make use of Western management know-how, at least at the THA management level, and to restructure the THA itself accordingly.

Autonomous Structural Change and Passive Privatization

By April 1991 this reorganization of the THA was more or less complete and the appropriate forms of corporate governance were put into place. But the time up to that date can be described as the *passive privatization and restructuring phase* because the THA's control and management function of its companies was still in the process of creation. During that time, however, the *Kombinate* had to a large extent been spontaneously restructured and a significant number of companies already privatized. This included the reprivatization of 3000 smaller companies under the Modrow government[22] and the privatization of a number of particularly attractive properties.[23] In some cases, individual managers had developed on their own cooperation agreements with Western German companies, often with the aim of an eventual merger. As a consequence, West German parties were able to exert their influence on these companies even before an official purchase contract with the THA had been signed.[24]

Table 7.2 Extent of Management Transfer to the THA

	1. Permanent staff numbers (Central Office, branches, and TLG)				
	30 June 1990	31 Dec. 1990	30 June 1991	31 Dec. 1991	30 June 1992
Total numbers employed	114	1140	2722	3604	3941
From Eastern Germany	112	1032	2048	2578	2716
From Western Germany/ Foreign countries	2	108	674	1026	1225
Administration Boards	18	22	24	24	24
From Eastern Germany	8	5	4	3	3
From Western Germany/ Foreign countries	10	17	20	21	21
Executive Board members	2	8	9	9	9
From Eastern Germany	2	2	2	1	–
From Western Germany/ Foreign countries	–	6	7	8	9
Branch managers	15	15	15	15	15
From Eastern Germany	15	–	–	–	–
From Western Germany/ Foreign countries	–	15	15	15	15
Senior managers	9	206	235	294	301
From Eastern Germany	9	31	33	24	25
From Western Germany/ Foreign countries	–	175	203	270	276
	2. Tempory staff numbers (Central office, branches, and TLG)				
	30 June 1990	31 Dec. 1990	30 June 1991	31 Dec. 1991	30 June 1992
Managers on secondment	–	38	70	48	51
From Eastern Germany	–	–	–	2	2
From Western Germany/ Foreign countries	–	38	70	46	49

Notes: Administration Board started to be appointed on July 15, 1990.

Source: Treuhandanstalt Informationen, various issues.

Some of the *Kombinate* were already commercialized and converted into joint-stock companies in early 1990, during the time of the Modrow government. They acquired the legal form of an AG-company, but generally retained the structure of the old *Kombinate*. The legally necessary Supervisory Boards were appointed following the West German principles of codetermination for the so-called 'Montan' industries (basically, major coal, iron and steel concerns).[25] In some cases this first step towards commercialization had been combined with a certain amount of autonomous unbundling, mainly horizontal, but in some cases vertical as well.[26] Other companies preferred to remain under the roof of the *Kombinate*'s holding company, waiting for the initiative of the THA.

This horizontal and vertical unbundling of business and product divisions during the commercialization of the *Kombinate* was carried out 'spontaneously' and did not always follow rationally comprehensible criteria, but were mostly designed to concentrate the company's activities on its core areas. But as some of plants or their managers were gripped to a certain extent by the feeling of 'every man for himself', they often believed they could survive better on their own and therefore parted their companies from the *Kombinate*. This significantly reduced the depth of production (vertical unbundling) and hived off separable parts of companies (for example, social services, the vehicle fleet, repair and construction departments, and so on), but in some cases the *Kombinate* did also lose important benefits of scope, such as from research and development units or benefits of internal coordination, and the hived-off parts were not always capable of survival on their own.[27].

This 'spontaneous' restructuring often also involved the dismissal of members of the companies' management. Some managers in politically exposed positions, or those with a particularly authoritarian style, were not able to hang onto their jobs and were often replaced in a process characterized by 'grass-roots democracy' by those in the management level below them (for example production manager, works manager, senior managers in sales, export or R & D, and so on). These were then the managers which the THA discovered when it eventually took effective control and in this process attempted to evaluate the company's management capability.

However, until the early summer of 1991 the THA tended more to operate in a passive role. It was not until the new organization was more or less in place, and some of the legal hurdles to privatization had been overcome by the necessary revisions to the Treaty of Unification or the Property Act[28], that the THA was able to make an effective start on fulfilling its task of supervising, reorganizing, restructuring and privatizing companies.

Move to Controlled Structural Change

The THA then started to look systematically at all the companies and to examine their structures for economic and administrative practicability.[29] Whenever possible, the THA acted as a holding company in the management of its companies. A Supervisory Board was installed in the larger companies, an Advisory Board in the smaller ones.[30] Each Supervisory Board then examined the company (with the assistance of the THA's Central Office) and his management, often replaced some of it, issued new management contracts, and assisted the management in the vertical and horizontal restructuring process.[31] It also assessed the new business plans that had to be filed with the THA headquarters, before any financial support to cover current deficits or new investment could be approved. As a consequence, the newly appointed Supervisory Boards had to intervene far more actively in the operational structure of the firms than is provided for in the German *Aktiengesetz*, the Companies Act for companies of the AG-type.[32]

The restructuring proposals prepared by the Executive and Supervisory Boards were then discussed and agreed with the THA in order to ensure that the operational units thus created were capable of being sold. In particularly difficult restructuring cases, such as for companies of great importance to their regions, the relevant Industry Directorate of the THA was also actively involved in preparing such restructuring proposals. Examples of this are found in the chemical industry, ship-yards, the steel industry and microelectronics.[33] In particularly complicated cases it was also necessary to consult the various state ministries, principally in order to permit the necessary accompanying measures to be taken to relieve the burden on the regional labor market.[34]

The horizontal, vertical, and geographical restructuring process in these crucial restructuring cases was often highly complicated. The most difficult step in preserving industrial locations was the decision as to whether the existing company, or companies could be restructured and sold or should be closed down. Another crucial question was whether after liquidation[35] preference should be given to the establishment of a new, 'greenfield' company near that site and/or if a third party would be permitted to take-over and develop the old production locations from the bankruptcy estate.

Private or State-controlled Restructuring?

After private ownership, contractual freedom and protection of private contracts had been legally underpinned after unification, the crucial step towards creating a new company and industry structure was privatization through the THA. The role of the state as the party ultimately responsible for the large *Kombinate* and their companies was to be replaced after privatization by the supervision of private providers of capital. This option is particularly important in the implementation of corporate restructuring. Although bureaucrats can prepare the corporate strategies related to the restructuring process, the question as to how much is to be invested for which products and where, in order to make the physical and human capital more productive, can only be decided on a decentralized basis. Private capital is the natural choice for this function.[36]

This restructuring through privatization is made up of two interrelated steps. A distinction needs to be made between the first step:

1. the *legal transfer*, that is, the change of owner and;
2. the subsequent *implementation of the corporate strategy* that adjusts the firm and its human and capital assets to the new micro- and macro-environment.

The legal transfer is strictly speaking the actual privatization, and means that the existing company (or part of one) is handed over as it stands, given the new environment. The proceeds of privatization (the 'transfer price') do not depend on the companies previous turnover or its present stock of labor and capital, but far more on present and expected market conditions. For some companies the transfer price obtained by the THA was very low, and if there was a heavy burden of historic debt, or a significant liability for environmental pollution, or large obligations to employees under 'social plans' (redundancy compensation) because of imminent lay-offs, the transfer price might even be negative. The THA therefore sold many companies for the purely symbolic price of DM 1.00, or even for a negative price, keeping in mind the associated restructuring subsidies provided.[37, 38]

On the other hand, the (upgrade and turn around) investments designed to reactivate the company and implement a corporate restructuring plan could be very high indeed.[39] However, only the two steps together will lead to the successful restructuring of the companies and the economy.[40] To use the low prices attained for some companies under these circumstances as an argument against rapid privatization is therefore a rather shortsighted view. The experience of the THA shows that the second phase of privatization, the restructuring process, was not solved until 'real' owners – proprietors, in fact – could be found, who had a long-term interest and sufficient control over the company that a sound corporate strategy could be implemented with the appropriate level of investment.[41]

Given these considerations the THA had to set priorities in the privatization process, since the large number of privatization cases to be handled resulted naturally in a time problem. For capacity reasons, it was not possible for the THA to privatize everything at once.[42] While time was passing, decisions still had however to be taken on changes in production methods, reorganizing the companies, structure and making investments.[43] Where restructuring needs were minimal, as for example in public utilities, privatization could be postponed without major dynamic efficiency losses, while in a rapid changing environment, restructuring and therefore privatization as a necessary first step was of the highest priority.

Another reason for the very low transfer price of companies is their associated risk, as their economic developments are very hard to forecast. If, however, the state holds on to part of a company via the THA, it has a stake both in the risks and in the possible increase in value that can arise when the individual companies improve. The demand for companies can then be increased by this policy of partial privatization and therefore of easier market access. The THA pursues this policy, for example in the case of an MBO, when the payment of the purchase price can under certain circumstances be postponed, and also when particularly risky companies are being privatized.

One possibility for lengthening the period of time over which privatization takes place, that is to keep companies for a longer time in state ownership, was to work with management contracts. This was done, necessarily, in the management contracts signed with power utilities, because of the long legal delay in implementing their sale. But under which criteria are the companies to be managed, and 'investor-neutral' investment plans drawn up, if they are shortly to be privatized? Clear targets have to be set and supervised. This was difficult during the enormous changes in the firms environment, which followed German unification, particularly in the manufacturing industry.[44] How was the THA to design an incentive scheme for top management when even an insider finds it hard enough to distinguish between external factors affecting the company and the management's success in managing it?

But the main reason for rapid privatization instead of restructuring under state control was the imperfect market for managerial talent. The THA's experience shows how difficult it is to 'buy in' good managers to handle the restructuring of the company. There were more than enough opportunists and managers who were unsuccessful in the West, but really effective experts are very hard to come by. The THA is therefore thrown back mainly on the managers who are already in Eastern Germany but first need to be familiarized with the new notions of a free market if it wants to pursue a policy of active restructuring.[45]

7.5 METHOD OF PRIVATIZATION USED BY THE THA AND BY OTHER PARTIES

Privatization by the THA

The quickest and most efficient way of restructuring and modernizing a company's structure is usually to allow the purchaser to do it. The quicker companies are privatized, the sooner they will have access to capital, modern management knowledge, and technology as a prerequisite for successful restructuring. These were the crucial factors for achieving competitiveness under the new economic condition. It is these arguments which primarily justified the THA's theory that rapid privatization meant rapid and more effective restructuring.

The radical changes in economic conditions brought about by the unification process led the THA to pursue fast privatization as the main strategy for restructuring and unbundling. Only in well-justified cases was restructuring of individual companies permitted before privatization.[46] By August, 1 1993, 7247 of the 12 142 companies had been privatized.[47] This also involved the reprivatization (restitution to the previous owners) of 1446 companies: 264 were communalized, or handed over to Eastern German regional administrative bodies, and 79 were assigned to new owners (Figure 7.1).[48, 49] In almost 2400 cases, privatization took the form of management buy-outs (MBOs), an instrument of particular importance for creating a structure of small- to medium-sized owner-operated businesses. Liquidation proceedings had been carried for 2880 companies, and created the possibility of a new start.[50]

Privatization was not run at a uniform pace in all the individual sectors. Those in attractive sectors, such as those in which the competitive pressure was not as tough, for instance because their markets were regionalized, could be privatized more quickly than those in industries like textiles, engineering, and electronics where the need for adaptation was greater and global competition more intensive.[51] This was not in line with our argument above, but also shows that the THA was behaving opportunistically with the aim to show quick results.

Up to June 1993 the progress of privatization was greatest (weighted by the number of employees) in the fields of construction and its ancillary trades, food, quarrying, and wholesale and retail trade. The problem areas had always been, from the start of privatization, in mining, agriculture and forestry, leather and shoes, and textiles and clothing (Figure 7.2). When measuring privatization based on the number of companies being privatized (Figure 7.3) an above-average progress was achieved in the fields of energy, quarrying, and construction, and also in wholesale and retail trade and services. In the construction and ancillary industry, the rate of privatization weighted by the number of employees is greater than that weighted by the number of firms, but the proportions are the other way round in the energy field, wholesale and retail trade, and services.[52]

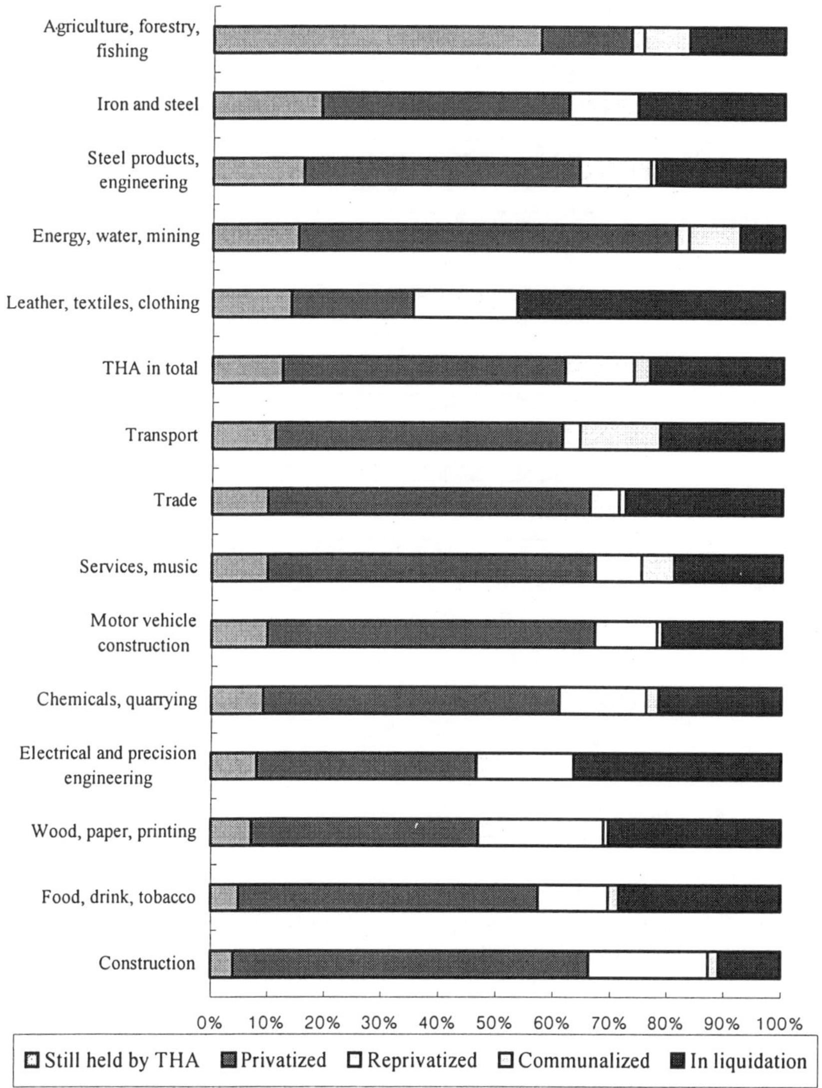

Figure 7.1 THA Companies' Status in Early 1993

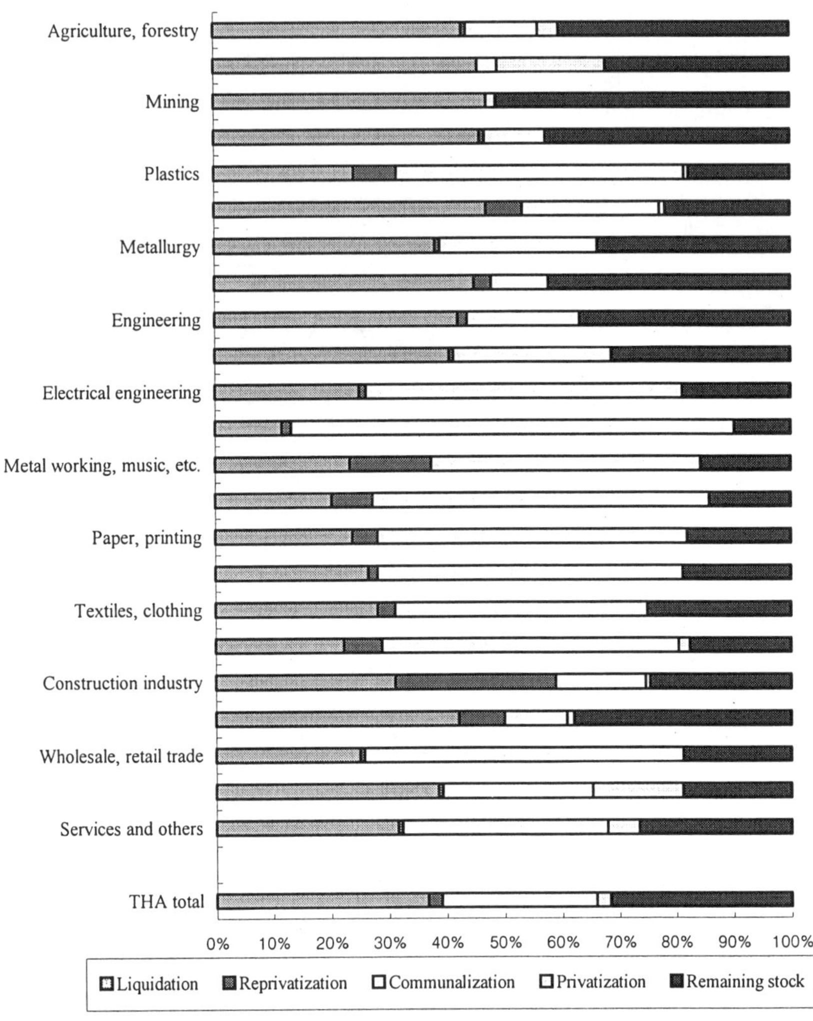

Notes: Shares weighted by the numbers of employees as of the second quarter of 1991. Companies undergoing liquidation were shedding employees particularly rapidly and they would thus have been underrepresented in these figures. Companies have not been included if they were only partially privatized and communalized, as this did not reduce the THA's stock.

Source: Treuhandanstalt Informationen, various issues.

Figure 7.2 Progress in Privatization until June 1993 Weighted by the Number of Employees of the Second Quarter of 1991

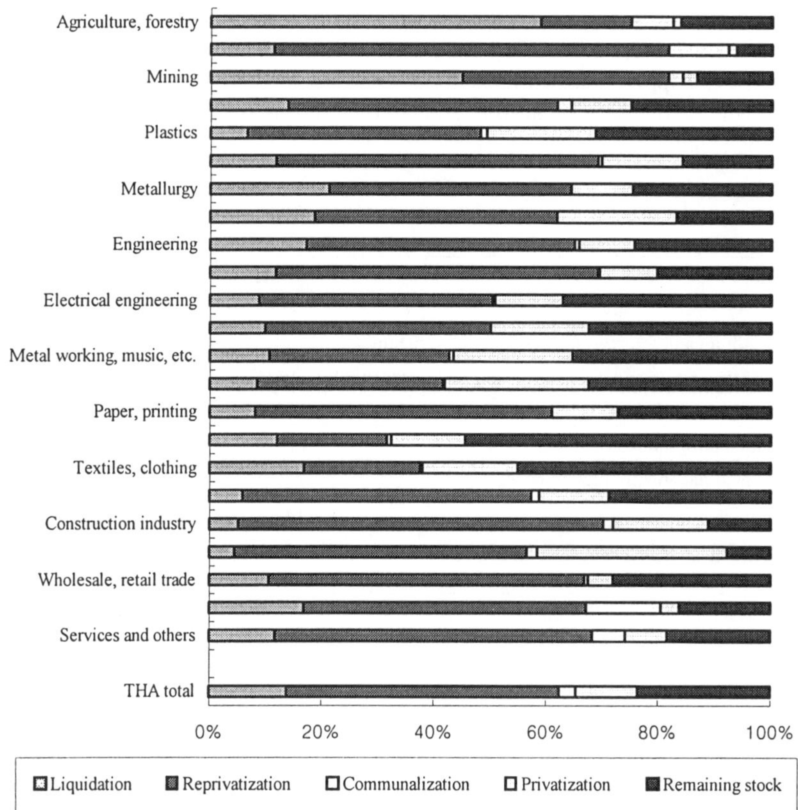

Source: *Treuhandanstalt Informationen*, various issues.

Figure 7.3 Progresses in Privatization Weighted by the Number of Firms, as of June 1993

Mergers and Diversification

By far the greatest proportion of Eastern German companies were taken over by Western German companies, and in some cases foreign companies.[53] Not only the distribution of company acquisitions between Western German and foreign firms is of interest, but also the distribution at the sectoral level and the horizontal, vertical, and conglomerate nature of these mergers. The THA's privatization balance sheet contains no indication of the sectoral origin of the purchasers of the various companies, but a statistical evaluation by the Federal Cartel Office allows these questions to be answered.[54] The sectoral distribution of mergers, weighted by the amount of turnover thus acquired, shows the following picture at the end of 1992: 28.5 per cent of the total turnover was accounted for by the power generation and distribution and gas and water supply industries, 26.7 per cent by manufacturing industry, 20.3 per cent by the service sector, and 20.0 per cent by wholesale and retail trading (Table 7.3).

Table 7.3 Distribution of Mergers[a] by Sectors

Sector	Mergers		Turnover acquired[b]	
	No.	in %	DM million	in %
Agriculture and forestry, animal husbandry, fishing	14	1.0	656	0.5
Power generation and distribution, gas and water supply	96	6.7	35 175	28.5
Mining	0		0	
Manufacturing industry in total	602	42.2	33 002	26.7
Raw material and production goods	275	19.3	15 517	12.6
Capital goods	195	13.7	11 289	9.1
Consumer goods	37	2.6	1 117	0.9
Foodstuffs and food products incl. drinks	95	6.7	5 079	4.1
Construction industry including real estate	98	6.9	4 639	3.8
Wholesale and retail trade[b] in total	400	28.1	24 727	20.0
Food and drinks trade	198	13.9		
Petroleum and fuel trade	44	3.1		
Building materials trade	28	3.1		
Metal trade	17	2.0		
Chemical products trade	20	1.2		
General and mixed trade	26	1.4		
Service trades in total	190	1.8	25 083	20.3
Financial services[b]	29	13.3	6 470	5.2
Publishing and newspapers[b]	67	2.0	16 145	13.1
Services for environmental and waste disposal	36	4.7	372	0.3
Transport and communications	26	2.5	276	0.2
Total	1426	1.8	123 558	100

Notes:

a. Mergers completed with Eastern German companies and reported to the Federal Cartel Office by the end of 1992.

b. Based on turnover as defined by the Distortion of Competition Act; trade turnover reduced by a quarter; publisher rated at one-twentieth of their turnover; banks at one-tenth of their balance sheet totals; insurance companies on their premium income; all taken from the most recent annual accounts. Turnover in East German Marks converted to DM at 2:1.

Source: Frisch (1993).

The Federal Cartel Office's figure on mergers also permits the purchasers and the companies they acquire to be identified by sector of origin. Horizontal mergers dominate totally with 92.6 per cent, 95.9 per cent, and 91.7 per cent in the years 1990 to 1992 respectively. The proportion of vertical mergers fell from 5.8 per cent in 1990 to 1.7 per cent in 1991, rising slightly to 2.9 per cent in 1992. Mergers of a conglomerate nature, meaning that the acquiring company was entering a totally new market, increased in the same period from 1.7 per cent to 2.4 per cent to 5.4 per cent. The dominance of horizontal mergers supports the theory of effective management and technological transfer through rapid privatization that we have advanced above. Companies acquiring others within their own industry were better able to evaluate its expected cash flow situation and to carry out the necessary restructuring more effectively than investors from outside the industry, and indeed better than the THA could. The very small but growing number of conglomerate mergers, however, gives rise to the assumption that over time it became easier to evaluate the profit potential of companies and their management teams. The growing involvement of foreign companies in mergers, rising from 16.5 per cent in 1990 to 16.7 per cent in 1991 and to 23.8 per cent in 1992, also appears to reflect a growing transparency in the evaluation of Eastern German companies' spotential profitability, and of course the redoubled efforts of the THA in finding buyers.

MBO/MBI

MBOs and MBIs became significant forms of privatization of the THA.[55] In an MBO, the employees or the managers in a company (and in an MBI from outside it) take over both ownership of and responsibility for managing the company or part of it having been unbundled before. This route enables a *Mittelstand,* a group of small- to medium-sized independent company owner–managers to be created and strengthened in Eastern Germany. Roughly one privatization in six took this form; the total achieved by June 1993 was 2364. This form of privatization was however concentrated on a relatively small number of sectors of the economy; most of them were engaged in services, and very few in the manufacturing sector. MBOs were of significance mainly for small and medium-sized businesses.[56] In the case of MBOs the purchasers came mainly from inside the company, where 93 per cent of them had held a leading managerial position before. Only 7 per cent came from outside the company, mainly in the case of MBIS: 74 per cent of these purchasers were West Germans.[57] The THA gave every possible support to this kind of privatization. However, these newly established business owners requested, and usually greatly needed, a more intensive consultancy assistance from the THA. This applied in particular to support and advice on financing and the prolongation of bank guarantees.

The use of the MBO/MBI as a novel instrument in the process of restructuring began under difficult conditions. The great majority of the buyers had very little market experience or knowledge and, in addition to this, the companies concerned were usually in a difficult economic situation anyway, as can be seen from the fact that no outside investor was interested in them. It therefore seems fair to say, in at least some of these cases, that the MBO teams took over the management of their company because they were forced into it. The success rate achieved was nevertheless surprisingly good, bearing the difficult initial circumstances in mind.[58]

Restitution

A further possible form of restructuring was the 'reprivatization' or restitution of firms or parts of them to their previous rightful owners. Such units were then unbundled from their *Kombinate* with the aim of reprivatizating them. In most cases, because of the great length of time during which the companies had been in state hands and because of changes in production methods and the economic environment, they too were not capable of surviving without restructuring in this form. Instead the former owners had to restructure them all over again.[59] In just the short time in which the Modrow government was in power, some 3000 companies were handed back to their former owners. Up to August 1993 the THA had reprivatized another 1360 firms. Figures 7.2 and 7.3 above show the sectoral importance of this form of privatization. Weighted by number of companies, reprivatized companies play an important part in the building industry, printing works and in the textiles field.

Private and Small and Medium-sized Enterprises (SMEs)

Private companies, especially of the SME or *Mittelstand* category were of little significance in the old East Germany, and only occurred in a few areas of the economy. They only attained a certain prominence in the craft and catering trades, and even then were limited to small or family companies. Great hopes were therefore set in the newly created *Mittelstand* in industrial and craft companies.[60] In 1990, there were a good 80 000 craft enterprises employing about 400 000 people. A survey carried out by the German national association for craft enterprises showed that at the end of 1992 there were already 131 500 craft enterprises providing jobs for about 850 000 people.[61]

According to the results from questionnaires analyzed by the economic research institute DIW,[62] *Mittelstand* companies have taken on considerable significance in the short time since the old East German economy collapsed. Apart from the establishment of new companies, this is mainly attributable to the shrinkage of the old companies and the process of vertical unbundling. Also access to the production capacity no longer needed, sometimes in conjunction with liquidations, were particularly important for the rapid development of the *Mittelstand.* They have gained great significance in the food industry, particularly in the bakery and butchery areas, in woodworking, in plastic products and in metal products and motor vehicles (particularly motor repair workshops). Their significance is small in those industries which produce in large-scale plant (chemicals, metals production): they are more important as small, mainly craft enterprises, and two-thirds of them employ less than 20 people each.

Companies Based on ABM and ABS Job Creation Schemes

Because of the high level of unemployment as a result of the recent restructuring, particularly widespread use was being made in Eastern Germany of such labor market policy instruments as ABM and ABS societies.[63] The THA saw these firms as an 'employment policy catchment basin' for temporary employment in *Qualifizierungsgesellschaften* (ABM), companies formed to train workers while employing them, and *Beschäftigungsgesellschaften* (ABS), companies formed to employ workers mainly in social and environmental activities, with the aim of making the process of the privatization of THA companies socially bearable. The companies funded under those schemes took in nearly 400 000 employees in 1993.[64] They concentrated their activities in the environmental and infrastructural area, followed by modernization and restructuring old company sites. Their main aim was thus to support public-sector activities in the environmental and infrastructural area until the situation on the labor market had returned to something near normal. If these 'artificial' job-creating organizations later develop into viable companies, this will at the same time be a contribution to creating more private companies.

However, this road was a long and hard one. It seems certain that greater support for hiving off parts of companies as part of the privatization program, for example through MBO or MBI, would have been a more promising policy than this indirect route.[65] The main point with THA activities in connection with ABM and ABS companies was therefore its temporary material support in making redundancy easier to bear.[66, 67] A study made by the Hans Böckler economic research foundation in 1992 showed that, in 57 per cent of the cases investigated, the initiative for such companies came from works management, often in collaboration with works councils and local or county authorities. The trade unions and the state governments played only a minor role in establishing them.[68] The THA companies were therefore the major shareholders.

Liquidation

For companies and parts of them, which even in the long term had very little prospect of becoming economically viable although much had been spent on restructuring them, there was no other alternative but liquidation. The only exceptions to this rule were for reasons of structural and regional policy. By the end of July 1993, closure had been initiated for 2880 companies because the THA no longer saw any prospect for effectively restructuring them. A total of 303 671 jobs were affected by liquidation up to that point in time. However, the hope existed for many companies that new commercial activities could arise out of the old structures after the close-down, for example through the establishment of new companies and by putting the old land, buildings and equipment to new uses. The THA estimates that some 25 to 30 per cent of the employees affected by liquidation were able to find a new job at the old location.[69]

Restructuring and the Retention of Industrial Core Activities

The THA itself describes the relative priorities in its transformation work in one motto: 'rapid privatization – resolute restructuring – considerate closure'. The first and the last aspect of this strategy have indeed been implemented in the first three years of its existence. The THA had sustained a pace of privatization that few would have considered possible, but for a host of reasons had been rather more cautious with liquidation, as we saw in the section above. However, controversy flared up, sometimes violently, over its restructuring work (or better lack of it) and the question of preserving jobs in the companies still on its books, before the THA was closed down and its remaining asset transferred to the successor organization EVS. Although the Federal government – as the institution behind the THA – on more than one occasion emphasized its general support for the task of restructuring the remaining central industrial sites with the aim of 'maintaining and further developing eastern Germany as a varied and diverse economic location', but the question was left unanswered as to the extent to which the maintenance of 'industrial core activities' was to be linked with the retention of 'old' companies in its restructuring and privatization policy.

What were the economic arguments of this debate? The discounted opportunity costs of one permanently unemployed person, amplified by the so-called multiplier effect, was then estimated at about DM 300 000.[70] On the other hand, an economic research organization had suggested a figure of about DM 110 000 as the typical investment needed per job for an average THA manufacturing company and nearly DM 160 000 if it was active in the field of transport and communications.[71] In capital-intensive industries the figures were considerably higher than this. The restructuring costs per job for the THA should therefore only exceed these figures if special consideration to special structural and social policy aspects were present. But in some instances, much larger investment grants were given, for example to the Eastern German shipyards at the rate of DM 800 000 per job, some of it subsidized by the EC. The expenditure incurred at *Carl Zeiss Jena* was of a similar magnitude: part of it was borne by the State of Thuringia; similar figures have been spent for the restructuring of the EKO steelworks in Brandenburg.

Two aspects based on structure political experience in West Germany over the past decades are worth considering here. It is easier to promote growth in regional centers than to hold back the deterioration of economically unattractive locations. On the other hand, it is more of a problem to create new centers of growth within a short time once the industrial infrastructure has completely disappeared because of the massive sectoral transformation referred to above. For this reason it was not possible for the THA to invoke economic criteria alone for the restructuring or close-down of large companies, which were important for the whole economic infrastructure of a region (such as the shipyards in the north, the *EKO* works near the river Oder, or *Zeiss-Jena* in Thuringia). Such decisions had to be supplemented by an examination of the macroeconomic opportunity costs. As unemployment was anyway high in the economically weak regions in Eastern Germany, the loss of each additional job was likely to lead to further long-term unemployment.

But subsidies on this massive scale, based on political decisions for conserving at least the core of a regional industry structure, could scarcely be justified in terms of the THA's task of restructuring.[72] A greater readiness to assume direct responsibility on the part of other political institutions, meaning the Federal and State governments, seems to be called for her.

On the other hand, in those companies that have been on the THA's books for rather longer it was possible to discern something of a 'wait and see' attitude to restructuring by the THA. Given the policy of only allowing 'investor-neutral investment' to take place, all the usual restructuring programs such as getting rid of redundancies, unbundling, and supporting investments in modernizing the production plant had to be carried out in the interests of an unknown outside party and without any commercial risk. Thus the THA companies, in comparison with those already privatized, were able to invest far too little in proportion to their numbers employed. Because there was no proper incentive system for restructuring (except for the Management KGs to be discussed below), it would be expecting too much of the THA, compared with an actively managed, private restructuring process.

Restructuring Through Management KGs

It was in order to find a way out of the problem of these difficult restructuring cases and to simplify institutional control that the concept of Management KGs (commercial limited partnerships) was finally introduced. The THA originally intended to complete its operational business by the end of 1993, but even after that date it still had a significant number of companies on its books which, although rated as capable of being restructured, would not be immediately able to find a buyer. This included also companies which because of their importance for their regions could not be considered for liquidation (for example *Deutsche Waggonbau AG or EKO-Stahl).*[73]

The THA developed the concept of the Management KGs outside the normal privatization procedure, since the possibility of these firms being restructured and privatized depended mainly on contracting a highly qualified management team and to privatize the management of these companies via a contingency contract. Experienced 'troubleshooters' were hired to each look after a group of companies and help them along the way to privatization. In June 1993, 58 such companies with a total work force of almost 25 000 were organized into five of these Management KGs.

According to Dyck (1993, 1997) the experience of these Management KGs organizations created by the Treuhand that used performance-related pay provides detailed evidence on the significant transaction costs in using this instrument during the transition period. In a Management KG, a management team was given broad rights to restructure and privatize a number of firms, while the Treuhand retained ownership of the firms' physical assets. Management was compensated with fixed pay and an incentive contract. To reflect the government's multiple goals of increasing sale price, employment, and investment, managers were rewarded based on 'social value' created in the restructuring and privatization. Social value was defined as a fixed combination of the sales price (less an initial estimate of firm value), and employment and investment committed by new private owners. For feasible levels of social value, compensation averaged between 5–10 per cent of 'social value' created. One of the advertised benefits of this organizational form was its ability to attract and retain highly qualified management. As the vice-chairman of the Treuhand argued, the Management KG concept provides small highly qualified teams the Treuhand could otherwise not make available.

Implementing this program was costly and difficult. For example political concerns with potentially large bonuses coinciding with massive employment reductions at some of the plants being restructured, so that government officials were forced to cap the performance bonus at DM 6 million per management team. Professional auditors were employed to establish an initial value for each firm at a cost of DM 1 million each. The Treuhand itself had great difficulty specifying and securing approval for a specific trade-off between sale price, employment, and investment. The specific performance bonus used for all KG organizations required the approval not only of the Treuhand management board but also the finance minister.

Perhaps most importantly, there was a significant administrative delay between the agreement to use performance-related pay and implementation of this system. The idea of the Management KG was first floated in November 1991, more than six months after unification. The proposal took six months to be approved by political representatives, Treuhand officials, and management, was announced in May 1992 and first introduced in September 1992 – 26 months following economic and monetary union. Three new management KGs were only introduced after a one-year trial in September 1993. While representing a small fraction of the firms under Treuhand ownership, these difficulties suggest wider problems in using performance-related pay.

7.6 EVALUATING THE PRIVATIZATION PROCESS

A First Assessment

When analyzing the role of the THA in the process of privatization and structural change it is necessary to take the macroeconomic and sectoral effects of the changed economic environment – over which the THA had no influence – into account in. In section 7.3 we demonstrated the difficult macroeconomic and sectoral adjustment effects of German unification and the structural shortcomings, which these brought to light. The decline of large parts of industrial production capacity as a result of their dependence on foreign trade, and also the lack of knowledge concerning the market economy within the companies, were the main characteristics of the new economic environment in which the THA's privatization strategy has to be evaluated.

The THA played a dominant role in the conversion of *Kombinate* and VEB companies under the old socialist planning system into a decentralized economy functioning on market principles. It not only had to restructure the old forms of organization completely, but also supervise the companies during this process of transition. Nevertheless, the establishment of a really independent and functioning privatization institution was very difficult to begin with, as the problems of the 'leaderless phase' up to the middle of 1991 have shown. The THA therefore had to work with highly simplified management instruments, such as the introduction of tight budget constraints on the individual companies, or the use of the holding company concepts as an instrument of corporate governance. Nevertheless the decentralized restructuring concept chosen by the THA, working through the appointment of Supervisory and Advisory Boards and decentralized support by the THA branches, proved to be an effective management model for management transfer and paved the way to successful restructuring and privatization, particularly since the middle of 1991. The horizontal, vertical, and geographical unbundling of the old *Kombinate* and their companies are important direct interventions on the company structures. In the first 18 months of its existence, however, uncontrolled, autonomous unbundling was of considerable significance. The different forms of privatization, (for example reprivatization, communalization or partial privatization) changed corporate structures further: their indirect structural effects can, however, only be seen as a by-product of the privatization process.

Despite its enormous size and the scope of the legal measures it employed, the THA's ability to influence each sector's industrial structures was limited. This is partly connected with the fact that, although large parts of the economy were subservient to it, not all were.[74] Its scope for exerting further restructuring influence of course declined with its own success as privatization progressed. Even in those sectors in which the THA had complete control its creative scope was partly limited by statutory requirements (such as communalization and restitution) or political considerations. For example in companies faced with inevitable liquidation decisions, statutory regulations and budget limitations often delayed such difficult decisions.

Through the policy of rapid privatization, the problem of effective company supervision and restructuring was quickly solved, especially through management and technology transfer from acquiring companies. But the question of a more active implementation of corporate restructuring strategies in the remaining companies took on a growing significance as time passed and its supervision tools continued to be improved. The development of more systematic reporting procedures, the systematic evaluation of remaining managers, and if negative their replacement were growing signs of improving corporate governance.[75] The development of the concept of Management KGs was also an initiative in this direction.

Similarly, where whole sectors had to be restructured, sector specific corporate strategies were prepared more frequently under direct THA supervision, for example for the shipyards, the chemical and the steel industry, then the decentralized approach suggests. This also included the task of creating effective sectoral competitive structures and reducing barriers to market entry, often after a little gentle pressure from the Federal Cartel

Office.[76] The active search for foreign investors not only improved the competitive situation in the various industries but also created additional demand for the companies still awaiting privatization. The release of property no longer required for operations as a result of spatial unbundling was helpful in facilitating market access for new companies. The exit from the market, or liquidation, of companies no longer capable of being restructured was also related to the creation of an effective competitive structure. Although the THA has often been accused that it subsidized unprofitable companies for too long, thus distorting competition.[77] this could sometimes be justified as part of the socially acceptable liquidation of moribund companies.

A further goal of privatization was to raise the proportion of independent owners of capital in Eastern Germany. However there was too little capital in the form of savings available in Eastern Germany, and even the banks tended to be cautious in financing the corporate strategies of East German SMEs. The THA's initiatives to encourage the growth of SME, principally using the instruments of MBO and MBI, together with so-called 'mini' privatization (retail trade, restaurants and cafés, hotels, and so on) became nevertheless an important building block in the creation of a true, local business-owning class in Eastern Germany.

The aim of also 'creating jobs through privatization' was impossible to achieve however, as private or public restructuring (via the THA) of companies tended to have just the opposite effect. On top of that, especially for tradable goods, came the effect of globalization and the politically supported increase of salaries towards Western German wage levels far beyond the growth in labor productivity. The resulting fall-off in production and employment, particularly in manufacturing industry, could hardly be compensated for by positive factors in the other sectors such as craft enterprises and the remaining services. By the middle of 1993, some 80 per cent of the old industrial jobs were lost.

Nevertheless, the THA's restructuring policy was a successful one particularly viewed against the background of the difficult macro economic conditions of the time and the need to establish itself first as a functioning institution. This is also showed by a glance at the sector privatization summary given in Figures 7.2 and 7.3, which make it clear that privatization, measured by the number of companies involved, and even more clearly when measured by the number of employees involved, was extraordinarily difficult and time consuming in exactly those areas in which, compared to West Germany, companies tended to have far too many employees anyway.[78] It was principally in the old industrial core areas of the East German economy, such as engineering, metal production, and steel processing that the rate of privatization (measured in terms of numbers employees) was slowest (see Figure 7.2).

The Difference with Germany

We have rationalized the THA policy of rapid privatization (rather than state-led restructuring) and privatization through sales – with openness to all purchasers (rather than a policy of voucher giveaways) as a superior solution, at least in terms of economic efficiency. This privatization model used by the THA, which relied on rapid privatization (and the associated private restructuring), often in the form of horizontal mergers with mainly West German firms on the one hand, and state-aided restructuring under the tutelage of the Western managers in the THA on the other (and the associated management transfer) can be explained with a model of management transfer, which is developed in more detail by Dyck (1993, 1997). But this THA model is less well suited to environments where a newly transferred manager also requires a knowledge of idiosyncratic features of a country including societal norms and language. Under those circumstances, indigenous Eastern managers arguably have a higher level of such skills than imported Western managers, so that restructuring with the old managers makes more sense. Even 'inside' Western managers transferred from within firms after a horizontal merger would have no information advantage relative to 'outside' managers hired by a privatization agency. This privatization model has, therefore, according to Dyck (1997, p. 581) greater applicability to countries where idiosyncratic knowledge is less important relative to functional and restructuring skills. Possible indicators of the importance of functional and restructuring skills are a greater degree of international openness, use of developed country standards and regulations, and a minimal governmental role in allocating goods, capital, and services. Eastern Germany's integration into Western Germany, the use of a common language, and the high level of management transfer from Western to Eastern Germany suggest that Eastern German idiosyncratic knowledge was relatively unimportant in this case. The importance of knowledge of the German language and institutional system perhaps account for the overwhelming dominance of Western German purchasers of Eastern enterprises.

Dyck's principal message which is reinforced with this analysis – that reformers need to consider how privatization programs affect the need to replace managerial human capital – has broad implications even though few Eastern European countries can replicate the German privatization strategy. The extent of management replacement in Germany, where incumbent managers lacked the ability to block such changes, is a strong signal of the importance of management replacement in successful enterprise restructuring.[79] This also suggests that privatization policies open to foreigners are likely to have a higher return in countries where functional skills such as marketing, distribution, sales, controlling and knowledge of market economy institutions are more important relative to idiosyncratic knowledge of domestic language and institutions.[80] This issue is also likely to come up if North Korea were trying to implement such a radical restructuring policy. The greater the change in the economic environments of firms, the greater the need for management transfer as a prerequisite for successful restructuring. A recognition of the link between the design of privatization programs and the ability to facilitate needed management change suggests that both issues have to be kept in mind. Otherwise, the benefits from privatization policies may be negative, or counterproductive, as can be seen by the experience in some Eastern European countries. It also suggests how countries aside from Germany can take steps in their privatization programs to encourage appropriate restructuring and management change.

NOTES

1. This paper is based on earlier work, while the author worked at the German Institute for Economic Research (DIW) Berlin. Part of the research was based on a study for the Federal Economics Ministry (Müller, 1993), whose support for this project is greatfully acknowledged. I thank Alexander Dyck, who was visiting at the time, for many conceptual discussions, that found their way into this paper (and led to his dissertation on this theme, Dyck, 1993), Georg Merdian and numerous officials at the THA and some of the officials of East German companies.
2. It was once the largest holding company in the world, employing four million people in more than 8000 firms (later 14 000 as some large firms were separated). In just four and a-half years, the Treuhand privatized more than 13 800 firms and parts of firms.
3. Such as the voucher process that became popular in a number of post-socialist economies.
4. See Besanko et al. (1996) for a more complete treatment of these issues.
5. Thus sorting industries into those exhibiting significant market failures, and those not, would help to make this choice more effective. In those industries without market failures we would want an ownership structure that produces internal efficiency, while in industries with market failures we want not only internal efficiency but also allocative efficiency. See models to evaluate specific trade-offs found in Vickers and Yarrow (1985). Such stuies help to make it clear upon which parameters a preference for public or private ownership lies, in particular emphasis should be on the strength of managerial incentives.
6. There were also some 2000 smaller companies at the *Bezirk* or District level, mainly serving regional markets. In the field social facilities, the trade unions and the political parties were particularly unusual economic organizations, which ran some sizeable operations.
7. Some of the large *Kombinate* were allowed to operate their own foreign trade, and were in some cases highly successful. However, they were subordinate to the Minister for Foreign Trade and were only independent to a limited extent.
8. Measured in terms of proportion of employment, the significance of the food, forestry, and fishing sector, for instance, was almost twice as great as in West Germany. Such a distribution of employment, and the serious differences in productivity, naturally emphasise the importance of such low-productivity sectors as agriculture.
9. On this point, see Müller (1976).
10. This element had been particularely important in the restructuring of the Polish economy after transformation started.
11. The companies within each *Kombinate* after their nationalization tended of course to specialize along lines of business that followed the centralization of production within the *Kombinate*.

12. However, the horizontal unbundling of industrial monopolies was more difficult in newly created industries and sectors, where the technical linkages within the *Kombinate* had been largely optimized between plants. This also applied to the newly created industries with supply links in the other Comecon countries, where East German firms often had a central supply function for the whole Comecon.
13. The vertically integrated activities of the Warnow shipyard in Rostock prior to restructuring covered such stages as steel processing, rust protection, insulation, scrap metal recycling, a factory kitchen, industrial cleaning, carpentry, repair work, plant construction, interior furnishing, upholstery work, transport services, staff training, kindergartens, and so on. After restructuring, only the central functions of planning and administration, ship-building and ship repair, and the production of several consumer goods were left within the company. All other activities were hived off as outside services and privatised separately; see Albach (1992).
14. The THA established the *Treuhand-Liegenschafsgesellschaft mbH* or TLG (the THA real estate company) to handle these aspects of 'site' unbundling separately from privatisation.
15. Experience in the Eastern German states showed in fact that for the short term, if a company's assets were substantial, stripping off assets and consuming the proceeds was often more attractive to management than carrying out the necessary restructuring and dismissing redundant staff. The attraction was often very great for the THA companies because the company's chances of being categorized as capable of being restructured were increased the lower the losses it reported (or the fewer funds the THA had to guarantee it). However, such a strategy has no prospect of success in the long term and led to more negative value creation and to further squandering of economic resources. All the same, if geographical unbundling is forced on a company, it is essential that the company should be supervised and assisted financially in the process in order to ensure liquidity through difficult times. An example for living off one's own assets was practised by Saxonia AG of Freiberg (a company processing precious metals) up to the end of 1991. They financed their ongoing losses by selling their working capital of available silver. The company was thus only a tiny cash-gobbler, but it was also one of the THA's biggest loss-making companies.
16. It took over all the VEB companies and state farms, but not the socialist cooperatives.
17. It was once employing four million people in more than 8000 firms (later 14 000 as some large firms were separated).
18. This is in addition to the 3000 SME companies already reprivatized by the Modrow government early in 1990.
19. The four 'THA AGs' (heavy industry, capital goods industry, consumer goods industry, and services) were to be structured so as to cover a number of branches of industry each; see § 5 section 2 of the THA Statutes and appendix to the Statutes.
20. *Treuhandanstalt Informationen* 6 (October 1991), p. 6; THA, PE Tl/ih/ March 19, 1992. The word 'manage' should be regarded here more in the legal sense because in the early days there was never much scope for exerting direct influence on the running of the companies.
21. The appeal from the Chancellor to major Western German companies to second managers on loan for the rapid restructuring of the THA played a certain role here. See also Letter from Hero Brahms to the Minister-Presidents of the States on March 18, 1993.
22. The East German Companies Act of March 7, 1990 covered the return to private ownership of the companies expropriated in 1972.
23. At this time well-informed purchasers who were interested in specific parts of various Kombinate, and particularly in the lucrative fields of non-tradable goods, such as energy, insurance, banks and hotels, were able to buy them at bargain prices.
24. In the energy sector, some of these privatization contracts were signed even before German unification, for example in the power generation field, although because of legal objections these could not be implemented until the summer of 1994. The time gap was bridged by working with management contracts. Also, some 20 municipal utilities were established with the participation of Western power companies. The same applies in the field of brown coal (lignite) and the gas industry. By 1994, about 20 Western German companies had taken holdings in the newly independent regional gas supply companies. On this point, see Frisch (1992, p. 9)

25. From July 1, 1990 the THG converted all the remaining *Kombinate* into AG companies and all VEBs into GmbH companies.
26. The legal basis for the break-up of the *Kombinate* (or for hiving off parts of the former *Kombinate* or the converted AG companies) was initially § 12 section 3 of the THG, and later the Splitting Act as applied to the companies administered by the THA, which included these possibilities:

    a. splitting up the old companies and selling the shares, or
    b. splitting off a new company from the old one which remained in existence but handed some of its assets to the new, small unit, See Priester (1991, pp. 2373 et seq).

27. Even later the THA's more organized restructuring efforts, however, preceded by extensive managerial investigations, often ran into the same kind of problem.
28. Legislation reacted to the difficulties caused to privatisation by the Property Act of September 23, 1990 (restitution before compensation) with an amendment; see new version of the Property Act dated April 18, 1991, and preamble to the Removal of Obstacles Act of March 22, 1991.
29. It was not until March 11, 1991 that the Companies Data Bank was complete, on the basis of which it was possible to categorize them; see article by Seibel in Fischer et al. (1996).
30. The THA had to appoint Supervisory Board Chairmen for about 550 companies; nearly all of them came from western Germany. These chairmen then had to set up their Supervisory Board teams, with the assent of the THA, with half the seats being filled, under German codetermination law, by the employees' side, meaning particularly by the trade union representatives.
31. The THA's Industry Directorates played a consultative role; they were asked for their views prior to any major investments or restructuring of firms under their responsability.
32. The situation here is a little closer to that created by US company law, in which the 'Chairman' often plays a very active part.
33. On this point, see articles by Seibel and by Kern and Sabel in Fischer et al. (1996).
34. However, as the States themselves were not able to make any significant financial contribution to the restructuring process (except in the case of Carl Zeiss Jena), their direct influence remained relatively small. The role of the States in maintaining 'industrial cores areas' was somewhat more active, for example with such projects as ATLAS in Saxony.
35. On this point, see discussion in the article by Kern and Sabel and the article by Schmidt in this volume.
36. The THA pursued this idea in its policy of rapid privatization to investors which offered a workable corporate strategy. In contrast to this policy there is the privatization model based on the distribution of equity holdings through voucher privatization in which the shares are rapidly distributed (as in the Czech Republic) to the population at large, so that at least initially the share ownership is very widespread.
37. On this point, see article by Küpper in Fischer et al. (1996).
38. A further reason for the slack demand for THA companies, particularly those producing tradable goods, is that companies in Western Germany and other EC countries often had ultramodern production facilities, often not running at full capacity. It would therefore have made little sense for Western German and West European companies to invest more heavily in Eastern German companies in the same industries.
39. If one compares the total proceeds from privatization realised up to June 30, 1993 of DM 43.5 billion with promised investment undertakings totalling DM 180.1 billion, the proportion is about 1:4.
40. On this point, see Hax, *Privatization Agencies.*
41. If privatization is carried out with vouchers, the concentration of decision making into a small number of hands first has to be carried out through the secondary market, for example through banks or investment trusts.
42. There were also financial reasons for lengthening the privatization phase. The mass of companies awaiting privatization – the 'stock' – is faced by a limited amount of savings in the population, which represents a 'flow'. Theoretically at least, this could mean that the

proceeds of a fast privatization should be very low indeed. On this point, see: G. and H.-W. Sinn, *Kaltstart*. This 'stock/flow' problem can, however, be solved by the THA selling more slowly and privatizing its companies only partly. On this point, see Neldner's discussion of G. and H.-W. Sinn's book *Kaltstart*. He does not consider this argument particularly convincing when looked at against the background of the THA's small revenue from sales; see also endnote 38 above. In the case of agricultural land, long leases are one way of dealing with this problem. It was for this reason that the BVVG, the THN's land sale and administration company, was established in September 1992. 75 per cent of its capital is held by banks.

43. But as a rule, the THA only permitted 'investor neutral' investments, which over the course of time and without privatization tended to worsen the companies' chances of survival.
44. As compared to the case of public utilities referred to above.
45. See Letter from Hero Brahms to the Minister-Presidents of the States dated March 18, 1993, and Müller, *Managementtransfer in die neuen Bundesländer*.
46. For a slightly different view on this, see G. and H.-W. Sinn, *Kaltstart*.
47. They had either been handed back to their previous owners (reprivatization) or sold on to new ones, with 1 481 000 jobs taken over or guaranteed and investments promised totaling DM 180.1 billion On this point, see also Figure 7.3 above; and Treuhandanstalt, *Monatsinformation der THA* as of July 31, 1993.
48. The THA companies grouped by status (communalized, reprivatized, liquidated or in liquidation, privatized, and still on the THA's books) in Figure 7.1, however, are just presenting number of cases privatized. They are not weighted by numbers employed or value created, so that the structural effects of the THA's activities are only vaguely indicated by these shares. Also, the status groups only partly match up with the three components of structural market change mentioned in section 7.3 above. We will go into this problem in more detail below.
49. On this point, see articles by König and by Willgerodt in Fischer et al. (1996).
50. See Treuhandanstalt, *Monatsinformation der THA* as of July 31, 1993.
51. See Figures 7.3 and 7.3 in this text.
52. On this point, see Gruhler (1992).
53. By the end of July 1993, foreign investors had acquired 732 THA companies or parts of companies (5.7 per cent of all privatizations), undertaking to invest a total of DM 18.9 billion (10 per cent of the total) and guaranteeing 140 779 jobs (likewise 10 per cent); Treuhandanstalt, *Monatsinformation der THA*, as of July31, 1993.
54. However, this only covers a proportion of the THA's privatization activitieis because this data set sets a threshold of DM 500 million for the purchaser. Frisch (1993).
55. This applies at least when based on the number of companies being privatized.
56. According to: Friedrich, *Management Buy-out,* 66 per cent of the companies privatised by MBO/MBI have fewer than 50 employees, and only 16 per cent of them employed more than 100 at the time they were taken over by their own management.
57. Op. cit.
58. An investigation carried out on behalf of the Federal Ministry for Economic Affairs in 1993 (see Friedrich, *Management Buy-out)* showed that in most MBOs the desire to preserve the participants' own job and those of their subordinates was the prime factor rather than any desire to become a self-employed business person. Some 74 per cent of these companies were, according to that survey in at least a satisfactory situation, although in some cases there was still a certain amount of risk attaching to them. Only 5 per cent of the MBOs/MBIs had failed, as of March 1993, although another 10 per cent were in difficult economic straits.
59. No statement is possible on the restructuring measures and the expenditure incurred by the former owners on adaptation to changed times in comparison with the new owners of 'freshly' privatized businesses, but they complain that, because of their having to accept the historic debt and the risk of historic environmental pollution of their companies, they are often more badly treated than investors in 'fresh' privatizations; the latter are partly or completely let off these obligations by the THA in order to bring the purchase price up above zero. In order to ensure that all business owners start on comparable terms, however,

the THA improved the position of some reprivatized companies retroactively if they are having a particularly hard time of it. On this point, see article by Willgerodt in Fischer et al. (1996).

60. The demarcation criteria for *Mittelstand* companies are supposed to be an upper limit of 500 employees, including the smallest companies with fewer than 20 employees and all craft enterprises.
61. The greatest growth in employment came in the branches of the economy associated with construction. On this point, see *Süddeutsche Zeitung* of June 8, 1993.
62. On this point, see DIW, *Wochenbericht* 11 (1992).
63. ABM is *Arbeits–beschaffungsmaßnahmen,* 'measures for creating jobs', and ABS is *Arbeisförderung, Beschäftigung und Strukturentwicklung,* 'promotion of work, employment, and structural development' On this point, see Kern and Sabel in Fischer et al. (1996).
64. The THA's role concerning these labor market policy instruments was laid down in a joint declaration dated April 13, 1991 by the THA, the DGB (the German Federation of Trade Unions), and the DAG (Trade Union of German Employees, for salaried staff, the largest union not affiliated to the DGB) on regulations for redundancy compensation plan (the so-called social plans): the THA 'gave particular support to companies in the use of the statutory instruments of promotion of work, especially in further vocational training, retraining, and work familiarization, and in job creation schemes in the companies in which the employees are threatened with the loss of their jobs'. Reprinted in *Treuhandanstalt Informationen* 3/4 (July/August 1991), p. 23.
65. See above, Section 7.5.
66. It supported major ABM projects by providing interest-free loans and bearing some of their costs (up to 10 per cent of total costs, and recently up to 20 per cent, to be used as a contribution to material costs). It regarded the limited (negotiable) allocation of some property and tangible assets of THA companies to them as one measure designed to this end; these assets have as a rule already been transferred to the THA's property agency, the TLG.
67. On this point, see Outline agreement dated July 17, 1991; Härtel et al. (1992).
68. See Hans-Böckler-Stiftung (eds): *Qualifizierungs und Beschäftigungsinitiativen*, p. 3.
69. In some cases liquidation procedures have shown that the separate parts of the company were capable of being privatized (for example *Pentacon Dresden, MZ Zschopau)* while whole companies could not. In other cases, when liquidation was ordered, it was road-blocked by the employees who thus forced a 'normal' privatization (for example *Addinol Mineral öl GmbH).*
70. See McKinsey & Company, *Überlegungen zur kurzfristigen Stabilisierung.*
71. See Gruhler, *Unternehmensbezogene Umstrukturierung in den neuen Bundesländern.*
72. On this point, see article by Schwalbach in Fischer et al. (1996).
73. On this point, see articles by Kern and Sabel, and by Schwalbach, in Fischer et al. (1996).
74. By way of a few examples: the railways, the post office, banks, health care, and libraries. Compared with a total number of people in employment in eastern Germany of about 7.7 million on January 1, 1991, even during the phase of the 'great' THA only about 3 million people were employed in its companies; by April 1, 1993 the proportion was down to 0.4 million out of a total of 6.2 million.
75. In an internal working document, the THA director of personel reported that 1800 Eastern managers had been dismissed, because of reported lack of skills or illegal activities (Wagner, 1991).
76. On this point, see Härtel et al., *Unternehmenssanierung und Wettbewerb in den neuen Bundesländern*; Frisch, *Untemehmenszusammenschlüsse in den neuen Bundesländern.*
77. For instance, the Bundesbank discovered in 1993, after analyzing the balance sheets of 863 Eastern German companies for 1991, that they had a return on sales of minus 13.5 per cent; the figure in manufacturing industry was minus 23 per cent.
78. Agriculture and forestry, energy, mining, leather/textiles, see Table 7.1 above.
79. For example, many East European privatization policies gave incumbent management significant stakes. This shareholding increased managerial incentives, but by entrenching management made it very difficult to introduce the replacement of human capital that is

critical to successful restructuring. Also costly were privatization plans that avoided managerial entrenchment by distributing a significant fraction of shares to the domestic populace through various voucher schemes. This suggests that unless voucher privatization was coupled with possible purchase of shares by foreign firms, the newly privatized state enterprises will have difficulty making the required changes with existing management, and will face additional costs in purchasing those skills on the labor market because of adverse selection. Relative to the government, the domestic populace has no better information about productivity levels of Western managers with the required functional skills (Dyck, 1997).

80. In countries where functional skills are important, but foreign direct investment on a large scale is not politically feasible or introduces additional costs, Dyck (1997) suggests that owners should recruit Western managers in the early stages of privatization and tailor their recruitment policies to overcome potential informational asymmetries. Potential mechanisms include screening, signaling, and rewarding managers through performance-contingent contracts. Attempts to recruit Western management for mutual funds in the Polish privatization scheme have exploited such policies.

BIBLIOGRAPHY

Albach, Horst (1992), *The 1992 Uppsala Lectures in Business*, WHU, Koblenz.

Barberis, Nicholas, Boycko, Maxim, Shleifer, Andrei and Tsukanova, Natalia (1996), 'How does Privatization Work? Evidence from the Russian Shops', *Journal of Political Economy*, August, **104** (4), 764–90.

Besanko, D., D. Dranove and M. Shanley (1996), *The Economics of Strategy*, John Wiley & Sons, Inc., New York.

Boycko, Maxim (1996), 'A Theory of Privatization', *Economic Journal*, March, **106** (435), 309-19.

Boycko, Maxim, Shleifer, Andrei and Vishny, Robert (1993), 'Privatizing Russia', *Brookings Papers on Economic Activity*, no. 2, 139–81.

Carlin, Wendy and Mayer, Colin (1994), 'The Treuhandanstalt: Privatization by State and Market', in Oliver Blanchard, Ken Froot and Jeffrey Sachs (eds), *The Transition in Eastern Europe*, vol. 2, Chicago: University of Chicago Press, 189–207.

Demougin, D. and Sinn, Hans Werner (1992), 'Privatization, Risk-taking and Communist Firm', *National Bureau of Economic Research* (Cambridge, MA) Working Paper no. 4205.

Deutsche Bundesbank (1993), 'Bilanzrelationen und Ertragsverhältnisse ostdeutscher Unternehmen im Jahre 1991', in: *Monatsbericht*, July, 27–39.

Deutsches Institut für Wirtschaftsforschung (DIW, ed.) (1992), *Analyse der strukturellen Entwicklung der deutschen Wirtschaft*, Strukturberichterstattung, *Gutachten im Auftrag des Bundesministeriums für Wirtschaft*, Berlin.

Deutsches Institut für Wirtschaftsforschung (DIW, ed.), 'Gesamtwirtschaftliche und unternehmerische Anpassungsprozesse in Ostdeutschland', Berichte 1 bis 8, in: *Wochenbericht* 12 (1991), 24 (1991), 39 and 40 (1991), 51 and 52 (1991), 12 and 13 (1992), and 13 (1993).

Deutsches Institut für Wirtschaftsforschung (DIW, ed.) (1992), 'Industrieller Mittelstand in Ostdeutschland', in *Wochenbericht*, 11.

Deutsches Institut für Wirtschaftsforschung (DIW, ed.) (1991), 'Subventionierung und Privatisierung durch die Treuhandanstalt – Kurswechsel erforderlich', in: *Wochenbericht*, 41.

Dyck, Alexander (1993), *Imperfect Information, Ownership and Incentives*, Dissertation, Stanford University.

Dyck, Alexander (1997), 'Privatization in Eastern Germany: Management Selection and Economic Transition', *American Economic Review*, **87** (4), 565–97.

Fischer, Wolfram, Hax, Herbert and Schneider, Hans Karl (eds) (1996), *Treuhandgesellschaft, The Impossible Challenge*, Berlin: Akademie Verlag.

Friedrich, Werner (1992), *Management Buy-out and Management Buy-in, Untersuchung im Auftrag des Bundesministers für Wirtschaft*, DIW, Cologne.

Frisch, Thomas (1993), 'Untemehmenszusammenschlüsse in den neuen Bundesländern' *HWWA-Report*, no. 119, Hamburg.

Görzig, Bernd and Martin Goming (1991), *Produktivitdt und Wettbewerbsfähigkeit der Wirtschaft der DDR*, DIW Report, Berlin.

Gruhler, Wolfram (1992), *Unternehmensbezogene Umstrukturierung in den neuen Bundesländern*, DIW, Cologne.

Hans-Böckler-Stiftung (ed.) (1992), *Qualifizierungs und Beschäftigungsinitiativen. Bericht über eine Umfrage in den neuen Bundesländern*, Düsseldorf, May.

Härtel, Hans-Hagen, Reinald Krüger, Joachim Seeler, and Marisa Weinhold (1992), 'Unternehmenssanierung und Wettbewerb in den neuen Bundesländern. Fünfter und sechster Zwischenbericht gemäß dem Forschungsauftrag des Bundeswirtschaftsministeriums Beobachtung und Analyse des Wettbewerbs in den neuen Bundesländem', *HWWA-Report* nos 100 and 103, Hamburg.

Hax, Herbert: Privatization Agencies (1992), 'The Treuhand Approach', in: Horst Siebert (ed.): Privatization Symposium in Honor of Herbert Giersch, *Tübingen*, 143–155.

Heseler, Herbert and Heike Löser (1992), *Die Transformation des ostdeutschen Schiffsbaus PIWIBastro*, Rostock.

McKinsey & Company (1991), 'Überlegungen zur kurzfristigen Stabilisierung und langfristigen Steigerung der Wirtschaftskraft in den neuen Bundesländern', Diisseldorf and München.

Meinhardt, Volker, Bernhard Seidel, Frank Stille and Dieter Teichmann (1993), 'Vorläufige Berechnungen zu den Transferleistungen in den NBL', DIW.

Müller, Jürgen (1976), 'The Impact of Mergers on Concentration', *The Journal of Industrial Economics*, December, pp. 113 et seq.

Müller, Jürgen (1993), 'Managementtransfer in die neuen Bundesländer Schwerpunktthema zum Gutachten: Gesamtwirtschaftliche und untemehmerische Anpassungsprozesse im Gebiet der früheren DDR', Berlin, July.

Neldner, M. (1993), 'Buchbesprechung', in Zeitschrift für Wirtschaftsund Sozialwissenschaften 13, p. 142.

Priester, Hans-Joachim (1991), 'Gesellschaftsrechtliche Zweifelsfragen beim Umgang mit Treuhandunternehmen', in: *Der Betrieb* 1, 2373–8.

Sappington, David E.M. and Stiglitzt, Joseph (1987), 'Privatization, Information and Incentives', *Journal of Policy Analysis and Management*, Summer, **6** (4), 567–82

Shapiro, Carl and Willig, Robert D (1990), 'Economic Rationales for the Scope of Privatization' Discussion Paper no. 41, Princeton University,

Siebert, Horst (1991), 'German Unification and the Economics of Transition', *Institut für Weltwirtschaft, Working Papers* no. 468, Kiel.

Sinn, Gerlinde and Sinn, Hans-Wemer (1992), *Kaltstart,* Volkswirtschaftlich Aspekte der deutschen Vereinigung, Tübingen.

Statistisches Jahrbuch der Bundesrepublik Deutschland (1989), edited by the Statistisches Bundesamt, Wiesbaden.

Statistisches Jahrbuch der Deutschen Demokratischen Republik 34 (1989), edited by

the Staatliche Zentralverwaltung fiir Statistik, Berlin.
Süddeutsche Zeitung, June 8, 1993.
Treuhandanstalt Informationen, various issues.
Treuhandanstalt (1993), Monatsinformation der THA as of July 31.
Vicker J. and Yarrow, G. (1985), Privatization and the Natural Monopolies, London: Public Policy Center.
Wagner, H. and Statusbericht (1991), Management-Transfer West-Ost, THA internal document, Berlin.

PART FIVE

The Availablability of Social Infrastructure

8. Transformation of the Telecommunications Infrastructure in North Korea

Chang-Ho Yoon and Young Soo Lee

8.1 INTRODUCTION

Many of the former communist leaders like Joseph Stalin were reluctant to extend telecommunication networks to private homes, believing that there could be no better counter-revolution than the telephone. It is no wonder that horizontal communication among households and businesses is still very limited in North Korea, where civilian contacts with the Western world have been banned for a long time and secrecy is mostly welcome as a means to avoid criticism and preserve authority. Out of its one million main telephone lines, only about 10 per cent are owned by individuals. No telephone directory is circulated in North Korea and telephone numbers for government offices are not publicly listed.

The severe restrictions on the civilian use of telecom networks discouraged commercial application of telecom services, and any investment in telecom infrastructure in North Korea had to be financed by the central government. Those who have private access to the public network, namely members of the privileged class, have been subsidized by very low tariffs. The revenue per telephone line in North Korea is less than one-tenth of the average revenue per line in OECD countries.

In addition to institutional limitations on the use of a telecommunications network, there are several industry characteristics that discourage investments in a poor country like North Korea. Telecommunication service is very capital-intensive and has a long pay-off period. The networks have to be internationally linked and must satisfy international quality standards. In fact, due to rapid technical progress, the most modern digital technology has the highest potential pay-off. Furthermore, to utilize network externalities, the network size has to be greater than a certain critical level. Unless the government takes the strong initiative to extend the scope of the civilian use of telecom services and utilizes foreign capital and technology to modernize infrastructure, North Korea is not likely to capture the benefits of technological progress in information technology in the global economy. The dilemma that North Korea confronts is that any credible measure toward this direction could threaten the very foundation of the incumbent regime.

As time passes, however, North Korea seems to have very few options other than to admit the importance of the information infrastructure. During the recent period of drastic and continuing economic decline triggered by the loss of Soviet aid and exports in the early 1990s, North Korea's foreign trade contracted sharply from US$4.71 billion in 1990 to US$2.18 billion in 1997. Foreign debt surged to US$12 billion, reaching a debt/GDP ratio of somewhere between 70 to 110 per cent. For better or worse, the economy has become more dependent on foreign trade and aid than ever, and is bound to be gradually integrated into the global economy. North Korea finds it increasingly difficult to extol the virtue of self-reliance and seems to be considering various reform measures to revitalize its collapsing economy by attracting foreign capital and technology. The incumbent regime seems to be walking on a tight rope, balancing the demands of both the hard-liners and the reform-minded technocrats.

Recently, North Korea undertook some measure to prepare for the global information society. The most ambitious project to modernize its information infrastructure started in the middle of the economic crises of the 1990s. North Korea invested quite heavily (by their standards) in the telecom infrastructure. With the support from UNDP, North Korea installed its first 300-km fiber-optical cable from Pyongyang to Hamheung in 1995, which is being extended to Rajin–Sonbong Economic and Trade Zone (RSETZ). As of September 1998, 35 major cities and counties were connected by fiber-optical cables and 15 more are scheduled to be added to this network, including an optical cable connecting Sinuiju, Pyongyang and Panmunjum. In fact, North Korea seems to have established its optical trunk lines connecting all the major industrial and urban areas in the west as well as the east.

These networks have been mainly used for vertical linkages from Pyongyang to local areas and upgrading of local networks for horizontal communication is still at the incipient stage. If North Korea attempts to revitalize its economy in a market-friendly way, however, it has to activate individual initiatives and let people have access to efficient means of exchanging their ideas. There began to appear some signs that North Korea was willing to recognize individual initiatives in rebuilding the collapsed economy. Reform measures such as a constitutional amendment to introduce cost accounting in economic management would increase managerial responsibility, and freedom of travel would eventually encourage horizontal communication.

Notwithstanding temporal inconsistency and erratic reversal of reform measures observed in recent times, one can pose the question whether North Korea can profitably transform its telecom structure in a market-friendly way. The experience of many transitional economies illustrates that the pattern of demand growth across sectors and regions is quite uneven. For example, in a developing economy like China, the tele-density in the largest city increased from 5 per cent in 1992 to more than 20 per cent in 1997, while the tele-density in rural areas still remained less than 1 per cent. A similar pattern of growth is also seen in Vietnam. In both countries, the average revenue per line now well exceeds the operating cost and will eventually pay back the initial investment costs.[1] It shows that North Korea can also start to build its local fiber networks in major industrial and urban areas, and can profitably charge cost-based tariffs for business users and relatively rich residential customers. It can then use these profits for universal connectivity in the later stage of development. Potential growth in demand for telecom service in North Korea is great enough to attract strategic investors. Especially, if both Koreas allow people to communicate freely, demand growth from network externalities will be astronomical.

If North Korea can carry out necessary legislative changes, it can consider several different versions of reform strategies that may be used as a vehicle for delivering higher investment and efficiency. The most dramatic strategy is a so-called competition strategy where all the telecommunications markets are fully liberalized at the earliest possible date. This strategy is currently unimaginable in North Korea and leaves the possibility that foreign investors will concentrate only on inelastic demand, and thus prefer projects with a short pay-off period to long-term projects with high initial investment. In such a scenario, the telecommunication needs of large businesses or foreign companies with an ability to pay in hard currency are satisfied first. As a result, once the urgent urban business demand is met, small businesses and individuals who cannot afford the expensive phones are left out of the market, and there will be less pressure to expand the backbone network. There is no assurance that the competition strategy will bring welfare optimal deployment of telecommunications infrastructure and lessen the burden of universal service responsibility in North Korea.

The alternative and more plausible reform strategy is to begin by commercializing Public Telephone Operator and eventually sell its shares to strategic foreign investors, granting a monopoly right in a specified region over a certain period of time. In specifying rights and obligations of the privatized carrier, the government may set the target for expansion of the backbone network as well as quality improvement. The government can also introduce competition in new service areas indirectly by auctioning off franchises in mobile or cellular services in several different industrial and urban areas. To sustain an efficient market structure several regulatory measures may be needed. Particularly, credible commitment to cost-based tariff adjustment is necessary to attract foreign investment. Foreign investors must have confidence in the regulatory framework for setting tariffs and in the autonomy of the regulatory agency for fair competition and efficient network interconnection among the service providers.

This paper explores the variants of the second strategy by examining the nature of technology and simulating structural imbalances between demand and supply that North Korea will experience after it begins to transform its economy. Based upon our estimate of the minimal initial investment level, we attempt to identify policy options for North Korea by evaluating various development strategies adopted in the other transition economies.

8.2 TELECOMMUNICATIONS DEPLOYMENT IN NORTH KOREA

Economic Growth and Telecommunications Infrastructure

Poor infrastructure is one of the major obstacles to economic development. Building infrastructure in North Korea, however, is a formidable task. Modern telecom infrastructure that connects major industrial and urban areas alone would require billions of US dollars. Such a huge amount of capital would certainly be difficult to mobilize domestically in a poverty-ridden starving economy. North Korea must make every effort to reform its economy and install advanced facilities and technologies from the developed countries.

Although the demand for telecommunications services used to be strongly dependent on the stage of economic development, telecommunications development itself has strong multiplier effects on economic growth by encouraging technological development not only in traditional manufacturing and agricultural areas but also in those sectors with high technological components. A basic information infrastructure, connected with the Global Information Infrastructure, will help North Korea transform its declining economy by facilitating trade and investment in an increasingly borderless economy.

Figure 8.1 shows the relationship between per capita income and tele-density. In an economy with over US$6000 per capita income, tele-density increases sharply relative to the gain in per capita income, while in a economy with less than US$6000 income, tele-density increases linearly with per capita income.

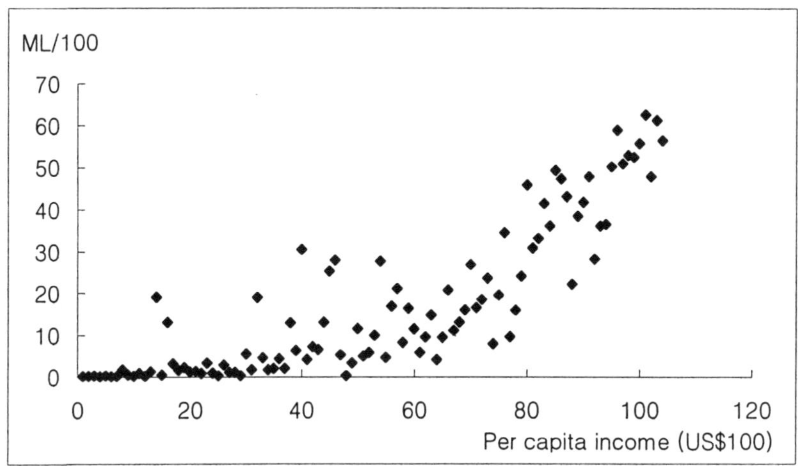

Figure 8.1 The Relationship between GDP per Capita and Tele-density

Table 8.1 Tele-density as a Function of GDP per Capita

ML/100 Inhabitant	Constant	GDP per capita	R^2
Lower income	−7.28 (−0.8)	1.58 (1.1)	0.003
Lower-middle Income	−63.33 (−2.8)	9.91 (3.2)	0.19
Upper-middle Income	−97.06 (−3.4)	13.66 (4.0)	0.35
High income	−118.17 (−2.9)	16.61 (4.2)	0.33

Notes: Figures in parentheses represent t-values.

To understand this relationship in more detail we divide countries into four groups and run the regression between tele-density and per capita income for each income group.[2] All variables are in log form so that the estimated parameters represent the elasticity of each variable. The estimation results are shown in Table 8.1. As per capita income increases, the tele-density increases at an ascending rate, except for the low-income group, whose estimated coefficient is only 1.58 and statistically insignificant. The estimated coefficients for the lower-middle, upper-middle and high-income classes are 9.91, 13.66 and 16.61, respectively. This shows that the income elasticity of tele-density turns out to be far greater than one, and accordingly the demand for telecommunications service will increase much faster than income growth. It also implies that any attempt to forecast social demands for telecommunications infrastructure must be based on the potential economic growth in the future rather than current income

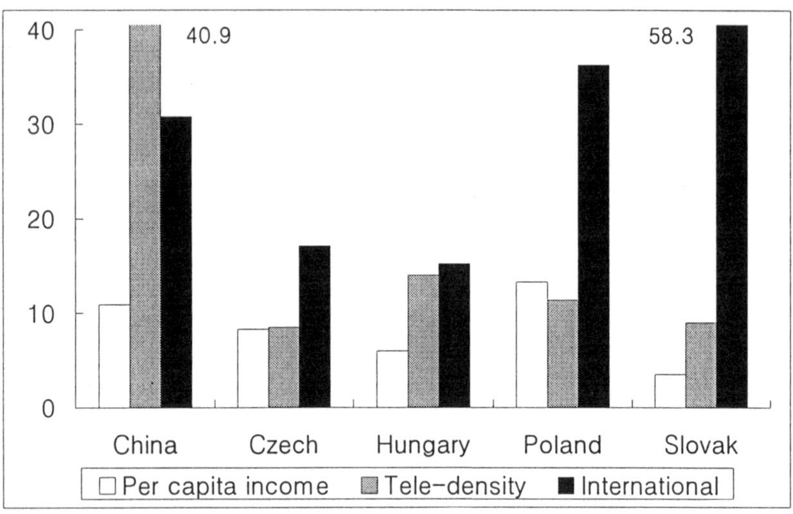

Source: ITU, *World Telecommunication Indicator Database.*

Figure 8.2 Per Capita Income, Tele-density and International Outgoing Traffic in Transitional Economies (1990–95 Annual Growth Rate)

The above argument holds strong for the successfully transforming economies in Central and Eastern Europe (CEE) as well as East Asia. Figure 8.2 shows the growth rates of per capita GDP, tele-density and the volume of outgoing international telephone traffic in transition economies from 1990 to 1995. In China, the annual growth rate of per capita income stays at 10 per cent, while the annual growth rate of tele-density reaches 40.9 per cent, and international outgoing traffic, 30 per cent. Hungary and the Slovakia Republic show a similar pattern of growth. In the Czech Republic and Poland, per capita income and tele-density grow more or less at the same rate, but the volume of international traffic shows a much higher annual growth rate.

Target Tele-density to Achieve International Competitiveness

Present situation of North Korea's telecommunications

North Korea once set a goal to install two million new lines through the third seven-year economic development plan (1987–1993). But in the absence of official performance records, it is difficult to obtain reliable information about the actual deployment rate. According to *Naewoe Press,* October 21, 1996, North Korea had 600 thousand main telephone lines as of late 1995.

Table 8.2 Telecommunication in North Korea

	1993	1995	1996
Main lines in operation	1 089 300	1 100 000	1 100 000
ML per 100 inhabitant	4.7	4.61	4.90
ML per 100 inhabitant of largest city	8.5	8.45	8.18
Number of local telephone calls (million)	2386	–	–
Interantional outgoing telephone traffic (thousand minutes)	3072	3100	3800
International incoming telephone traffic (thousand minutes)	3127	–	–
Residential telephone connection charge (US$)	47.4	47.4	47.4
Business telephone connection charge (US$)	47.4	47.4	47.4
Residential monthly telephone subscription (US$)	7.1	7.1	7.1
Business monthly telephone subscription (US$)	11.4	11.4	11.4
Telecommunication revenue (million US$)	0.58	–	–
Telecommunication investment (million US$)	3.00	–	–

Source: ITU (1997f, 1998a), *World Telecommunication Development Report*; ITU (1998b), *World Telecommunication Indicator Database.*

But ITU (International Telecommunications Union) recently reported that the number of main lines in operation in North Korea reached 1 million in the early 1990s (Table 8.2). These statistics are contradictory and certainly not reliable. It seems that many lines are outdated, 400 000 of which are operating through manual switching.[3]

The telecommunications network in North Korea is characterized by a centralized system of vertical linkages connecting Pyongyang with 9 provinces (*do*), 24 cities (*shi*), 139 counties (*kun*), 3311 villages (*ri*) and 251 labor districts. The vertical network is used mainly for administrative purposes connecting various regional jurisdictions and major industrial bases. The telephone network in North Korea consists of optical cables connecting major cities and counties through Pyongyang, and copper wire and coaxial cable for the other trunk lines and local loops. Wireless network is reserved for the case of mainline breakdown and used in mountainous areas where no fixed lines are available. Despite the limited use of the telecom network and capital shortage, North Korea has invested rather surprisingly in expanding its fiber-optic network and upgrading its network for digital communication such as ISDN. In fact, with support from UNDP, North Korea installed its first 300-km fiber-optic cable from Pyongyang to Hamheung in September 1995, which has recently been being extended to RSETZ.[4] To facilitate telecommunication services in RSETZ, North Korea established a joint venture, called Northeast Asia Telephone and Telegraph (NEATT) on a BOT basis with Roxley Pacific Company (Roxpac) and granted a monopoly right for 27 years starting in 1995. NEATT has installed 95-km of fiber-optic cable connecting Hunchun of Gilim, China, with the Rajin–Sonbong Area, which is eventually connected to Pyongyang. Roxpac initially planned to install 400 000 mainlines that would cost US$500 million. But as the foreign direct investment in RSETZ fell short of initial expectations, Roxpax ended up installing only 5000 fixed mainlines, 500 lines of mobile phones and 80 public phones. To cope with the financial burden of risky long-term investments in North Korea, Roxpac is now seeking a partner, possibly in South Korea.

In addition to this adventurous joint venture in RSETZ, North Korea expanded its backbone network rather rapidly. The government recently advertised in *Naewoe Press*, September 28, 1998, that it had already established an optical-fiber backbone network linking 35 major cities and counties, and 15 more cities and counties would be connected to this network by the end of 1998. This includes trunk lines from Pyongyang to Sinuiju, and from Pyongyang to Kaesung via Sariwon (Figure 8.3).

The international telecommunications network in North Korea consists of the fixed-line network connecting Pyongyang, Peking and Moscow and the fixed-line network connecting Chungjin and Vladivostok. North Korea depends on satellite networks to connect Pyongyang to the USA and Japan, and relies on a microwave network to connect Singapore and Hong Kong. Since joining INTERSPUTNIK in 1984, North Korea is operating 22 lines of FDM, and 10 lines of SCPC for communication with East Europe. Thanks to the technical assistance from France in 1986, North Korea established a branch of INTELSAT satellites over the Indian Ocean and is operating 36 lines of FDM and 18 lines of SCPC, through which satellite communication and TV transmission from Western countries are possible. In November 1990, an agreement was reached between North Korea and Japan to open 3 telephone lines, 10 telex lines, and 1 telegram line. In addition, 24 microwave and 15 cable network lines began to operate. In 1995, AT&T arranged a direct telecommunication link between North Korea and the USA. According to *Rodong-Shinmoon,* October 6, 1996, North Korea is now well equipped with computer facilities to digitalize satellite communications.

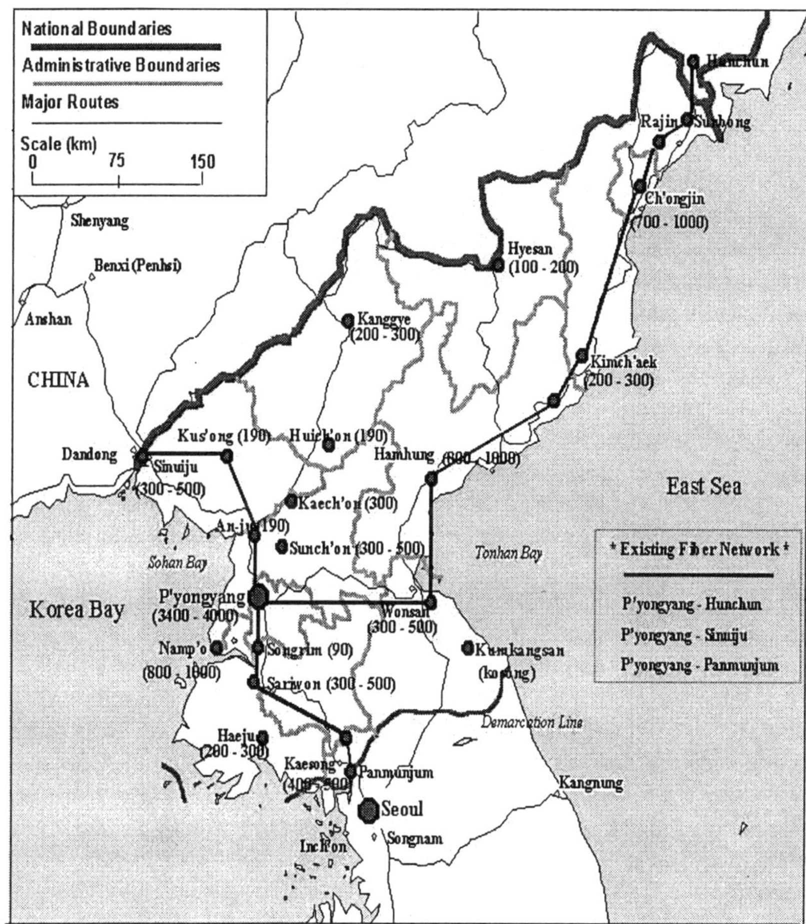

Figure 8.3 Fiber-optical Trunk Lines in North Korea

Public phones, which are the people's main access to telecommunication, are installed on the main streets and in department stores and hotels of large cities like Pyongyang and Hamheung. In towns and counties, two or three public phones are located in postal offices. Where public phones are not available, people use the telephones in local public offices or business centers, which report their calls. However, a telephone directory is not yet available in North Korea, and the telephone numbers and addresses of ministries are kept secret. Only a few firms publish their telephone and fax numbers.

Potential demand for North Korea's telecommunication services

To determine the social demand for North Korea's telecommunication services and define the target tele-density to be achieved within a reasonable period of time, we first need to analyze some demographic information and industrial locations. The population of North Korea had reached 23.8 million in 1997, 37 per cent of which is living in rural areas. The number of households in 1995 was 5.4 million and the average number of members per household stood at 4.4.

The western part of the nation, including Pyungan-*do*, Hwanghae-*do*, and the metropolitan area of Pyongyang, Nampo, and Kaesung city, is under direct government control. This region is heavily populated with 15 million people and a population density of nearly 300 per square kilometer. About a quarter of the whole population is spread throughout the metropolitan areas of Pyongyang and Nampo. The population of the eastern part of the nation, such as Hamkyung-*do* and Kangwon-*do*, is 7 million with a population density of 150, while the northern mountainous areas such as Jagang-*do* and Yanggang-*do* are sparsely populated with only 2 million people and have a mere population density of 60. In order to achieve fast mobilization and easy organization of the labor force as well as control, people usually live in collective habitations.

The Pyongyang industrial area is the major export-oriented industrial area in the west and consists of Pyongyang (population 3.4–4 million),[5] Nampo (population 0.8–1 million) and Sariwon (population 300–500 thousand) cities. Labor-intensive middle-tech industries such as textiles and electronics have been developed in this region. In the Shinuiju industrial area, which includes Shinuiju (population 300–500 thousand), Ungampo, Yongchun and Kusung, textile and petrochemical industries have gained competitiveness thanks to the region's locational advantage in terms of access to oil pipelines from China. The Haeju industrial area, which has developed around Haeju city (population 200–300 thousand) and Kaesung city (population 400–500 thousand), is also anticipated to become an industrial complex.

The export-oriented industrial and tourist areas of the east are the Hamheung–Wonsan industrial area that consists of Hamheung–Heungnam (population 0.8–1 million) and Wonsan (population 300–500 thousand) and the Chungjin (population 0.7–1 million)–Rajin–Sonbong area. Auto, chemical, steel and refining industries are to be located in the Hamheung–Wonsan area, while shipbuilding, steel and chemical industries are expected to develop in the Chungjin area.

We can now divide the whole North Korean territory into three regions in terms of demographic perspective and industrial location. The first region consists of export business areas, resort areas and large cities. The upper bound for population of these areas combined is estimated at about nine million. The second region consists of domestic business areas, and small and medium-sized cities, which include Kanggye, Hyesan, Kimchaek, and Dandchun. The population of this region is estimated at 6.6 million. The third region consists of the rural areas where the estimated population is about 8.4 million (Table 8.3).

Table 8.3 Basic Indicators of North Korea's Population and Households

Basic year: 1997	Population (10 thou.)	Average size of household	Number of household (10 thou.)	Ratio of population (%)
Export business areas, resort areas and large cities	900	4.4	220	37.5
Domestic business areas, and small and medium-sized cities	660	4.4	150	27.5
Rural areas	840	4.4	190	35.0
Total	2400	4.4	540	100.0

Source: Comparison on the South–North Korean Socio-Economic Situation, National Statistical Office, Republic of Korea, 1997.

Target tele-density should vary from region to region. If North Korea is to introduce market economy to promote economic growth and expand trade with the outside world, it will eventually start competing with the coastal cities and the free economic zones of China. For example, the telecommunication infrastructure of modern industrial and tourist areas of North Korea should be at least comparable to that of the major coastal cities of China. And in other areas like domestic business and rural areas, the telecommunications deployment can be planned based on the overall growth potential of the North Korean economy.

Table 8.4 Urban and Rural Mainlines and Tele-density

	Ratio of urban population (%) (1995)	Ratio of urban ML(%) (1995)	Urban ML per 100 inhab. (1995)	Ratio of rural population (%) (1995)	Ratio of rural ML (%) (1995)	Rural ML per 100 inhab. (1995)
Low income	28.1	80.7	4.30	71.9	19.3	0.40
Low-middle income	55.7	82.2	10.72	44.3	17.8	2.92
Upper-middle income	73.7	77.1	26.03	26.3	22.9	9.13
High income	77.7	87.0	38.98	22.3	13.0	–
World	45.1	83.7	7.74	54.9	16.3	1.24

Source: ITU (1998a), *World Telecommunication Development Report.*

Table 8.5 Demand Projection

	Population (10 thou.)	Urban and rural ML per 100 inhabitants		Total ML (10 thou.)	Residential ML (10 thou.)	Business ML (10 thou.)
Export business areas, tourist areas and large cities	900	Scenario 1	38.98	351	233	118
		Scenario 2	52.00	468	312	
Domestic business areas, small and medium-sized cities	660	26.03		172	115	
Rural areas	840	9.13		77	77	–
Total	2400	Scenario 1	25.00	600	425	175
		Scenario 2	29.88	717	504	213

For experimental studies, we present two scenarios that are based on the hypothesis developed in the previous section. In scenario 1, the target tele-density of the major industrial and urban areas is assumed to be the tele-density of the urban areas of the high-income group. As shown in Table 8.4, the average tele-density of urban areas in these countries is 38.98 per cent. The target tele-density of the other areas is based on the optimistic estimation of growth potential in the forthcoming decades. We assume that the target tele-density of domestic business areas including small and medium-sized cities is 26.03 per cent, which is the tele-density of the urban area of the upper-middle income countries. The target tele-density of the rural areas is set to the average rural tele-density of the upper-middle income countries.

Table 8.6 Residential, Largest City and Rest of Country Tele-density, 1996

	ML residen-tial (%)	Resi. Of ML per 100 household	Largest city tele-density	Rest of country tele-density	Overall country tele-density
Low income	74.0	8.9	6.53	2.31	2.48
Low-middle income	75.9	31.1	22.16	7.20	9.41
Upper-middle income	72.1	39.7	25.73	11.51	13.74
High income	69.9	102.7	52.85	43.77	45.95
World	71.4	39.9	21.54	6.59	8.66

Source: ITU (1998a), *World Telecommunication Development Report.*

In scenario 2, the target tele-density of business and tourist areas is set to 52 per cent, which is equivalent to the tele-density of the largest cities of high-income countries. The assumption is not unreasonable since the tele-density of the largest cities of transition economies (except China and Vietnam) ranges from 36 per cent to 52 per cent. Table 8.5 exhibits the required mainlines in North Korea in each scenario.

We can be more specific in this estimate by distinguishing business lines and residential lines. We assumed in this experimental study that the average ratio of residential mainlines to business mainlines is 2. In fact, as seen in Table 8.6, the ratio of residential mainlines to total mainlines in various income groups fluctuates around 70 per cent. Table 8.7 shows that the ratio of residential lines in transition economies, except Vietnam, also ranges from 65 per cent to 83 per cent. Accordingly, our assumption on the ratio of residential mainlines in North Korea seems reasonable.

Table 8.5 summarizes the required infrastructure for North Korea's telecommunication needs. In Scenario 1, a total of 6 million mainlines are needed. And in this case, the tele-density will reach 25 per cent. 3.51 million mainlines need to be supplied to the major industrial and urban areas, of which 2.33 million and 1.18 million are residential and business lines, respectively. Domestic business areas including small and medium cities require 1.72 million mainlines, 1.15 million of which are residential lines, while 0.57 million are for businesses. In the rural areas, 0.77 million lines are required, all of which are assumed to be residential. According to scenario 2, 7.17 million lines are required to achieve a 30 per cent level of tele-density. 4.68 million mainlines will be needed for major industrial and urban areas, 3.12 million of which are residential and 1.56 million are for businesses.

Table 8.7 Urban and Rural Mainlines and Tele-density in the Transition Economies

	Resi. ML (%) (1996)	Largest city tele-density (1996)	Urban ML (%) (1995)	Urban ML per 100 inhab. (1995)	Rural ML (%) (1995)	Rural ML per 100 inhab. (1995)
China	75.2	18.97	80.2	9.26	19.8	0.94
Czech Republic	65.9	52.12	–	–	–	–
Hungary	82.9	36.89	81.6	26.55	18.4	10.97
Poland	83.0	–	71.1	17.04	28.9	11.27
Russia	75.7	42.86	86.6	20.11	13.5	8.49
Slovak Republic	73.8	52.06	78.7	27.88	21.3	10.79
Vietnam	50.0	8.96	50.0	0.85	50.0	0.22

Source: ITU (1998a), *World Telecommunication Development Report.*

Investment Requirements for North Korea's Telecommunications Deployment

Investment level for telecommunications deployment

The total number of mainlines needed to accomplish the target tele-densities of several strategic areas is six million lines in scenario 1 and 7.17 million lines in scenario 2. To get a rough idea about the cost of the telecommunications infrastructure, we need to distinguish between business mainlines and residential lines. Business lines are designed to achieve a global standard of international competitiveness and must be capable of handling multimedia information. On the other hand, for residential mainlines, immediate emphasis is put on simple voice and data transmission.

There are many ways to expand the business networks. A relatively less costly method to expand transmission capacity is to install twisted pair telephone wires utilizing compressing techniques such as xDLS. Where this method is not suitable, optical fiber cables or hybrid fiber-coaxial cables can be used to provide wide band services.

Amstrong and Fuhr (1993) have estimated the cost per subscriber for this type of deployment, and report that a cable cost of US$700–1200 per subscriber will be required in the USA. Considering that a significant portion of outside plant investment consists of capitalized labor cost, and taking into account the much lower wage rates in developing countries, outside plant investment in the developing countries (including inside wire) will be accomplished with less than US$500 per subscriber.[6] As a reference point, we assume that per subscriber cost for constructing business mainlines is US$500.

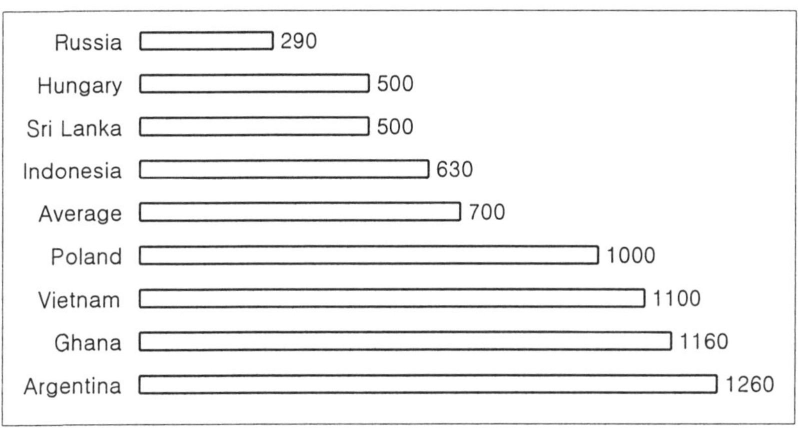

Source: ITU (1998a), *World Telecommunication Development Report.*

Figure 8.4 Cost of WLL per Subscriber

Wireless Local Loop (WLL) can be an alternative for residential fixed lines in North Korea. WLL, invented in the early 1970s, is a wireless network connecting a telephone station to the subscriber thereby saving installation costs. This method has a number of merits; the service can be provided much faster, and the bandwidth is still relatively broad enough while the cost is only a half of fixed wire networks. Besides these, it has all the functions of telephone voice service, facsimile, modem and ISDN. And there is also a variety of techniques developed for WLL satellites systems including applied fixed microwave systems, applied cellular systems, and cordless techniques. If WLL is to be chosen for residential connection, the cost would lie somewhere between US$200–500 per subscriber, as Hills and Yeh (1996) forecasted. Figure 8.4 shows the cost of WLL per subscriber in each country. It ranges from US$290 in Russia to US$1260 in Argentina. The average cost per subscriber is US$700. This difference is a result of variances in population density, demographic spread and the differential quality of WLL service. In this study, the cable cost of residential mainline construction is assumed to be US$300.

Table 8.8 Required Level of Investment

Unit: million US$	Demand projection					
	Cost of residential mainlines		Cost of business mainlines		Total cost	
Cost per line (US$)	682		1 136		–	
	Scenario 1	Scenario 2	Scenario 1	Scenario 2	Scenario 1	Scenario 2
Export business areas, tourist areas and large cities	1590	2128	1340	1772	2930	3900
Domestic business areas, and small and medium-sized cities	784	784	648	648	1432	1432
Rural areas	525	525	–	–	525	525
Total	2899	3437	1988	2420	4887	5857

To estimate the total cost per subscriber, we divide the total cost of deploying telecommunication networks into four categories.[7] A typical classification of the main forms of expenditure on telecommunications equipment is given as follows: 32 per cent of the total cost for switching equipment for public exchange, 44 per cent for cables and local network, 17 per cent for transmission equipment, and 7 per cent for telephone and PABX. But these categories could be altered depending on the economic environment or other conditions of the country in question. However, in this study, we calculated the total cost per subscriber using these ITU standards. Our estimates of the cable cost for business lines and for residential lines were US$500 and US$300, respectively. Since the cable cost accounts for 44 per cent of the total per subscriber cost, the total cost becomes US$1136 for business lines, and US$682 for residential lines.

Table 8.8 shows the expected investment level of North Korea's telecommunications infrastructure. Under scenario 1, the total cost of telecommunications deployment is US$4.887 billion, with the cost of business mainlines being US$1.988 billion and the cost of residential mainlines, US$2.899 billion. Export business areas will require US$2.93 billion, of which US$1.34 billion is for business mainlines and US$1.59 billion for residential mainlines. Domestic business areas and small and medium-sized cities will need US$1.432 billion, of which US$0.648 billion and US$0.784 billion will be for business main lines and residential main lines, respectively. Rural areas will require US$0.525 billion of investment.

Under scenario 2, total investment will be US$5.857 billion. US$3.9 billion is required for export business areas and tourist areas, of which US$1.772 billion is needed for business main lines and US$2.128 billion for residential mainlines.

Table 8.9 Time to Attain Different Tele-density (by Years)

	Stage 1	Stage 2	Stage 3	Stage 4	Stage 5	Stage 6
Tele-density (%)	1–5	5–10	10–20	20–30	30–40	40–50
Number of countries (1996)	37	29	28	22	17	19
Best years	5	3	3	3	3	4
Average years	14	7	9	6	7	7

Notes: 'Average' refers to the mean number of years taken by countries, which have made the transition from one tele-density category to another. 'Best' refers to best practice, in terms of the shortest length of time taken. It is logically not possible to provide an average transition length for 0 to 1 as many countries still have a tele-density of less than one.

Source: ITU (1998a), *World Telecommunication Development Report*, p. 17.

Investment perspectives in North Korea's telecommunications

In order to draw a picture for financial flows, we need to have at least a rough idea of the time schedule for North Korea's telecommunications deployment. Since it takes enormous costs to establish modern telecommunications infrastructure, it is important to determine where the priorities lie and what sector of the economy needs telecommunications infrastructure most.

Table 8.9 shows the number of countries at each category of tele-density, and the transition time required from one category to another. The average time required for tele-density to increase from 5 to 10 per cent, according to the table, is seven years. And to increase tele-density either from 20 to 30 or from 30 to 40 requires 6 or 7 years on average. Given the rapid pace of technological development, the required time period to reach a certain stage must have been considerably shortened. In fact in New Zealand, it took more than 30 years, from 1937 to 1970, to increase tele-density from 10 to 30. But in Japan, during the period from 1960 to 1977, tele-density had increased by 8 times from 3.9 to 30.6. And in South Korea, Singapore and Taiwan, thanks to technology development and the learning effect, tele-density increased from 10 to 30 in only a 10-year time period from 1975 to 1985.

During the 1990s, the amount of time required for tele-density to reach a certain stage has been considerably reduced, especially in large cities of transition economies such as Czech, Slovak, Hungary, China and Vietnam (Figure 8.5).

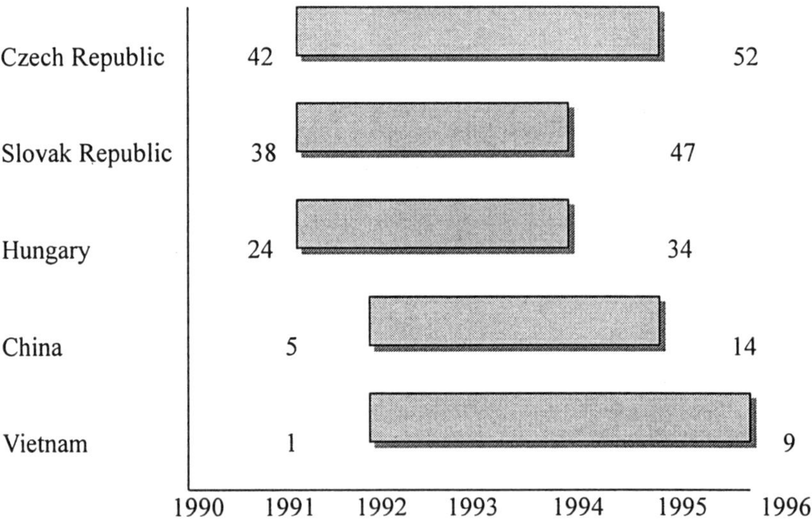

Source: ITU (1998a), *World Telecommunication Development Report.*

Figure 8.5 Changes in Tele-density (Economies in Transition)

Tele-density in Prague (Czech Republic) had increased from 42 per cent in 1991 to 52 per cent in 1994. In Bratislava (Slovak), tele-density rose from 38 per cent in 1991 to 47 per cent in 1994, and in Budapest (Hungary), from 24 per cent in 1991 to 34 per cent in 1994. In the largest cities of those countries with low tele-density to begin with, such as China and Vietnam, tele-density has multiplied by several times in three or four years. Hence, the required time for North Korea's tele-density to reach a certain target level is likely to be even shorter than in these economies in transition. For planning purposes, it is convenient to divide the investment horizon into three successive stages.

First of all, North Korea has to install backbone networks connecting various strategically important areas such as export-oriented industrial areas and major urban areas as soon as possible. For this purpose, it needs to install 1.28 million residential lines (30 per cent of total residential mainlines) and 1.4 million business mainlines (80 per cent of total business mainlines). That is, a total of 2.68 million lines need to be deployed during this stage. Considering that 2.33 million residential and 1.18 million business mainlines are required in major industrial and urban areas, we see that in stage 1, almost all of the business areas and almost half of the residential areas are covered in this region. After the first stage, the tele-density will rise from 4.7 per cent to 11 per cent. The required investments during this stage are US$1.59 billion for business lines and US$0.873 billion for residential main lines. It is not yet clear how much investment has been made in North Korea. Inferring the size of backbone networks from a recent *Naewoe Press* (September 28, 1998) issue, and applying the same cost formula as above, the upper bound would not exceed US$0.5 billion.

In the next stage, we assume that 50 per cent of all the residential main lines and all of the business mainlines will have to be deployed. All business lines for small and medium-sized cities and domestic business areas will be deployed during this stage. Through the second stage, most of the urgently needed residential mainlines for large cities and business areas will be completed. The required investment at this stage for residential lines is US$0.58 billion, and for business lines, US$0.397 billion. After the second stage, the tele-density will reach 18 per cent. In the final stage, the rest of the residential mainlines in both urban and rural areas will be deployed. US$1.446 billion of investment will be needed during this stage. Assuming North Korea has access to the current best practice, each stage will take about three years to complete (Table 8.10).

The other factor to be considered in North Korea's telecommunications deployment is the price of telecommunication services. In most developing countries, the price of residential telephone installation is much lower than the actual cost and especially tariffs for local calls are very low. On the contrary, the installation price and basic tariff for business telephone lines as well as domestic trunk and international lines are generally much higher than costs.

We examine revenue per mainline of transition economies for each income group. As shown in Figure 8.6, and in Figure 8.7 for country comparison, the revenue per line in low-income countries is US$343 and, in the lower-middle income countries, US$296, while in upper middle and high-income countries the revenue per line is more than US$700. In those transition economies, revenue per line is surprisingly higher than the world average of the income group to which these countries belong. For example in Vietnam, revenue per line exceeds US$500, and in Hungry, Poland and the Slovak Republic, it reaches US$400. China's average revenue per line is around US$300.

Table 8.10 Number of Lines and Additional Investment Required for North Korea

	Division	Cumulative percentage (%)	Mainlines (10 thou.)	Additional mainlines (10 thou.)	Additional cost (M$)
Stage 1	Residential lines	30.0	128	128	873
	Business lines	80.0	140	140	1590
	Total lines	44.7	268	268	2463
Stage 2	Residential lines	50.0	213	85	580
	Business lines	100.0	175	35	397
	Total lines	64.7	388	120	977
Stage 3	Residential lines	100.0	425	212	1446
	Business lines	100.0	175	–	–
	Total lines	100.0	600	212	1446

According to the ITU reports, the annual average operating cost per telephone line in 1995 falls in the range of US$200–750. The median value is US$300 while the lowest value, which could be considered as the outcome of the best practice, is US$200. Suppose the operating cost per line is US$300 in North Korea. Under the political pressure to satisfy universal connectivity, the government is not likely to set the residential revenue per line above the operating cost. Let's assume that the average revenue per business mainline and residential line in North Korea will eventually reach US$700 and US$300, respectively, after stage 1. The average revenue per line will then be US$460. Assuming that the annual operating cost per line is US$300, and considering a 5 per cent interest rate and 16.5 per cent depreciation allowance for switching and transmission equipment while neglecting for the moment the value of past investments, we can draw a time profile of annualized investment costs, revenue and profits, as shown in Figure 8.8. It shows that under this optimistic scenario for the revenue stream, it would take more than six years to recoup the total investment costs.

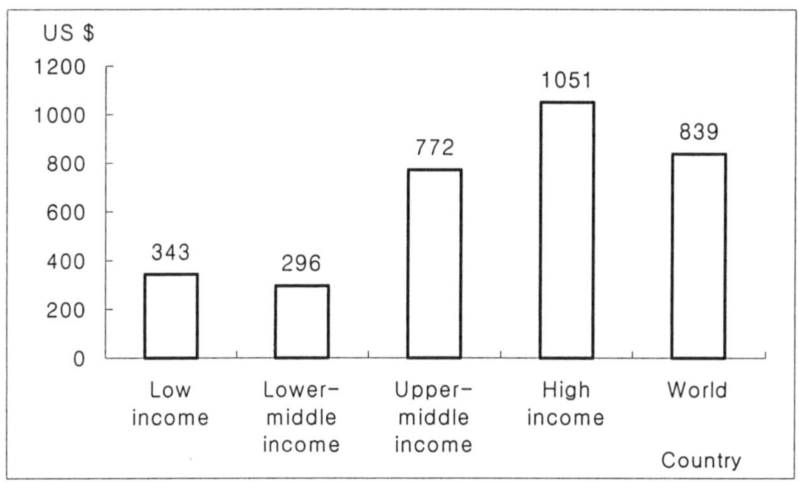

Source: ITU (1998a), *World Telecommunication Development Report.*

Figure 8.6 Revenue per Mainline ($), 1996

If we breakdown the revenue into business revenue and residential revenue, we see a wide discrepancy between the two streams of profits, as seen in Figure 8.9. As experienced in many other transition economies, profits from the business sector have to be great enough to cover the deficits in the residential sector. At least during the initial phase of network expansion for universal connectivity, cross-financing seems to be indispensable. Of course as the average revenue per line varies, the gestation period also varies, as can be seen in Figure 8.10. If the average revenue falls short of the operating costs, it will become more difficult to cover the costs of universal connectivity.

It is interesting to notice that if either the North Korean government or foreign strategic investors focus only on strategically important areas targeted in stages 1 and 2, the profit stream becomes more attractive (Figure 8.11 and 8.12). In fact, in the absence of universal connectivity obligations, investors are likely to focus on lucrative business demands in metropolitan areas, leaving out small businesses and residential demands.

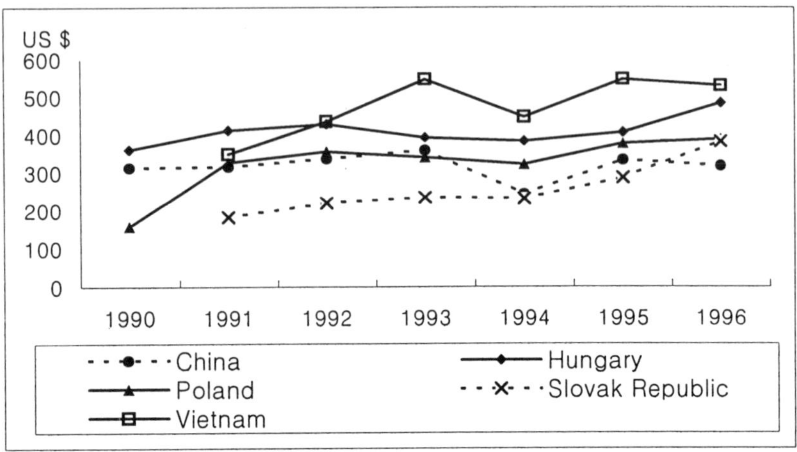

Source: ITU (1998a), *World Telecommunication Development Report.*

Figure 8.7 Revenue per Mainline (Economies in Transition)

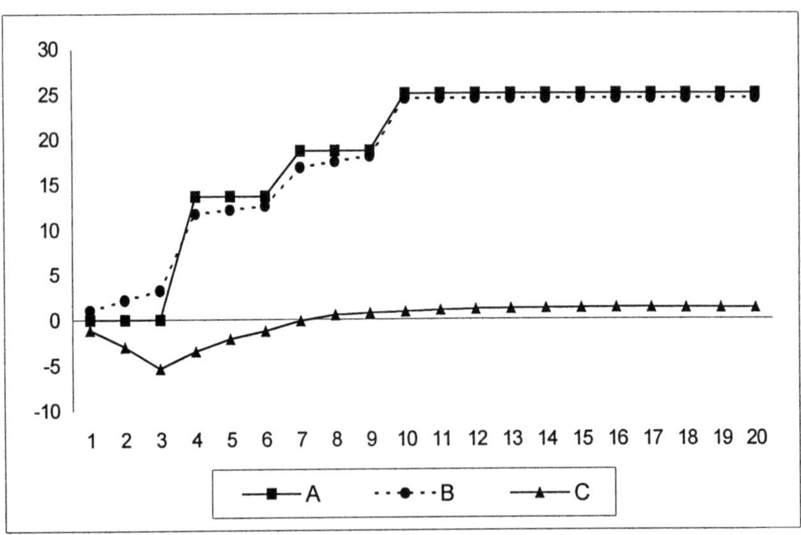

Notes: A; Revenue, B; Capital cost + Operating cost, C; Cumulative profit.

Figure 8.8 Time Profile of Cost, Revenue and Profit (Residential Revenue per Line = US$300, Business Revenue per Line = US$700)

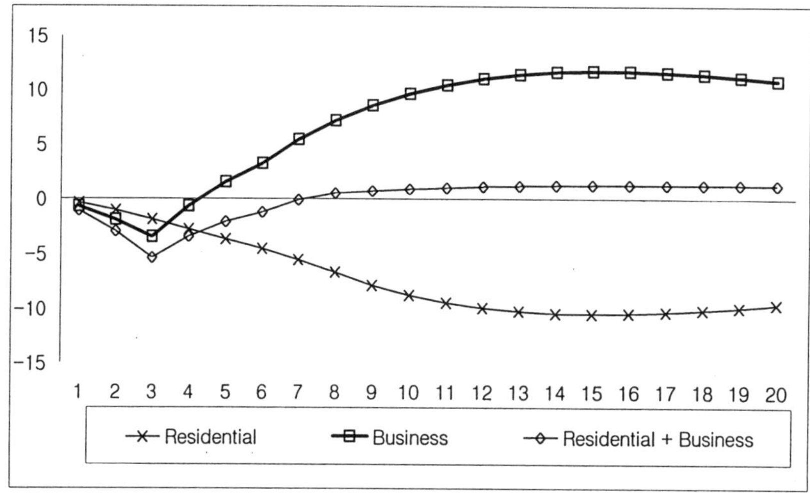

Figure 8.9 Decomposition of Time Profile of Cumulative Profits (Residential Revenue per Line = US$300, Business Revenue per Line = US$700)

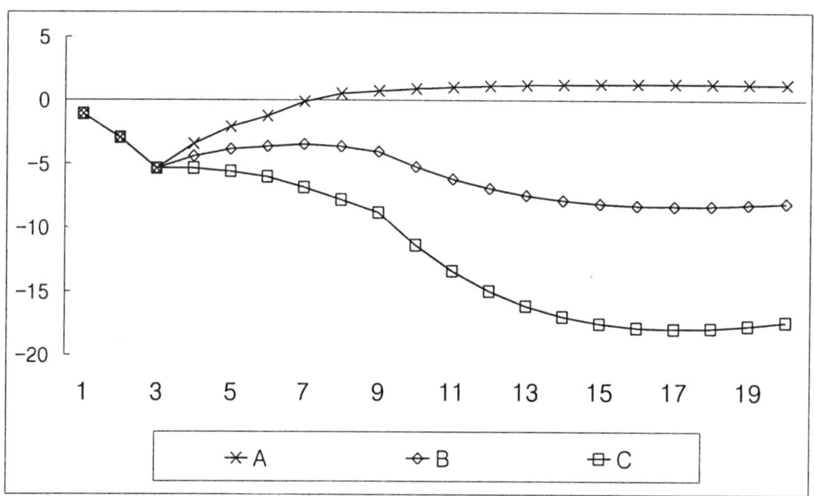

Figure 8.10 Time Profile of Cumulative Net Profits (Business Revenue per Line = US$700, Residential Revenue per Line = US$300 (A), Residential Revenue per Line = US$200 (B), Residential Revenue per Line = US$100 (C))

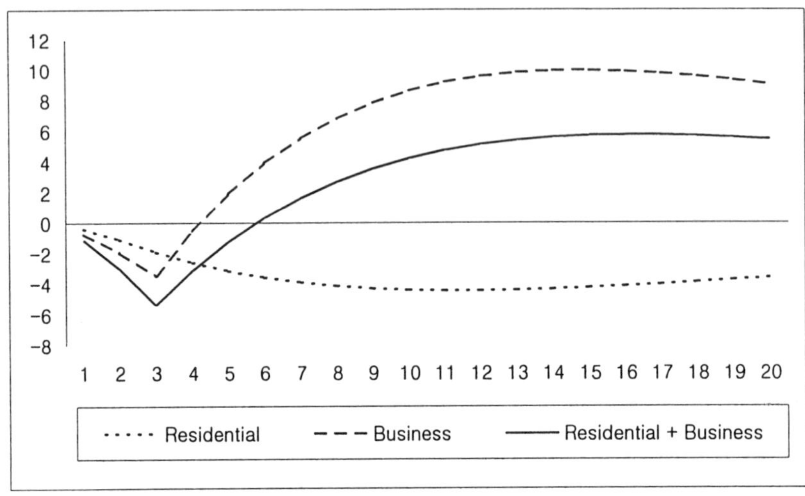

Figure 8.11 Decomposition of Time Profile of Cumulative Profits (A) (First Stage Investment Only: Residential Revenue per Line = US$300, Business Revenue per Line = US$700)

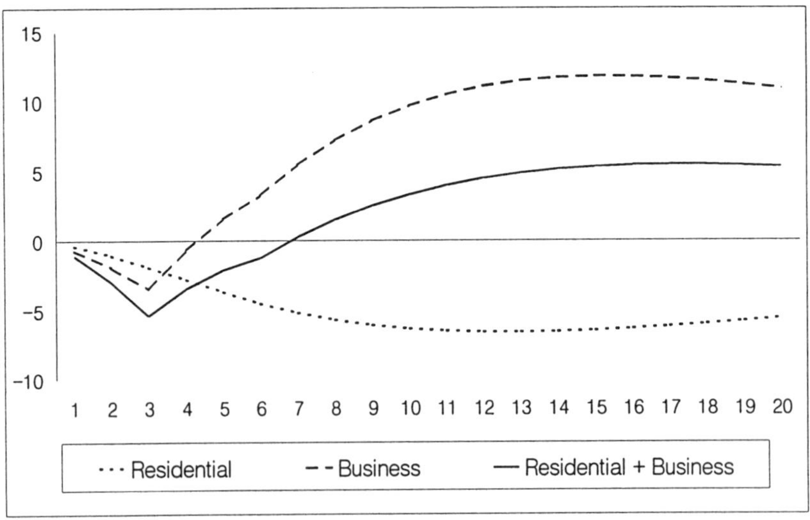

Figure 8.12 Decomposition of Time Profile of Cumulative Profits (B) (First and Second Stage Investment Only: Residential Revenue per Line = US$300, Business Revenue per Line = US$700)

8.3 DEVELOPMENT POLICY FOR TELECOMMUNICATIONS INFRASTRUCTURE

Financing the Modernization Project

As was explained in detail in the previous section, the required amount of capital to establish backbone networks is formidable. But without the economy-wide information networks, North Korea will not be able to let people exercise their individual initiatives to save their collapsed economy. The critical question is whether the current militant regime will accept a telecom reform that may help produce an individualistic knowledge-based economy. Even if the incumbent regime does not regard these developments as threatening, the question still remains whether the state-owned traditional PTT system can attract enough capital to finance a modernization project. Leaving aside the first issue for a while, let us focus on the financial problems that North Korea will be faced with.

First, like any other government in transition economies, the North Korean government will be susceptible to pressure from various interest groups during the transitional phase, and is likely to pursue non-economic objectives using telecommunications service as a means to achieving them. The telecommunication authority will then need various types of subsidies from the government. But since the government often runs out of budgetary resources, the telecom authority can hardly rely on the state budget alone to finance the modern information services and must eventually establish a cost-based pricing system to increase revenue. In fact even in Albania, which is one of the poorest countries in Eastern Europe, the telecom authority raised residential connection charges six times, and the cost of intercity calls by seven times, between 1992 and 1994. Even the tariff for local calls was doubled during the same period.[9] Since telephone service is virtually free to most of those who have access in North Korea, the required amount of an increase in tariffs would be astronomical. But again, for the same reason that the government is likely to be subject to political pressure, it would be very difficult to reform the existing tariff system in a credible and sustainable manner. To accomplish a tariff reform, the government has to commercialize state provision of telecommunications services and structurally separate telecommunication from post by abolishing cross-financing and establishing an autonomous system of management. These steps seem to be imperative and need to be undertaken in the soonest possible way to achieve modernization of the information infrastructure in North Korea. In addition, the telecommunication ministry has to play a role of an impartial regulatory agency to monitor the incumbent carrier.

Second, even if the North Korea government reforms the tariff successfully and meets the inelastic but growing business demands at high prices, it still has to wait at least five or six years to recoup the investment costs.[10] In fact, the North Korean government needs to finance the telecom project by issuing either debt or equity. Generally, debt is well suited for financing projects whose assets can be flexibly transformed into other businesses in the event that the initial project fails. Priority claims against such assets provide debt holders with considerable security. But unfortunately, most of the important investments in telecom assets such as switches and fiber-optic cables are relation-specific investments with limited flexibility. Coupled with political uncertainty and risks of repatriation, these assets can be debt-financed only under unfavorable terms. To reduce the cost of capital, the government may have to change the governance structure so that those who supply financing also run the carrier and thus bear the residual claimant statue. In other words, the telecom operator has to be privatized by issuing equities.

Privatization not only helps the government to finance the project at better terms, but also enables the telecom operator to focus on efficiency by freeing the operator from political pressure and bureaucratic rigidities and exposing it to competitive pressure. But the question is whether privatization strategy is viable in North Korea where the individual right to own even a small piece of agricultural land has hardly been allowed. In addition, there are simply not enough funds in North Korea to support mass ownership of a large modernized enterprise. Unless foreign investors exhibit great enthusiasm, privatization would not be possible, and to achieve privatization, the North Korean government has to provide an attractive investment environment to strategic foreign investors by letting market selection prevail and altering the perception that the telecommunications industry is a social welfare sector.

The strategic investors are most likely to come from South Korea, Japan and China. If North Korea adopts a liberalization policy, the traffic volume around this region will increase at an unprecedented rate. Also, telecom operators in North and South Korea will have incentives to obtain maximum benefits from network externalities by connecting networks from both sides. But unless there is a significant improvement in North–South relations, complementarity between the two networks may not be substantiated. If North Korea can successfully lift the US economic embargo and improve diplomatic relationships with neighboring countries, strategic investors may flow from the Western developed countries. As the global networks become seamless, North Korea will then have plenty of options when selecting business partners.

Privatization and Market Structure

In any part of the Western world, the efficiency of an economy is largely dependent on the institution of a well-functioning system of private property rights and competitive markets. But these two complementary institutions often develop at different paces, at least in the early phase of transition towards a market economy. Depending upon the socioeconomic and political situations, each country in transition has chosen different strategies. For example, Russia placed more emphasis on privatization than on legal structure for competitive markets and regulatory bodies, while China extended first the scope of competition without privatizing the telecommunication authority (Ministry of Post and Telecommunication (MPT)).

The telecom activities in many countries are still highly integrated, ranging from local services to domestic and international long-distance services. The critical policy issue is whether to retain integrated monopoly structure or restructure it before privatization. A continued monopolistic environment enables North Korea to utilize both economies of scale and scope, and coordinate various investment decisions. A monopoly market may also look more valuable to foreign investors.

But a monopoly operator who inherits the arrogantly rigid tradition of the bureaucratic authority is likely to perpetuate the 50-year legacy of communism. Moreover, it is not yet clear whether foreign direct investment flowing into the monopoly supplier will bring more capital into the industry than a competitive market.

The so-called monopoly versus competition dilemma posed difficulties to privatization in a potentially non-competitive industry.[11] It has been argued that in this type of an industry, competition-oriented restructuring must precede privatization since private businesses will not be willing to promote competition at the expense of their profits. By separating the local loop in the upstream stage and introducing competition in the downstream long-distance service, vertical divestiture could produce pro-competitive effects. But this policy of vertical divestiture and fragmented ownership reduces benefits resulting from economies of scale and scope. Unless this reduction is offset by dynamic technical progress driven by competitive market forces, too much emphasis on competition and diffuse ownership from the beginning stage of development is not likely to be welfare optimal. Furthermore, new carriers may enter only relatively profitable segments of the industry, and as a result, those demands of local business and residential areas are likely to be neglected. A regulated monopoly is often in a better position to accomplish universal connectivity through cross-financing among different services and regions.

The monopoly versus competition dilemma caused confusion in some CEE countries in the early 1990s. A rather unfortunate example can be observed in Russia. Russia vertically divested the ministry of telecommunication into many small regional monopolies and a nationwide monopoly,

Rostelcom, in the long-distance and international market. To utilize scale economies, however, Russia did not introduce competition in the downstream long-distance market, and the formerly integrated monopoly was merely converted into two successive monopolies that produced inefficient double-marginalization effects. Vertical divestiture merely produced another set of monopolies. In fact the Russian regulatory agency confronted many transitional difficulties setting standards in network management and encouraging compatibility of new technologies between local loops and long-distance networks.

Smaller countries like Hungary and the Czech Republic did not adopt a divestiture strategy and left an integrated monopoly structure intact. In fact, both countries guaranteed monopoly profits to foreign investors by credibly promising a monopoly position for a certain period of time. As of 1995, Ameritech and Deutsche Telecom hold a controlling block of shares (67 per cent) of Hungarian Telecom, Matav, which was incorporated at the end of 1991. The Hungarian government has provided a monopoly right and in return demanded Matav to expand the fiber backbone network on a planned basis. In fact, the number of direct lines per citizen in the Matav region rose from 15 to 28 in the three-year period from 1993–96. Privatization of Matav, which was completed in December 1995, was the single largest foreign investment in Hungary and the biggest privatization of the Central and East European region at that time. After privatization, Matav established itself as an international traffic hub by jointly initiating the TEL (Trans European Lines) and TET (Trans European Telecom Network) projects, through which 19 countries of CEE are connected by optical fiber.

In both Hungary and the Czech Republic, foreign investors undertook the restructuring of the privatized monopoly operator and improved management. They were both able to eliminate the legacy of state socialism inherited by the former telecom authority while obtaining synergy effects by utilizing economies of scale and scope. Both countries introduced competition in the mobile services industry, and to a certain extent, competition between land and mobile networks curbed the monopoly power of the incumbent. In fact, when the two international consortia were selected for 900 MHZ GSM service in Hungary in the early 1990s, they both promised 90 per cent coverage of the country in two years and offered prices that were competitive with regular land services.

In North Korea there is an undoubted need for foreign capital and technology, production management and professional skills. To attract foreign resources in an efficient manner, North Korea needs to avoid duplicated development that dissipates scarce resources. As discussed earlier in the previous simulation study, cross-financing between the business sector and the residential sectors seems to be indispensable for the modernization project. The government can also ask the privatized monopoly carrier to expand universal connectivity in return for guaranteeing monopoly profits for a certain period of time. Moreover, if the scope of the decentralized market expands too rapidly, North Korea will need sophisticated regulatory rule and competence, both of which take a considerable amount of time to prepare and are not expected to be accomplished in the short-term period. Efficiency-oriented restructuring must precede competition-oriented restructuring of the existing telecommunications authority. Still, the integrated incumbent carrier can be challenged from other directions including mobile and many other niche services, which have been successfully implemented in China in the 1990s.

8.4 CONCLUSION

The telecommunications policy in any developing country must achieve broad policy targets such as provision of modern high-tech services in the strategically oriented industrial and urban areas as quickly as possible, and basic services to all within a reasonable time framework. The policy targets must also include enhancement of dynamic efficiency by guaranteeing proper incentives. The telecom authority in North Korea may also like to maintain close contact with the outside carriers, especially those in the South, to maximize network externalities. But currently, North Korea has neither the technological expertise nor the sufficient amount of capital to achieve such policy targets. Without reforming the current age-old PTT system, North Korea will not be able to establish modern information infrastructure and lose its role in international division of labor. Reforms can proceed toward privatization and competition.

Privatization helps in two respects. It provides not only a channel for a strategic foreign investor to introduce capital and modern technology, but also an opportunity for foreign management to help restructure the bureaucratic organization of the communist government. Also at an earlier stage of development, an integrated monopoly structure seems desirable at least in the fixed-line services to utilize economies of scale and scope and to expand backbone networks throughout the country. In fact, as long as the government can enhance credibility of temporary protection in operating the backbone network, the current integrated structure system of the incumbent monopoly carrier need not be separated.

But apart from the monopoly versus competition controversy, it would be very difficult and painful for the power élite in North Korea to establish and run a so-called state privatization agency in a transparent and autonomous way. Also, as experienced in Russia, misguided policy toward privatization and competition produces inefficiency. The government has to assure that in the later stage of development competition (even with the government-owned carrier) will be unavoidable. The government promise can be made more credible, as in the case of the Czech Republic and Hungary, by preparing a supporting legal structure and introducing mobile phone competition on a gradual basis.

Although privatization is a long-run policy goal, North Korea may like to adopt a different path. It can still structurally separate telecommunications from the PTT system, but does not have to privatize for the time being. Instead, it may run a state enterprise by commercializing the state provision of telecom services and establishing management autonomy, and at some point announce that it will eventually privatize the state enterprise. During the transitional phase, the government could also introduce institutional competition from the other branches of related ministries or from the mobile phone entity. It is well known that China has been successful in building information infrastructure by adopting this type of development strategy. Once the groundwork for the national information infrastructure was successfully built, China later on reorganized related government agencies into the unified Ministry of Information Industry and is expected to split its government functions, thereby reducing direct control over business. The restructured China Telecom will then compete with many competitors on a fair basis. It is not yet clear whether North Korea will be able to maintain foreign investor credibility for such a strategy. But compared to the privatization strategy, the government will confront more difficulties in attracting foreign resources.

NOTES

1. For the related statistics, see ITU (1998a), *World Telecommunications Report.*
2. All the data used in our estimation are from the 1996 ITU database.
3. Recent Survey of Infrastructure in North Korea, Institute for Economic Research, Korea University, winter, 1997.
4. The complete extension of optical cables has not been publicly confirmed yet.
5. Since the population statistics of North Korea often show inconsistencies, we indicate only the upper and lower bounds for regional population. The lower bound is quoted from KRIHS, 1992, and the upper bound, from the Korea Trade-Investment Promotion Agency, 1995. In estimating the demand for telecommunications services, we use the upper bound.
6. Hills and Yeh (1996), p. 453.
7. ITU, Telecommunication Development Bureau, Document 1/197-E, 1997b, 26–7.
8. For the first three years, we assume, that on average, only half of the target revenue is collected.
9. See Manxhari et al. (1998) for telecom reforms in Albania.
10. See Figures 8.2 and 8.3 for illustrative cases.
11. See Tirole (1991) and Choi (1995) for comprehensive application of this concept to privatization policy in transition economies.

BIBLIOGRAPHY

Armstrong, T. and J. Fuhr (1993), 'Cost considerations for Rural Telephone Service', *Telecommunications Policy*, **17** (1), 80–83.

Choi, J. P. (1995), 'Telecommunications Reform in Central and Eastern Europe', Wien Institute for Advanced Studies.

Comparison on the South–North Korean Socio-economic Situation (1997), National Statistical Office, Republic of Korea.

Economist Intelligence Unit (1998), Country Profile.

Everstadt, Nicholas (1998), 'North Korea's Interlocked Economic Crises: Some Evidence from Mirror Statistics', *Asian Survey*.

Gareth Davies, Steve Carter, Stuart McIntosh and Dan Stefanescu (1996), 'Technology and Policy Options for the Telecommunications Sectors', *Telecommunications Policy*, **20** (2), 101–23.

Hills Alex and Hung-Yao Yeh (1996), 'Using Wireless Technology to Provide Basic Telephone Service in the Developing World', *Telecommunications Policy*, **20** (6), 443–54.

ITU (1997a), *Broadband Transmission Over Existing Cooper Wire Loops-Special Concerns of Developing Countries in Relation to the Work of the Radio-communication and Telecommunication Standardization Sectors*, Telecommunication Development Bureau, Document 2/263-E.

ITU (1997b), *Draft Final Report – Industrial and Transfer of Technology*, Telecommunication Development Bureau, Document 1/197-E.

ITU (1997c), *Handbook of New Technologies and New Services*, Telecommunication Development Bureau, Document 2/265-E.

ITU (1997d), *Handbook on New Development in Rural Telecommunications*, Telecommunication Development Bureau, Document 2/261-E.

ITU (1997e), *Report on Communications for Rural and Remote Areas,* Telecommunication Development Bureau, Document 2/224-E.

ITU (1997f), *World Telecommunication Development Report*, ITU.

ITU (1997g), *Yearbook of Statistics – Telecommunication Services Chronological Time Series 1986–1995*, ITU.

ITU (1998a), *World Telecommunication Development Report*, ITU.

ITU (1998b), *World Telecommunication Indicator Database*, ITU.

Korea Research Institute for Human Settlements (1992), *A Study on the National Spatial Development for the 21st Century: Potentiality and Problem after Korean Reunification.*

Korea Trade-Investment Promotion Agency (1995), *Industry in North Korea.*

Manxhari, M., N. Levine and D.C. Pitt (1998), 'Central and Eastern Europe – Convergence, Development and the New Competitive Paradigm – The Case of Albania', mimeo, Strathclyde Business School, Scotland, *Telecommunications Policy*, **22**(6), 519–39.

Milne, C., 'Universal Service for Users: Recent Research results – An International Perspective', Paper for the 25th Annual Telecommunications Policy Research Conference.

Preston, Paschal (1995), 'Competition in the Telecommunications Infrastructure – Implications for the Peripheral Regions and Small Countries in Europe', *Telecommunications Policy*, **19** (4), 253–71.

Tan, Zixiang (1995), 'China's Information Superhighway: What Is It and Who Controls It', *Telecommunications Policy*, **19** (9), 721–31.

Tirole, Jean (1991), 'Privatization in Eastern Europe: Incentives and the Economics of

Transition', in Oliver Jean Blanchard and Stanley Fischer (eds), *NBER Macroeconomics Annual.*

Welfens, Paul (1995), 'Telecommunications and Transition in Central and Eastern Europe', *Telecommunications Policy*, **19** (7), 561–77.

Yoon, Young H., Young S. Kwun and Han S. Yoo (1993), *A Study on the National Spatial Development for the 21st Century: Potentiality and Problem After Korean Reunification*, Korea Research Institute for Human Settlements (in Korean).

9. Strategies for Developing Transport Infrastructure in North Korea

Jae-Hak Oh

9.1 INTRODUCTION

In North Korea, transportation is thought of not as part of the social infrastructure, but as an element of production, the purpose of which is to take care of demand derived from other economic activities. Based on this principle, North Korea nationalized all of its public transport infrastructure and related assets. Furthermore, freedom for travel is tightly controlled and people can travel only with official travel permission. Also, the government allocates residences to be within walking distance of one's workplace. As a result, passenger transport demand is extremely suppressed. Most of available capacity of transport facilities is allocated for freight movements. It can be said that the transport system in North Korea has been developed mainly for freight transportation.

Transport infrastructure is an important factor in economic development. It is widely known that there is a close link between transport infrastructure and economic growth. South Korea has invested more than 2 per cent of its annual GNP every year throughout its past 30-year economic development period in order to provide and maintain an efficient transport system. Likewise, North Korea will have to provide an efficient transport system if it is to attract foreign investment and survive intense competition with other economies.

The major problems of North Korea's transport system are a deficiency in transport infrastructure, poor maintenance, inefficient institutional structure and an unbalanced modal share structure. At present, North Korea has 23 000 km for roads, 5100 km for railway, an annual seaport handling capacity of 35 million tons and an annual airport handling capacity of 20 million passengers. The total number of motor vehicles is reported to be about 270 000 (1 vehicle for every 85 persons). Transportation by rail accounts for 80 to 90 per cent of total transport demand. Transportation by road is extremely limited and road plays a minor role. North Korea has devoted major efforts to develop an electrified railway-oriented transport network.

The major challenges facing North Korea's transport sector are to increase the stock of transport infrastructure and to improve the operating performance of existing transport facilities. The present stock of transport infrastructure in North Korea compares with that of South Korea in the mid-1970s. South Korea has invested more than US$50 billion (about 2 per cent of annual GNP) in the transport sector every year for the past two or three decades. These statistics suggest that transport investment requirements for North Korea's economic development will amount to at least several billion dollars.

As social infrastructure to support other economic activities, investment in transport infrastructure is very capital-intensive and requires a long pay-back period. There are two possible strategies for development of transport infrastructure. The first strategy is to carry out intensive investment in transport infrastructure at the beginning of the economic development period. Constructing an efficient transport system in anticipation of high growth in future transport demand will provide a favorable investment environment. However, in this case, North Korea will take a high risk and experience difficulty in mobilizing a large amount of investment financing. The second strategy is to make investment gradually, to satisfy the level of transport demand. From the viewpoint that the role of social infrastructure is to invoke other economic investments, this approach has a limited effect on economic development. Considering the progress of economic reform in North Korea, for a strategy of investment in transport infrastructure, the second strategy of making gradual investments is the better option. However, this study will investigate future transport investment requirements for two contrasting scenarios of economic development: high growth and low growth.

Transport infrastructure in North Korea is owned and operated by the state. Although transport infrastructure has strong public properties, an investigation of various reforms, such as decentralization, privatization and corporatization, might be necessary to mobilize financing sources for transport investment and to reduce costs. Port and terminal facilities, for example, are regarded as potential investment items for privatization and private sector participation.

It is widely expected that once railway and road networks between South Korea and North Korea are connected, and train services are extended into Chinese and Russian railway networks, much of the long-distance freight and passenger demand for transport to China, Russia and even Europe may be converted into railway. There is a good possibility for North Korea to operate part of the transport network as a commercial business. For this purpose, enhancement of the transport network and operations might be necessary for North Korea to play a key role in running international transport services in the Northeast Asian Region.

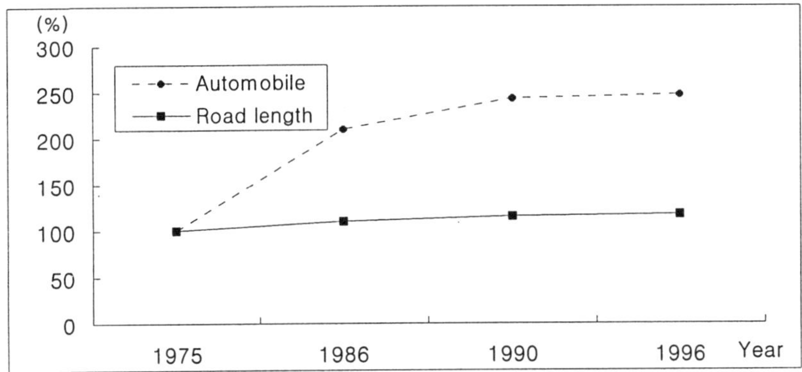

Figure 9.1 Trends in North Korea's Vehicle Ownership and Road Length

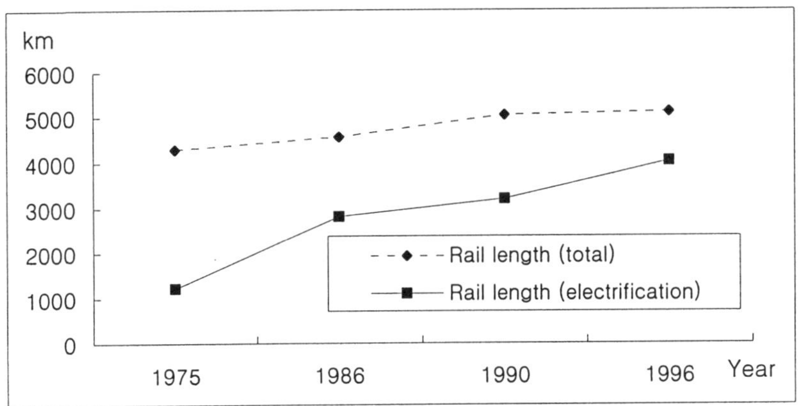

Figure 9.2 Trends in North Korea's Rail and Electrified Rail Length

North Korea must find ways to increase the stock of its transport infrastructure and identify measures that can finance needed infrastructure investments and improve the performance and use of existing transport capacity. This study will discuss these issues. The study's objectives are (a) to review the present state of transport infrastructure in North Korea; (b) to examine strategies suitable in North Korea's future development of an efficient and competitive transport system; (c) to assess financial resource requirements for transport investments; and (d) to examine options for financing and institutional reforms for developing North Korea's future transport system.

Table 9.1 North Korea's Transport Infrastructure

Mode		Year			
		1975	1986	1990	1996
GNP (US$ billions)		6.56	17.35	19.37	21.40
Population (1000 persons)		16 172	20 340	21 720	23 558
Road	Road length (km)	20 000	22 000	23 000	23 369
	Paved road length (km)	499	1 418	1 717	2 500
	Expressway (km)	–	–	–	682
Rail	Rail length (km)	4 292	4 561	5 045	5 112
	Electrified (km)	1 223	2 813	3 194	4 030
Seaport	Cargo handling capacity (10 000 tons/year)	2 835	3 390	3 490	3 501
Airport	Passenger handling capacity (10 000 persons/year)	–	–	–	2 000
Number of vehicles by mode	Motor vehicles (1000)	109	229	265	269
	Locomotives	854	1 094	1 182	1 153
	Passenger wagons	700	860	1 050	1 045
	Freight wagons	16 400	22 300	23 920	21 271
	Ships (10 000 tons)	12	50	54	92
	Civilian airplanes	–	–	–	21

Source: Korea Development Institute (1996), *North Korea's Economic Statistics*; Korea National Statistical Office (1997), *Comparison on Socio-economic Indices of South Korea and North Korea*; The Korea Transport Institute (1995), *Integrating the Transport Systems of the Korean Peninsula in Preparation for Unification.*

9.2 PRESENT CONDITIONS OF NORTH KOREA'S TRANSPORT INFRASTRUCTURE

Within the limitations imposed by the country's mountainous terrain, North

Korea has developed a national transport network along the east and west coasts. Because of high mountain barrier, which divides the western and eastern regions, the transportation link between the western and eastern regions is weak. Railway-oriented transport network has been built since rail transport is believed to be more efficient in the mountainous terrain. As a result, road, maritime and aviation transportation were not adequately developed. The share of railway transportation amounts to 80 to 90 per cent of total transport demand. Passenger travel demand is tightly suppressed by controlling the freedom of travel. Freight movements occupy more than 80 per cent of the total traffic volume. Existing transport capacity available is poorly maintained and underutilized due to a decline in economic growth in recent years.

The major transport problems of North Korea's transport sector can be summarized as deficiency in transport investment and capacity, unbalanced modal structure, poor maintenance and inefficient management. Table 9.1 shows the stock of transport infrastructure and the level of vehicle and train ownership in North Korea, along with trends in GNP and population. Figures 9.1 and 9.2 graphically depict trends in rail and road length, respectively. A detailed analysis of present conditions of railway, road, seaport and airport is described in the following section.

Railway

Starting with the railway network left by Japanese Imperial Rule, North Korea has developed a national transport network that is railway-oriented. North Korea's railway network comprises about 60 main and local railway lines. The total length of the railway network is approximately 5112 km. Of this, about 1100 km were built after 1960. Also, North Korea has electrified its railway network to improve operations: more than 4000 km (79 per cent) have been electrified since 1958. Railway electrification has helped in overcoming operational difficulties in mountainous sections. However, despite a high level of electrification, about 98 per cent of the railway network is single-track and, therefore, very inefficient in terms of operating speed (average train speed: 30–40 km/hr). Overall, railway transport in North Korea has failed to make use of rail transport's advantages over long-distances and in carrying large and heavy cargo.

North Korea's railway network primarily consists of three routes: Gaesung–Shinuiju, Wonsan–Rajin and Pyongyang–Wonsan. Since 1945, North Korea has constructed two new railway lines: Gangge–Unbong–Musan, in the northern region, along the Korea–China border; and Poyngsan–Sepo, an alternative route to Pyongyang–Wonsan. For international railway connections with China and Russia, there were originally six rail links to

China and one rail link to Russia. Three rail links with China (Shinuiju–Dandong, Namyang–Tomun, Manpo–Jiban) and one rail link with Russia (Tumangang–Hassan) are currently in use. In particular, the rail link Chongjin–Namyang–Tomun is used as a major transpiration route for freight movements and trade with China. China expressed its keen interest in utilizing North Korea's ports, Rajin and Chonjin, as well as its railway for trade with Japan and North American countries. Also, Rajin Port and the rail link Rajin–Tumangang–Hassan are used for trade with Russia. A mixed-gauge railway link between Tumangang and Rajin was built in 1974, and in 1987 was extended to Chongjin Port.

Road

Compared to railway, the role of road transport in North Korea is minor. The demand share of road transport is less than 15 per cent. Road investment in North Korea was small in the past. As a result, the total length of 2.4 m wide roads on which vehicles can drive is only 23 000 km, while the length of paved roads is 2100 km (road pavement rate: 9 per cent). Since the 1980s, North Korea has newly constructed 682 km of semi-expressways. But, at present, expressways are underutilized due to low traffic volumes. The total number of registered motor vehicles in North Korea is reported to be approximately 270 000 vehicles. This is evidence of how underdeveloped North Korea's roads network is compared to its rail transport network. The use of automobiles in North Korea is very limited. Even the major roads are extremely poor because of low traffic volume and poor maintenance.

The major road network in North Korea consists of four main routes: Gaesung–Poyngyang–Shinuiju (connected to China); Gosung–Wonsan–Choengjin–Rajin (along the east coast); Nampo–Pyongyang–Wonsan (east-west crossing); and Shinuiju–Manpo–Heassan–Musan (along the Korea–Chinese border area). North Korea's expressway network was built around the capital city, Pyongyang. Presently, there are five expressway lines: Pyongyang–Soonan; Pyongyang–Gaesung; Wonsan–Keumgangsan; Pyongyang–Hyangsan; and Sariwon–Shincheon.

Seaport

Because the North Korean economy does not rely greatly upon international trade, North Korea has invested very little in seaports. Also, since land rail and road transportation to China and Russia (North Korea's two major trading partners) is available, investment priority in maritime transport is relatively low. Maritime transport's share is less than 2 per cent. Currently, North Korea has about 22 seaports, including 8 trade ports. Table 9.2 shows the facility dimensions and uses of these trade ports. North Korean seaport's total annual cargo handling capacity is estimated at approximately 35 million tons.

Table 9.2 Existing Trade Ports in North Korea

Port			Length (m)	Depth (m)	Berthing capacity (10 000 tons)	Loading capacity (A) (10 000 tons)
East coast	Chon-jin	E/P[a]	754	9	1	87
		W/p[a]	1 384	10	1	713
	Rajin		2 515	10	1	300
	Sonbong		455	23	25	200
	Heungnam		1 850	13	3	450
	Wonsan		2 520	6.1–7.9	1	170
West coast	Nampo		1 890	13.5	2.5	800
	Songlim		700	10	2	160
	Heju		1 350	12	1	240
Sum			13 198	–	–	3 120

Port			Volume (B) (10 000 tons)	Utilization (B/A, %)	Freight items to treat	Remarks
E/C[b]	Chon-jin	E/P[a]	300	37.5	Grain, bulk	Chinese freight
		W/P[a]			Ore, iron	Kimchek iron factory
	Rajin		110	36.7	Coal, fertilizer	Russian freight
	Sonbong		200	100	Petroleum, chemical	Power plant
	Heungnam		450	71.1	Fertilizer magnesia	Chemical factory
	Wonsan		40	23.5	Cement, fishery	Navy, fishery
W/C[b]	Nampo		300	37.5	Coal, cement, bulk	Gateway to Pyongyang
	Songlim		130	81.3	Ore, coal	Iron factory
	Heju		100	41.7	Cement	Cement factory
Sum			1 500	48.1	–	–

Notes: a. E/P = East port, W/P = West port, b. E/C = East coast, W/C = West coast.

Source: Jun (1994)

Airport

North Korea is known to have about ten airports for use by civilian airplanes. The major international airport is Soonan International Airport, which has two runways (3500 m × 70 m, 4000 m × 50 m). Soonan International Airport is located along the outskirts of the capital city, Pyongyang, and is linked to Pyongyang by a four-lane semi-expressway. The annual passenger handling capacity of Soonan International Airport is estimated at about 20 million passengers, in view of the capacity of runways and other airport facilities such as the terminal facilities and the control and security systems. Due to low travel demand, however, existing airport facilities are underutilized. There are presently about 21 civilian airplanes in North Korea.

9.3 NORTH KOREA'S TRANSPORT INFRASTRUCTURE INVESTMENT POLICIES

As discussed in the previous chapter, the present situation of North Korea's transport infrastructure requires substantial improvement in the near future in order to support the transformation of the economy effectively. This chapter aims to identify investment policies for the development of an efficient national transport system in North Korea that can support transport demand generated from economic growth.

In general, social infrastructure investments are very capital-intensive and require a long time for planning and construction. Once infrastructure is built, it is very difficult to reverse. Thus, the development of transport infrastructure is generally based on a comprehensive transport planning process. In particular, transport planning takes account of national economic growth projections and land use development plans.

North Korea should increase its stock of transport infrastructure. Also, the present unbalanced structure of its rail-oriented transport system should be improved gradually by prioritizing investment in road, maritime and aviation transport. Once land transport routes between the two Koreas are connected, long-distance transportation's demand share will grow rapidly. Accordingly, the share of rail transport, which is more competitive for long-distance (longer than 250 km) movements, is expected to increase in the intercity transportation sector. Because of the special properties of each transport mode, railway will be a major transport mode for long-distance transportation and road transport will be responsible for short-distance transportation within regions. Single-track railway lines should be converted into double-track lines. In particular, railway train control and communication systems should be modernized to improve operational performance. For road transport, new four-lane motorways should be built to provide nation's mobility in major corridors centering around Pyongyang. Based on the basic direction of transport investment policy, investment projects with a higher priority are listed as follows:

Railway

Rehabilitation of disconnected transportation routes There are 4 railway routes between South Korea and North Korea. Transport routes that were disconnected in the border zone should be restored to facilitate interaction and trade between the two Koreas as soon as possible.
Double-tracking of single-track lines Major railway lines should be double-tracked to reduce waiting time and increase operational capacity. Candidate lines for double-tracking are Gaesung–Shinuiju, Pyongyang–Wonsan, Wonsan–Rajin, and so on.
Modernizing train control and communication systems All trains and stations should be provided with advanced automatic train control and communication systems. Modernization of outdated control and communication equipment can be made to enhance operational efficiency at a minimal investment cost.

Road

Preparation for motorization
The experiences of developed countries show that rapid motorization will occur as the economy grows. Rapid motorization causes traffic congestion and high logistics costs, which may disturb rapid economic growth. Thus, it is very important to expand transport infrastructure in a timely manner in preparation for rapid motorization.

Building an expressways network
Corresponding to South Korea's expressways network, an extensive expressways network should be built to support truck movements and intercity passenger travel.

Improving local road networks in cities and rural areas
Local road networks in cities and rural areas should be improved by widening or paving them. In particular, roads in rural areas need substantial improvement. Busy intersections at which major arterial roads meet need to be modernized with advanced traffic control systems in order to increase operational capacity and reduce traffic accidents. Advanced transport technologies, such as Intelligent Transport Systems (ITS), are available at

low cost, making it now possible to improve the operational capacity of existing facilities without constructing new infrastructure facilities.

Seaport

In the first phase of North Korea's economic development, maritime transportation is expected to play a useful role, while land transport modes take a long time to improve. As traffic volumes increase, major ports in North Korea need to be expanded and improved through a structure for role-sharing with ports in South Korea. In particular, high priority should be placed on enhancing access transport links to existing ports.

Airport

As domestic travel distances increase, aviation transport will be a more competitive transport mode, especially for long-distance trips (that is longer than 500 km). A rapid growth of international and domestic aviation demand is expected. For Soonan International Airport, high priority should be placed on improving terminal facility and control systems. Also, local civilian airports need to be improved in preparation for the increase of domestic air travel demand such as tourists, home visitors, business travelers, and so on. In the case of a rapid increase in domestic air demand, military airports may be easily converted into civilian airports.

9.4 PROJECTED INVESTMENT REQUIREMENTS OF TRANSPORT INFRASTRUCTURE IN NORTH KOREA

Projected Transport Demand

North Korea should undertake substantial investment in transport infrastructure. Transport demand will grow rapidly and transport problems such as traffic congestion and expensive logistics costs might become one of the biggest barriers to economic development. Rapid economic growth is usually accompanied by rapid increases in transport demand. Dealing with this will require planning and investing in transport infrastructure in advance before transport problems appear.

Although the railway sector represents the major transport mode of both passenger and freight movements in North Korea, rapid motorization is expected to occur at a very rapid growth rate. At present, the total number of automobiles is estimated to be about 270 000. An analysis of motorization trends experienced in South Korea suggests that the projected level of North

Korea's automobile ownership in the future will reach 0.65 million vehicles by the year of 2005, 1.5 million vehicles by 2010, 3.5 million vehicles by 2015 and 6 million vehicles by 2020. Figure 9.3 depicts the predicted growth of North Korea's automobile ownership. If motorization makes progress at the projected speed, the importance of planning and investing in roads to cope with rising demands in road traffic will increase. Transport investment policy to cope with motorization in a timely manner will be the most important issue in the development of North Korea's transport sector.

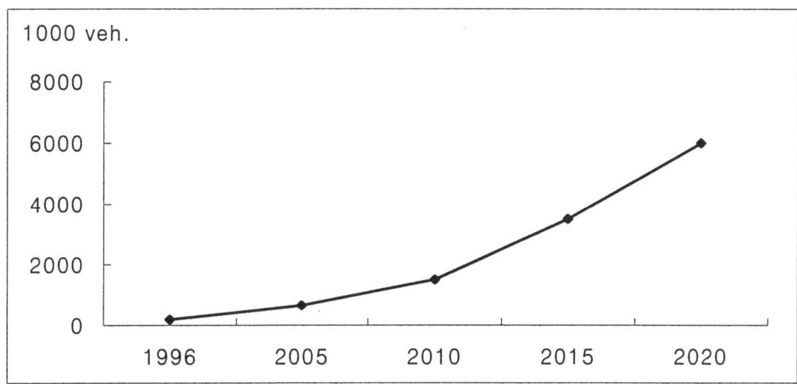

Figure 9.3 Motorization Projections for North Korea

For urban transport, passenger demand for bus and subway will increase. Taxis will also be an important passenger transport mode in cities. For intercity transport, currently railway transport is dominating, but intercity bus and domestic aviation demand will rise sharply. In particular, domestic air transport demand, such as the demand for long-distance passenger trips and time-sensitive freight movements, will increase sharply.

In maritime transport, once North Korea adopts an open economy policy, import and export-related transportation demand will increase tremendously. The share of international and coastal shipping will increase. The increase in maritime transport demand will require a further expansion of port facilities.

Projection of Transport Investment Requirements

In general, the projection of transport investment requirements in the future should be based on comprehensive long-term land-use development and transport investment planning. This study attempts to predict transport investment requirements in an unconventional way. It is quite different from the conventional transport planning process, which is conducted with scientific demand modeling. To predict investment requirements of transport infrastructure, this study started to investigate the trend and performance in South Korea's transport investments made over the past 20 years. This approach was based on the assumption that there is a close relationship between economic growth and transport development. After examining various indices on trends in population and economic growth, and on the transport development of South Korea and Japan, Oh (1997) identified that there is a close link between transport investment and economic growth and also a consistent gap of 20 to 30 years in transport development between South Korea and Japan. It is widely known that Japan motorized significantly in the mid-1960s, while South Korea did it in the mid-1980s and early 1990s.

First, this study compared the trends in the population and GNP of the two Koreas, using trend data for the past 30 years. As shown in Table 9.2, the GNP of South Korea reached US$20 billion, the GNP level of North Korea in 1996, around 1975. This study assumes that the state of North Korea's transport infrastructure in terms of transport capacity and motorization level is similar to that of South Korea in 1975. Also, Table 9.3 shows the stock of transport infrastructure and vehicle ownership level of the two Koreas, in 1975 for South Korea and 1996 for North Korea.

It can be said that, other than the road sector, transport facilities in the two Koreas are quite similar. Also, comparison suggests that South Korea has a better road infrastructure, while North Korea has a better railway infrastructure. However, motorization level and port cargo handling capacity are strikingly similar.

As the next step of the projection analysis, the study assumed two scenarios for North Korea's future economic development: high economic growth (optimistic) and low economic growth (pessimistic). Furthermore, it is assumed that for both scenarios, North Korea will achieve economic growth in the same step in which South Korea has experienced. Four target years for North Korea to achieve economy growth in terms of GNP level were set: 2005, 2010, 2015 and 2020. The indirect estimation method to calculate transport investment requirements adopted in this study might lead to an overestimation of transport investment cost, since construction costs in North Korea, in particular land acquisition and labor costs, are much lower than that of South Korea.

For the scenario of high economic growth, the first target year is 2005 (which South Korea reached in around 1982) by which time North Korea will reach 15 per cent of South Korea's 1996 GNP level. The second target year is 2010 (which South Korea reached around 1986) by which time North Korea will reach 30 per cent of South Korea's 1996 GNP level. The third target year is 2015 (which South Korea reached around 1990) by which time North Korea will reach 50 per cent of South Korea's 1996 GNP level. Finally, North

Korea is projected to reach 70 per cent of the 1996 GNP level of South Korea by 2020, which South Korea reached around 1993.

Table 9.3 Stock of Transport Infrastructure in South Korea and North Korea

		North Korea	South Korea					
Mode and item	Year	1996	1975	1982	1986	1990	1993	1996
GNP	GNP ($ billions)	21.4	20.9	71.3	128.9	251.8	330.8	480.4
	GNP per capita ($)	910	594	1 824	3 110	5 883	7 513	10 548
Road	Total length (km)	23 369	44 905	53 935	53 654	56 715	61 295	82 342
	Paved (%)	10.7	26.9	35.8	54.2	71.5	84.7	72.7
	Expressway (km)	682	1 142	1 245	1 415	1 550	1 602	1 886
Rail	Total length (km)	5 112	5 618	6 045	6 324	6 434	6 517	6 559
	Electrified (km)	4 030	424	428	441	524	530	577
	Double track (km)	–	563	714	773	847	852	901
Port	Cargo handling capacity (10 000 tons/year)	3501	3 164	9 600	15 401	22 435	26 894	29 526
	Container cargo handling capacity (10 000 TEU)	–	38	59	105	165	207	341
Airport	Handling capacity passengers (10 000 persons/ year)	2000	–	–	9 031	20 690	43 138	64 210
Number of vehicles by mode	Motor vehicles (1000)	269	194	647	1 309	3 395	6 274	9 553
	Locomotives	1 153	793	1 004	1 162	1 345	1 851	2 194
	passenger wagons	1 045	1 717	2 152	2 213	2 108	1 921	1 900
	cargo wagons	2 1271	15 866	16 702	15 858	15 601	16 238	14 048
	Ships (10 000 tons)	92	208	565	665	711	638	699
	Civilian airplanes	21	75	102	109	179	188	245

Source: Korea Research Institute for Human Settlements (1997a), *Social Overhead Capital Statistics & Information Yearbook*; Korea National Statistical Office (1997), *Comparison on Socio-economic Indices of South Korea and North Korea*.

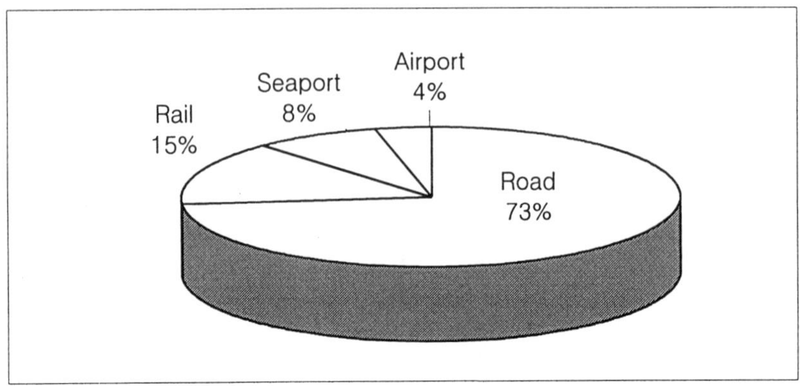

Figure 9.4 Share of South Korea's Transport Investment, by Mode, from 1975 to 1996

Table 9.4 Trends in Transport Investment of South Korea from 1975 to 1996 (Billions of US Dollars)

Mode Period	Road	Rail	Seaport	Airport	Total
1975–82	4.52	1.81	1.32	0.10	7.76
1983–86	5.69	1.68	0.79	0.10	8.27
1987–90	12.84	1.60	1.33	0.24	16.01
1991–93	8.25	1.49	0.51	0.35	10.60
1994–96	11.49	2.00	0.71	1.37	15.56
Total	42.78	8.59	4.66	2.16	58.19

Source: Korea Research Institute for Human Settlements (1997a), The Korea Transport Institute (1998).

Table 9.4 summarizes the transport investment performance trends of South Korea from 1975 to 1996, divided into five periods, (1975–82, 1983–86, 1987–90, 1991–93 and 1994–96) as described above. The cost is calculated at the current price in US dollars to avoid inflation effects. As shown in Table 9.5, South Korea has invested US$7.76 billion for 1975–82, US$8.27 billion for 1983–86, US$16.1 billion for 1987–90, US$10.60 billion for 1991–93 and US$15.56 billion for 1994–96. In total, South Korea has invested about US$58 billion during the period from 1975 to 1996. The expenditure invested in the transport sector occupies about 2 per cent of the total annual GNP, on average. Figure 9.4 shows the share of transport investment performance by mode. It shows that the share of road investment accounts for more than 70 per cent, while the share is 15 per cent for railway, 8 per cent for seaport, and 4 per cent for airport.

Table 9.5 Projected Stock of Transport Infrastructure in North Korea (High Economic Growth)

Mode		Target year				
		1996	2005	2010	2015	2020
GNP (US$ billion)		21.4	70	120	250	330
Number of motor vehicles (10 000)		27	65	150	350	600
Road	Total road length (km)	23 369	40 000	50 000	56 000	61 000
	Expressway (km)	682	1 000	1 400	1 500	1 600
	Paved (%)	10.7	30	50	70	80
Rail	Total rail length (km)	5 112	5 600	6 000	6 300	6 400
	Double track (km)	–	400	700	800	850
	Electrified (km)	4 030	4500	4 800	5 040	5 120
Seaport	Cargo handling capacity (10 000 tons/year)	3 501	9 000	15 000	22 000	26 000
	Container cargo handling capacity (10 000 TEU)	–	50	100	150	200
Airport	Terminal capacity (10 000 passengers/year)	2 000	3 500	5 000	10 000	15 000
Target investment (US$ billion)		–	7.76	8.27	16.01	10.60
	Cumulative	–	7.76	16.03	32.04	42.64

This study applies the trend of South Korea's transport investment to the future investment scenario for North Korea. For the scenario of the high economy growth, if North Korea reaches 70 per cent of the 1996 GNP level of South Korea by around 2020, the total financial requirement for North Korea's transport infrastructure development over the next 20 years is estimated to be about US$40 billion. For the scenario of the low economy growth which assumes to achieve roughly half the GNP level of the high growth scenario, the total financial requirement for North Korea's transport infrastructure development over the next 20 years is estimated to be about US$28.5 billion. Tables 9.5 and 9.6 show projected automobile ownership, transport infrastructure and financial requirement by mode and by target year for both of the scenarios, respectively. Taking into account the present level of land and labor costs in North Korea, the construction costs simply based on South Korea's past investment record might be overestimated.

Table 9.6 Projected Stock of Transport Infrastructure in North Korea (Low Economic Growth)

Mode		1996	Target year 2005	2010	2015	2020
GNP (US$ billion)		21.4	34	54	100	170
Number of motor vehicles (10 000)		27	50	90	170	300
Road	Total road length (km)	23 369	26 000	30 000	40 000	52 000
	Expressway (km)	682	750	850	1 100	1 500
	Paved (%)	10.7	15	20	40	60
Rail	Total rail length (km)	5 112	5 200	5 300	5 600	6 100
	Double track (km)	–	60	150	370	700
	Electrified (km)	4 030	4 110	4 200	4 500	5 000
Seaport	Cargo handling capacity (10 000 tons/year)	3 501	4 700	6 500	11 000	18 000
	Container cargo Handling capacity (10 000 TEU)	–	150	500	1 000	2 000
Airport	Terminal capacity (10 000 passengers/year)	2 000	2 500	3 000	5 000	7 500
Target investment ($ billion)		–	3.8	5.5	8,0	11.2
	Cumulative	–	3.8	9.3	17.3	28.5

According to the projection, major investment priority should be given to road expansion and pavement, the double-tracking of single-track rail lines, the expansion of ports and the modernization of airports. Although the share of North Korea's future transport investment by mode can be different from South Korea's, it is true that North Korea needs to improve its road network with a higher investment priority. In general, the direction of North Korea's transport investment policy should be established through long-term comprehensive transport planning. A long-term comprehensive transport plan should be established by taking into full consideration the forming of a unified transport network in preparation for unification of two divided Koreas and the future role of the transport network of unified Korean peninsular within the framework of the Northeast Asian transportation network.

9.5 FINANCING AND REFORMING OF NORTH KOREA'S TRANSPORT SECTOR

In section 9.4, this study projected more than US$40 billion for North Korea's transport infrastructure investment over the next 20 years. The development of North Korea's transport infrastructure will require an intensive investment over the next 20 years. If North Korea goes through the similar development stages as identified in the development program experienced by South Korea, financing resources of about US$10 billion for each of four development stages should be mobilized. Considering the present financial situation of North Korea' economy, it is quite uncertain whether North Korea will be able to mobilize this amount of financial resources in accordance with planned investment schedule. This study outlines various possible alternatives that can be taken to mobilize financial resources for North Korean transport infrastructure investment.

The most important issue concerning the financing of transport investment is the timely provision of transport capacity and efficient transport service needed for economic growth by mobilizing financial resources. In theory, it is always possible to find financial resources for projects for which there is enough demand and for which people are willing to pay. The problem is how to associate user willingness with financing. In general, transport infrastructure requires capital-intensive investment and requires a long pay-back period. Because of such difficulties, the public sector generally plays a major role in the planning and financing of transport investment. Here are some basic suggestions on how to mobilize financial resources for North Korea's transport infrastructure investment.

Introducing Market-oriented Pricing Reform

To motivate greater private sector participation and foreign investment, pricing structures, which in North Korea are entirely regulated by the state, should be reformed to reflect costs and market conditions. Pricing reform is a basic precondition for the financing of transport infrastructure and the efficient utilization of existing infrastructure assets. Individual investment projects must be able to generate revenues according to forecast market conditions. To attain revenue projections, prices need to be determined in relation to market conditions, capital and operating costs. It is necessary to clearly identify revenues from user fees or subsidies from government sources. Market-oriented pricing is generally recognized as an effective tool to help balance supply and demand, for example to ration congested facilities and to divert traffic to underutilized capacity. Market-driven pricing would not only generate new revenues of existing transport facilities, but would also help distribute the demand among the modes to maximize the utilization of existing facilities at all times.

Table 9.7 Overseas Loans to South Korea from 1962 to 1992 (Millions of US Dollars, Percentage)

Type	1962–65	1966–72	1973–78	1979–85	1986–92	Total
Public funds	63 (4.29)	1 130 (32.2)	3 431 (30.6)	10 105 (28.9)	4 688 (15.4)	19 417 (24.2)
Commercial funds	71 (48.3)	1 950 (55.5)	5 858 (52.2)	7 937 (22.7)	5 206 (17.1)	21 022 (26.2)
Foreign investments	13 (8.8)	227 (6.5)	704 (6.3)	1 157 (3.3)	5 684 (18.7)	7 785 (9.7)
Bank funds	– (–)	205 (5.8)	1 007 (9.0)	11 892 (34.1)	4 318 (14.2)	17 422 (21.7)
Commercial agency's bond	– (–)	– (–)	219 (2.0)	2 989 (8.6)	5 978 (19.7)	9 186 (11.5)
Company's overseas bond	– (–)	– (–)	– (–)	834 (2.4)	4 515 (14.9)	5 349 (6.7)
Total	147 (100.0)	3 512 (100.0)	11 219 (100.0)	34 914 (100.0)	30 389 (100.0)	80 181 (100.0)

Source: Ministry of Finance, Korea Development Bank (1993).

Utilization of Overseas Loans

South Korea has utilized overseas loans for social infrastructure development during the past three decades. As shown in Table 9.7, South Korea's total overseas loans from 1962, the commencing year of the first five-year economic development plan, amounted to about US$80 billion. In particular, the contribution of overseas loans for transport infrastructure investment such as Seoul–Pusan Expressway Construction Project, which is considered one of the most successful projects in the history of Korea's economic planning, was immense. Among types of loans used by South Korea, public loans and commercial funds were dominant in the 1960s and 1970s. From the 1980s, the share of foreign investment and bank funds increased. The ESCAP country report for social infrastructure development of developing countries prepared by the Korean government suggests some useful policies for mobilizing overseas loans. The report recommends the need to establish new overseas loan policy based on the principles of market economy, with respect to interest rates, profit rates, marginal productivity, and so on. Also, foreign investments needs to be liberalized and effective management system of overseas loans relating to inflow and outflow of foreign currency needs to be set up.

Encouraging Private Sector Participation

To relieve financial burden of public sectors in transport investment, private sector participation in transport infrastructure is an effective option to raise additional resources to finance major infrastructure projects. Also, private sector participation may also improve the managerial and operational efficiency of the infrastructure. As discussed earlier, market-driven pricing reform and public subsidies should be made more explicit to stimulate greater private sector participation on a project-finance basis. Various arrangements of private financing forms, including 'build–operate–transfer' (BOT) and leasing and management contracts, are available, and they differ in financing arrangements and risk-sharing. Tendering public infrastructure assets through leasing or management contracts could yield increased managerial efficiency and cost savings, along with higher revenues. As shown in Table 9.8, the Korea Transport Sector Study Report (World Bank, 1995) discusses the feasibility of private sector participation of transport infrastructure components, and quantifies marketability of transport infrastructure for each type of facility. Transport infrastructure services such as rail freight and passenger services and ports and airport services are rated as investment projects with the highest marketability.

Utilizing Existing Transport Infrastructure Assets

In North Korea, all transport infrastructure and related assets are owned and operated by the state. The most immediate and potentially attractive options for North Korea to generate new sources of capital may be the franchising, securitizing or refinancing of existing transport infrastructure assets currently owned and operated by the state. Compared to privatizing new facilities, capitalizing the revenue streams of existing assets involves lower risk levels in terms of future demand and construction risks. Potential candidates may include franchising congested roads, leasing multi-purpose shipping berths, leasing train rolling stocks, franchising the operations and maintenance of airports, and so on.

Developing Government Tax Revenues Earmarked for Transport Investment

In order for North Korea to develop transport infrastructure according to an investment schedule, various sources of tax revenues, which can be allocated for transport investment, need to be developed. In particular, this study will examine financial resources from oil taxes and vehicle-related taxes. If motorization of North Korea in the future is to be proceeded as projected in this study, revenues from these vehicle-related taxes will provide substantial contributions for North Korea's transport investment. In this study, the possibility of financial aid from tax revenues is investigated by examining the examples of South Korea.

Table 9.8 Feasibility of Private Sector Delivery of Infrastructure Components

Key to marketability ratings 1: least marketable 3: most marketable	Potential for competition[a]	Characteristics of good or service	Potential for cost recovery from user charges	Public service obligations (equity concerns)	Environmental externalities	Marketability index[b]
Urban roads	Low	Common property	Medium	Few	Few	1.8
Port and airport facilities	Low	Club	High	Few	High	2.0
Port and airport services[c]	High	Private	High	Few	High	2.6

Notes:
a. Due to either absence of scale economies or sunk costs, or existence of service substitutes.
b. Marketability index is average of ratings across each row.
c. Including cargo handling, shipping and airlines.

Source: World Bank, Korea Transport Sector (1995).

In 1994, South Korea introduced earmarked motor-vehicle-related taxes and set up a special account for transport infrastructure investment from these revenues. As the number of registered vehicles dramatically increased at an annual average growth rate of more than 25 per cent since the mid-1980s, the revenues from earmarked oil taxes and vehicle-related taxes constitute a major financial source for transport infrastructure investment. In recent years, revenues from petrol and diesel taxes accounted for about 70 per cent of the special account. Earmarked tax revenue provided around 24 per cent of the total transport sector investment in South Korea. Also, revenues from vehicle-related taxes, such as the vehicle excise tax, vehicle acquisition taxes, vehicle registration fees, road taxes and license taxes, provided other potential financial sources for transport infrastructure investment, especially by local governments.

9.6 CONCLUSION

The timely construction of transport infrastructure is an important factor for successful economic development in developing countries. In particular, North Korea needs to put a high priority in providing an efficient transport system in order to attract foreign investments and survive in the hard international economic competition.

The major problems of transport infrastructure in North Korea are summarized as capacity deficiency, poor maintenance, unbalanced modal share, and inefficient institutional structure. The major challenges in the transport sector faced by North Korea are to increase the stock of transport infrastructure and to improve the managerial and operational efficiency of existing facilities by adopting various measures.

This study identified that the present (1996) state of North Korea's transport infrastructure in terms of transport capacity and motorization is similar to that of South Korea in 1975. Based on the analysis of South Korea's past performance in transport investment (from 1975 to 1996), it is projected that transport infrastructure investment in North Korea over the next 20 years will be about US$42 billion, assuming the high growth scenario, and about US$28 billion, assuming the low growth scenario. The indirect estimation based on the historical investment record of South Korea might lead to overestimation. However, considering the present financial situation of North Korea, it is quite doubtful that North Korea will provide transport infrastructure as envisioned in this paper.

North Korea should introduce various practical measures to mobilize financing sources for transport investment and to help stimulate private and foreign investment. Current pricing structures that are entirely regulated by the state should be reformed to reflect actual costs and market conditions. Some of public transport infrastructures and relating assets that are viable under commercial business need to be franchised and capitalized. Private sector participation and foreign investment will be an effective option to raise additional resources and improve the managerial and operational efficiency of the infrastructure. Overseas loans combined with the assistance of advanced technologies in construction and operation from developed countries may be useful. Finally, as motorization makes progress, tax revenues such as oil taxes and vehicle-related taxes earmarked for transport investment will make a great contribution.

BIBLIOGRAPHY

Jun, I. (1994), 'Present Condition of Maritime Transport and Ports in North Korea', *Journal of North Korea Studies*, **5** (2), 60–82.

Korea Development Institute (1996), North Korea's Economic Statistics, 137–41.

Korea National Statistical Office (1997), *Comparison on Socio-economic Indices of South and North Koreas.*

Korea Research Institute for Human Settlements (1997a), *Social Overhead Capital Statistics & Information Yearbook.*

Korea Research Institute for Human Settlements (1997b), Policy Agenda for the Unified National Development after Korean Reunification (in Korean).

Korean Ministry of Construction and Transportation (1996), *Infrastructure Development and Prospects in Korea*, 1996.

The Korea Transport Institute (1995), *Integrating the Transport Systems of the Korean Peninsular in Preparation for Unification*, (in Korean).

The Korea Transport Institute (1997), *Reform of Transportation Facilities Management with Focus on Privatization*, (in Korean).

The Korea Transport Institute (1998), *Transport Investment Requirements and Financing Policies*, (in Korean).

Ministry of Finance, Korea Development Bank (1993), *The History of Korean Overseas Loans for 30 Years.*

Oh, J. (1993), 'Present Transport Conditions in North Korea and Policies for Development of Unified Korea's Transport Network', *Journal of Social Science*, **32** (2), Sungyunkwan University, 289–318 (in Korean).

Oh, J. (1997), 'Comparison of Transport Conditions and Policies between Tokyo and Seoul: Using Time-series Data', *Journal of the Eastern Asia Society for Transportation Studies*, **2** (1), 781–94.

World Bank, Korea Transport Sector (1995): 'Resource Mobilization Challenges and opportunities', Report no. 13847-KO, p. 113.

10. Practical Approaches for Energy Sector Cooperation between South and North Korea

Jeong-In Kim and Seung-Jun Kwak

10.1 PROBLEM STATEMENT

The government of North Korea had shown impressive economic gains in the 1960s and the 1970s, but economic growth slowed down in the 1980s. Since the early 1990s, North Korea (or the Democratic People's Republic of Korea: DPRK) has suffered a diminishing gross domestic product (GDP) for six consecutive years. According to the Bank of Korea (BOK, 1997), South Korea's central bank, North Korea's economic growth rate in 1997 was negative 6.8 per cent and nominal GNP was US$17.7 billion; meanwhile South Korea's nominal GNP was US$437.4 billion in 1997.[1]

The consecutive years of economic recession were related to the foreign debt incurred in purchasing industrial equipment, shortages of energy and raw materials as well as sharp decreases in grain output from the agricultural sector. However, despite the fact that North Korea has substantial reserves of energy resources such as anthracite and brown coal, the main cause of economic sluggishness stems from the problem of energy shortage and therefore low plant operation rate.

In addition to these problems, there are also other problems – outdated equipments for power plants, lack of energy control management and technology, and old electric distribution lines and parts. Because of such combined reasons, the energy intensity in North Korea has been quite low compared to South Korea. As of 1990, the energy consumption per unit of value added was 1650 TOE per thousand dollars, which was four times higher than the South Korea's energy intensity.

Most of the hydroelectric facilities in operation are antiquated and little water is impounded behind the dams. For thermal electricity generation, whether they are coal-fired or oil-fired plants, there is a lack of coal supply and money to buy petroleum. As a result, it is suspected that around 37 per cent to 40 per cent out of the total electric power could only supply for the industrial sectors.

Even though North Korea is being given support to build a Light Water Reactor Nuclear Power Plant (LWRNL) by the year 2003 through the Korea Energy Development Organization (KEDO), the energy shortage problem faced by North Korea in the near future will not be totally resolved. Besides, smooth operation for LWRNL will be difficult considering an insecure power system (Yoon, 1996). North Korea also still faces sticky problems such as financial sources, technical transfer problem, and political issues with other participants KEDO such as the USA, Japan, and South Korea.

Lack of interconnection in power and infrastructure in transport are other obstacles to use electric power from the LWRNL through KEDO. Furthermore, since a nuclear power plant usually works at base-load purpose, it is hard to adjust supply of electric power whenever demand is increasing. Therefore, it is necessary to check whether it is technically appropriate to use the electric power system from LWRNL in conjunction with an existing power system.

Besides the problems related to the LWRNL operation, North Korea should consider the following activities: (1) re-engineering of existing power plants to improve energy efficiency; (2) interconnection of power systems between South and North Korea; (3) construction of dispersed generation systems such as gas turbines combined with thermal power plants or small-scale power plants; (4) full-fledged analysis of energy efficiency and substitute energy use for renewable energy like wind power; and (5) looking into other types of energy cooperation with other countries.

So far, studies pertaining to the North Korean situation for energy cooperation have been quite limited because of the limited availability of data. There have been few studies of North Korean energy economics: Jang (1994), KEPCO (1993), Chung et al. (1994), Hayes (1994), Hippel and Hayes(1995), Yoon (1996), Kim and Park (1997).

Since there are few economic cooperatives between North and South Korea, progress has been very slow. The reasons for dragging economic cooperation come from the fact that both countries overlooked the fundamental factors to be considered. Namely, the success of economic cooperation will depend on the effectiveness of cooperation, mutual interests and economic benefits, and finally financial availability. Among these factors, mutual interests and economic benefits are the most important factors for economic cooperation. As shown from the case of the construction for (LWRNL), energy cooperation is also closely related to political and economic cooperation.

As we have seen with the reunified Germany, the socioeconomic costs of reunification are tremendous. Therefore, it is highly desirable to study in greater depth the issue of economic cooperation between North and South Korea. At the same time, while taking into consideration the shortage of necessary energies for the industry, it is necessary to examine the opportunities for economic cooperation between South and North Korea through energy cooperation. Since the main cause of economic sluggishness stems from the problem of an energy shortage, it is therefore urgent that the energy problem for North Korea is solved.

Most East Asian countries already have a common interest in securing an adequate energy supply. China plans to construct both a natural gas-based power plant and a nuclear power plant in order to resolve its energy shortage problem. Russia, which has huge reserves of natural gas, has been interested in exporting natural gas to earn foreign dollars. Based on its world-best energy technology, Japan is also trying to export its energy industry to the East Asian region.

In order to solve the energy shortage problem in North Korea, it is desirable to have short- and long-run strategies. For the short-run solution, it is necessary to examine the current electric transmission network in North Korea, and assess the possibility of a power network connection between North and South Korea. According to the Nautilus Institute, which is well known for North Korean economic analysis, replacing old electric distribution lines and parts will allow much room for raising energy efficiency without entailing large investments in North Korea.

Since the wave and electric networks are technically similar to each other, it is possible for South and North Korea to initiate electricity trade within a short period of time with small investments. Of course, something must be done before the actual electric system begins; namely, setting up a network operation plan, securing financial sources, setting electricity prices, and strengthening the network connection with KEPCO (Korean Electric Power Company), and so on.

As a long-term solution, it is desirable to use Russian or Chinese natural gas. The natural gas industry has remained the most successful sector in Russian economy, retaining economic preeminence and providing main source of income for Russia. Even North Korea has shown a strong interest in using Russian natural gas.

The overall goal of this study is first to review the current status quo of energy supply and demand in North Korea, and to analyze the energy problems in North Korea and to suggest some ways of energy cooperation between North and South Korea. Another purpose of the paper is to look carefully at the energy market situation in Russia and China, and to suggest near and medium-term economic strategic plans to implement energy cooperation between North and South Korea in relation with those countries in the future.

10.2 CURRENT STATUS OF ENERGY SUPPLY AND DEMAND IN NORTH KOREA

Current Status of Energy Supply and Demand

Over the past 23 years, growth rate of energy supply per year was only 0.6 percent, meanwhile the growth rate for South Korea was 8.9 per cent (see Table 10.1). As of 1996, among the primary energy sources, coal was the main energy source and occupied 66.3 per cent, hydroelectric was 19.7 per cent, 9.15 per cent for petroleum, and the other resources were made of 4.9 per cent out of total primary energy.

Table 10.1 Trends of Primary Energy Sources in both North and South Korea (Million TOE)

	1972	1976	1985	1990	1995	Average growth rate (%, 1972–96)
North Korea	21.67	26.68	36.25	36.22	24.6	0.6
South Korea	21.29	30.19	56.30	93.19	150.44	8.9

Source: IEA (1997).

North Korea's energy policy is not based on economic efficiency or comparative advantage of international trade but rather on a self-energy policy. Its major source of energy is domestically produced coal, which holds 81 per cent share of the total primary energy and 83 per cent of the final energy consumption (see Table 10.2). On the other hand, North Korea has fairly extensive potential for hydroelectric power development. Since the primary source of energy is coal, North Korea's petroleum consumption is very low, and used only in the transportation sector. It seems North Korea has shown stable energy security; however, lack of diversification for energy sources is causing an energy security problem, since the price of oil has decreased, which resulted in a relatively higher energy price for coal. The lack of diversification also causes an inefficient industrial structure, because it is hard to substitute coal for other energy sources. There is very little reliable data to describe the supply and demand of energy in the country. Data on coal production in the DPRK comes from the North Korean government report, the Ministry of National Unification (MNU) in South Korea, and IEA, all of which provide different data estimations. Official coal production data from the DPRK's annual report until 1989 are two times higher than the Ministry of National Unification's report in South Korea. However, the estimation from the DPRK is hard to take as being accurate.

Table 10.2 Trends of Coal Production in DPRK (Million Ton)

		1975	1980	1985	1986	1987	1990	1993	1994	1995
DPRK		–	–	–	78	80	–	112	–	–
MNU		27	30.2	37.5	37.5	39	33.1	27.1	25.4	23.7
IEA	Hard coal	32	36	39	39.5	39.5	40.5	41	–	–
	Lignite	9	10	12	12.5	12.5	13	14	–	–

Source: Ministry of National Unification (1995).

It is hard to say whether the data from the MNU is more reliable than that of the others. However, if we assume data from the MNU is correct and accounts only for hard coal, the estimation from both IEA and the MNU is the same up to 1988. However, figures in IEA after 1989 (55 000 thousand TOE) shown have an increasing trend in coal production (see Table 10.2). Relying on the MNU report, the main reasons for the downswing in coal production are: (1) most underground mines are getting deeper than before; and (2) mining equipment is quite old, and hard to develop new mining fields. For example, financial support from the USSR and China stopped after the Cold War was over, and therefore it is hard to develop the construction of power plants in Taechon and Youngbyn in the past.

Meanwhile, even if North Korea has large deposits of iron ore, it imports bituminous coal and coking coal from China and Russia and supplies the coals to the steelmaking companies in Kimchaek and Hwanghae, which are the main suppliers in the country. Hence, the imports of bituminous and coking coals are essential for the steel industry and for industrialization. Table 10.3 shows the import trend of those coals. Until 1989, North Korea imported 2.574 million tons of coal, but after 1989 imports from Russia sharply decreased.

Even though some scientists have maintained that North Korea has some offshore reserves of petroleum, these have not been yet confirmed. The main petroleum exporters to North Korea are the former Soviet Union, China, Iran, and Hong Kong. North Korea imported around three million tons of crude oil from these countries until 1988. However, due to the restriction of foreign credit and the changing contract to hard currency from the former Soviet Union and China, oil imports decreased sharply after 1990.

Table 10.3 Imports of Coal (Bituminous, Cokes) in DPRK (Thousand Ton)

		1976	1985	1987	1989	1990	1991	1992	1993	1994	1995
Coal	Russia	167	212	790	749	682	184	–	326	167	–
	China	–	–	1910	1597	1702	1515	1369	1567	1468	1120
	Sub-total	–	–	2700	2346	2384	1699	–	1893	1635	–
	IEA	170	2500	2500	2500	2500	2500	2500	2500	–	–
Coke	Russia	150	–	231	190	145	–	–	–	–	–
	China	–	–	–	38	64	–	123	83	51	–
	Japan	–	–	14	–	–	–	–	2	–	–
	Sub-total	–	–	–	228	209	–	–	85	51	–
	UN	222	300	300	300	300	300	–	–	–	–
Total imports		–	–	2945	2574	2593	–				
IEA, UN(Total)		392	2800	2800	2800	2800	2800	–	–	–	–

Source: Ministry of Foreign Trade of USSR (1996); Ministry of Foreign Trade of China (1996); IEA (1995).

The DPRK has two major oil refineries, one of which receives crude oil from China through a pipeline. Various estimates have placed the total refining capacity at these plants between 3 million and 3.5 million tons. Capacity in this range would be adequate to process the volume of imported crude oil. In estimating the operation rate given per ton of crude oil input, the maximum operation rate was 89 per cent in 1986, and as of 1994 it decreased to 26 per cent (see Table 10.4). In addition to refining crude oil in its own refineries, the DPRK purchases refined products such as diesel fuel, heavy oil, gasoline, and kerosene on the open market.

For electric power generation, North Korea supplies electricity from hydroelectric power plants and thermal power plants, which are mainly coal-fired plants. According to the report from the MNU, North Korea's electric power capacity was 7.38 million kW as of 1996 (BOK, 1997), which is four times as much as in 1960. Actual power electricity generation increased from 9.1 billion kWh in 1960 to 29.2 billion kWh in 1989. But after 1989, power generation kept decreasing until 1997. In 1997, actual electric power was 19.3 billion kWh (see Table 10.5).

Table 10.4 Operation Rate for Crude Oil Refining Facilities (Thousand Ton, Percentage)

	1975	1986	1987	1988	1989	1990	1991	1992	1993	1994
Refined capacity	3500	3500	3500	3500	3500	3500	3500	3500	3500	3500
Oil used	2590	3119	2904	3020	2485	2520	1880	1520	1360	910
Operation rate	74	89	83	86	71	72	54	43	39	26

Source: ERINA (1996).

Table 10.5 Electric Power Generation in DPRK (Billion KWh)

Year	South Korea				North Korea			
	Generation	Hydro (%)	Coal (%)	Nucl. (%)	Generation	Hydro .(%)	Coal (%)	Nucl. (%)
1965	3.3	21.2	75.8	–	13.2	54.5	45.5	0.3
1975	19.8	8.6	91.9	–	18.3	53.6	46.4	1.1
1985	58.0	6.4	64.8	29.0	25.1	49.0	51.0	2.3
1990	107.7	5.9	44.9	49.1	27.7	56.3	43.7	3.9
1995	184.7	3.0	60.7	36.3	23.0	61.7	38.3	8.0
1997	224.5	2.4	63.3	34.3	19.3	55.4	44.6	11.6

Source: Ministry of National Unification in South Korea (1992); United Nations (1980).

Due to political reasons, DPRK has been interested in nuclear power generation since it has quite good quality of uraniums. In 1986 the DPRK started the first experimental nuclear power generation plant at Youngbyn, which has 5000 kW power generation capacity. Although the DPRK had tried to build a second nuclear power generation plant of 50 000 kW power electric capacity at Youngbyn, and 200 000 kW power electric capacity at Taechon, the project was cancelled. Instead, with the help of KEDO, the LWRNL is under construction.

It is certain that North Korea has a very high loss of energy due to poor electricity transmission and distribution systems since electrical components of the generating facilities are quite old. If the DPRK can replace old electric distribution lines and parts, it will allow much room for raising the energy efficiency without entailing large investments in North Korea. Official estimates of losses in transmission and distribution systems were 16 per cent of total power generation; however, the MNU in South Korea argues that the loss should be close to 50 per cent or above.

Estimation of Future Electric Power Demand

Even though the DPRK has more than 500 electric power generating facilities, only 62 generation facilities were operating as of 1996. Among them, there are 42 hydroelectric power generation plants, and the rest are coal-fired power plants.

Table 10.6 Future Estimation of the Electric Power Demand

		2000	2005
Recovery	Electricity supply (TWH)	36.74	62.78
	Per cent of supply (%)	40 : 60 (Hydro : Coal)	38 : 40 : 22 (Hydro : Nuclear : Coal)
	Electricity demand (PJ)	90	132
Decline PJ (Petajoules)	Electricity supply (TWH)	23	38
	Per cent of supply (%)	40 : 60	36 : 32 : 32
	Electricity demand (PJ)	52	64

Source: Hippel and Hayes (1997).

Von Hippel and Hayes (1997) estimated the DPRK's electric power demand based on two different scenarios. The first scenario was a recovery case. It assumed that in the year 2000, the Sun-Bong refinery plant will be operating again, and in the year 2005 the operation capacity will be twice higher than before. During 1995 and 1996, most of the hydroelectric power plants were severely damaged by floods. Therefore, with the recovery scenario they assumed that 50 per cent of the damaged hydroelectric power plants will be operating until 2000; after that plants will be fully operating, and the DPRK will have high energy efficiency in coal-fired plant until 2005. Meanwhile heavy oil (B-C) usage in coal-fired plant was 9.5 per cent out of total power plant in the year 2000, and down to 3.5 per cent in 2005 out of total coal-used plant.

The second scenario is a somewhat dark case. It is assumed that the DPRK's economic situation will stabilize only after year 2005. It assumed that the Sun-Bong refinery plant will shut down, and most of the hydroelectric power plants will only be recovered by 25 per cent in year 2000, and that 50 per cent of the damaged hydroelectric power plants will be operating in 2005. Meanwhile B-C oil usage in coal-fired plant will reach 10.6 per cent in the year 2000, but down to 5 per cent in 2005. Based on the 'recovery' and 'decline' scenarios, H-H estimated the DPRK's electric power demand in 2000 and 2005, respectively (see Table 10.6).

H-H argued that if the North Korean government can overcome the severe flood damages within a few years, then it could supply enough electric power to the industry as well as the other sectors. Therefore, in 2005, the DPRK need a new transmission and distribution system and more electricity demand. In that case, the DPRK may consider the electric power import from South Korea. On the other hand, with the decline scenario, it is enough to supply electricity with current power generating capacities and expect to depend more on the coal-fired power plant in the year 2005.

As we mentioned before, the wave and electric networks are technically similar to each nation but have a different pattern of peak time demand, so it is possible for South and North Korea to exchange electricity within a recovery scenario. However, both countries need to examine more carefully how much electric power will be traded in the future.

Energy Supply and Demand Problems in North Korea

Institutional problems

Even though the DPRK set a self-sufficient energy policy as a national goal, the DPRK's energy supply mostly depends upon Russia and China. Most of the crude oil and coking coal and energy-related facilities were from former allies. The fragmentation of institutional responsibility in the energy sector is another problem in controlling the energy management system. There is no single institution responsible for energy supply and demand analysis, integrated planning, and management. For example, ministries and other government organizations involved in the energy sector are scattered and the role of energy management is also dispersed. In addition, coordination among the organizations is quite restricted, and not fully utilized.[2]

Besides these institutional problems, the financial burden in purchasing crude oil was tremendous. As we discussed before, North Korea bought crude oil on a barter (soft) basis. However, after 1990, crude oil imports decreased sharply as export countries changed the settlement fund to hard currency. As a result of the changing settlement fund, the price of crude oil increased three times for Russian crude oil and two times for Chinese crude oil.

One aspect to keep in mind is that North Korea has a very high loss of energy because of poor electricity transmission and distribution systems, inadequate maintenance and control systems, and antiquated transforming equipment. The DPRK has 62 power plants, 58 substations, and 11 regional transmission and dispatching centers, which are controlled by the EPPDCC (Electric Power Production and Dispatching and Control Center). However, EPPDCC communicates with regional centers by telephone and telex without the aid of computer systems, which results in poor frequency control problems, and hence frequent outages occurs. Therefore, repairs are urgently needed for transmission and distribution lines located underground.

Table 10.7 Summary of Quantitative Evaluation of Energy Efficiency and Renewable Energy Options for DPRK (1999–2000)

Measure	Estimated energy savings potential	Total estimated investment cost
Total coal supply savings	377 043 TJ/year	1 271 730 269
Industrial boiler and furnace improvements	158 267	6 104 005 542
Residential and public/commercial military	–	–
Boiler improvement	41 091	88 480 469
Building envelope improvements	27 513	54 306 490
Domestic stove/heater improvements	31 935	22 921 595
Electric utility boiler improvements	114 505	441 621 174
Avoided cost of coal during transport	3 733	–
Investment required, $ per TCE/year of coal saving	–	US$95
Total electricity supply savings/generation	51 132 TJ/year	1 614 162 370
Industrial motors and drives	8 719	339 561 095
Motors and drives in other sectors	1 574	61 311 299
Residential lighting	2 572	100 182 798
Non-residential lighting	10 267	285 183 258
Own use reduction in power plants	2 752	128 592 305
Reduction of emergency use in power plant	6 420	187 530 445
Transmission and distribution	10 675	311 801 170
Wind-powered electricity generation	3 492	200 000 000
Additional avoided T & D losses	4 211	–
Investment required, $ per mWh/year of electricity supply savings	–	US$114

Notes: One terajoule is equal to one trillion joules, which is the equivalent of 24 tons of crude oil.

Source: Hippel and Hayes (1995).

The IEA estimated 16 per cent energy losses, but in reality the percentage is probably much higher. Assuming a 30 per cent energy loss, equal to 7 billion kWh in losses, which exceeds the annual electric power consumption in the city of Daegu, Korea in 1995. The Nautilus Institute in the USA estimated that with a small investment, coal consumption would save about 37 million TJ, and 50 000 TJ for electric power plants (see Table 10.7).

Floods in 1995 and 1996 caused most of the hydroelectric power plants to stop operating. The capacity of reservoir water in dams was reduced because of landslides. It is expected that it will take a while for the DPRK to dredge through the landslides given the lack of equipments in the country. Dependency on coal-fired power plants, consisting of Chinese and the former Soviet Union's electrical parts such as boilers and generators, which could not burn North Korean coal at optimal combustion, exacerbated the low energy efficiency. Lack of spare parts and boiler turbines has caused coal-fired power plants to record lower energy efficiency.[3]

Interconnection problem to other power system

Currently, the DPRK uses 60 Hz in its electric power system. However, sometimes, difficulties in wave control forces it to use 57 Hz or 59 Hz. If North Korea tries to export electricity from the LWRNL to Russia and China, there is also an interconnection problem since those countries use 50 Hz. In order to change the frequency to 50 Hz, it will require a large investment. For example, to supply 1000 mW, it will cost approximately US$4.6 billion (Hippel and Hayes, 1997).

There is also a problem in terms of connection to the South Korean electric power system. First of all, a transformer substation should be built near the demilitarized zone 38th parallel in order to change AC (alternating current) into DC (direct current), then back again into AC to supply electric power to the South Korean power system. The system will cost around US$1.2 million (Yoon, 1996).

The biggest problem is related to use electric power from the LWRL. At present, the DPRK's electric power system is not a standardized network system for all regions but rather a district-based network system. Therefore, it is necessary to build up the network system as a singular unit.

Environmental problem in North Korea

Since the DPRK has heavily relied on coal as a primary energy, but has outdated equipment for power plants, the air quality has deteriorated over the past years. It is reported that industrial areas such as Hungnam, Hamheung and Wonsan have a serious air pollution problem. Among these industrial areas, Hungnam is well known for a serious air pollution problem since there are lots of chemical industries. However, very little research has been conducted to investigate the levels of air quality, emission amounts, and impacts of air pollution on health.

North Korea's reliance on coal to fuel its large energy system raises concern over the large amount of sulfur dioxide emissions (SO_2), which can be transported over hundreds of kilometers before it is deposited and is the main cause of acid rain problems. Of course China has the most serious problems of SO_2 emissions nowadays. Acidity of rainfall has increased remarkably in many areas, and damaged lakes, forests, and people's health in Northeast Asian countries, particularly in North and South Korea, and Japan. Of course, the biggest victim of acid rain is China (see Table 10.8).

Table 10.8 Country-to-country Source Receptor Relationship (Percentage)

Receptor source	S. Korea	Japan	N. Korea	Mongolia
China	13	96	35	48
South Korea	83	7.1	3.7	0.01
Japan	0.5	36.8	0.05	0
North Korea	1.2	0.6	29	0.01

Source: Shin, Eui-Soon (1997).

Thus far, the RAINS-ASIA model is the most comprehensive and elaborate transboundary pollution model.[4] According to the summary report of the RAINS-ASIA project, Northeast China, Japan, and South Korea are highly vulnerable to acid deposition and are expected to be a greater risk in the future.

Table 10.8 shows the country-to-country, source-receptor relationship among Northeast Asian countries. North Korea is responsible for 1.2 per cent of South Korea's sulfur dioxide deposition and 0.6 per cent of Japan's sulfur dioxide deposition. North Korean's own contribution is 29 per cent while China is responsible for 35 per cent of sulfur dioxide deposition. All of these, so called export–import matrix, figures are not yet conclusive. Therefore, we should be very cautious in interpreting the result of the matrix.

However, it is clear that acid deposition has significant potential to impact the Northeast Asian regions. Therefore, firm and sound empirical evidence is urgently needed to verify this and to provide early warning of increase in the magnitude and spread of acid deposition and its effect throughout Northeast Asia. In this regard environmental cooperation will become one of the top priorities in the Northeast region.

10.3 ENERGY COOPERATION BETWEEN NORTH AND SOUTH KOREA

International Energy Cooperation

Formal international energy cooperation started at the meeting of the Ministry of Economics in Indonesia in 1980. In the following year, ten projects were suggested during the meeting. Among these projects, the third project was 'A Project for the Interconnection of Electric Power System in Asia Countries'. According to the project, eight Asian countries' electric power systems were planned for interconnection. But only two lines have been interconnected thus far, since there have been problems related to the allocation of the financial burden among participating countries, low electric power demand in some regions, and an uncertain plan for the construction of fire plants, and so on (see Table 10.9).

Table 10.9 A Case of Interregional Electric Power System Connection

Interregional power connection	Methods	Characteristics
Malaysia–Singapore	230 kV, 2 circuits	Simultaneous operation setting up the wave
Malaysia–Thailand	132 kV, 1 circuit	Weak for the connection thinking of HVDC
Sarawak–Malaysian Peninsular	In process	In Bakun, Murum, large-scale hydro. power
Sumatra–Malaysia Peninsular	In process	Need for HVDC cable in ocean
Singapore–Bakun Island	Distribution center for gas, coal	Need large investment
Singapore–West Killimantan	Share of reserve power	More than 100 mW electric power capacity
Sawara–Sava–Philippine	Development of hydro power	Possible for project
Sawara–Sava–Brunei	Long transmission line	Not feasible

Source: Korean Electric Power Company (KEPCO, 1995).

European and North American countries have already interconnected their electric power systems and expanded the connection area. For the East Asian region, the Eastern Siberian and Chinese Southeast areas are the most promising areas for electric power generation and have rapid growth in electric power demand. Hence, there is a strong possibility for the trade of electricity with other countries in the future. East Siberia has abundant water for hydroelectric power generation. The potential capacities for hydroelectric power generation are 849 billion kWh. It is assumed that China also has about 1000 billion kWh in water hydraulic power. In recent years, privatization of the electricity sector has been established in these countries.[5] Therefore foreign investors for the East Siberian area will accelerate developing a hydroelectric power plant in the future.

It seems that the interconnection of power systems among East Asian countries will be an economically profitable project. There is a feasibility study concerning the connection of power systems from the Primorye nuclear power plant in Russia to South Korea by way of China. Yoon (1996) maintained that if government or business groups are to invest US$876.5 billion to construct and US$109.5 billion for operation costs, it is possible to connect the electric power system between Far Eastern Russia and the Northeast region of China.

Bilateral Cooperation: North–South Korean Electric Power System Connection

As of 1994, if we calculate the total amount of energy supply for the DPRK and South Korea, the size of energy use is quite large, and there is a high possibility of complementary effects between each country. By using 1990 data, KEEI (Korean Energy Economics Research Institute) estimated the future energy demand in 2000.

KEEI anticipated that if North Korea could resolve its energy shortage problem, the difference of energy demand might increase to as much as four times in the year 2000. However, since the estimated figures in 1990 do not reflect the energy shortage problem after 1990, the gap will be much wider if we re-estimate the future energy demand for the year 2000.

The first beneficiary of electricity trade should go to North Korea. However, South Korea can also benefit from exchanging electric power. Since the peak load for both countries are at different times of the year, it is estimated that South Korea can export about 700 000 kW to North Korea during the winter season, and North Korea can export about 1 million kW to South Korea during the summer season. By trading electricity, South Korea can save the development cost for electric power plants, and solve the NIMBY (Not in My Backyard) situation for selecting power plant locations.

So far, there are various approaches to energy cooperation; electricity trade, exchange South Korean's B-C oil for North Korean's coal, develop hydraulic power generation and build up petrochemical plants jointly, develop coal reserves, and gas field jointly, and construct gas pipelines through the DPRK's territory. Among these options, the first three ideas can be done within a short period of time.

Table 10.10 Comparison of Future Energy Demand between North and South Korea in Year 2000 (Thousand TOE)

	South Korea	DPRK	Difference (DPRK= 1)
Total energy demand	176 334	52 173	3.3 : 1
Energy use per people	3.80 TOE	2.26TOE	1.7 : 1
Coal	39 793 (23.6)	36 049 (68.3)	1.1 : 1
Oil	99 282 (56.3)	5 198 (9.9)	19.1 : 1
Gas	12 414 (7.0)	–	–
Nuclear	23 889 (13.5)	3 300 (6.3)	7.2 : 1
Hydro power	956 (0.5)	8 166 (15.5)	0.1 : 1

Source: Chung et al. (1994).

North Korea is already receiving B-C from KEDO since in South Korea industrial use for B-C has decreased and has been replaced by high-quality oil. Therefore, South Korea can export the remaining B-C oil to North Korea. From the South Korean view, petrochemical industries should invest further to prepare for the high demand of petrochemical products domestically, hence building petrochemical plants in North Korea with low labor cost is feasible. This will give[6] South Korean industries low economic cost effect. From the DPRK's point of view, they can hire many skilled laborers, and supply petroleum products to consumers.

For the development of coal mining, since the primary source of energy in DPRK will be coal for several decades in the future, it is worthwhile for South Korea to develop coal mining projects, and exports to other countries such as Mongolia, and Northern China might be a good alternative.

In order to have energy cooperation between South and North Korea, private sector cooperation might be the best at this time considering the political situations. For that purpose, it is desirable to obtain financial support from the international bank such as ADB or IBRD. Regarding project financing, both parties should look at BOT (build–operate–transfer) approaches, which are commonly done in Africa and Asia region.

Table 10.11 Small-scale Electric Power Connection between North and South Korea

Region	Connection Line (kV)	Distance (km)	Volume (kW)	Enhancement of network
Western	Monsan–Kasung– (154) (66) Pyungsan (154)	65	200 000	Yangjoo–Kumchon– (345) (154) Moonsan (154)
Central	Pochun–Woonchon– (154) (66) Choulwon (154)	70	700 000	Yeijungboo–Kumoh– (345) (154) Pochon (154)
Eastern	Sokcho–Gansung– (154) (154) Kymgangsan (66)	83	800 000	Sangnam–Inje– (154) (154) Gansung (154)

Source: KEPCO (1993).

Another way of cooperation is making a consortium among the South Korean companies such as KEPCO, Hyundae Construction Company, et al. In this case, a North Korean partner should be involved in a consortium to guarantee the project. It is reported that the Hyundae group will establish an industrial complex at HaeJoo in Kaesung in the near future.[7] If this kind of economic cooperation progresses smoothly, power plant constructions to supply electricity is essential for the complex. In this case, North and South Korea can jointly build a power generation plant of at least 100 000 kW capacity. The type of plant will be either a coal-fired or combined cycle power plant for LNG.

In the long run, North Korean should increase the portion of oil-based power plants, hence it is highly desirable to have energy cooperation for the construction of oil-fired power plants and management control between the countries.

So far we have discussed several options for energy cooperation. Among these options, electricity trade might be the most practical and possible option to solve the energy shortage problem in the DPRK. Of course, it is essential for both parties to reach an advanced agreement for energy cooperation. The basic rules of electricity trade should be determined before. The rules should include the scale of electric power trade, who will be the financial supporter, and the electric power pricing mechanism. Since the bulk of the electric power trade will be done by KEPCO (Korean Electric Power Company) in

South Korea, KEPCO should obtain enough capacity of electric power based on the level of electric power trade. At the same time, KEPCO should enhance the electric network and think of other ways of operating the network after the interconnection of the electric power system has been established.

At the same time, if both parties can resolve the low quality problem of electric power, standardize the electric equipment, and set up an electric pricing mechanism, then the interconnection of electric power will boost the operational efficiency of power plants in North Korea.

If the DPRK needs a small scale of electric power, KEPCO expects that the volume of electric power trade would be around 300 000 kW. In this scenario, a 154 kV transmission line will be used, and it will take about two years to set up the connection. Table 10.11 shows the regional interconnection line for the electric power system.

Table 10.12 Large-scale Electric Power Connection between North and South Korea

Region	Connection Line (kV)	Distance (km)	Volume (kW)	Enhancement of network
Western	Yangjoo– (345) Pyungyang (220)	200	1.5 million	Shingapyung– (765) Shinyangjoo– (765) Yangjoo (345)
Eastern	Donghae– (345) Yangyang– (345) Hamheung (345)	70	700 000	Yeojungboo– (345) Kumo– (345) Pochon (220)

Source: KEPCO (1993).

However, if a large-scale electric power system need to be connected, it is also possible to connect the system by using 345 kV (see Table 10.12). In this case, the volume of electric exchange would be around 1 to 2 million kW, and will take three years to achieve an exchange of electric power, and the optimal plant having 50 000 – 1 million kW will be located near the DMZ (KEPCO).

Perhaps the most immediate problem for the interconnection of the electric power system is that an uncertain system connection in North Korea may cause an unstable electric power system, and trigger unreliable control of the network system in South Korea. It may even become a source of bilateral dispute if there are frequent stops after the connection. In order to cope with these problems, it is necessary to increase the capacity of power plants in North Korea. That is, in the long run both countries need to construct more power plants whether it is either coal-fired plants or nuclear power plants, or hydroelectric power plants. In doing so, the DPRK can achieve a balance of electric power supply and demand.

In the matter of nationalization of devices, we can resolve the problem by allotting separate roles. While South Korea is responsible for the operation and technical management, the DPRK can take responsibility for financial liability. Another way of preventing nationalization is to connect the lines with Northern China, which also has a serious energy shortage problem.

Multilateral Energy Cooperation: Use of Russian Gas

Background

Natural gas consumption in the world has been rapidly increasing, and the trend will continue during the 21st century since it is an environmentally friendly fuel, and new gas reserves are being found. Also, technologies to use natural gas have been developing faster in recent years. The share of natural gas in the world in terms of primary energy consumption increased from 18 per cent in 1990 to 23.1 per cent in 1995. Meanwhile the consumption of natural gas in South Korea has been increasing at more than 30 per cent on average due to high consumer preferences in the past decades, and the extension of a nation wide natural gas trunk line to be completed in 2002.[8]

North Korea has been interested in using natural gas for quite some time. In 1986, North Korea hosted an international seminar related to natural gas. The Energy Center had studied natural gas projects regarding how to transport the gas through a gas pipeline, which was planned to be built along the East Coast in DPRK.

It is natural for the DPRK to show interest in natural gas. Compared to other fossil fuel types, power plants using natural gas have definite advantages; high-energy efficiency, short construction period, easy operation, and smaller land requirements for construction than coal-based power plants. At the same time, the construction cost of natural gas power plants is cheaper than the other types, and it is easy to disassemble and maintain the equipment. Therefore, with cheap fossil fuel prices, and low environmental pollution emissions, natural gas power plants are economically feasible and efficient for the North Korean economy. That is why the DPRK has shown a strong interest in using natural gas.

Gas supply to DPRK

Russian Gas The former USSR as a whole contains more than 40 per cent of the world's proven gas reserves. Because of these abundant gas reserves, 65 per cent of the fuel in power plants is natural gas, and gas consumption in Russia increased from 48.7 per cent in 1985 to 53.1 per cent in 1994 due to high demand from the electric power plants and the large gas storage facilities. During the 1980s, gas demand from the iron and steel industry, chemical industries, and petroleum refinery industry were also increasing. As a result of high demand from these industries, gas for commercial and residential purpose was quite low. However, it is expected that demand for residential and commercial use will increase since those energy-intensive industries will experience industrial restructuring in the future.[9]

Russian gas specialist Matthew (1995) expected that natural gas production will increase after 1998/9 up to 640 billion cubic meter (BCM), and will keep increasing until 2020 by 950 BCM. However, there is no gas development project planned until the year 2000, except in the Western Siberian region such as Astrakhan, Timan–Pechora region after 2000.

The proven reserves (commercial grade) of natural gas are 49 million cubic meters as of January 1994, and 219 million cubic meters if we include total potential reserves. Almost 80 per cent of Russian's commercial grade gas reserves are located in West Siberia, especially in northern Tyumen Oblast (in the Yamal Nenets Autonomous Okrug), which account for 80 percent of the total reserves.[10] Sizeable reserves (10.6 per cent) remain in the European Russia (Volga–Urals) and Timan–Pechora Basin (2 per cent) of the northern European Russia. East Siberia and the Far East (Yakut–Sakha republic and Sakhalin) account for 4.2 per cent of Russia's onshore reserves (2 trillion cubic meters). However, Sakhalin's potential offshore reserves are rated at 4.5 trillion cubic meters. Remaining reserves are found offshore on the continental shelf.

West Siberian gas production has not increased in recent years due to decreasing internal demand for gas in Russia, frequent labor union strikes, and technical problems in developing the gas fields. East Siberian natural gas was not developed extensively even though the region has 2 trillion cubic meters of natural gas. However, there is high potential for export to Asian countries if a natural gas pipeline is laid from East Siberia to Japan by way of China and North Korea. Japan has already performed the economic benefit and cost analysis for different routes from the Koviktinskoye gas field – the major gas field for the Irukutsk project – to Japan in the Northeast Asia pipeline projects.

Russia has emerged as the world's most prominent gas exporter, with gas exports outside the territory of the former USSR jumping from a mere 3.3 BCM in 1970 to 109 BCM in 1990. Russia has usually exported natural gas to the major Eastern European countries and the former Soviet Russian Federation (CIS). However, as we can see in Table 10.13, exports to the CIS since 1994 has decreased while the amount of export to non-CIS has increased. One cause of reduced exports to CIS countries is the difference of prices between CIS countries and non-CIS countries. Export price per 1000 m^3 for the CIS countries were US$51.5, but for the non-CIS countries it was US$80.1.

Table 10.13 Status of Russian Gas Export (m^3, Percentage)

	1992	1993	1994	1995
Production	640	618	607	595
Total export	195	185	187	192
To non-CIS	88	96	109	121
(% out of total production)	(14)	(16)	(18.1)	(20.5)
To CIS	106	75	74.7	70.3
(% out of total production)	(17)	(12)	(12.3)	(11.8)

Source: Whurr Publishers (1996).

Russian Gas Exports to Northeast Asian Countries in the Future Plans of Russian gas exports to Northeast Asia, mainly to Japan, date back over 30 years to 1966. The plan was to develop a gas pipeline or to export LNG from Sakhalin to Japan. During the 1970s, there were also plans for a much larger-scale pipeline and/or LNG projects from gas fields in the Yakutia region of Eastern Siberia (Sakha Republic). However, Russian gas exports to Northeast Asian countries had not progressed much over 30 years. The principal problem was political reason. Japan did not want to rely on a single country for its energy source. Japanese buyers preferred to purchase their gas from a variety of other suppliers in the Asia-Pacific region and the Middle East (see Table 10.4).

No significant progress towards Russian gas trade with Asia-Pacific countries has been made since the break-up of the former Soviet Union. However, at present, several projects are under consideration. The first and most interesting project is based on the gas condensate field 'Kovyktinskoye (900 billion m^3 deposit) in the Irukutsk region'.[11] Plans have been established for a large-scale gas exploitation base connected by a main pipeline not only to East Siberia (Kovyktinskoye gas field, Yaraktingskaya mining lot), and southern part of the Far East but also to Mongolia, China, DPRK and South Korea. Another exploitation project is the Sakhalin continental shelf exploitation project. It is expected to exploit 20 billion m^3 by the year 2010.

Besides the gas pipeline construction plan, oil exploration in East Siberia and the Far East is another promising area for the energy problem after the year 2010. Currently, some large-scale oil deposits have been discovered and examined: Yurubchensckoye, Verkhnecheonskoye, Talakanskoye oil fields, and so on.

Considering these plans, it is highly possible that after the year 2010 the natural gas and oil flow from Russia's western Far East and the East to the Asian countries will form the foundation of an integrated gas transport system in East Russia. If the Russian government can remove legal obstacles, and attract foreign capital, the development of these projects will be accelerated. Therefore, it is necessary for the Far Eastern countries to look carefully and constantly at Russia's political and economic situation.

Table 10.14 Future Gas Export in Far Eastern Region (BCM)

Countries	2005	2010	2020
China	10–15	16–23	30–45
S. Korea	8–10	10–23	12–14
N. Korea	2–4	3–5	5–6
Japan	5–8	10–18	10–15
Taiwan	2–3	3–4	4–5
Mongolia	0–2	1–3	2–3
Total	27–42	41–58	63–88

Source: Siberian Energy Institute of Russian Academy of Sciences (1996).

Multilateral Energy Cooperation among the East Asian Countries

Gas pipelines

In 1997, Russia and China agreed on the construction of two PNG gas pipelines between Russia's Iruktsk and Northern China. The amount of gas to be supplied is 2 to 3 million BCM at a cost of US$4–5 billion dollars. South Korea and Russia agreed in September 1992 to jointly study the feasibility of developing natural gas deposits in Russia's Republic of Sahka. A consortium of South Korean and Russian counterparts is presently undertaking a preliminary feasibility study of a project which would involve building a gas export line from gas fields in Sahka to South Korea. The APEC had planned to connect a gas pipeline, which is a 42 500 km pipeline from Yakustk to Dampier in Australia via four ASEAN countries (China, Japan, Taiwan, and South Korea).

The NPRSJ in Japan has a long history of pipeline development plans to use Russian gas. It was Japan that introduced the idea of the 'Trans-Asian Natural Gas Pipeline Network' in 1990, and the NPRSJ was established to pursue this project. Dr. Asakura from the NPRSJ had examined the economic feasibility for different routes via the Korean Peninsula to Japan (Kovitsinskoye–KitaKyushu).

The key assumptions in the study were as follows: 80 per cent operation rates, 5-year construction periods, 8 per cent interest rate for the invested capital, 5 per cent profit rate, and 0.03 \$/MMBTU/100 km for penetration fee. Table 10.15 shows the economic feasibility study of the final gas prices.[12]

Table 10.15 Different Routes and Final Gas Prices with and without Passing Fee (US\$/MMBTU)

Without passing fee	Kovitsins-koye (0.5)	Iruktsk (0.72)	Beijing (1.59)	Shenyang–Pyongyang–Seoul (2.31)	KitaKyushu (2.90)
				Inchon (2.57)	(3.18)
				Mokpo (2.73)	(3.96)
With passing fee	Kovitsins-koye (0.5)	Iruktsk (0.72) + 0.36	Beijing (1.59)	Shenyang–Pyongyang–Seoul (2.31) + 0.66 + 0.1	KitaKyushu (4.02)
				Inchon (2.57) + 0.54 + 0.1	(4.85)
				Mokpo (2.73) + 0.53	

Notes: The numbers in parenthesis denote final price.

Table 10.16 Summary of PNG Projects in Asia-Pacific Region

Project	Turkmenistan	Yakutsk	Irkutsk
Pipeline route	Turkmenistan–China–Korea–Japan	Yakutsk–Vladivostok–Hasan–(N. Korea)–S. Korea	Irkutsk–Mongolia
Total length	On shore 6000 km Off shore 2000 km	5000–6000 km	4000 km
Related companies	CNCP, Mitubishi, Exxon	Korea Sakha Consortium Russia Consortium	KGC, Halla, Kohap
Cost	?	US\$20 billion	US\$10 billion

Source: Korea Pan-Asian Natural gas pipeline Association (1996).

The most economically and technically efficient line was the the first pipeline connection as we can see in Table 10.15, originating in Russia and passing through China, North Korea (Pyongyang), South Korea (Seoul), and Japan (Kitakyushu) regardless of taking into account the passing fee for the third country.

Besides these pipeline connections, the Trukmenistan PNG project and Yakutsk project were being considered by Mitsubishi, CNPC, and Exxon and so on. Natural gas can be transported via a newly constructed long-distance pipeline from Turkmenistan to the East Coast of China. It will either be liquefied or transported by LNG vessels, or transported by submarine pipeline directly from the east coast of China and marketed in the Far East Asian market (see Table 10.16).

Benefits from multilateral energy cooperation between North and South Korea

Russia also considered laying down a gas pipeline from Irkutsk to Vladivostok via Qitar, and Komsololsk to Vladivostok via Habalovstk. If the Yakutsk and Irkutsk project begins, the DPRK will connect the pipeline from Hasan to Chungjin with relatively low investment. The pipeline to Chungjin would play an important role to supply enough energy for the Tumen River Area Development Program (TRAP) through the United Nations Development Program (UNDP).

However, Russia alone cannot proceed with the project. The project requires international cooperation. However, if the Russian natural gas pipeline passes through the North Korean area, then North Korea will have much to benefit from it. First, the project will create many employment opportunities. Second, it will obtain foreign currencies from the passing fees for the pipeline, and most of all, North Korea can use the pipeline to meet its energy demands. That is why North Korea has shown great interest in the Project. If North Korea's labor and South Korea's technology can mutually combine, it will create huge economic benefits for the DPRK in the long run, and both parties will obtain a greater level of energy security.

Both South Korea and North Korea need to cooperate closely in the energy sector as an essential prerequisite for the two Koreas to begin full-scale economic exchange. The cooperation is urgent in view of the planned natural gas pipeline linking Russia, China and Japan via the Korean Peninsula.

In order to use the Russian gas in South Korea, passage of the DPRK is an essential condition. Even if North Korea permits the passing of a natural gas pipeline, labor is needed to construct the pipeline. Thinking about the reunification costs, it is highly desirable to build the social infrastructure in advance. Therefore, both parties can think about a joint venture at Chungjin Harbor, which is a free harbor and close to the Rajin–Sonbong Economic and

Trade Zone.[13]

After the Vostok Program[14] planned by the former Soviet Union during the Gorvachev ruling period, and the Asian gas pipeline project from the Siberian gas field, the DPRK has shown interest in the natural gas pipeline project. After Russia announced the Vostok Program, it was reported that the DPRK had planned to use 5 billion BCM natural gas per year after 2000. It was also reported that the DPRK had established an association to study the natural gas issue in recent years.

If we assume reunification, a pipeline connection through the natural gas industry will give several benefits to both countries. First, avoiding coal-dependency will restructure the energy industry in North Korea. At present, North Korea's energy policy is a coal-oriented policy, but it leads to an inefficient energy system, which further results in an ineffective economic structure across the whole economy. However, if reunification occurs between the nations, a lot of inefficient coal mining projects would be shut down, and hence bring the problem of a shortage in coal supply. In response to the potential crisis, it is urgent to have a sufficient source of energy such as natural gas.

The second benefit will come from the gas–electric power exchange system during the peak times for both countries. That is, natural gas demand occurs during the winter in South Korea; therefore, the South Korean gas industry needs gas storage facilities during the summer, which requires a lot of investment. However, demand for natural gas in North Korea might come from the power plant operation. Therefore, the DPRK can supply electric power to South Korea, and receive power during the winter. In this manner, the South Korean gas and electric industry will increase their economic efficiency and North Korea will secure an energy supply year-round.

Thirdly, by having a pipeline through North Korea, the cost paid by the South Korean government would be reduced if reunification were to happen in the future. Therefore, it is worth while to study the Russian Gas Project more closely as a possible economic option for resolving the North Korean energy problem. In order to study the natural gas situation in Russia and China it is desirable to establish a so-called 'Northeast Gas Development Research Center' in the near future.

Of course, there might be some obstacles hindering the development of the gas pipeline. Because of the uncertain economic situation and legal problems, foreign investors hesitate to be involved in the gas development project. The first problem is Russian law, namely the Producing Sharing Contract (PSC).[15] The attraction of PSC for private investors lies in the fact that it replaces any energy-specific taxes and eliminates many uncertainties about future tax rates and rules. The law outlines the relationship between the state and domestic and foreign investors concerning the use of mineral resources, royalties, sale of products, and taxation. The most hard element is the Russian tax shield. Investors transferring a portion of the product to the state will be exempt from taxes, customs, duties, excise, and other fees, with the exception of the profit taxes, and royalties. However, there is still disagreement among the Duma's Committee.

10.4 CONCLUSION

North Korea's gross national product (GNP) was reported to suffer a 25 per cent drop over the past six years and is recording a six-consecutive year decline (BOK, 1977). It has suffered bad harvests and floods. The reasons for the consecutive economic recession were related to foreign debts incurred in purchasing industrial equipment, shortages of energy and raw materials as well as a sharp decrease in grain output from the agricultural sector. However, the main cause of economic sluggishness stems from the problem of energy shortage.

It is true that economic cooperation between South and North Korea has not been productive because they could not find mutually beneficial areas to explore. However, since the main cause of economic sluggishness stems from the problem of an energy shortage, the practical approaches for economic cooperation must first be through energy cooperation.

In order to solve the energy shortage problem in North Korea, both short- and long-run strategies are necessary. For the short-run strategy, it is desirable to have bilateral cooperation between the DPRK and South Korea, which involves the connection of an electric transmission network in North and South Korea. In the long-run strategy, multilateral cooperation is needed to use natural gas from the Russian Republic of Siberia through the gas pipeline project. All the participating parties will derive economic benefit from the projects. Therefore, it is necessary for the Far Eastern countries to look carefully at Russia's gas-related political and economic situation.

In summary, solving the energy shortage problem in North Korea in a short time period is desirable but difficult, and in some cases, it can be very sensitive to address. However, it should be understood that it might not be possible to obtain the ultimate answer to some of the questions raised in this paper. Sound analysis of energy issues based on reliable data, nonetheless, will provide a firm foundation for practical economic cooperation approaches through energy sector cooperation. It is definite that South and North Korea's energy cooperation will give North Korea a chance to boost its economic growth again.

APPENDIX

Estimation of Fixed Costs and Construction Costs for Different Lines

Table 10.A.1 Fixed Cost for A, B Line (Millions of US Dollars)

Line	A, B	A	B
Supply	Kovyktinskoye	Irkutsk	Irkutsk
Consumer	Irkutsk	Beijing	Beijing
Length (km)	400	3 550	2 400
Volume of gas (million m^3)	38 000	28 000	28 000
Construction cost	1 988	9 786	6 614
Interest period	477	2 349	1 587
Total fixed cost	2 465	12 135	8 201
Pipeline construction cost (US$/$m^3$)	4 969.4	2 756.6	2 755.7

Table 10.A.2 Interest Rate

Interest of construction (%)	24.00	24.00	24.00
Rate per annual of construction cost (%)	10.19	10.19	10.19

Source: Korea Pan-Asian Natural Gas Pipeline Association (1996).

Table 10.A.3 Fixed Cost for C Line (Millions of US Dollars)

Line	C1	C2
Supply	Beijing	Seoul
Consumer	Seoul	KitaKyushu
Length (km)	1 600	585
Volume of gas (million m^3)	20 000	10 000
Construction cost	3 487	1 252
Interest period	837	300
Total fixed cost	4 323	1 552
Pipeline construction cost (US$/$m^3$)	2 179.1	2 139.6

Table 10.A.4 Fixed Cost for D Line (Millions of US Dollars)

Line	D1	D2	D3
Supply	Beijing	Sandong	Inchon
Consumer	Sandong	Inchon	KitaKyushu
Length (km)	1 100	370	585
Volume of gas (million m^3)	20 000	20 000	10 000
Construction cost	2 371	1 855	1 252
Interest period	569	445	300
Total fixed cost	2 940	2 300	1 552
Pipeline construction cost (US$/$m^3$)	2 155.4	5 013.2	2 139.6

Table 10.A.5 Fixed Cost for E line (Millions of US Dollars)

Line	E1	E2	E3
Supply	Beijing	Rizhao	Mokpo
Consumer	Rizho	Mokpo	KitaKyushu
Length (km)	1 050	620	750
Volume of gas (million m^3)	20 000	20 000	20 000
Construction cost	2 030	3 152	3 005
Interest period	487	756	721
Total fixed cost	2 517	3 908	3 726
Pipeline construction cost (US$/$m^3$)	1 933.3	5 083.6	4 006.7

NOTES

1. North Korea's nominal gross national product in 1996 was US$21.4 billion.
2. The Ministry of Coal Mining is responsible for coal exploration, the Electric Power Industry Commission for electricity generation, dispatching, and sale, the Transport Commission for energy use in the transport sector, and the State Committee for Energy for decision making for the energy plan.
3. In case of Load Center, maintenance is poor and outdated.
4. RAINS-ASIA model was performed to analyze and assess the relative vulnerability and natural environments to acid deposition.
5. North Korea also maintained that the possible capacity of water hydraulic power, if they cooperate with other countries, is 100 billion kWh.
6. As of 1995 40.24 million barrels were exported.
7. Another candidate for the industrial complex may be Nampo near to the Pyungyang province.
8. South Korea started using LNG in 1986 and take 10.3 per cent of the world LNG trade.

9. It is expected that gas consumption for commercial and residential sectors will be increased from 15.4 per cent in 1995 to 16.3 per cent in 2010 to 16.6 per cent in 2020.
10. These include, so called, six giant fields such as Urengoy, Yamborg, Medvezh'ye, Zapolyarnoye, Bovanenko, Kharasavey, which account for the 92.7 percent of Russia's total production.
11. The possible annual exploitation is estimated at 32 billion m^3.
12. For the estimation of fixed and construction costs, see appendix.
13. The Chungjin Harbor has the simultaneous berthing capacity of 11 ships in the 5000 or 10 000-ton class.
14. The main purpose of the program was to boost up the Eastern Siberian economy by attracting foreign investment and export East Siberian natural gas to the East Asian countries.
15. The Russian State Duma (the lower chamber of parliament) enacted the PSC on June 14, 1995; the Federation Council should approve the law and signed by the President. Its approval by the Council and President for the Irutsk region has not been passed, but expected to pass soon.

BIBLIOGRAPHY

Bank of Korea (1997), *Economic Situation in North Korea*, Annual Report (in Korean).

British Petroleum (1997), *Statistical Review of World Energy.*

Choi, Soo-Young (1994), *Energy Cooperation in Preparation of Reunification between the North and South Korea*, Monthly Report in the Petroleum Association, vol. 4, 32–36 (in Korean).

Chung, Young-Hun (1997), *The Northeast Asian Natural Gas Project: Prospects and Problems*, Paper presented at the Northeast Asian Economic Conference in Nigata '97.

Daewoo Research Institute and KEEI (1995), *North East Asian Energy and the Global Context*, Policy Paper, Seoul (in Korean).

Economic Research Institute Northeast Asia (1996), *Current Status of Energy Supply and Demand*, Research Paper, vol. 8, 26–32 (in Japanese).

Hayes, Peter (1994), *Economic Dimensions of Restoring North Korea's Environment,* 4th North Korean Economy International Conference.

Hippel, D.V. and Peter Hayes (1995), *The Prospects for Energy Efficiency Improvements in the Democratic People's Republic of Korea: Evaluating and exploring the Options*. California.

Hippel, D.V. and Peter Hayes (1997), 'Current Status of Energy Industry and Future Perspectives in North Korea', Paper presented at Economic Integration in Korean Peninsular, Washington D. C.

International Energy Agency (1996), *World Energy Outlook.*

International Energy Agency (1995), *Energy Statistics and Balances of Non-OECD, 1992–1993.*

International Energy Agency (1997), *Energy Statistics and Balances of Non-OECD.*

International Trade Administration (1996), *China: Environmental Technologies Export Market Plan*, Washington D.C.

Jakobowicz, Jean M. (1994), 'Acid Rain: An Issue for Regional Cooperation' in J. Rose (ed.), *Acid Rain: Current Situation and Remedies*, Gordon and Breach Science Publishers.

Jang, Young-Sik (1994), The Economics of N*orth Korea's Energy*, KDI, Seoul (in

Korean).

Korean Energy Economics Institute (1995), *A Study on the Economic Cooperation between North and South Korea for the Natural Resource Development*, Seoul (in Korean).

Korean Energy Economics Institute (1997), 'Current Status of Energy', *KEEI Bulletin*, December (in Korean).

Korean Electric Power Company (1993), 'Interconnection of Electric Power System between North and South Korea', unpublished paper (in Korean).

Korea Institute for Internatioanl Economic Policy (1994), *Chinese Annual Report*, Seoul (in Korean).

Kim, Jeong-In (1997), 'Energy Problem in North Korea and Future Respects', *North Korean Economy*, vol. 2, 35–56 (in Korean).

Kim, Jeong-In and Park Chang-Won (1997), 'Current Status of Environmental Pollution and Estimation of Future Pollution Emissions in North Korea: Case of Air Pollution', *Korean Environmental Economics Journal*, 7 (1), 29–60 (in Korean).

Kim, Jeong-In, Choi Dong-Joo, Kim Kap-Chul and Kim Seung-Woo (1997), 'Energy Consumption in East Asian countries and Transboundary Pollution Problem', Korea Environmental Policy and Impact Evaluation Research Institute (KEI), *KEI Research Paper*, RE 97-12 (in Korean).

Korea Pan Asia Natural Gas Pipeline Research Association (1996), *Current Status of Gas Development Project*, Annual Report.

Lin, Xianuan (1996), *China's Energy Strategy*, London: Praeger.

Mathew J. Sagers (1995), *The Russian Natural Gas in the Mid-1990s*, Post-Soviet Geography, no. 9, 521–64.

Ministry of Foreign Trade of China (1996), *Yearbook of Imports in China*, Annual Report.

Ministry of Foreign Trade of USSR (1996), *Foreign Trade of the USSR*, Annual Report.

Ministry of National Unification (1992), *Economic Indicators between DPRK and South Korea*, Annual Report (in Korean).

Ministry of National Unification (1997), *An Overview of DPRK: 1995* (in Korean).

North Korea Research Institute (1996), *North Korea Annual Report* (in Korean).

Paik Keun-Wook (1996) 'Northeast Asian Energy Cooperation' in Royal Institute of International Affairs, *Northeast Asian Energy and the Global Context*, London, 19–26.

Science Technology and Policy Research Institute (1993), *Energy Use and Forecasting of Environmental Pollution Emissions*, Tokyo (in Japanese).

Sameer Nawaz (1995), *Natural Gas in Asia*, London: FT Energy Publishing.

Shin, Eui-Soon (1997), 'Cost Sharing Approach toward Acid Rain Problems in Northeast Asia', Paper presented at the Northeast Asia Acid Rain workshop, Bejing University.

Siberian Energy Institute of Russian Academy of Sciences (1996), *Large Scale Development of the Gas Industry in the Eastern Direction as the Priority of the Modern Russian Energy Strategy*.

Smil Vaclav (1996), *Environmental Problems in China: Estimates of Economic Costs*, East-west Center.

Street, D. (1997), *Energy and Acid Rain Projections for North Asia*, Nautilus Institute for Security and Sustainable Development, California.

United Nations (1980), *Yearbook of World Energy Statistics*.

Whurr Publishers (1996), *Russian Economic Trends*, vol. 4, 64–7.

Yoon Kap-Goo (1996), 'Interconnection and Security Enhancement of Power System in North Eastern Asia Region related to the TRAP', Paper presented at the 26th Korean and Japanese P.E. Symposium, (in Korean).

Zarsky, L. (1995), 'The Prospects for Environmental Cooperation in Northeast Asia', *Asia Perspectives*, **19** (2), Fall–Winter, 103–30.

PART SIX

The Importance of Industrial Location

11. Industrial Location Planning in North Korea

Duk Hee Lee

11.1 INTRODUCTION

Locational factors play an important role in the locational choice of industries. Above all they are most advantageous for acquiring the critical resources for production. For instance, the production sites of natural resource-oriented industries tend to be located in regions close to natural resources, while skilled labor-intensive industries have an incentive to be situated near the metropolitan areas in which skilled laborers are abundant. In addition to these deterministic factors, indeterministic factors also have an important influence on the locational choice of industry. Locations are also the result of 'chance effects' which induce agglomeration effects, or externalities, accruing to a group of similar industries at a certain place. Silicon Valley, for instance, was largely the outcome of chance. Certain key players happened to set up near Stanford University in the 1940s and 1950s, and the local expertise and inter-firm market followed them, making Santa Clara County an extremely advantageous location for the high-tech industry.

Location theory and its principles in this paper are applied to the industrial location planning in North Korea. Different country-specific aspects must be considered in the case of North Korea. First, a plan should be devised to facilitate linking the strong points of the two Koreas' industrial development. Second, the plan should aim to achieve balanced development in North Korea through the efficient utilization of the territory. Third, the plan should generate externalities with the adjacent countries. Moreover, the newly located industries in North Korea should be cooperatively developed with those of China, Russia and Japan.

This paper suggests the several candidates for industrial zones, basic locational plans of each zone and further suggests factors to be considered in industrial location planning of North Korea. Such factors are classified into two groups. One consists of industrial location theory factors and the other concerns specific situation factors. The former includes production-specific factors of industry, agglomeration effects, economies of scale, central place development, and so on. The latter consideration includes the balanced development of North Korea, linkage to the industrial clusters of South Korea, and cooperative development with the North East Asian countries' (China, Russia, Japan) industries. Attributing equal weight to each of these factors regardless of industry is incorrect because the relative importance of each factor is different across industries. Accordingly, weighing the importance and relevance of each factor for individual industries is the most appropriate approach.

In this context, an optimal methodology to create locational plans is herein suggested. First, according to Central Place Theory, establishing several industrial zones is necessary in order to guarantee the balanced development of a nation. Also, to induce agglomeration effects, the existing industrial zones should be considered. Second, evaluating the industrial location theory factors of each zone is required. Third, it is important to match these evaluations with the production technology characteristics of industries and make priorities for all industries and zones. The next step is to rearrange the priorities considering the specific situational factors.

Based on the above methodology, the detailed industrial location plan for North Korea must be initiated by the establishment of several industrial zones. Most of existing major industrial zones will form the center for the development of North Korea, and their growth will diffuse over the entire North Korean region. The recommended industrial zones are: Pyongyang-Nampo, Shinuijoo, Hamhung–Wonsan, Cheongjin–Kimchaek, Rajin–Sonbong, Anjoo–Suncheon, Kaeseong–Haejoo (new) and Kanggae–Manpo. Specific industries can be matched with these zones based on the industrial location theory factors and the specific situation factors.

Finally, we suggest an action plan for implementing the location plan. The plan calls for constructing industrial location plan by stages, which deliberate the existing conditions of the North Korean economy including its comparative advantage and long-term prosperity.

11.2 INDUSTRIAL LOCATION THEORY FACTORS

Two factors generally account for the locational choice of industry. One is geographical necessity, and the other is chance. Since both are associated with shaping the locational pattern of industry, the relative importance between both factors matters across industries.

Industrial Characteristics

Production-specific factors

Various factors are incorporated in the determination of industrial location. Since factors crucial for the production activities of a particular industry are exclusively specific to that industry, however, determinants of industrial location also are different from one industry to the other. The first step in the determination of industrial location is to associate the characteristics of production factors with industrial location. For instance, a high-tech industry may achieve the best performance when related businesses are located collectively to exploit its synergy effect and when adjacent to research institutes or universities to capitalize human capital in R & D. For the petrochemical or steel industries, which are dependent on imported raw materials, a seaport would be considered the most important industrial location. Hence, industry-specific production and technology factors should be regarded as the first criterion in determining industrial location.

Though numerous studies have analyzed location factors by industry, they are similar in their methodological approach in analyzing factors by dividing industry into two categories, market-oriented and resource-oriented. In this study, industry is classified into three categories: urban-oriented, resource-oriented, and free type (see Table 11.1). The urban-oriented type is market-oriented, and it can be divided into urban consumption type and agglomeration type. Urban consumption type is an industry in which substantial market demand is an important production factor as in clothing and furniture. In other words, this type is a demand-pull industry. Agglomeration type is a group of industries wherein synergy effects among producers belonging to similar or the same business is highly important. This type is classified as a supply-agglomeration industry rather than only as an urban-oriented industry. Resource-oriented type is a group of industries for which success is dependent on timely supply and transportation of raw materials. It is divided into foreign and local resource-oriented types according to the source of raw materials. Seaside locations including seaports are preferred by foreign resource-oriented type industries while local resource-oriented industries are attracted by regional sources of raw materials. Finally, free type industries such as information and telecommunication, and software are indifferent to location.

The above classifications are not absolute but are based on the relative importance of specific factors to individual industries. One industry may be classified as both urban consumption-oriented type and agglomeration type or regarded as agglomeration type as well as resource-oriented. Moreover, rapid changes in production technologies have altered industrial location factors. As a whole, transportation factors have become less important than in the past due to improved transportation technologies while labor costs impose a heavier burden on producers. Efficient use of raw materials and introduction of substitute materials have lessened the dependency ratio on raw materials in general.

In addition to these shifts in location factor theory, some factors are newly emerging as important requirements. For example, the environment is now highlighted as a critical factor though it was not regarded as important in the past. Therefore, the agglomeration effect, labor force, transportation cost, electricity, water, land, transportation, port and the environment, are considered major industrial location factors.

Table 11.1 Industrial Location Pattern by Production Characteristics

Market-oriented	Urban consumption type	Shoes, apparel, furniture, printing, publishing
	Agglomeration type	Rubber product, machinery, metal, electric product, electronic product
Resource-oriented	Foreign resources	Paper and paper product, chemical, petrochemical, steel
	Local resources	Food and beverages, textiles, woods, leather, glass, transportation machinery
Free type	Information and knowledge-based industry	

Transportation-oriented versus production factor-oriented

Among the various factors of production determining industrial location, transportation and production factors (labor, capital, and raw materials) have been reviewed heretofore. According to transportation cost, industries are divided into resource-oriented and market-oriented industries. If the cost of resource transportation is relatively important in an industry and it tends to locate its production facilities near the source of raw material, the industry is resource-oriented. On the contrary, an industry is called market-oriented when the cost of product transportation is relatively important in an industry, and so it is likely to be near markets (see Table 11.2).

Let's consider the factors of production specific to a product. Production factors are specific to the region since they can be supplied efficiently to a particular region and are moved to other regions with difficulty. Typical examples of such factors are energy, labor, intermediate capital goods, and services specific to regions. If the portion of a certain production factor is given much weight in total expenditure, a firm should be attracted by the region where the price of the factor is relatively low. For instance, a firm using energy intensively would locate its production line in an area where energy is cheap. Labor-intensive industry would move to a region with low labor cost or with low unit labor cost including labor productivity.

Over time in industrial development the relative importance of the two factors has changed. Production factors rather than transportation is becoming more important. That is, the advance in transportation and production technology encouraged the tendency for an industry to choose a region close to cheap production factors specific to the industry more than a region near raw material or markets. Advances in transportation technology reduced transportation costs of raw materials or products. High-speed sea transportation and technological development of containers drastically cut transportation costs, and the introduction of express railroads, super trucks and air cargo, among others, also contributed to the curtailment of expenditure. Therefore, a firm would be motivated to move its location if the amount of increase in transportation cost brought about by changing location is less than the amount reduced in other expenditures.

Table 11.2 Transportation-oriented versus Production Factor-oriented Industries

	Characteristics	Industry
Transportation-oriented	Large portion of transportation cost of total	
Resource-oriented	Decreasing weight	Wood products
Market-oriented	Increasing weight	Beverages
Production factor-oriented	Small portion of transportation cost of total	
Energy	Energy-intensive	Aluminum
Labor	Labor-intensive	Textiles
Intermediate goods		
Specific intermediate good	Localization	Tailor/dress shop
business service	Urbanization	Company's HQ

Source: O'Sullivan, A. (1993), *Urban Economics*, 2nd ed., Boston, MA: IRWIN. 55–9.

Advances in production technology have also contributed significantly. Actual unit input has decreased due to efficient utilization and substitution by technological progress. That led to reductions in total transportation expenditure, and changed location patterns from transportation-oriented to production factor-oriented. The steel industry illustrates this tendency. Improved manufacturing processes and using scrap iron substituted for iron ore have continuously decreased the amount of coal and iron ore needed to produce steel. As a result, transportation costs relative to labor costs fell, and the steel industry moved to regions with low labor cost in some cases.

A few case studies were conducted to demonstrate this phenomenon. Analyzing location patterns of the semiconductor industry Castells (1988) found that not transportation cost but abundant skilled labor is the major determinant of industrial location. Most leading semiconductor manufacturers are located in Oregon, Arizona, or Texas or surrounding the Silicon Valley. Bartik et al. (1987) tried to analyze the background for the location of General Motor's Saturn line in Nashville, and defined the main reason as cheap and stable supply of labor.

Regarding industrial location in North Korea, the following matters should be considered in advance. Firstly, proper location should be chosen according to the relative importance of transportation and production factors by industry. Secondly, transportation conditions should be deliberated. If transportation is not developed sufficiently, it will be impossible for the production factor-oriented tendency in industrial location to evolve. As the transportation system in North Korea, except railway transportation, has lagged behind, each industry should be located based on the above considerations.

Agglomeration Effects

We frequently witness in markets that the same or similar businesses or products gather on one site. In some cases, a single market is specialized in a specific item. In South Korea Kumi Electronics Complex and Changwon Machinery Complex are examples of such clusters in which similar businesses operate together though the clusters were developed artificially. What is the reason for such clustering? The businesses may have come together at the same location to exploit advantages arising from clustering. The simplest reason behind this is that clustering contributes to demand generation. On the demand side, consumers are guaranteed to benefit by visiting a spot where relevant suppliers are gathered.[1] This would lead to a market search cost reduction. Therefore, suppliers are enticed to locate their business where there are many similar businesses operating.

On the supply side, clustering is beneficial since suppliers can share information and save costs by acquiring information through dynamic communication in business activities. In addition, suppliers can improve efficiency by pooling production factors, such as skilled labor, capital goods, among others, which are abundant within a cluster.

Various studies have been conducted on the importance of agglomeration effects as a determinant of geographical industrial location. Krugman's (1991) explanation emphasizes the motives of consumers. That is, he puts an emphasis on the role of the consumer while explaining that the geographical pattern of an industry is determined by interaction between supply factors (increasing returns to scale, transportation costs, and so on) and demand factors (the number of consumers). According to his explanation, firms are likely to be near a highly populated region where there exists abundant demand.

Arthur (1989, 1990) accounts for this in a different way. He explains clustering as an indeterministic chance factor, rather than a result of deterministic factors like increasing returns to scale, transportation costs, economies of scope, and so on. If a firm chooses a particular region for some reasons, whatever they are, then another firm would choose the same region to exploit the advantages generated by locating near the first firm. A third firm would willingly select that region expecting benefits arising from being near the two firms already established there. Lots of firms form a cluster in the region through this process, which is regarded as an evolutionary process initiated by chance. If a certain region draws more firms than other regions in the early stage of evolution, the probability for that region to attract more firms than other regions would be higher in the later stage as well. The final probability that a specific event will occur rests on the present probability that the same event will occur. Arthur, Ermoliev and Kaniovski (1984) call this phenomenon a 'path-dependent process' and prove it mathematically. In conclusion, when a firm selects one of many possible regions to locate, the probability that a particular region would be chosen is dependent on the number of firms located in that region.

Agglomeration effects have been studied in great detail. Agglomeration effects consist of the localization effect – externalities caused when firms in the same business gather in one region – and the urbanization effect, which signifies the externalities, derived from diversity of a city embracing various businesses. An industry is located near urban areas because the agglomeration effect is relatively prominent despite the negative externalities of the urban area such as congestion, high production cost, and so on (Mills, 1967).

Recently, the two effects have been as the outcome of a dynamic accumulation of knowledge and information. In this view, the localization effect is defined as an effect called Marshall–Arrow–Romer (MAR) externalities derived from the knowledge accumulation acquired from various interchanges of information between firms in the same line of business. Urbanization effect is an effect called Jacobs Externalities derived from the accumulation of knowledge and ideas from historical diversity.[2] High-tech industries, which are highly dependent on the synergy effect from the infusion of different technologies, show higher Jacobs externalities than MAR externalities.

Through the researches mentioned above, industrial location patterns based on agglomeration effects can be said to be veracious. In order to maximize agglomeration effects in the locational plan of North Korea, it would be effective to establish the same or similar business as the existing businesses of an industrial region or in adjacent areas.

11.3 SITUATION FACTORS

Balanced Development of North Korea

The metropolitan area including Seoul, the capital of South Korea, as a huge overpopulated region has symbolized unbalanced development of Korea. An astounding 45.1 per cent of the total population lives in this area as of 1995. In addition to the population density problem, the phenomenon of concentration in a metropolitan area is serious in other social activities. According to data of 1991, 76 per cent of economic activity, 93.6 per cent of information, and 92.7 per cent of international activity occur in Seoul. Hence, the problem of Korea can be reduced to that of the metropolitan area surrounding Seoul.

Though lots of entangled factors produced the situation mentioned above, above all, a tendency of overemphasis on efficiency can be pointed out. In other words, the agglomeration effect has been overly emphasized. As a result, it exacerbated inefficiency, contrary to expectations. Any region will benefit from the agglomeration effect (economies of scale, and so on) exceeding various congestion costs, and so accelerate agglomeration. However, benefits of agglomeration are absorbed by congestion costs because the latter would prevail as agglomeration proceeds beyond a certain degree. The metropolitan area including Seoul has suffered from numerous counter productive conditions caused by congestion costs that surpass the agglomeration effect.

Imbalance in national development is directly connected to factors blamed for weakening the competitiveness of Korean industries. The first problem is land price. A large population in a limited small area raises the price of land. High value of land leads to high rent and high prices, and it results in high wages, high interest rates, and finally high production costs. As a consequence, high land prices undermine price competitiveness. Another problem is high logistics costs. Overpopulation and concentration of city functions in a certain region bring about excessive traffic congestion. In 1995, the average logistics cost of Korea was 14.3 per cent[3] of sales, which was high compared to that of Japan's 8.55 per cent.[4] Moreover, the problem is being aggravated since logistics costs have been increasing by 19 per cent annually. The third problem is related to the quality of products. Tension builds up in the state of overpopulation, and excessive competition is brought about accordingly. This deters normal and fair competition, and consequently, procedures that ought to be followed are ignored or substituted by abnormal ones. In this situation, it is natural that the quality of products deteriorates since resources are concentrated on managing and maintaining output already produced rather than being used to create competitiveness. In a word, excessive concentration results in low quality.

In the above discussion, the importance of physical plot planning of a country was highlighted. Considering the significance of production activities, the spatial arrangement of industries is highly important. The importance of industrial location was verified already through the fact that overpopulated regions lie upon major industrial regions, such as Seoul–Kyunggi industrial area and southeastern industrial area. Therefore, it goes without saying that regional balance should be considered in the industrial mapping of North Korea.

North Korea is a new opportunity for Korea's future. Careful policy coordination is needed to avoid excessive imbalance in development as happened in South Korea. According to statistics, the population of Pyongyang was 3.3 million, 15.1 per cent of the total population in 1990.[5] Compared to Seoul, Pyongyang is not overpopulated. However, we should remember that Seoul was not overcrowded in the past but experienced a rapid growth in population during its economic development. As cities in North Korea may follow suit, special consideration is necessary on this point. Above all, industrial locational plans should foster balance among regions so that no region is excluded. Especially, core industries like steel, machinery, and electronics should be given with more weight since they have pervasive effects on regional development. If satisfied, these conditions would guarantee efficient use as well as lasting development of land in the long term.

In order to satisfy these conditions, a basic plan is suggested to prepare a few large central industrial zones including existing industrial complexes of North Korea in the first place, and to develop several medium-sized industrial central places surrounding the large central industrial zones. Ultimately, the effects will spread over many small regions.

Linkage to SOC Plan and the Industrial Zones of South Korea

Methods to develop a region can be classified into two: one is to interlink regions already developed by expanding infrastructure projects like roads, transportation, ports, and so on, and the other is to expand infrastructure projects in advance and to develop the region centering around these. In this paper, the latter is discussed. It goes without saying that industrial location and social overhead capital (SOC) plans should be correlated. In the first place, well-constructed roads, railways, and ports interlinking industrial sites will reduce tremendous logistics costs. As relations between different industries grow, and outsourcing from other firms prevails, logistics is becoming a more critical matter. Secondly, it is inefficient to construct new SOC after the industrial location plan is executed without relation to existing SOC. Since SOC construction requires an enormous expense, it would be a waste of resources.

In Korea, the Ministry of Construction and Transportation and the Korea Institute for National Land Development Planning have taken the responsibility of long-term plans. A recent announcement of a plan for cooperation in industrial location in North and South Korea provided a framework for cooperation in industrial locational plans and basic SOC plans in North Korea.

According to the plan, the basic line of national development of Korea is U-shaped along the coastline. Inland industrial zones are also included. The line coincides with the basic SOC plan. According to the basic SOC plan, the role of the railway would be tremendous after unification since 90 per cent of total material mobilization in North Korea is undertaken by rail.[6] Moreover, rail transportation is expected to be very important because it can be connected to the Trans-Siberia Railway (TSR) and the Trans-China Railway (TCR). The railway expansion plan comprises four lines in all: two lines connected both to the TRS along the east coast and to the TCR along the west coast and two inland lines a little to the west and the east. Associated with the industrial location plan, the west coast line closely borders already established industrial zones such as Shinuijoo, Chungchunkang, Pyongynag, and so on. It is desirable to plan to develop Haejoo as a new industrial zone considering its location near South Korea. In the same way, the east coast line is overlapping with existing industrial zones: Cheongjin, Rajin–Sonbong, Kimchaek, Hamhung, Wonsan, and others. Shinpo could be considered as a small- or medium-sized industrial zone between Kimchaek and Hamhung. The west line is represented by Kanggae Industrial Zone. Close to Seoul, Kaeseong may be specialized in one industry. The east line goes through a mountain area and so there are hardly any industrial zones. However, a small industrial zone would be desirable in Haesan as it borders China and Russia.

In terms of roads, the basic plan is not much different from that of the east and west railway, except that Shinyang, between Pyongyang and Wonsan, is supposed to be an industrial zone.

Upon unification, connection between industrial regions within the Korean Peninsula would be a very important factor in constructing an efficient production system. North Korean industrial zones might produce the same products that South Korean industrial zones produce, or there would be a system of vertical or horizontal specialization. In the case that both produce the same product, the two industrial zones should consider carefully the demand and supply of the product to decide production capacity. For vertical–horizontal specialization, industrial location plans for North Korea should put an emphasis on the geographical contiguity with South Korea. For example, Kimchaek may cater to the steel-related industry for connections with Pohang by sea. It would be possible to locate machinery, automobiles, chemical industries in Hamhung, and Wonsan industrial zones in consideration of the connections with the southeast coast region of South Korea. Besides, an industrial zone connecting Pyongyang, Haejoo, and Kaeseong can be developed into a high-tech and light industrial site to gain agglomeration effects thanks to the Seoul–Incheon Industrial Zone situated adjacent to the region.

Harmony with the Northeast Asian Countries

North Korea will have new opportunities by its neighbors China and Russia. Most of all, North Korea will have both opportunities to develop new markets and to utilize the abundant resources like minerals, timber, petroleum, among others of China and Russia. Geographical closeness as depicted in Figure 11.1 will facilitate economic cooperation including trade and investment with adjacent countries. Thus, it is important to connect industries in North Korea to general conditions and industries of China and Russia in industrial location planning because such well-built connections are crucial for the long-term development of North Korea.

The far eastern area of Russia has plentiful resources. Energy resources such as hydropower, petroleum, natural gas, coal, and others of the former USSR amount to 28.3 per cent of the total. Mineral resources like iron ore, gold, diamonds, copper, lead, nickel, mercury, and tungsten are also copious. Forest resources of good quality are so abundant that it amounts to 26 per cent of the total of the former USSR. Production of fur is very prosperous in the forest area; one third of world supply is produced in this area.

The northeastern area of China bordering North Korea possesses substantial amounts of major resources. Though it has simpler combination of resources than far eastern Russia, 45 per cent of petroleum and 23 per cent of iron ore in China are in this region. Different from the far eastern area of Russia, this region has, in addition to agricultural products, some heavy industries developed to a certain degree producing machinery, and automobiles.[7]

It is desirable to deliberate actual situations in the adjacent areas – China and Russia – in the industrial location plan for North Korea. Among the existing industrial zones in North Korea, Cheongjin–Rajin–Sonbong industrial zone is supported by Musan with the greatest production of iron ore to develop heavy industries like iron, steel, machinery, chemical industry and is expected to play a key role associated with far eastern Russia. Petrochemical or the non-ferrous metal industry is likely to be appropriate for this area because of abundant resources in the far eastern area of Russia associated with the industrial base in the area.

Shinuijoo will function as an industrial center linked to northeastern China. Machinery and textile industries are major businesses in this area, but the machinery and petrochemical industries are likely to prosper since they can get resources from northeastern China where abundant petroleum, petroleum refineries, and machinery and automobile industries exist.

Figure 11.1 East Asia Economic Zone Plan

Table 11.3 Locational Factors by Industry

Product	Labor		Raw material	Agglomeration effect	Land	Market	SOC		
	Quality	Quantity					Transportation	Water supply	Electric power
Food and beverages	×	×	○	△	×	○	○	○	△
Textile and clothing	×	○	△	○	△	○	△	△	△
Wood, paper, and pulp	×	△	○	△	△	△	△	○	△
Petrochemical	○	×	○	○	○	△	○	○	○
Non-metallic mineral material	×	○	○	×	○	×	○	○	△
Iron and steel	×	○	○	×	○	×	○	○	○
Non-ferrous metals	–	–	–	–	–	–	–	–	–
Machinery	○	△	×	○	△	△	×	×	×
Electrical and electronic products	○	△	×	○	×	△	×	×	△
Automobile	○	△	×	○	○	△	○	×	△
Shipbuilding	○	△	×	○	○	×	×	×	△

Notes: O implies the factor is important, △ medium, and X unimportant.

Another anticipated industrial zone is the Kanggae Industrial Zone, which specializes in machinery. It can be converted to new industries since it was established for military purposes rather than economical location factors. As Kanggae is a mountain area and forest resources are abundant in the far eastern area of Russia, the timber industry can be added.

So far, we have considered the inland industrial zones. Now, what is the locational plan for the coastline? When it comes to the industrial location plan on the coastlines of North Korea it should be reviewed with regard to the East Sea Rim Economic Zone Plan and the Yellow Sea Rim Economic Zone Plan. Though it is uncertain whether the plans would be realized, what is certain is that Korea would activate economic cooperation with Japan, China, Russia, Southeast Asia, and Mongolia. The form of economic cooperation may be vertical or horizontal specialization depending on the resource endowments and comparative advantage of each participant. Trade in goods as well as direct or indirect investment will increase among the countries. Consequently, the role of industrial zones on the coastline is gaining importance. In the East Sea Rim Economic Zone plan, underdeveloped regions of Japan, Hokuriku and Niikata will take a leading role. Recently, the region is proactively developing high-tech industry like the information industry. Wonsan–Hamhung Industrial Zone seems apt to correspond with the Hokuriku and Niikata regions. To conduct active interchange, Wonsan–Hamhung should invite high-tech industries such as the electronics, and information industry

Dalian, Qingdao, Shanghai will play a leading role in China's Yellow Sea Rim Economic Zone Plan. Dalian has a relatively high ratio of heavy industry, while Qingdao has a specialty in light industry, and Shanghai in the banking and service industry. The compatible areas of North Korea would be: Dalian–Shinuijoo, Qingdao and Shanghai–Pyongyang and Haejoo.

11.4 BASIC INDUSTRIAL LOCATION PLANS

Industry Candidates and Locational Factors

Since manufacturing industries are the foundation of industrial development, they are the first to be considered as industry candidates to be located in North Korea. Eleven basic industries among them are analyzed for the locational plan and summarized in Table 11.3.

Food products and beverages

The most crucial locational factors are transportation and water supply. Labor is not an important locational factor but raw material can be critical for some products. Because sales activities are concentrated on local markets rather than the national market, it is advantageous to be situated near a city center in a local area.

Textile and clothing

Among locational factors, water supply has much influence on upstream lines of the textile and clothing industry while labor is an important factor in downstream lines. Quantity of labor is more important than quality of labor. Because the textile industry has an inter-industry diffusion effect to a large extent within industry it is affected by economies of agglomeration. The clothing industry is likely to adjoin the local market.

Wood, paper and pulp

As wood industry handles and processes wood, locating in raw material sources is advantageous. However, the industries should be situated around seaports since Korea imports most of its raw lumber. In the case of paper and pulp industries, raw materials and water supply constitute important locational factors as they uses large amounts of both. Labor is not a critical factor in the paper industry, which is regarded as capital intensive. However, other industries like wood products require a large labor force to some extent.

Petrochemical

The petrochemical industry requires a large site for the installation of gigantic production facilities and storage of raw materials and products. Since the industry has close connections with both forward and backward industries, it is advantageous for it to locate near those industries. In addition, it is quite important to form an industrial complex according to the production process.

For transportation of raw materials and products, ports and roads in good condition are prerequisites. The industry calls for large amounts of freshwater and seawater to generate steams necessary for the production process and cooling process. A power plant should be near the petrochemical industrial site for it uses a large quantity of electric power. However, it does not need a large amount of labor because it is a capital-intensive industry requiring lots of equipment and facilities. However, well-trained engineers should be available.

Non-metallic mineral material

The non-metallic mineral industry should be located near raw materials source since raw materials are too heavy to be transported. Transportation conditions are important for the distribution of end products. The industry uses a large labor force and a large amount of water as well as needing an appropriate industrial site for production.

Iron and steel

The iron and steel industry is one of the key industries, which provide basic materials to industries of various kinds. It consumes lots of energy and requires large-scale facilities as a capital-intensive industry. The industry is also characterized by high transportation expenses, which account for a large portion of sales because of heavy raw materials and end products. For this reason, locating near seaports is advantageous for the industry.

Non-ferrous metals

Energy, especially electric power, is the most crucial factor in deciding the location of non-ferrous metal industry for it consumes tremendous amounts of energy. If it is highly dependent on imported raw materials, seaport facilities are indispensable requirements. If there are mines, however, locating near mines can be more desirable. Being a capital-intensive industry of large-scale facilities, it needs a relatively large industrial site. In addition, ample water supply and good drainage are required.

Machinery

Demands for machinery arise from every industry in the manufacturing sector. Therefore, the machinery industry should have the capacity to produce various product lines to meet diverse needs of users. In the case of consigning production to other producers, the cost in machinery industry is high relative to that of other industries. In addition, the industry uses components and parts of which size and type is highly varied. Hence, it is favorable for the machinery industry to be adjacent to the component industry and related industries. Concentrated location in such a form as a machinery industrial complex is desirable.

In terms of labor force, the machinery industry requires skilled labor and specialized labor particularily. Considering the trend of technological progress in the machinery industry, the importance of a specialized work force is expected to increase further as time goes on. Locational factors like land, transportation, electric power, water supply, and so on, are not critical factors with respect to the characteristics of the industry.

Electrical and electronic products

The electrical and electronics industry represents free type industries unregulated by specific locational factors. However, economies of agglomeration among similar industries may be regarded as an important locational factor since the inter-industry diffusion effect is necessary for some products using lots of components. That implies that it is beneficial to situate related industries together in a region.

In addition, a region where the job transfer rate is low and workers with advanced education are supplied in a stable manner can be an appropriate candidate for the location of the electrical and electronics industry, which uses lots of components and has a complicated manufacturing process. For the stable supply of excellent engineers, the best candidate should be well equipped with housing, education, medical services, cultural facilities, and so on. Environmental aspects like clean air, mild climate, rare chance of natural disasters such as heavy snowfalls and floods are vital conditions for a desirable location of the industry.

Automobile

Economies of scale are a crucial determinant in the automobile industry because it requires a tremendous amount of capital investment in facilities. On the other hand, however, it needs advanced specialization and division of labor. Economies of scale in the automobile industry imply that it physically requires huge factories. Consequently, a large industrial site constitutes a critical location factor. As an overall assembled machinery industry, specialization and division of labor, which demands systemically cooperative relations with numerous material and component firms, characterize the automobile industry. Therefore, it is necessary to secure industrial sites for the components and parts industry. Supply of labor is also an important locational factor since the automobile industry needs abundant skilled work forces and engineers.

Shipbuilding

The shipbuilding industry must locate in seashores with deep water for building, repair and the breaking-up of various ships. Because a ship is built by assembling lots of equipment and parts it is difficult to automate the manufacturing process, thus the industry has a feature of labor-intensiveness. At the same time, the industry is also regarded as technology-intensive since it requires highly advanced technologies in some parts. Considering these features, it is expedient for the industry to be placed along seashore and in a region where technical workers can be supplied in a stable manner. As this industry is mutually complementary with industries such as machinery, steel, electrical and electronics, and so on adjacent location of these industries will promote the shipbuilding industry.

Industrial Zones and Locational Conditions

Eight industrial zones

Central place development, as a basic principle of the locational plan, has been previously discussed. Based on this principle, and considering the industrial location theory factors and the specific situational factors, candidates for industrial clusters can be established as in Figure 11.2.

Several criteria are associated with determining the candidates. First, big cities in which the population size is large and industries are developed are likely to be the best candidates. This criterion will best utilize broad agglomeration effects including the urbanization effect. Second, geographical adjacency rather than administrative districts has a priority in establishing the zones. It is often the case that although two cities are situated in different administrative districts, they are geographically adjacent and formulate one economic bloc. For example, Songrim and Sariwon are members of Hwanghaebukdo, their administrative district; however they are geographically closer to Pyongyang–Nampo than to Kaeseong–Haejoo, and thus have a closer economic relationship with the former. Also, Dancheon of Hamkyungnam-do is located closer to Cheongjin–Kimchaek than to Hamhung–Wonsan. Consequently, Songrim and Sariwon, and Dancheon were respectively incorporated into Pyongyang–Nampo and Cheongjin–Kimchaek zones. Third, the perspective on regional development was considered. If a region has many favorable characteristics to be a large industrial zone but currently it is not developed enough to be a zone, it is likely to be a candidate for the zone. Kaeseong–Haejoo and Kanggae–Manpo zones are examples because their future is promising in developing a relationship between China and South Korea. Fourth, transportation infrastructure is another important factor. For example Huicheon of Jagangdo belongs to the same administrative district as Kanggae-Manpo, but communication and transportation between Huicheon and Anjoo–Suncheon is easier than with Kanggae–Manpo, which is a mountainous area. Huicheon was thus included in the Anjoo–Suncheon zone.

Since Pyongyang–Nampo, Anjoo–Suncheon, Hamhung–Wonsan, and Cheongjin–Kimchaek have been major industrial zones in North Korea, they were selected again as candidates in order to take advantage of the agglomeration effects. As well, the locational factors such as market, labor force, and social overhead capital (SOC) in the zones are superior to other zones. Regarding the balanced development and the East Asian Economic Zone Plan, Kanggae–Manpo and Rajin–Sonbong will be expected to play a crucial role. Both are isolated mountainous areas but easily access water from the adjacent Tuman and Abrok rivers. Developing them will contribute to the balanced development of North Korea. Furthermore, both regions will be important in trading with Russia and China because the two countries border them.

Hamhung–Wonsan and Cheongjin–Kimchaek have many advantages with respect to the East Sea Rim Economic Zone Plan. They can develop high-tech industries corresponding to Hokuriku and Niigata of Japan. Similarly, Haejoo–Kaeseong is expected to escalate its importance in the Yellow Sea

Rim Economic Zone Plan and South Korea's industrial zones. Its location between Pyongyang–Nampo and Seoul–Incheon Industrial Zone retains the high possibility that it be developed as a large industrial zone to connect the two huge industrial zones. In particular, Haejoo, facing the West Sea, has great potential to be a center able to cope with the fast-growing areas of China, Dalian, Tianjin, Qingdao, and Shanghai. Kaeseong is geographically close to Seoul and so may be incorporated into the Seoul–Incheon zone.

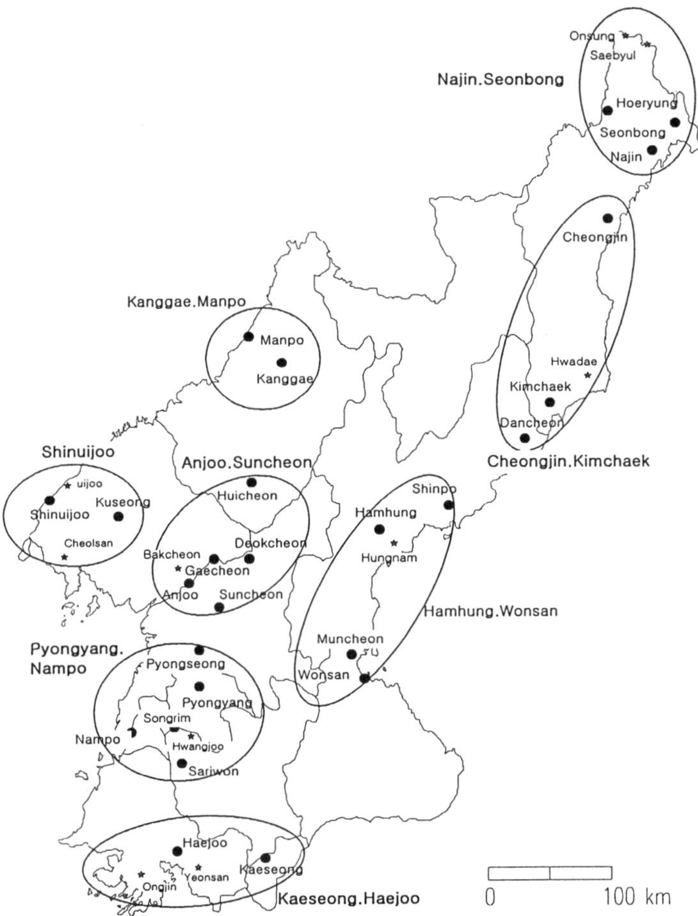

Figure 11.2 Eight Candidates for Industrial Zones

Locational conditions of each zones[8]

The results of assessing locational conditions of the eight zones synthetically are summarized in the following table. Nine factors are considered including labor in terms of quality and quantity, raw materials, agglomeration effect, land, market, transportation, water supply, electric power. Among these factors, raw material and agglomeration effect are applied to the overall manufacturing sector not to a specific industry. Therefore, they need to be assessed differently with respect to individual industries in the following analysis of locational suitability in terms of industry and zone.

As an assessment method, a relative evaluation process was adapted to assign scores from one to five to each zone as shown in Table 11.4. The assessment resulted in the following recommendations. Pyongyang–Nampo was the best candidate with favorable locational factors because it gained high scores in most items including quality and quantity of labor, agglomeration effect, market, transportation, but not in raw materials such as mineral resources. Hamhung–Wonsan, the largest industrial region in the east area of North Korea, followed Pyongyang–Nampo marking a second best score. The result reflects the advanced heavy chemical industry like machinery, chemical, and so on and favorable market environment as one of the most populated regions, and well-furnished transportation facilities including seaports.

Cheongjin–Kimchaek, representing the heavy chemical industry in eastern area of North Korea took the third place in the assessment. Thanks to abundant underground resources like iron ore, Cheongjin–Kimchaek gained a high score with respect to raw materials. However, it had less favorable conditions in terms of land or transportation because of its geographical features as a mountainous area. Shinuijoo zone ranked the fourth place because of its plentiful water supply and electric power form the Abrok River and transportation connected to the Trans-China Railway.

Both Anjoo–Suncheon and Kaeseong–Haejoo zones received the same score. Anjoo–Suncheon has several merits such as abundant underground resources, water supply from the Chungcheon and Taedong Rivers, favorable market conditions owing to geographical closeness to Pyongyang–Nampo zone. It lacks in the rest of the factors, though. However, its rapid population growth casts a light on the possibility of market expansion. Kaeseong–Haejoo zone also has good prospects. Particularly, it is expected to play a crucial role in trade with China. Moreover, it will serve as a link with Seoul and the Metropolitan area. Without developed industries, however, it failed to get high scores in other factors except land, quality of labor, market, and electric power.

Rajin–Sonbong and Kanggae–Manpo were given a low rank. Rajin–Sonbong zone has good pontential as a transit trade base or a processing trade site targeting North East Asian market. However, locational factors are not so favorable because it is in a mountainous area and transportation conditions are poor. As a result, it received low scores in general except raw materials and quality of labor. Kanggae–Manpo zone is a mountainous area and not easy to access. Accordingly, this zone received the lowest evaluation in most criteria except raw materials and water supply.

Table 11.4 Synthetic Assessment of Locational Factors by Zone

Zone	Labor		Raw material	Agglo-meration effect	Land	Market	SOC			Total score
	Quality	Quantity					Trans-portation	Water supply	Electric power	
Pyungyang–Nampo	5	5	3	5	4	5	5	4	4	40
Kaesung–Haejoo	4	3	2	3	4	4	4	3	3	30
Shinuijoo	4	3	3	3	3	4	4	4	4	32
Anjoo–Suncheon	3	3	4	3	4	4	3	4	3	31
Hamhung–Wonsan	4	4	4	4	4	4	4	3	4	35
Cheongjin–Kimchaek	4	3	5	4	3	4	3	4	4	34
Rajin–Sonbong	3	2	4	2	3	3	2	3	3	25
Kanggae–Manpo	2	2	4	3	2	2	2	4	3	24

Industrial Location Plans by Zones

In this section, locational policy directions are suggested in full consideration of industrial location theory factors, situational factors, and efficient spatial allocation in North Korea. Locational factors are summarized in Table 11.5 and candidte industries in Table 11.6. First, North Korea can be easily divided into east and west areas in view of the geological and transportation conditions. The east is mountainous, not easily accessible, and not populous, whereas the west is relatively flat, easily accessible, and populous. Heavy and chemical industries are developed in the east and light industry in the west. The industrial location should be planned in consideration of all these basic characteristics and aim at balanced development in North Korea.

Second, developing a representative industry in each zone will be necessary. Several zones have established dominant industries: electronics in Pyongyang–Nampo, machinery and chemicals in Hamhung–Wonsan, steel in Cheongjin–Kimchaek, petrochemical in Anjoo–Suncheon, and so on. Utilizing these given endowments will maximize the agglomeration effect within the same and similar industries.

Third, maximizing the linkage effect between the industrial complexes of South and North Korea will be a prerequisite. In particular, heavy and chemical industries located in South Korea's southeast coast and high-tech and light industries in the west coast can vertically or horizontally link to the new clusters in the east and west coast of North Korea. This linkage will further support a smooth structural adjustment of South Korea's industries which has been a key issue for South Korea's economic revitalization.

Table 11.5 Locational Factors of Eight Candidates of Industrial Clusters

Clusters	Industrial location theory factors	Situation factors	Existing industries
Pyongyang–Nampo	Agglomeration effect, labor, market, SOC	Yellow Sea Rim economic zone	Machinery, steel, electric/electronic, shipbuilding, cement, fertilizer, Textile/clothing
Kaeseong–Haejoo	Market, labor, land, SOC	The Yellow Sea Rim economic zone, linkage to South Korea's industrial zones (Seoul–Incheon)	Cement, fertilizer, textile
Shinuijoo	Market, SOC, labor	Trade with China	Machinery, metal, chemical textile, paper/pulp
Anjoo–Suncheon	Market, raw material, land		Petrochemical, chemical fertilizer, machinery, telecommunication equipment, Automobile
Hamhung–Wonsan	Agglomeration effect, labor, market, raw material	The East Sea Rim economic zone, linkage to South Korea's industrial zones (southeast coast)	Chemical, machinery, non-steel metal, cement, ship building
Cheongjin–Kimchaek	Raw material, agglomeration effect, market, labor	The East Sea Rim economic zone, linkage to South Korea's industrial clusters (southeast coast)	Steel, metal, machinery, automobile, shipbuilding
Rajin–Sonbong	Raw material, Market	Balanced development of North Korea, trade with China and Russia	non-steel metal, petrochemical, coal
Kanggae–Manpo	Raw material	Balanced development of North Korea, trade with China	Machinery, lumber, glass

Fourth, North Korea's location provides an exceptional opportunity to trade with the adjacent countries – China, Russia and Japan – in the usage of natural resources, and other market expansion activities. Therefore, the location plan should sufficiently exploit this opportunity and locate the industries with a high import and export potential near the zones geographically close to the countries.

Since Pyongyang–Nampo is the center of national affairs such as politics, economy, and social activities, it is not desirable for industries to excessively concentrate near that zone. In light of this point, light or non-polluting industry rather than heavy or polluting industry will be appropriate for the Pyongyang–Nampo zone. Food and beverage, textile and clothing, electric and electronics, glass, plastics, precision chemical industries are selected as appropriate industries for the Pyongyang–Nampo zone. They will fully utilize the large market and abundant labor of high quality, which are the merits of Pyongyang–Nampo zone. The locational factor of raw materials allows cement industry to be selected for this zone thanks to abundant limestone buried around the region. Shipbuilding is chosen as a proper industry for Nampo, which is the largest port in the west coast and has an advantageous environment for developing ports.[9]

Table 11.6 Candidate Industries by Zone

Clusters	Candidate industries
Pyongyang–Nampo	Electric-electronics, textile and clothing, food and beverage, cement, precision chemicals, plastic and rubber, glass, and shipbuilding
Kaeseong–Haejoo	Electric-electronics, textile and clothing, food and beverage, cement, and chemical fertilizer
Shinuijoo	Precision chemicals, plastic and rubber, textile and clothing, food and beverage, wood, paper, and pulp, and glass
Anjoo–Suncheon	Petrochemical, plastic and rubber, precision chemicals, automobile, glass, and cement
Hamhung–Wonsan	Machinery, shipbuilding, automobile, steel, non-ferrous metal, petrochemical, plastic and rubber, precision chemicals, chemical fertilizer, food and beverage, clothing, cement, and glass
Cheongjin–Kimchaek	Steel, non-ferrous metal, machinery, and electric products
Rajin–Sonbong	Wood, paper and pulp
Kanggae–Manpo	Lumber

Kaeseong–Haejoo is geologically flat so that traditionally agricultural and light industries have been developed. Although its population size is small, the industrial location conditions are similar to Pyongyang–Nampo. Similarly, the location of light or non-polluting industry rather than heavy or polluting industry will be desirable in this area. This zone is also well located in such a place as to maximize the market pooling effect linking the large zones, as it is geographically close not only to the Seoul Metropolitan area but also to the Pyongyang–Nampo cluster. Haejoo port will play a very crucial role in trading with China in the future. Food and beverage, clothing, and so on, which are sensitive to market conditions, seem to match the locational factors of Kaeseong–Haejoo. The electronics industry proved to be appropriate considering the connection with Seoul and the Metropolitan area as well as market conditions. Kaeseong–Haejoo will play an important role in textile export to China. The cement industry will be profitable in this zone thanks to the adjacent limestone sources, and the chemical fertilizer industry is also promising for the agricultural area.

Shinuijoo is a traditional industrial area of sufficient electric power and potable water. Here, machinery, metal, chemicals, textiles, fabric, and paper/pulp have been developed for a long time. Its present market size is not large, but its future is bright with the opportunity of trading with China. In other words, Shinuijoo will be an important window to make inroads into China's market including Beijing, Shinjang, and Tianjin. Accordingly, the industries that are based on the already developed industries and are expected to play an important role in trading with China should be specialized in this zone. For this, the central port of the zone has to be developed. Shinuijoo has a favorable environment to develop textile and clothing, wood, paper and pulp industries not only because they have already been in operation but because the zone has advantages in utilizing rich forest resources of north-east region of China. Trading with China makes the region more attractive. Plastic, rubber and precision chemical industry may be able to develop based on a close cooperation with Bonghwa Chemical Factory located in Pihyun. Considering the market size of this zone, food and beverage and glass industries are also viable.

Anjoo–Suncheon is a newly industrialized area. This area is populous relative to its land size, and the growth rate of population high, making this one of the most promising areas. Its transportation infrastructure, railways, roads, canals, and so on, are satisfactory owing to the proximity to the Pyongyang–Nampo zone. Various industries are able to locate in this zone, however the petrochemical industry, which is already developed, is more advantageous than others. Namhung Youth Chemical Combined Corporation of Anjoo, the largest petrochemical industry complex in North Korea, produces many petrochemical commodities with naphtha which is produced at the Bonghwa Chemical Factory based in Pihyun, Pyunganbukdo. China provides petroleum to the company through pipelines. In addition to this agglomeration effect, the zone is appropriate for petrochemical and related industries with respect to raw materials. Therefore, petrochemical, precision chemical, plastic and rubber industries should be considered in the first place. The automobile industry is likely to be located in this zone, too. As the only integrated automobile plant, Seungri Automobile Factory, is operating in Dukcheon the zone has advantages in supplying vehicles to the western region. In addition, Anjoo–Suncheon is suitable for glass and cement industries since the market conditions and raw materials are appropriate.

Hamhung–Wonsan is a representative industrial complex in the eastern area of North Korea specializing in heavy industries such as machinery, shipbuilding, metal, chemicals, and so on. Its population represents 13.1 per cent of the total and is the second largest next to the Pyongyang–Nampo area. Hamhung–Wonsan's transportation infrastructure is well developed, so that it is a gateway to connect the western areas. In the east coast, Hungnam and Wonsan ports will be windows to trade with Japan and South Korea. In regard to balanced development, this zone should be considered as a center, which will be a counterpart to the Pyongyang–Nampo cluster, center of the eastern area. It can also specialize in heavy and chemical industries to link the southeast industrial complex of South Korea. Considering the linkage with the south east industrial complex of South Korea, machinery, shipbuilding, and automobile industries should be selected with first priority among the heavy industries prospering in Hamhung–Wonsan zone. Steel and non-ferrous industries are also viable since there are great inter-industry diffusion effects between them and machinery, shipbuilding and automobile industries. In deciding items and scales of those industries located in Hamhung–Wonsan, it is important to consider the field of specialization with regard to Cheongjin–Kimchaek and the south east industrial complex of South Korea, in which the same industries are operating. The chemical industry including petrochemicals, plastic and rubber, precision chemicals, land chemical fertilizer industries has been developed to a certain extent in the zone. It is necessary to build plants of a considerable scale as a supply source for Cheongjin–Kimchaek and Rajin–Sonbong as well as the zone itself. Furthermore, Hamhung–Wonsan has advantages in water transportation between this zone and the oil refinery in Ulsan. Food and beverage, clothing, cement, glass, and so on, are adequate items to be located in this zone for market and raw material factors.

Cheongjin–Kimchaek is also a representative heavy and chemical industrial complex in the east and competitive in steel, non-steel metal, machinery, chemicals, and shipbuilding. This zone is seemingly similar to the Hamhung–Wonsan. However, it has a unique aspect in that it is close to not only the Rajin–Songbong Economic and Trade Zone, but also to Killim,

Hukryonggang in China and far eastern areas in Russia. Therefore, this zone is expected to specialize in heavy industry, particularly intermediate capital goods for other industries related to the already developed metal industry. Steel and non-ferrous metal industries represent such industries, and there are several production lines in the Cheongjin–Kimchaek zone. They are Kimchaek Iron Mill, Cheongjin Steel Mill, and Dancheon Refinery. Steel and non-ferrous metal industries are most suitable to this zone since Moosan Mining Company and Kumduk Mining Company are here. In North Korea, the former is the largest production site of iron ore and the latter is the largest for non-ferrous metals. Furthermore, the zone has a quite advantageous position to make use of the rich mineral resources from the far eastern area of Russia. It is needless to say that proper division of labor should be considered with respect to steel and non-ferrous metal industrial sites in South Korea and Hamhung–Wonsan. Producing capital and intermediate goods, machinery and electrical products are highly related to steel and non-ferrous metal industries producing raw materials. As such products are required by heavy and chemical industry developed in Hamhung–Wonsan, it is beneficial to locate machinery and electrical industries in Cheongjin–Kimchaek. To facilitate the interchange between the industrial zones and to promote trading with China and Russia, it is essential to expand and improve the facilities of Cheongjin and Kimchaek ports.

Rajin–Sonbong is mountainous, not populous, and far away from the west. The industries are limited to chemicals (Sungri, Aoji), shipbuilding (Rajin), machinery (Hoiryung Coal Machine). North Korea is currently establishing this area as a center for transit trade and export-oriented manufacturing in northeast Asia by inducing foreign capital. In order to attain this goal, developing infrastructure including ports and roads is a priority concern. Wood, paper and pulp industries are the strongest candidates for suitable types of industry in this zone, which has abundant forest resources and can exploit the rich forest resources of the far eastern area of Russia. Besides this, the chemical industry related to petrochemical products, machinery and shipbuilding industries could be located in a small or medium scale by taking advantage of existing industries.

Kanggae–Manpo is very mountainous and not easily accessible. As a result, most industrial location factors, that is labor, land, market, transportation, water, and electric power, except raw materials such as minerals and lumber, are not well established. This area is not appropriate for the location of industry. The machinery industry known to be located in this area is for military purposes. Because of these reasons, this zone proves to be unsuitable for most industries. The lumber industry may be the only viable industry in this area, but it is not clear how the industry would be profitable from an economic point of view. Other industries of a small and medium scale may be situated to meet the demand within the zone.

11.5 ACTION PLANS

Following the economic cooperation between North and South Korea, South Korean corporations will actively participate in investment in North Korea, human resource exchanges will increase, and SOC will be expanded. Accordingly, it is expected that industrial development of North Korea will proceed gradually. In the process of industrial development in North Korea it is desirable to improve South Korea's industrial structure as high value added and a more competitive one as well so as to increase employment and income level in North Korea. This can be achieved by encouraging North Korea's industrial development to be coordinated with and complementary to South Korea's industrial development in order to generate synergic effect and ultimately to maximize the economic potential of the Korean Peninsula. For this purpose, the industrial location plan for North Korea should be constructed on the basis of the following three fundamental concepts.

Firstly, North Korea's industrial location should be designed to promote complementary industrial restructuring in both North and South Korea based on comparative advantages of each economy so that it can connect most efficiently with the existing industrial structures and planned blocs of North and South Korea. That is, by combining the cheap labor cost and relatively abundant resources of North Korea with the advanced technology, capital, and marketing capacity of South Korea, mutually complementary industrial structures will be achieved without unnecessary overlapping or competitive relations between North and South Korea.

Secondly, to accomplish effective industrial development in North Korea, constructing an industrial location plan by stages is needed, which takes into account existing conditions of the North Korean economy. In North Korea industrial activities are sluggish due to the recent aggravation of the food situation, deterioration of production facilities, lack of energy, and weak SOC construction. In particular, North Korea is suffering from an electric power shortage, rendering the operation rate of factories quite low. Therefore, it is desirable to avoid locating industrial sectors inappropriate to industrial conditions of North Korea in the early stage. For instance, chemical, metal, and non-metal mineral industries, which consume lots of electric power, should start operating within North Korea in earnest when the electric power supply conditions improve there.

Thirdly, the industrial location plan should eliminate regional imbalances in development and promote economic cooperation in Northeast Asia. Not only should the industrial location plan encourage efficient utilization of national land and balanced development, but also it should direct the Korean Peninsula to obtain comparative advantages in terms of geography and politics within the Northeast Asian region.

Table 11.7 Industrial Location Plan by Stages

	Candidate industries	Distinctive features
Early stage	Labor-intensive light industries Textile, shoes, sewing, toys, home appliances, etc. Agricultural productivity and SOC-related sectors Chemical fertilizer, agricultural chemicals, agricultural machinery, cement, etc. Resource and energy-related sectors Electric power, lumber, mining Some service sectors Sightseeing, logistics, restaurant, hotel, etc. SOCs; roads, railways, ports, telecommunications, etc.	Focusing on industries of comparative advantages and fortifying industrial foundation Entry of small and medium-sized enterprises with capital of a small scale No industries consuming lots of electric power Locating agriculture-related sectors
Middle stage	Capital, technology-intensive heavy and chemical industries Steel, non-metal mineral products, machinery, chemical, electronics, paper, pulp, etc.	Industrial development and income growth in North Korea Promoting development of endurable consumer goods (washing machine, refrigerator, color TV, etc.) targeting the domestic market in North Korea Encouraging division of labor in production between North and South Koreas (division of labor in process and product differentiation) Considering balanced development over regions Encouraging the location of industries in the fields of economic cooperation in Northeast Asia
Last stage	High-tech industries; information and telecommunications, aerospace, precision machinery, optical, medicinal material, etc. Service sectors; finance, insurance, logistics, distribution, advertisement, etc.	Narrowing the gap between North and South Koreas in economic and industrial development Promoting export industries

The following are the main features of each industrial location plan stage based on the three basic concepts and summarized in Table 11.7. In the first stage, labor-intensive light industries, which can utilize cheap labor in North Korea and need a relatively small amount of capital investment, should be located. Such industries are, for example, food and beverage, textiles, shoes, sewing, toys, home appliances industries. Small and medium-enterprises will be able to advance in the area. At the same time, some heavy and chemical industries (agricultural chemicals, agricultural machinery, chemical fertilizer, cement, and so on), service industries (hotel, restaurant, sightseeing, logistics, and so on), energy or resource related industries (electric power, lumber, mining, and so on), and the SOC sector (roads, railways, ports, and telecommunications) will likely be planned in this stage because these industries will break the bottleneck of industrial development in North Korea.

The economic and industrial development in North Korea in the first stage will be accomplished to a certain extent to increase the purchasing power of North Korean residents and to narrow the gap of economic capacity between North and South Korea. Following this, the second stage will implement an industrial location plan to situate energy-consuming industries and heavy and chemical industries including steel, non-ferrous metal, machinery, and chemical industries, which require large-scale investment, advanced technologies, and high-skilled workers. These industries will be developed adequately in connection with abundant underground mineral resources in North Korea. In particular, the industrial sectors such as wood, paper and pulp and underground mineral resources can be located to promote cooperation with Russia and China. This would enhance the regional economic cooperation in Northeast Asia.

The second stage will bring about expansion of productivity and competitiveness by the division of labor or product differentiation of North and South Korean industries based on individual comparative advantages even in the same line of business. Economic development and income level growth in North Korea will allow the endurable consumption goods industry (washing machine, refrigerator, color TV, and so on) of a high income elasticity to actively operate in North Korea.

In the final stage, technological and structural gaps between North and South Korea will be narrowed considerably. In addition, industrial development in North Korea will have been preceded quite extensively while the overall industrial foundation including skilled labor and SOC will have been established to a much higher degree. Therefore, the final stage will witness the advancement of some high-tech industries (for example, information and telecommunications, aerospace, precision machinery, and so on) and certain service sectors (for instance, finance, insurance, distribution, logistics, advertising, and so on) into North Korea. Besides, production and investment for exports targeting global market will be launched on a full scale because the synergy effects of North and South Korea's industrial coordination will enable industries to enhance their competitiveness in the world market.

11.6 CONCLUSION

Two basic sets of factors have been discussed as prerequisites of the industrial location plan in North Korea. The two sets of factors function properly when they are harmonized with each other through checks and balances. While industrial locational factors put an emphasis on efficiency in the market, situational factors specific to the Korean Peninsula regard equity of great importance. Overemphasis on industrial locational factors is very likely to cause excessive concentration in the region by strong centripetal force to certain regions, which have comparative advantage. In other words, a spatial plan for industry based on the market mechanism only will bring about congestion in a region and consequently deter efficiency in the market. Therefore, policy should complement the market mechanism with equity so that an industrial locational plan could guarantee efficient use of land in the long term.

The suggested locational plans by zones serve as a long term plan that can be implementable even after unification. However, in the short term, one or two zones should be developed prior to other zones based on the industrial location plan to be implemented in stages. In that sense Kaeseong–Haejoo and Pyongyang–Nampo zones in the western area can be promising candidates for the prior development zones. Since the zones are not only suitable for the labor intensive and light industries, which have a priority as the first stage of development, but also they are located close to China the zones are well positioned to take advantage of their environments.

Finally, it might hinder the long-term development of national land to locate industries based on excessive vertical or horizontal specialization in linking North and South Korea industrial zones. For example, to locate only labor-intensive industries in North Korea would be profitable in the short term, but will ruin the competitiveness of North Korea in the long run. Therefore, developing future industries like the information and telecommunication industry would be an adequate measure to ensure the long-term prosperity of North Korea and balanced development of national land.

NOTES

1. Krugman (1991) describes this as demand externalities.

2. Henderson, V., A. Kuncoro and M. Turner (1995).
3. The Korea Chamber of Commerce and Industry (1995), pp. 33–4.
4. Japan Association of Logistics System (1996), p. 6, Average of manufacturing sector.
5. The Board of National Unification (1991).
6. KIET, Korea Research Institute for Human Settlements, and Korea Institute for Industrial Development (1995), 470–2
7. Kim, Hwaseob (1991), 38–49.
8. Each zone's geological conditions are based on The Board of National Unification (1993).
9. The locational and industrial conditions of each zone are based on The Korea Research Institute for Human Settlement (1992), Yoo, Y. and Kwon, Y. and Yoo, S. (1993), and KOTRA (1995).

BIBLIOGRAPHY

Arthur, W. B., Y. M. Ermoliev, Y. M. Kaniovski (1984), 'Strong Law for a Class of Path-dependent Stochastic Processes', Arkin and Shiryayev and Wets (eds) (1984) *Proceedings International Conference on Stochastic Optimization: Lecture Notes in Control and Information Sciences 81.*

Arthur, W. B., Y. M. Ermoliev, Y. M. Kaniovski (1989), 'Competing Technologies, Increasing Returns, and Lock-in by Historical Event', *Economic Journal*, vol. 99, 116–31.

Arthur, W. B., Y. M. Ermoliev, Y. M. Kaniovski (1990), 'Positive Feedback in the Economy', *Scientific American,* Feb. 92–9.

Bartik, T. J., C. Becker, S. Lake, J. Bush (1987), 'Saturn and State Economic Development', *Forum for Applied Research and Public Policy,* Spring, 29–40.

The Board of National Unification (1991), *Social and Cultural Index in South and North Korea* (in Korean).

The Board of National Unification (1993), *North Korea's Geography and Geology* (in Korean).

Castells, M. (1988), 'The New Industrial Space: Information Technology Manufacturing and Spatial Structure in the United States', In G. Sternlieb and J. Hughes (eds), *America's New Market Geography*, New Brunswick, NJ: Center for Urban Policy Research.

Henderson, V., A. Kuncoro, M. Turner (1995), 'Industrial Development in Cities', *Journal of Political Economy*, vol. 103, 1067–90.

Japan Association of Logistics System (1996), *1995 Survey on Logistics of Industries* (in Japanese).

KIET, Korea Research Institute for Human Settlements, and Korea Institute for Industrial Development (1995), *New Industrial Location Plan of Korea* (in Korean).

Kim, Hwaseob (1991), *NorthEast Asian Economic Zone and Cooperation Plan*, KIET (in Korean).

Korea Research Institute for Human Settlements (1992), *Development of North Korea* (in Korean).

The Korea Chamber of Commerce and Industry (1995), *1995 Survey on Logistics of Firms* (in Korean).

KOTRA (1995), *North Korea's Industries* (in Korean).

Krugman, P. (1991), *Geography and Trade*, Cambridge, MA: The MIT Press.

Mills, E. S. (1967), 'An Aggregate Model of Resource Allocation in a Metropolitan Area', *American Economic Review Papers and Proc*, vol. 57, 197–210.

O'Sullivan, A. (1993), *Urban Economics*, 2nd ed., Boston, MA: IRWIN.
Research Institute for North Korea (1994), *Survey on North Korea* (in Korean).
Yoo, Younghwui, Kwon, Youngseob and Yoo Sunghan (1993), *Korea's Unification Potential and Issues,* Korea Research Institute for Human Settlements (in Korean).

12. The Rajin–Sonbong Economic and Trade Zone (RSETZ): the Sources of Difficulties and Lessons for the Future

Icksoo Kim

12.1 INTRODUCTION

The Tumen River Economic Development Area (TREDA), consisting of Hunchun in northeast China, Rajin–Sonbong in North Korea and Posyet in the Russian Far East, has attracted the attention of outside investors since the inception of the UNDP in 1992. The UNDP's vision is to transform the TREDA into the international trade center and transportation hub of Northeast Asia.[1]

Notwithstanding the UNDP's ambitious vision and the long-term development potential of the TREDA, however, the three riparian governments, with the exception of China, have yet to see success in attracting foreign direct investments (hereafter 'FDI'). In particular, North Korea, which set up a free trade and economic zone at the Rajin–Sonbong area in December 1991, attracted only a total of US$67 million during a seven-year effort until the end of 1997, to the disappointment of the pragmatic bureaucrats.

The much publicized obstacles are characterized by political ones: North Korean leadership's political subjectivism, overindulgence in 'Juche' ideology, insistence of economic self-reliance, intransigence about sovereignty, fear of economic domination by Japan and South Korea over the program,[2] and persistent yet legitimate worries about the systemic collapse following partial opening of the restricted region. Pyongyang's obsession with its own conditions attached to FDI is another major obstacle.

However, there are nonpolitical yet more persistent barriers, too. Wrong location decisions made by the North Korean authorities at the very outset of establishing the Rajin–Sonbong Economic and Trade Zone (hereafter 'RSETZ') is the one factor constraining the development potential of the zone. At a more practical level, backward, inefficient transportation and telecommuni-cations infrastructure has impeded the rapid expansion of foreign trade of and FDI into the zone. This, combined with other institutional constraints, resulted in the arrival of an insufficient amount of FDI into the region.

Multitudes of papers have dealt with the systemic problems of the North Korean economy, and there are some papers dealing with the changes in the legal and institutional framework of the RSETZ based primarily upon the North Korean and Japanese sources.[3] However, to date, no paper has dealt with the geo-economic ramifications of wrong location selection decision, poor transportation infrastructure of the RSETZ, and the Stalinist price fixing practices, which led to the unsatisfactory performance of the zone, far short of expectations of the North Korean leadership.[4]

This paper is a modest attempt to fill this gap. It examines at first the locational specifics and triple role of the RSETZ envisaged by the North Korean authorities, looks at the performance in each respective role, with focus on the attraction of FDI, then analyzes various sources of the poor record, particularly negligible arrival of FDI in transport infrastructure, which is so critical to the realization of North Korean objectives and the prosperity of the zone in the long term. The paper concludes that economic reform is the inevitable course of action North Korea should take to remedy the deadlocked situation and realize the development potential of the zone.

12.2 LOCATION AND ENVISAGED ROLE OF THE RSETZ

Before we look at the problems of the RSETZ, the discussion should start with the geographical merits and diverse role of the zone envisaged by the North Korean government.

Location of the RSETZ

To speak of the locational specifics, the Rajin–Sonbong zone is located in the northeastern part of North Korea, and it is 400 km away from Pyongyang.[5] Jurisdiction-wise, it belongs to Hamkyongbuk-do, a province bordering Jilin Province of the PRC and the Primorsky of Russia. Rajin–Sonbong City itself is adjacent to the cities of Hunchun and Yanji of China and Khasan and Zarubino of the Russian Far East.

Such idiosyncratic locational characteristics of the RSETZ provide various advantages with regard to the role and development prospects of the zone.

Firstly, based on purely locational specifics, the zone may work as a transit center between Asia and Europe. In particular, the prospected completion of the disconnected part of the Sino–Mongolian railway would enhance the role of the RSETZ as a land-bridge between Europe and Northeast Asia. Being ice-free year-round and its location at the northwestern corner of the East Sea (or the Sea of Japan) may be a clear advantage for the zone. However, this locational advantage would be realized in the long term only if and when appropriate transport infrastructure is in place in the zone.

A second merit related to the first one is that the RSETZ may serve as a competitive export-processing base if other conditions are fulfilled. Its wages are lower than in the coastal cities of China where nominal wages are rising very rapidly in the mid-1990s.[6]

Therefore, by attracting cost-seeking FDI into the zone, North Korea may be able to earn the desperately needed hard currency, and help revitalize the country's rapidly deteriorating economy. Indeed, North Korean authorities have been highly enthusiastic about the potential of the export processing zone, and expanded the space of the zone from the original 621 km^2 to 746 km^2 in 1993.[7]

Thirdly, given the rich natural resources endowed in Northeast China and the Primorsky region, the RSETZ may provide potential foreign investors with good opportunities to develop and process natural resources, including forest, energy, and rare mineral ore, targeting the nearby export markets of Northeast Asian countries (notably, Japan, South Korea, and China).

Finally, because of the very fact that it is a self-contained zone 400-odd km (19 hours by train) away from Pyongyang, the RSETZ may serve as a laboratory for North Korean leaders to test a partial open door policy. At the same time, the location provides the North Korean leadership with the theoretical possibility to experiment with more radical market-oriented reform measures, without any political backlash or resistance.

Diverse Role of the RSETZ

Entrepôt trade and center of tourism and finance

The diverse roles of the zone, envisaged by the North Korean government, reflect the locational advantages mentioned in the above. As a matter of fact, Article 2 of the Economic and Trade Zone Law manifestly states that the RSETZ plays the triple role as the hub of an *entrepôt* and cross-border trade, the center for tourism & finance, and finally the base of export processing.

Transhipment hub Firstly, the RSETZ, with the three ports of Rajin, Sonbong and Chongjin in the RSETZ, is required to play the role of future transport hub of the Northeast Asia. In particular, the Rajin port, to be developed as a container port, is expected to serve as a base of *entrepôt* trade with major Northeast Asian countries. Customs duty, other than usage fees and commissions will not be imposed upon the goods transhipped to China and Russia through the Rajin port. Sonbong is planned to be transformed into a modern port specializing in the trade of crude oil and petrochemical products, while Chongjin port shall deal primarily with bulky cargo including cement, iron ore, coke, and grains.

Cross-border trade Being adjacent to Primorsky of the Russian Far East and the Jilin Province of the PRC, the RSETZ is also required to work as a base for cross-border trade with China and Russia. It is certain that the completion of the Wonjong Bridge across the Tumen River in 1997 is expected to promote cross-border trade with Hunchun (the PRC) and Rajin (North Korea).

Tourist center Thirdly, the RSETZ has an advantage of an uncontaminated coast (120 km), three beautiful lakes (Manpo, Seobanpo and Dongbanpo), Mt. Chilbo (659 m high) and hot springs. Such natural beauty could be used to produce a booming tourism industry, provided that the zone is equipped with sufficient accommodation and recreation facilities. The opening of the new sightseeing routes via North Korean ports of Rajin or Yanji to Mt. Paektu would pave the way for the zone to develop into a promising tourist base.

Export-processing zone

Secondly, in addition to the aforementioned role, the North Korean authorities envisioned the zone as the base of export processing, which is evidenced by their naming of the zone as 'the Free Economic and Trade Zone', initially.[8] One easy conjecture is that they might have attempted to emulate the Chinese SEZ or 'Special Economic Zone' model of Shenzhen. As a matter of fact, there are many circumstantial reasons to believe that the RSETZ was modeled after China's SEZ.

Firstly, the North Korean leadership since the mid-1980s dispatched high-ranking government officials and party cadres on many occasions to Shenzhen and other SEZs to check the pros and cons of the partial opening up and learn from their experience. Strapped by the lack of hard currency, North Korea might have felt the need to expand exports.

Secondly, location-wise, the Rajin–Sonbong is the carbon copy of the Shekou Industrial District, an export-processing zone (EPZ) at the initial experimental stage of the Shenzhen SEZ, which performs the dual role of a port and the production base of light industry goods.[9]

To increase the synergy effect between ports, North Korea declared the certain delineated area of Chongjin port as a free trade port to import raw materials and capital goods duty-free, and export-processed goods.

Thirdly, the North Korean authorities' strong wish for the EPZ role is also supported by the partitioning of the industrial estate of the RSETZ into seven different industrial estates, each of which is required to specialize in the processing of a certain industry such as textile, foodstuff, daily goods, and home appliances. Preferential corporate income tax rate of 14 per cent, as compared to 25 per cent in other places, is also an incentive for export-processing investments. Foreign-invested firms in the zone are also eligible for reduced tariffs, duty-free import of capital goods, flexible labor and wage policies and less bureaucracy than elsewhere in North Korea.

Internal and External Efforts

Increased resource allocation to the zone

As a follow-up to their plans, and also because of competition with China and Russia, the North Korean government made serious efforts to make the zone successful, both internally and externally.

Internally, the North Korean authorities have introduced and amended various laws and regulations related to the foreign firms and also to the operation of the RSETZ. At the same time, the central as well as local governments in the RSETZ began to place the topmost priority on the development of the RSETZ, probably second only to the defense-related sector, in the allocation of human and investment resources. In particular, the 1996–97 period is the time in which North Korean authorities allocated a total of 200 million North Korean won to budget expenditures to the construction of roads, railways, and other infrastructure.[10]

In addition, '*tolkyokdae*', a highly efficient military construction regiment formed to serve the special purpose of building residential complexes in the Pyongyang area, was redeployed to the RSETZ to expedite the construction work. A total of 50 000 people, mostly youngsters, were also ordered to move to the zone to be utilized as potential labor and construction force.

This all reflects the strong degree of North Korean government's commitment to the zone, and its serious efforts to make it successful.

Investment promotion forums

In addition to the domestic efforts, the North Korean government has also strived to attract the much needed foreign capital. Several occasions of investment promotional seminars and forums were held in various places, including Yanji, Hamburg, Hong Kong, Nikata, and so on mostly with the assistance of international organizations such as the UNIDO and the UNDP.

The first forum took place in the Yanbian Autonomous Prefecture (China) in 1995. The Yanbian Forum, which South Korean businessmen could not attend due to North–South political conflicts, attracted 430 foreign investors and resulted in the conclusion of 142 agreements and letters of intent for foreign investment with an estimated valuation of US$600 million.[11] Extensive follow-up work by local authorities and companies in 1997 resulted in nearly 100 of these projects being finalized and approved.

A particular success was the Second Investment Promotion Forum held in mid-September 1996 in the Rajin–Sonbong City, at least in terms of the number of foreign participants and the amount committed or contracted during the Forum.[12] A total number of 460 foreign participants attended the forum where a total of US$268 million of FDI contracts were concluded. The largest contract was US$28 million by Thailand Loxley telecommunication consortium, and other projects included investments in hotels, tourist facilities, a bank and several manufacturing industries. In addition, 11 partnerships worth US$560 million were concluded in the form of the Memoranda of Agreements.

However, the majority of the memoranda or the letters of intent negotiated did not develop into contracts, and only 18 to 20 per cent of the 109 contracts signed during the 1995–97 period were actually realized. In particular, investment projects of large amounts primarily in transportation, telecommunication and construction projects were given up afterwards for various reasons. Moreover, most of the investments realized went to service sectors including trade, hotels, restaurants, taxi service and tourist facilities, and more importantly, only a fraction were channeled into transport and other infrastructure sectors.

12.3 POOR PERFORMANCE OF THE ZONE: PROBLEMS AND SOURCES

Cross-border Trade

Given the nonexistence of the relevant statistics, it is impossible to confirm if the RSETZ is playing the diverse role as the center of *entrepôt* and transhipment trade, the center of tourism and international finance, and the EPZ in a manner as originally planned. Therefore, with regard to the assessment of the first role, suffice it to analyze the growth in the volume of cross-border trade between the zone with the two neighboring riparian countries.[13]

As shown in Table 12.1, cross-border trade volume was meager at US$97.2 million in 1991, but it jumped to a peak of US$471.3 million in 1993. Since then it has recorded negative growth. In particular, the border trade volume dwindled sharply by 66.9 per cent in 1995 to US$150 million from US$454 million a year earlier. The sharp drop is due to two factors: firstly, the Jilin Provincial government's request since 1995 to settle the trade balance in US dollars, in lieu of local currencies they had accepted in the past; and secondly, to the virtual crumbling of the production base of the North Korean economy, which made the diversity as well as quantity of commodities to trade decrease sharply.

Table 12.1 Cross-border Trade between Jilin and Hamkyongbuk-do (Millions of US dollars, Percentage)

Year	Total border trade		Export to DPRK	Import from DPRK	Trade balance
	Amount	Growth (%)			
1991	97.20	–	48.43	44.27	4.16
1992	217.57	123.84	97.92	119.65	−21.73
1993	471.26	116.60	229.40	241.86	−12.46
1994	454.00	−3.66	250.00	204.00	46.00
1995	150.09	−66.94	89.27	60.82	28.59
1996	116.38	−22.46	75.59	40.29	35.30
1997	(104.57)*	(−10.15)	37.00	24.00	13.00

Notes: The 1997 figure was estimated through the method of extrapolation given the first seven months' performance is US$61 million.

Source: Yanbian Tongji Nianjian (1998); Unpublised mterials by Foreign Trade Council of Jilin Province, PRC.

Although it was not possible to obtain the most recent figures, it is safe to estimate that the 1997 figures would not far exceed the US$105 million, or the annualized extrapolation of the seven months' trade performance. One big achievement in 1997, which will affect positively the future prospects of cross-border trade, is that in July 1997, both the Jilin Provincial and North Korean governments agreed to open a border trade market at Wonjong-li in the zone. The restoration and reopening of the Quanhe in October 1995 was also a boost to the revitalization of border trade between the RSETZ and Hunchun City of Jilin Province on the Chinese side.[14]

As far as the border trade with the Primorsky Territory of Russia is concerned, it is very difficult to discuss the trade volume because of the lack of detailed trade statistics. Neither the Russian nor the North Korean side discloses such information. However, scattered evidence from newspapers suggests that North Korea's border trade with Russia fell by 50 per cent from 1991 when the Soviet Union's disintegration started. Considering that the North Korean economy contracted further in the post-1995 period, and that the Russian traders show an increasing interest in trade with the market economies, North Korea's border trade with the Primorsky Territory might have continued to record negative growth since 1995. The Russian request for the settlement of trade balances in hard currency since 1993 might have accelerated the diminishing growth rate of border trade.[15]

This indicates that North Korea's cross-the-border performance is not expanding, but shrinking with both trading partners. In addition, its major border trade partner is China, not Russia, which implies that development priority should be given to the transport/logistical infrastructure supporting the cross-border trade with the Yanbian Autonomous Prefecture.

Financing and Tourism Activities

When assessing the performance of the center of finance and tourism, there is no evidence that the RSETZ is working properly as originally envisaged. First of all, ING Bank, a Dutch bank as well as the only foreign bank registered in the zone, has in fact operated in the Pyongyang area, and in April 1999 decided to pull out of North Korea, frustrated by the worsening operating environment and bleak business prospects.[16] Peregrine Daesung Bank, joint venture between Peregrine Investment Securities and the state-owned Daesung Bank, which showed some interest in business in the zone, left Pyongyang in early 1999, because its parent company in Hong Kong went bankrupt amidst the Asian economic crisis and was taken over by the BNP (Bank Nationale de Paribas).

Tourism activities via the zone are also in the doldrums, but the prospects of tourism seems to be brighter than the goal of becoming a finance center, which has become a laughing stock in the international business community. Some international arrangements have been made with regard to the institutional framework of tourism, and discussions are also under way for further improvements. For instance, Jilin and Liaoning provinces of China and North Korea have discussed the possibility of tourism expansion since the early 1990s. Finally in 1997, North Korea approved the diversification of travel routes, thus increasing the number of the border crossings in addition to the two existing crossings of Tumen (Jilin)–Samjiyon (DPRK), and Tumen–Rajin–Sonbong (DPRK). In addition, in August 1997, a tourist train service was re-established between Tumen City of the Yanbian Autonomous Region and Rajin after the 52-year closing.[17] Only South Korean passport holders are not allowed to take the tourist train. As a consequence of the improvement of the institutional arrangement, the number of foreign visitors to the RSETZ, which was minimal at 3400 in 1996 and 5800 in 1997, rose to 8200 in the first 7 months of 1998.

Yet there are some caveats in order. The majority of the visitors are not genuine tourists, but the Korean-Chinese who are dropping by for business purposes. The number of tourists from Japan, Taiwan, and Hong Kong, though increasing, is extremely small. The complex visa procedure, inefficient and ill-equipped transportation facilities and the lack of lodging and entertainment facilities are prohibiting a big rise in the number of foreign tourists.

A more serious obstacle to the expansion of tourists, however, is a security concern. This is particularly true of South Korean tourists, who account for a lion's share of tourists once political restrictions are lifted. To take the case of the Mt. Kumkang incident as an example, a South Korean tourist was held for ten days by the North Korean authorities for the alleged charge that she was inciting the defection of a North Korean guide, but in fact without any particular reasons other than a political leverage purpose, following the clash between North and South Korean naval forces in the West Sea. This incident, although it took place in Mt. Kumkang, may have considerable negative repercussions on the prospects of cross-border tourism through Rajin–Sonbong.

There are strategic or situational obstacles, too. North Korean officials in charge of the management of the RSETZ are particularly frustrated by the fact that they are attracting only several hundred genuine tourists annually despite the seven-year efforts, whereas the Mt. Kumkang area is earning US$125 million in a big deal with Hyundai within a space of four months in January to April 1999.

Attraction of FDI

Despite the North Korean government's strenuous efforts to attract FDI, the RSETZ's record is rated to be the poorest performer of the three TREDA regions, including the Yanbian Autonomous Prefecture and the Primorsky Territory of Russia, as shown in Table 12.2. The RSETZ absorbed a total of US$67 million of FDI during the 1991–97 period in comparison to US$465.2 million by the Yanbian Prefecture and US$384.3 million by the Primorsky Territory.

However, if one looks at the trend growth of yearly volume of investment attracted, North Korea is not hopeless since the record is improving. In particular, the year 1996 saw a sharp jump to US$30 million from US$4 million a year earlier, and the following year of 1997 also witnessed an investment inflow of US$29 million. This owed substantially to the successful launch of the investment promotion forums in major foreign countries. The problem is that North Korea could not keep this momentum unless politico-economic, and institutional environments are not substantially improved.

Table 12.2 The Amount of FDI Attracted into the RSETZ in Comparative Perspective (1991–97, Millions of US Dollars, Percentage Share)

Country /Area	Actually realized figures					Forecast Figures
	During 1994	During 1995	During 1996	During 1997	Accumul-ated inv. amt. 1991–97	Accumul-ated inv. amt. 1991–98
RSETZ (DPRK)	1.34 (2.1)	4.0 (3.1)	30.0 (13.9)	29.0 (13.3)	67.0 (7.3)	100.0 (9.3)
Yanbian prefecture (PRC)	60.7 (94.9)	78.3 (59.7)	133.9 (62.2)	94.0 (43.1)	465.2 (50.8)	550.0 (51.4)
Primorsky territory (Russia)	1.87 (2.9)	48.8 (37.2)	51.2 (23.8)	95.0 (43.6)	384.3 (41.9)	420.0 (39.3)
Total TREDA	63.9 (100.0)	131.1 (100.0)	215.1 (100.0)	218.0 (100.0)	916.5 (100.0)	1,070 (100)

Source: UNDP (1997a); the Tumen Secretariat (1999).

The low realization of the investment contracts is another problem. The analysis based on the figures disclosed at the international conferences by North Korean officials and the information revealed by a Korean-Japanese close to the DPRK (*chochongryon*), who is a frequent visitor to North Korea, shows that the total volume of the investment North Korea attracted during the 1993–97 period is known to be US$750 million over 111 projects on an accumulated contract basis.[18] Of these, actually realized investments were a meager US$63 million over 77 cases, with the realized to contracted investment ratio reading only at 8.4 per cent in terms of amount. Moreover, of the realized investments, only 44 firms are confirmed to be in operation, after cross-checking with other sources.

The lopsided composition of FDI by investing country and by industry is another serious problem to North Korea. The analysis of the 44 foreign-invested firms in operation by the country of origin (see Table 12.3), indicates that about 54 per cent (24 firms) of the total number of FDI are from the PRC, with 58 per cent (14 firms) of them being the Korean-Chinese firms in the Yanbian Autonomous Prefecture. The next biggest investors are Japanese, but again, half of the Japanese firms are *chochongryon.* Other marginal yet genuine foreign investors are Hong Kong (7), Singapore,

Thailand, and the Netherlands (1 each).

The majority (over 68 per cent) of the investments were small and medium-sized, with the average amount per project being only US$750 000. In particular, the scale of FDI made by the Korean-Chinese were minimal at US$300 000 on average, and their major line of investments were in such service sectors as trade, taxi, restaurants, karaoke bars, shops, small inns and so on.

Table 12.3 FDI into the RSETZ by Investing Country (as of the 1997 Year-end)

	Japanese		Chinese		Hong Kong	Singa- pore	Thai- land	Nether- lands
	Total	Korean Japanese	Total	Korean Chinese				
Total (44)	10	5	24	14	7	1	1	1
% share	22.7	11.4	54.5	31.8	15.9	2.3	2.3	2.3

Source: Lee Kyong-il (1998); Korea Investment and Trade Promotion Corporation (1998); Tumen Secretariat (1999).

Another characteristic feature is that not a single South Korean firm was on the list. This indicates that despite all the rhetoric of South–North economic cooperation, there is a big gulf between the two sides as far as FDI is concerned. Filling in the gap were small and medium- investments made by overseas Koreans living in China or Japan, who seek to maximize their economic profits by using 'blood ties' or 'personal connections' with North Korean people.

By investment pattern, equity joint ventures accounted for 63.6 per cent (28 firms) of the total, followed by contractual joint ventures (13.6 per cent; 6 firms) and wholly foreign-owned firms (22.7 per cent; 10 firms).

By industry, as shown in Table 12.4, the service industry (30 firms) accounts for 68.2 per cent of the total number, followed by manufacturing industry (27.3 per cent; 12 firms) and primary sector (4.5 per cent; 2 firms). Of the tertiary sector, trading firms accounted for one-third of the total, with the remaining firms distributed in such service sectors as restaurants and merchandizing (4), hotel (4), tourism (2), bank (2), taxi (3), trucking service (3), telecommunication (1), and road construction (1). In particular, telecommunications and transportation infrastructure saw the arrival of only two investments: one by Thailand Loxley in telecommunications, and the other by Hong Kong Tyson Trading in the road construction and local transportation businesses. In the manufacturing industry, the processing of marine products was the most popular sector for FDI, followed by foodstuff and beverage (2), building materials (2), and herbal products (2).

Table 12.4 FDI into the RSETZ by Industry (as of the 1997 Year-end)

Total	Primary sector (agriculture, etc.)	Secondary sector (manufacturing)	Tertiary sector (service)
Firms (44)	2	12	30
% share	4.5	27.3	68.2
Industries (number of firms)	Animal husbandry (1) Vegetable farm (1)	Marine products processing (5) Foodstuff and beverage (2) Herbal products building materials (2) Soap (1)	Trade (8) Restaurants and shops (4) Hotels (4) Bank (2) Tourism (2) Taxi service (3) Trucking service (2) Oil sale, car repair (1) Ocean transport (1) Container (1) Road construction (1) Telecom (1)

Source: Lee Kyong-il (1998); Korea Investment and Trade Promotion Corporation (1998); Tumen Secretariat (1999).

Overall Assessment

Overall, the above analysis shows that far from the North Korean authorities' ambitious goal of transforming the zone into the export-processing zone and future transportation hub of North East Asia, the RSETZ did not perform the role as laid out by the plan. In particular, the zone as a center of financing is found to be illusory, given North Korea's economic collapse, insufficient infrastructure, lack of knowledge and skills and insurmountable institutional problems. Its role as a center of tourism, though limited for security reasons, is considered to have better prospects. The recent major obstacle, however, is its disappointing results, as compared with the Mt. Kumkang sightseeing project, in attracting potential tourists from South Korea.

The role as an export-processing base has been partially achieved owing chiefly to North Korea's aggressive FDI promotion efforts. However, the majority of the small investors were those petty investors like Korean-Chinese and Korean-Japanese, and over half of them were concentrated in the service sector, while the transport, telecommunication or manufacturing sectors suffer from underinvestment. Although these 'relationship-based' investments are better than nothing, this type of FDI will not only exhaust soon, but also distort the industrial structure of the zone.

Indeed, North Korea has yet to see the consistent, stable inflow of FDIs into the zone. Relatively better results in 1996 and 1997 were a temporary phenomena due to the holding of Investment Promotion Forums, but North Korea cannot continue in this way in attracting FDI. Still, the majority of potential investors, those particularly from the USA and South Korea, are either indifferent to or losing interest in investing in the zone.

Having witnessed the foreign investors' withering interest in the zone, the North Korean government in 1996 came up with a more realistic proposal after restructuring the scale and scope of investment plans. At the Northeast Asian Economic Conference held at Nikata in the fall of 1996, Kim Eungryol, vice-chairman of the Foreign Economic Cooperation Council of North Korea, made it clear that given the budget constraints, it would have to minimize the new infrastructure investment while making the most of the existing facilities in the development of the RSETZ. He also stressed that they will place a priority on the economically feasible projects in transit transportation, tourism, and manufacturing industries, which would bring immediate benefits in terms of employment and hard currency acquisition.

However, in order to attract a big chunk of investments from South Korea or from other countries, North Korea needs to identify the real sources of the poor record and come up with more pragmatic solutions.

Sources of the Poor Record

Then why is the performance of the RSETZ so poor? Why do major potential foreign investors keep aloof from the investment promotion initiatives proposed by Pyongyang? There are many reasons. Moreover, probably the most formidable obstacle to the expansion of FDI would be North Korea's non-conciliatory attitude about the four-party peace talks, and its belligerent attitude towards the outside world as evidenced by the launch of medium-range missile over Japan.

Pyongyang's ambivalence shown in its missile negotiation with the USA is another factor that makes the USA government hesitant about delisting North Korea from the list of terrorist nations. The recent naval incident touched off by Pyongyang in the West Sea threw a cold blanket over the good mood of bilateral economic cooperation formed after the 'Sunshine policy' initiative made by the South Korean (Kim Dae Jung) government, and Hyundai's cattle-diplomacy.

What aggravates the situation is the political infighting between hard-liners and pragmatic technocrats within North Korea and the subsequent policy swings and attitudinal ambivalence toward consistent engagement with the South. This, combined altogether, constitutes a formidable obstacle to the expansion of trade with and FDI into North Korea. Without North Korea's strong commitment to reform and the opening of the economy, there will always be sharp, on-and-off discontinuities in the inflow of FDI into North Korea.

12.4 INCORRECT LOCATION SELECTION DECISIONS

Demerits of the RSETZ

Apart from the political constraints, what inhibits the massive arrival of foreign investments into the zone is that North Korean authorities made a wrong decision about the selection of a site for a free trade and economic zone at the initial stage of setting up a plan. The reality is that various locational merits of the zone introduced earlier in the previous section, in fact, gave rise to various disadvantages stated below.

Firstly, the fact that the RSETZ is secluded not only from the economic growth pole of other Asian countries but also from the economic center of Pyongyang, combined with the isolation of the North Korean economy itself from the global market, makes it impossible for the zone to develop into a major trading center and/or transport hub in the subregion. Potential foreign investors would choose to invest in Vietnam or the small and medium-sized coastal cities of China rather than going into the secluded zone where political and economic risks are high.

Secondly, although the size of the RSETZ (746 km^2) is more than twice the size of Shenzhen (327.5 km^2), the real space available is much smaller than that of Shenzhen because approximately 70 per cent of the zone is mountain-ous area, swamps or lakes. Moreover, the zone is a long way from the major trading ports of China, Korea and Japan. This, combined with the notoriously poor transport infrastructure, works as an unequivocal stumbling block to the attraction of any significant volume of FDI.

Thirdly, as far as the low-cost export-processing is concerned, more populous cities in the West Coast such as Nampo–Haejoo would serve as a more or at least equally competitive export platform. The reason is that they not only enjoy the same advantage of low-cost labor inputs, but also have the advantage of geographical proximity to the export markets of the PRC and South Korea. In addition, according to the survey made by the Korean business conglomerates, the West coast cities are known to be equipped with a better transport infrastructure. The recent move by the Hyundai group to establish an industrial complex in the Haejoo area confirms this argument.

Fourthly and more critically, the RSETZ does not have a core economic center like Hong Kong in its vicinity. As a matter of fact, the success of the SEZs in China is related closely to the existence of and close interaction with the economic center of Hong Kong, which has provided the SEZ with capital, imported raw materials, technology, and management know-how. In fact, the SEZ was designed to maximize the cooperation potential with a neiboring free trade port city, Hong Kong, and this is evidenced by the fact that the Guangdong Provincial government accommodated the suggestions for the creation of the SEZ made by the China Merchants' Steam Navigation Company in Hong Kong.[19] The absence of a core economic center like Hong Kong is considered as a critical defect of the RSETZ in North Korea because the shock effect of the partial opening may soon diminish and cannot be sustained without the core center in the vicinity of the zone.

Lastly, the RSETZ adjacent to the borders of China and Russia is a politically sensitive area. Although the territorial issues surrounding the border with China have basically been resolved as of the end of 1998, the riparian governments, particularly North Korea, more often than not, overreact to trivial immigration or border-crossing issues. This, coupled with the possibility of recurrence of border disputes, diverts the attention of foreign firms away from the zone.

Given these tremendous geo-economic disadvantages, simple, symbolic provision of corporate income tax incentives would not be sufficient to induce the massive influx of FDI into the RSETZ.

Comparison with Shinuijoo

However, the situation might have been different if the North Korean authorities set up a similar zone in one of the west coast cities like Nampo–Haejoo, or Shinuijoo. In particular, Shinuijoo shares many characteristic features with Rajin–Sonbong. It is a port city in the northwestern coast of Jakang-do, bordering the Chinese city of Dandong, Liaoning Province, across the Yalu River.

Shinuijoo, as summarized in Table 12.5, has many geo-economic merits over Rajin–Sonbong. The RSETZ has advantages over Shinuijoo only in policy-related factors, which include the strong central government's policy support, tax benefits, existence of foreign joint venture laws and regulations, and the possibility of establishing wholly foreign-owned firms. Thus Shinuijoo might have been a more promising destination of FDI or a better alternative for export-processing should North Korea designated Shinuijoo as a 'border economic cooperation zone' or an EPZ open to foreign trade and investment.

Firstly, the location of Shinuijoo at the river-mouth of the Yalu is considered favorable to the expansion of *entrepôt* or cross-border trade with the PRC. As a matter of fact, in August 1996 the Shinuijoo government was allowed to set up a free market on the island between Dandong and Shinuijoo. It is also convenient to transhipment trade. It is only seven to ten hours away by sea from the port of Inchon, a gateway to Seoul, whereas it takes more than a full day to reach the Rajin–Sonbong area from Inchon. This signals a definite locational advantage of Shinuijoo over the Rajin–Sonbong in the development potential of cross-border trade and in transportation convenience.

Secondly, Shinuijoo has better conditions for an export platform base. It has a richer labor force than the Rajin–Sonbong area, and it is close to the resource-rich provinces of Liaoning and Heilongjiang, from which it can source cheap raw materials and process them for export to the nearby markets of South Korea or China.

Thirdly, Liaoning Province, to which Dandong belongs, boasts of a high per capita GDP of 8519 yuan, even higher than Jilin Province (with a per capita GDP of 5515 yuan), major trading partner to the Rajin–Sonbong city.[20]

Moreover, the sum total of the population of Shinuijoo (with a population of 321 000) and Dandong (with a population of 700 000) constitutes a market of one million people. This indicates that Shinuijoo, once given a formal status of a free trade port, can enjoy the 'halo effect' of fast-growing Dandong, and that as a consequence the Dandong and Shinuijoo economies, when informally integrated, may become a 'natural economic territory', thereby providing incentives to pull market-seeking FDIs from major Northeast Asian countries.[21]

In addition, unlike the RSETZ, necessary capital, technology and management know-how can easily be imported from Dandong, which can work as a core city or mini-Hong Kong. In support of such a possibility, there are several hundred foreign-invested firms in Dandong, including those of South Korean origin.

Overall, as far as geo-economics is concerned, Shinuijoo has better qualifications than Rajin–Sonbong to develop into a prosperous economic and trade zone.

Background of the Location Decision

Precedence of geo-political logic

The question is how and for what reason North Korean authorities settled on the Rajin–Sonbong of Hamkyongbuk-do as the final site for the free economic and trade zone in the secluded area of Hamkyongbuk-do, a long way away from Pyongyang, instead of western coastal cities including Shinuijoo.

Table 12.5 Comparison between Shinuijoo and the RSETZ

	Shinuijoo area	Rajin–Sonbong zone
Location	• Belongs to Jakang-do • At the mouth of the Yalu River • Bordering Dandong of Liaoning Province, China • Convenient for export to China and Korea	• Belongs to Hamkyongbuk-do • Riparian to the Tumen River • Close to the border with Russia and China • Remote from major consumer markets
Population	• Shinuijoo (321 000) • Dandong (700 000)	• Rajin–Sonbong (200 000) • Hunchun (300 000), Yanji (500 000)
Nature of the zone/area	• Mainly for trade between North Korea and China • Good harbor with natural trading	• Mainly for multilateral economic cooperation • Laboratory of market economies
Major target markets	• Korean domestic market • China's domestic market	• Markets of Russia, Japan and China • Access to USA market prohibited at this stage
Industries for FDI	• Light industries for export processing	• Light industries for export processing • Infrastructure
Central government's support	• Weak because of security concern	• Strong policy and institutional support
Political sensitivity	• Very sensitive • Frequent intervention by the party and the government	• Insensitive as it is remote from Pyongyang • Little political intervention
Infrastructure	• Relatively good infrastructure for ocean, railway, and road transportation	• Less developed than Nampo–Haejoo area • Ambitious plan for infrastructure expansion and improvement
Sourcing of raw materials	• Advantageous for the out-sourcing of raw materials	• Disadvantageous for the sourcing of raw materials
Tax benefits	• 25 per cent corporate income tax • No tax holidays	• 14 per cent corporate income tax • No corporate tax for three years, 50 per cent for the next two years
Labor supply	• Uncertain policy	• Priority in the supply of labor
Currency for settlement	• North Korean won	• Foreign exchange certificates abolished in June 1997
Immigration procedures	• Visa needed	• Required only when a foreigner wants to cross the zone border
Cross-border trade	• Border trade with liaoning Province	• Border trade with Primorsky and Jilin Province

Source: Based on various North Korean laws and regulations related to the establishment and operation of the RSETZ.

There are three possibilities. Firstly, the North Korean government might not have seriously examined the geo-economic merits and demerits of the Rajin–Sonbong while focusing on the geo-political merits of the zone.

Secondly, even if they had tried to evaluate, they might have suffered from the lack of methodological know-how or experience in making location decisions. Lastly, but most convincingly, although the North Korean leadership might have known about the superiority of Shinuijoo to Rajin–Sonbong in geo-economic aspects, they might have refrained from choosing Shinuijoo for political reasons or for security considerations in reflection of their fear of the adverse impact of its opening on the system collapse.

In fact, Shinuijoo has one critical geo-political disadvantage of bordering a more prosperous city of Dandong, Liaoning, which North Korean leaders regard as an area seriously contaminated by 'bourgeois capitalism'. North Korean leadership might have thought that once Shinuijoo is open, it might work as an effective conduit to import capitalist contamination and spread it through North Korean society. Such worry is reinforced by a recent sharp increase in the number of North Korean defectors or illegal immigrants across the Yalu to the adjacent Liaoning Province.

Competition with the Hunchun

Another argument is that the location of RSETZ was the product of the combination of two factors: that is, to learn from the Chinese Special Economic Zone model, and to catch up with the China's Hunchun Border Cooperative Zone for a better record in the attraction of FDI.

As a matter of fact, in desperate need to earn hard currency, North Korean administration (*Zhengmuwon*) ordered the North Korean Academy of Social Sciences to study the merits and demerits of the Shenzhen Special Economic Zone. The North Korean leadership might have been impressed by the fact that sleepy coastal towns of negligible economic significance in Guangdong turned into modern export-processing bases in such a short span of time.

However, they had worries about the adverse impact of the partial opening-up on their systemic security. In particular, they might have been struck by the prevalence of undesirable byproducts such as corruption, smuggling, prostitution, and so on and felt the strong need to take some policy measures to prevent the spread of capitalist contamination into the North Korean system. Given the hard-liners' opposition to the politico-economic ramifications the partial opening-up will bring about, the technical complexities of the issue, and the inexperience and the concomitant lack of confidence, neither North Korean leadership nor bureaucrats in charge of the practical task were fully prepared for the partial opening-up. However, the rapid progress on the Chinese side forced them to establish the RSETZ in a rather haphazard manner. In fact, during the 1990–91 period, Hunchun was already prospering with the increased arrival of foreign firms.[22]

With insufficient time left in competing with China in the attraction of FDI, and also under equally strong pressure to prevent the capitalist contamination, Pyongyang in December 1991 decided to set up the zone in the Rajin–Sonbong area, and in July 1995 installed the barbed wire around the boundary of the zone to tighten the immigration control over the zone.[23] By so doing, they were able to contain undesirable byproducts within the boundary of the zone, and feel comfortable with the alleviated security burden.

Haphazard location decision

Given the lack of detailed information about the internal decision-making process within the North Korean party administrative bureaucracy, it is difficult to analyze the decision process. However, scattered evidence and the author's discussions with North Korean officials in international conferences and meetings related to the TRADP support the development of the two arguments, which worked interactively to push North Korean leadership to establish the zone.[24]

Whatever the true reason may be, it is worth noting that the geo-political logic has preceded over the geo-economic rationality. However, the wrong, haphazard location decision, without due attention being paid to geo-economic elements, has become one of the major sources of causing the poor performance of the zone in the attraction of FDI and constitutes a serious inherent limit that constrains the future growth potential of the zone. Had North Korea established the zone in the west coastal cities, either at Nampo–Haejoo or at least Shinuijoo, taking some degree of political risks, then foreign investors might have paid greater attention to the economic and trade zone and considered investment in a more positive manner than in the present situation.

12.5 TRANSPORT SHORTAGES: STATUS, SOURCES, AND REMEDIES

Good Infrastructure as a Precondition for FDI

In the above, we have mentioned how the North Korean leadership ended up making wrong decisions as to the selection of the location for an economic and trade zone. However, with the location decision being irreversible and the political constraints being irreparable, North Korean leaders attempted to send other positive signals to potential foreign investors by disclosing ambitious plans to modernize and expand the infrastructure of the zone.

Keenly aware of the harsh reality that many foreign investors regard modern, well-functioning transport and logistical infrastructure as a pre-condition for their investments, the North Korean authorities had to do something to improve backward, insufficient transport/logistical infrastructure. Indeed, a non-negligible number of foreign investors turned away from the zone simply because they considered the zone without proper transport and logistical infrastructure might not even guarantee the normal operation of the plants, particularly in energy, sourcing of raw materials and the in-time delivery of finished products.

The following is a brief description of the current status and problems of the transport infrastructure of the RSETZ and the subsequent North Korean efforts to cope with the problems by major modes of transportation.

Current Status of the Transport Infrastructure

Railways

North Korean efforts to expand and modernize the transportation infrastructure in the RSETZ started with the railway system, which accounts for over 70 per cent of total inland cargo volume handled into and out of the zone. The railway network stretches approximately 218 km from Chongjin to Rajin, Sonbong, Saetpyol, and finally to Onsong. Completion of the electrification of the 168 km of railway in Hamkyongbuk-do in October 1998 was a great achievement in expanding the transportation capacity. Construction of the Namyang Railway Marshalling Yard, which upon completion would handle the transfer of 20–40 ft containers from vehicles to the train bound for Rajin, was another sincere effort to give confidence to foreign investors.[25]

Roads

Roads are the next important means of inland transportation in North Korea, but the situation is no better than in railways. In particular, road networks in Hamkyongbuk-do are so inefficient that it takes almost twice the time normally required to deliver the goods for the same distance in South Korea. Lack of capital, bad management, neglect of maintenance works are major culprits.

Transhipment trade and cross-border trade is the victim of poor road systems. One major achievement is the reopening of the Quanhe Bridge (in October 1995), which had been closed in 1953 for safety and security reasons. The reopening of the bridge has enabled the RSETZ to expand the cross-border trade with the neighboring Jilin province of China via the Wonjong-li free market. In addition, the construction of a new 50-km road linking Wonjong-li with Sonbong is under way to facilitate the delivery of imported container cargo to Jilin province via North Korean ports.[26]

The pavement of the existing roads between Rajin and Wonjong-li began in 1996 and the reconstruction of major town roads in the Rajin–Sonbong city are also under progress with the participation by Tyson Construction Company of Hong Kong. At the same time, in order to develop transport networks linking major cities along the border, North Korea put up US$19 million for the expansion of transportation and tourism, out of the total US$37 million investment expenditure earmarked for the RSETZ from 1992 to 1996.

Ports and ancillary facilities

Port situations are slightly better than in the cases of roads and railways. The natural conditions of Rajin, Sonbong, Woongsang, and Chongjin are such that they are regarded as good harbors which do not freeze over during the winter. In particular, Rajin has natural breakwaters like Socho and Daecho islands.

In order to take advantage of such good natural conditions, the North Korean government has announced plans to transform Rajin into a modern container port and also expand the Sonbong and Chongjin ports, but there are no signs that Rajin port is being transformed into a modern container port. North Korean ports, with most of the port facilities built in the 1950s and 1960s, are notorious for an outdated, inefficient cargo handling system, antiquated storage facilities, and their malpractice of not returning the outbound containers.

A modest consolation comes from the construction of a Rajin fertilizer terminal by Russian and Japanese investors through an equity joint venture agreement. However, it is hard to expect any further arrivals of Russian investments in the zone due to the domestic financial difficulties culminated by their announcement of the moratorium of non-repayment of loans denominated in foreign currency in August 1998. A Competing relationship with the Russian ports for cargo is another factor depressing FDIs from Russia. As shown in Figure 12.1, four ports/harbors of Vladivostok, Vostochini, Nakhodka, and Zarubino in the Russian Far East, equipped with modernized transport and logistical infrastructure, are taking away a substantial proportion of cargo which otherwise would have been chaneled through North Korean ports.[27]

The completion of the Hunchun–Zarbino railway in 1997 made the positions of Russian ports more competitive in handling the *entrepôt* trade cargo, and enabled the Chinese traders in Jilin and Heilongjiang provinces to choose between the more efficient, economical Hunchun–Zarbino route and the notoriously inefficient Hunchun–Rajin route, with the outcome being mostly to the benefit of Russian ports. From the pragmatic Chinese point of view, what counts is the economics of transport and logistical costs, not historical friendships with North Korea.

Faced with the decline of locational advantage of the RSETZ, the Rajin port authorities have entered into an agreement with the Yanbian Hyuntong Shipping Company concerning the lease of the port for 25 years.[28] However, we have yet to see any solid evidence that the Rajin port is utilized more intensively than before by the Chinese traders.

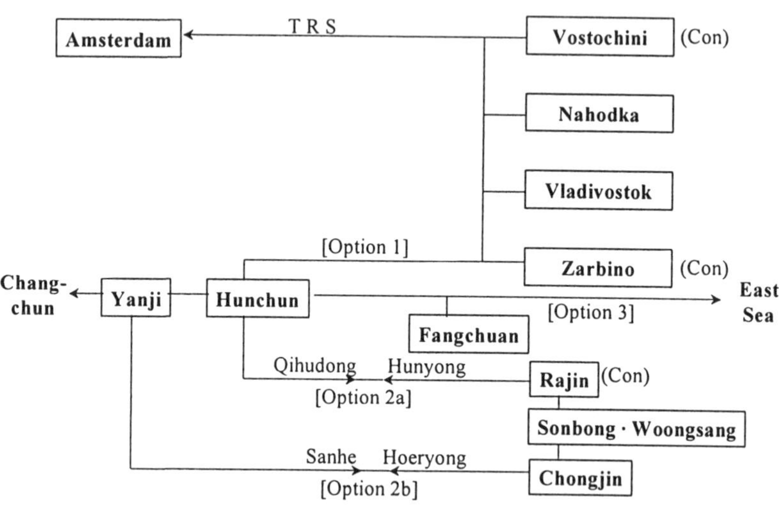

Notes: (Con) represents the container ports.

Figure 12.1 Fork-type Transport Network Linkage in TREDA and the Competitive Positions of North Korean Ports

No access to the zone by air

Fourthly, when getting access to the RSETZ for feasibility studies, negotiations, and actual investments, one may think the fastest means would be by air. However, such means are not available to the RSETZ as there is no civilian airport in the neighborhood of the zone.

Only under special circumstances, the Wolyang military airport, one and a half hours away by car from Chongjin, is used for VIP visitors. However, ordinary visitors, not given such a luxury, have to endure a 19-hour train ride to reach the zone, after entering Pyongyang. This discourages potential investors from coming to the RSETZ.

A simple reason for the poor status of air transportation is that not enough financial resources are left for the construction of civilian airports since the railways and roads take up a comparatively greater share of investment resources. The North Korean authorities plan to build an international airport at Bupo-li, Sonbong, with a handling capacity of 8 million passengers and 1 million tons of cargo per year, still remains wishful thinking, as financing problems have not been resolved. In the meantime, potential investors have two options: suffer from the inconvenience, or delete the zone from their list of FDI destinations.

Sources of the Poor Transport Infrastructure

Thus far we have reviewed the problems of transport and logistical infrastructure in the RSETZ. Our finding is that despite the North Korean government's efforts, the transportation infrastructure in the RSETZ is notoriously poor. Many potential investors might have turned away from the zone to the alternative destinations of Hunchun and Primorsky.

Then what are the primary sources, other than lack of capital, causing the poor transport infrastructure? One obvious source would be the political and institutional impediments to attracting FDI in the zone. There are, however, more fundamental sources imbedded in the North Korean economic system, as stated below.

Subjectivism and the Stalinist accounting

The first and most formidable obstacle is the North Korean leadership's growth-biased subjectivism biased towards new investment projects in heavy and defense-related industries. The theoretical underpinning of the voluntaryism is related to the Fel'dman growth model espoused by the Soviet economy in the 1950s.[29] This, coupled with the dysfunctions of the rationing system, results in insufficient allocation of investment resources to the transport or logistics-related sectors. By contrast, heavy and defense-related industries enjoy more than necessary resources. Although such subjectivism is often exposed to perfunctory criticism by pragmatists, the hard-liners prevail in most cases.

Secondly, the Stalinist accounting practice, which defines national income as 'net material product' and hence treats fixed investment in transport and logistical services as a nonproductive component, reinforces this subjectivist tendency. An equally strong bias is the North Korean bureaucrats' strong psychological attachment to 'new' rather than 'replacement' fixed investment.

The reason is that new investment is the legitimate component of net material product, whereas maintenance is not. For this reason, more often than not, the financial resources earmarked for the technical renovation or maintenance of transport infrastructure are diverted by powerful state organizations and agencies to new investments in producer goods or defense-related manufacturing sector.[30]

The natural consequences are industrial dislocations of the economy, as characterized by the chronic transportation shortages, poor quality of transport/logistical services, and the extremely low efficiency in the inter-modal linkage and management of transportation systems. As a matter of fact, the growth of cargo handled by the railway system has been stagnant, if not decreasing, since the mid-1980s, and this has been far below the required level to keep up with the relatively faster growth of the heavy industry sector.

The congestions and delays in the delivery of important raw materials, energy and investment goods exacerbate the supply constraints already existing in the economy and cause what Brus (1982) called the 'bottleneck multiplier' to be set in motion. Thus, material shortages in one industry or region are spilled over to other sectors and regions through the channels of backward and forward linkages and input–output relationships, thereby reproducing shortages and affecting adversely the North Korean economy.[31]

Lack of economic incentives and investment security

Other important factors that cause shortfalls of transport investments are the lack of economic incentives and investment security. First of all, in North Korea the prices and fees are fixed by the planning authority regardless of the relative scarcity of goods and services. Extremely low tollgate fees and port usage charges would, however, not guarantee an economically appropriate level of profit margins, while preventing foreign investors from recouping investment principal plus profit margins within an expected period of time. By contrast, transport infrastructure projects, by nature, require a comparatively large amount of capital (and hence huge financing costs) over a long gestation period, which translates into high risks but with low return.

More seriously, given the nonexistence of lucid or transparent investment protection treaties, be they multilateral or bilateral, and the oft-observed vagaries in North Korea's attitude towards the honoring of international treaties or agreements, potential foreign investors are not assured of the security of their investment assets, not to mention the timely remittance of profits generated in projects. This is particularly so in the case of investment by South Korean investors. The two Koreas have yet to sign an investment protection agreement.

Many old South Koreans, who fled to South Korea before or during the Korean War, have strong aspirations to invest in their home-towns, regardless of the level of profits. Their initial enthusiasm, however, will diminish if their investment assets are not protected from the incidence of confiscation or unlawful seizure. This threat is not purely imaginary, but a possible contingency as evidenced by North Korea's recent seizure of a woman who was on a sightseeing tour to Mt. Kumkang.

Jurisdictional conflicts and insufficient coordination

Poor transport services and inefficient transport systems are not merely caused by the lack of foreign capital, but also by insufficient cooperation between different transport authorities, possibly due to jurisdictional conflicts. Lack of coordination between riparian governments also impedes or decreases the possibility of the harmonious or joint development of roads, railways or telecommunication networks encompassing different regions and countries.

In Hamkyongbuk-do, it was quite common in the past that rolling stocks and cargo carriages did not return to the original place of departure, which impeded the on-time delivery of coals and cement and other freight. Unclear demarcation of authority between different railway authorities was the major culprit. In 1995, the existing five railway bureaus were merged and integrated into one to ease the jurisdictional conflicts between railway authorities. In June 1997, the North Korean government elevated the Rajin railway branch bureau to a higher position in the Bureau in order to help them exercise centralized control over Namyang, Tuman and other branch bureaus in Hamkyongbuk-do. In addition, to enhance transport efficiency, the express cargo train was put into operation between Namyang and Rajin in November 1997.

Coordination between riparian governments is the more difficult part. More often than not, China, the Russian Far East, and North Korea all came up with their own respective plans to build airports far in excess of the transport demand in the subregion. Even in the expansion of Zarubino, Vladivostok, Rajin, and Chongjin ports, the functional merits/demerits or the comparative advantages/disadvantages of ports were not fully assessed in comparative perspectives, not simply because of lack of data but also because of the lack of a willingness to coordinate. To take Rajin and Zarubino ports as an example, both are presumed to play a similar role as specialized container ports. The only difference is that the former handles primarily the Korean cargo, while the latter handles primarily the Japanese cargo, all bound for Europe. However, the socialist practice of keeping the policy confidential hampers any possibility of coordinated development of the ports.

The natural outcome is the waste of scarce resources in overlapping investments, and inefficient transport inter-modal linkage between countries. This gives foreign investors negative implications concerning the long-term prospects of the zone in terms of economic feasibility.

Grandiose investment plans without financing scheme

Last but not least, the poor transport infrastructure of the zone is attributed also to the inexperience and lack of knowledge and skills related to the design and management of investment projects. More often than not, North

Koreans disclose grandiose investment plans full of a list of projects wanted by the North Korean government, but not reflecting the preferences or demand of foreign investors.

More seriously, the plans are not supported by any detailed financing schemes or technical feasibility studies. The consequence is that those plans end up becoming useless, illusory and unrealizable.

Need for Institutional Changes

International financing prospects

The foregoing analysis of the problems and sources of the poor transport infrastructure gives rise to the need for the North Korean leadership to eliminate or at least alleviate various institutional hurdles, while searching for available investment funds.

The success of the former hinges upon the sincerity and consistency of North Korea's own reform efforts, whereas the success of the latter shall be determined not only by North Korea's own efforts but also by the international politico-economic situation, which is often beyond their control. In particular, as far as international financing is concerned, the USA stance would be a critical factor impinging upon North Korea's prospects of obtaining international financing.

One important reason is that as long as the USA, the major shareholder to the IBRD and the ADB, opposes North Korea's membership, borrowing soft-term loans from these international financial institutions is not a viable option.[32] However, given the US's strong suspicion of North Korea's subversion of the Geneva Accord, and considering that North Korea is still on the list of terrorist nations subject to the restriction of a trade embargo, North Korea's acceptance by the international financial organizations will not be easy. In addition, given the uncertain prospects of establishing diplomatic links with Japan, particularly following its launch of medium-range missiles, obtaining reparation funds from Japan has also become a remote possibility.

The only remaining option is to attract FDI from Southeast Asia, the PRC, Japan and South Korea. However, Southeast Asian countries, with the value of their wealth substantially reduced by the Asian economic crisis, and Japanese and Korean firms under painful corporate restructuring, have very little free capital left to invest in such high-risk countries like North Korea.

Overall, with the international politico-economic situation being unfavorable to North Korea, North Korea may have to adopt a two-track strategy: on the one hand, it may keep making diplomatic efforts towards the USA and Japan for the establishment of formal relationships in order to get larger chunks of investments; on the other hand, they may have to think about introducing much bolder reform measures in the RSETZ, while increasing nonpolitical or civilian contacts with the South in trade, investment, and tourism so as to keep the secluded zone of Rajin–Sonbong afloat.

Economic reforms and investment protection

Having discussed the financing problems and inherent constraints of the RSETZ, the next question would be how North Korea can get out of this quandry caused by wrong location selection decision, acute transportation shortages, and the Stalinist price fixing practice. This question, however, boils down to the issue of what kind of incentives and confidence North Korea should provide to buy the trust and confidence of potential investors.

In addition to conducting transportation investments North Korean leadership may need to provide stronger economic incentives for FDIs in manufacturing and transport investments than those in ordinary service industries. In this regard, tax incentives are one thing. However, at a more fundamental level, unreasonably low prices (including user and transportation fees) need to be liberalized within certain bounds. Otherwise, foreign firms will not be able to attend the bidding of BOT (build–operate–transfer), one of the most popular forms of inviting foreign construction firms to infrastructure projects in the PRC.

However good the rationale may be, it may not be easy for North Korea to refrain suddenly from the old practice of the Stalinist practice of price fixing even at the restricted area of the RSETZ. However, this is the price the North Korean leadership has to pay for its future prosperity. To build confidence in North Korea's full commitment to the zone, North Korean leadership should consider introducing the Chinese-type gradual reform measures at least in the zone, starting with price and taxation reforms.

In this regard, North Korea's abolition of foreign exchange certificates of North Korean won in the zone and the concomitant implementation of managed floating exchange rates in the zone in 1997 is a good move in the right direction.[33] Entering into investment protection treaties with major potential investing countries including South Korea would be an additional requirement for North Korea to see the arrival of the economically meaningful volume of FDIs into the zone.

12.6 CONCLUSION

In the above, we have evaluated the location, envisaged role and actual performance of the RSETZ. The preliminary conclusion is that North Korea did not achieve the goal or outcome it had originally sought.

The role of the RSETZ as a center of financing and tourism has turned out to be imaginary, and this is all the more so as the Mt. Kumkang sightseeing project took away potential tourists from South Korea and the ING Bank, the single foreign bank, left the country. The role as the transhipment hub of Northeast Asia is also fraught with inherent limitations related to the incorrect location selection decision made at the initial stage and the lack of appropriate transportation and logistical infrastructure.

The role as an export-processing base, although situations are marginally better, has only been partially achieved. Most investments are in service industries rather than in manufacturing, transportation and telecommunication infrastructure, which are regarded by foreign investors as a precondition for conducting FDI. In particular, there were only two infrastructure projects realized during the 1993–97 period.

Such a poor record was caused by a combination of sources, including political ambivalence, wrong location selection decision, and backward transport infrastructures. However, with political factors irreparable and with the wrong location decision already irreversible, the North Korean leadership has to focus on the expansion/modernization of the transport infrastructure.

Holding external investment promotion seminars alone, in the absence of internal reform measures, would not lead to the same results as achieved in the 1996–97 period, because Asian investors have become more prudent and risk-averse following the economic crisis. Moreover, with the impact effect of the partial opening tapering off, the domestic financial resources having been exhausted, and the international politico-economic environment unfavorable to them, North Korea is left with only one option. That is, to give up its non-conciliatory, ambivalent attitude toward the partial opening-up, to commit itself to the incremental reform down the Chinese road, and to implement a more consistent, and economically meaningful open-door policy, although it may be restricted to specific locations.

Without dismantling various economic and institutional hurdles, more specifically, without providing sufficient economic incentives and appropriate investment security, the RSETZ will not see any significant increase in the arrival of investments in manufacturing and the transport infrastructure.

NOTES

1. The United Nations Development Program (UNDP) first launched the Tumen River Area Development Program (TRADP) in 1992 at the request of five countries, namely China, North Korea, South Korea, Russia, and Mongolia, which then became signatory members of the program. According to the UNDP's rather optimistic projections, Tumen River Economic Development Area (TREDA) or small delta will be one of the fast-growth regions in Northeast Asia. From 1992 to the year 2000, the economy will grow about 8 per cent per annum and will reach 16 per cent thereafter. It is estimated that about 35 million people live within 500 km of Hunchun, one of the projected fast-growth centers of TREDA.

See Lavallee, Michael P. (1997), 'The Tumen River Development Area: A Future Trade and Transportation Hub in Northeast Asia', July 5.

2. There is an extremely long legacy of mistrust and animosity in the region, stemming from the Japanese colonization, which makes the political barriers very difficult to break. In addition, the on–off political clashes or antagonistic relations between the two Koreas and the widespread suspicion about Pyongyang's nuclear development have blocked major investment coming into North Korea for now.
3. For the institutional aspects of the TREDA and the RSETZ, see M. Clifford (1993), M. Clifford et al. (1992), M. J. Valencia (1996), M. Noland and F. L. Gordon (1997), N. Cowee (1998), Icksoo Kim (1994a, 1994b, 1994c, 1995b, 1995d), KIEP (ed.), (1994), UNDP (1997a, 1997b), to name a few. For the comparative analysis of the differing positions of the countries interested in the TRADP, please refer to Icksoo Kim (1994d, 1995a).
4. Choe Sang-Chuel (1992) dealt with the issue of acute transportation shortages in the North Korean economy from a macroeconomic perspective. M. P. Lavellee (1997) examined the transportation infrastructure and development potential of the TREDA as a future transportation hub of Northeast Asia.
5. In 1995, the North Korean government decided to combine Rajin city with Sonbong county in a bid to enhance the synergy effect and elevate the status of the Rajin–Sonbong city to the city under the direct control of the National Council, Jungmuwon. Now the city enjoys the economic management authority of the province-level, that is, the same level of authority as Hamkyongbuk-do.
6. In major coastal cities of Tianjin, Shanghai, Guangzhou, Shenzhen, Dalian, and Qingdao, the level of nominal wage is already high when compared with small and medium-sized coastal cities or inland cities, but the wage is rising at the rate of 20 to 30 per cent a year, owing primarily to the increased entry of foreign-invested firms since 1992.
7. In 1993, North Korea, in the hope of attracting more FDI into the zone and promoting border trade with China, expanded the zone to 746 km2 from the original 621 km2. As a result many cities, villages, and townships alongside the Tumen River began to engage in border trade with Chinese cities including Hunchun and Tumen.
8. The original formal title of the zone is 'the Rajin–Sonbong Free Economic and Trade Zone'. However in September 1998, the North Korean authorities dropped the term, 'Free', from the title of the 'Rajin–Sonbong Economic and Trade Zone' to prevent the hard-liners' criticism and to get rid of any misleading connotation that 'everything is free from state control'.
9. Shekou Industrial District is an industrial park established at Baoan county, Guangdong Province, at the very early stage of establishing Shenzhen SEZ. It served as a showcase of China's experimental open-door policy, but it became part of the Shenzhen Special Economic Zone at a later stage.
10. This fact was revealed by North Korean officials in the Investment Promotion Seminar held under the auspices of the UNIDO and the ERINA (Economic Research Institute of Northeast Asia) in Nikata, Japan between September 16 and October 17 1997.
11. UNDP (1997a), 'Tumen Secretariat Analysis,' p. 5.
12. The second forum was also due to the operational and financial support of the UNIDO and the Tumen Secretariat, and to financial assistance from the UNDP. In particular, help from the UNDP was instrumental to the successful launch of the forum as it provided North Korea with the integrated program of project profiling (over 100 industrial projects were identified, screened and profiled), preparation of publicity, and promotional missions abroad.
13. The history of North Korea's border trade with China goes back to as early as 1954. Border trade came to a complete halt during the Cultural Revolution period (1966–76), but it was resumed in 1981.
14. The Quanhe Bridge, partially damaged by the US bombardment during the Korean War, has been closed since 1953 for safety and security reasons. Since 1984, however, the North Korean authorities in close consultation with the Chinese side began reconstruction work in 1993 on an on-and-off basis, and reopened the bridge in October 1995. The bridge is the sole road link between China's Hunchun to Hamkyongbuk-do's Wonjong-li.
15. The only exception is the import of raw materials, particularly bauxite from Australia,

which is still conducted through Rajin to Khazanski of Russia.

16. Crampton, T. (1999), 'North Korea to Lost Main Foreign Bank', International Herald Tribune, April 18.
17. Yanbian Ribao, August 25, 1997; UNDP (1997b).
18. The North Korean government does not reveal the related statistics by investment pattern, industry and the country of origin. This compels us to rely on the scattered information. For detailed information, see Lee Kyong-il (1998), 'General Introduction of the RSETZ' and Korea Investment and Trade Promotion Corporation (1998), 'Current Status of FDI into the RSETZ of North Korea', 18–22.
19. The China Merchants' Steam Navigation Company is an enterprise under the Ministry of Communications with offices and interests in Hong Kong. For an excellent account of how the Chinese special economic zones were created and managed in the midst of power politics, see Chapter 2 of Crane, G.T. (1990) and Falkenheim, V. (1986) to name a few.
20. As a matter of fact, Liaoning province has the highest income per capita, of the three Northeastern Provinces of China, which include Heilongjiang and Jilin. Zhongguo Tongji Zaiyao (China Statistical Abstract), 1998, p.19.
21. 'Natural Economic Territory' is a term used to depict the zone composed of countries that have close economic interdependence with each other in trade and investments, despite the nonexistence of any formal regional agreements like free trade area (for example AFTA, NAFTA), customs union, or economic integration (for example EU).
22. The Hunchun Border Economic Cooperative Zone was established by the Hunchun City government in the latter half of 1989 after obtaining the approval of the Jilin provincial as well as central governments. The Zone enjoys the economic management authority of the city level, although it is under the jurisdiction of Hunchun.
23. The barbed wire fence around the zone (80 km) is 40 km long and 2.2 m high.
24. During the June 1992 to February 1995 period, the author used to work as the non-governmental coordinator of the Korean National Team concerning the Tumen River Area Development Program (TRADP) as well as the manager of the research project of 'The Studies of TRADP' published in 1993 by the UNDP. The author attended various TRADP-related meetings and conferences including the PMC (Program Management Committee) meetings in New York, Beijing, Seoul, and Moscow to have first-hand views of North Korean officials.
25. Valencia M.J. (1994).
26. To link with the North Korean road, the Chinese side is also building another 50 km of first-class road linking Wonjong-li to Hunchun.
27. In particular, Nakhodka has been the most efficient container port, and Vostochini is the Estern-most terminal of the TSR (Trans-Siberian Railway) equipped with modern facilities like 'roll-on, roll-off' system.
28. The lease contract also stipulates usage fees, charges, handling procedure, and various financing alternatives for the gradual expansion of crane capacity at Rajin Port.
29. According the two-sector growth model of Fel'dman, a greater proportion of resources should be allocated to the producer goods sector at the initial stage in order to achieve a faster growth in the second phase. The now defunct Soviet Russia, Cuba, and North Korea all rely on the Fel'dman formula in the allocation of scarce resources.
30. According to the Marxist accounting practice, transportation itself is classified as a materially productive sector, and so on but logistical services such as warehousing and other ancillary services are regarded as nonproductive sectors. Investment in the nonproductive sector decreases the possibility to enhance performance, power, and productive capacity.
31. According to Wlodzimierz Brus, Polish economist, the 'bottleneck multiplier' indicates how the bottleneck effect of a cut in imports or similar unfavorable occurrence in one sector spreads to other sectors, reducing overall production. See Brus, W. (1982), p. 43.
32. The membership into the IMF should precede the membership into the IBRD or the ADB.
33. In June 1997, Pyongyang began to float exchange rate in the RSETZ, in a certain bound. Thus the North Korean won trades at 200 to the dollar as at the end of 1997, as compared to the official 2.16 to the dollar in the rest of the nation.

BIBLIOGRAPHY

Anderson, Arthur (1994), Northeast Asia Railway and Port Group Co. Ltd. (mimeo), June1994.

Brus, W. (1982), 'To-o-shakaishugi no genjitsu' (The Reality of Socialism in Eastern Europe), Ekonomisuto, Tokyo.

Choe, Sang-Chuel (1992), 'Transportation Problems and Policies in Northeast Asia', in Kim, Won Bae et al. (eds), *Regional Economic Cooperation in Northeast Asia* (Proceedings of the Vladivostok Conference), Ch. 13, 195–210.

Clifford, M. (1993), 'Send Money: North Korea Appeals for Investment in -Trade Zone', *Far Eastern Economic Review*, September 30, 1993, p. 72.

Clifford, Mark, de Rosario, Louise, and Kaye, Lincoln (1992), 'Trade and Trade-offs', *Far Eastern Economic Review*, 18–19.

Cowee, Neizel (1998), 'Significance of Recent Changes Made in the Rajin–Sonbong Economic Trade Zone', Tongil–Kyongjae (The Unified Economy), 105–8, (in Korean).

Crampton, T. (1999), 'North Korea to Lost Main Foreign Bank', *International Herald Tribune*.

Crane, G.T. (1990), *The Political Economy of China's Special Economic Zones*, Armonk, NY: M.E. Sharpe Inc.

Falkenheim, V. (1986), 'China's Special Economic Zones', in US Congress, Joint Economic Committee, *China's Economy Looks to the Year 2000*, vol. 2, Washington: GPO, 348–370.

Jang, Young (1998), 'Border Trade between the PRC and North Korea: Recent Trends and Major Characteristics', Tongil–Kyongjae (The Unified Economy), 94–104 (in Korean).

Kawata, Takuji (Yomiuri Shimbun Correspondent), 'Pyongyang Views Border Area As Key To Survival', *The Daily Yomiuri*, February 23, 1995, p. 4.

Kaye, Lincoln (1992a), 'Hinterland of Hope', *Far Eastern Economic Review*, January, 16–17.

Kaye, Lincoln (1992b), 'Casualty of History', *Far Eastern Economic Review*, January, 19–20.

KEI (1996), 'Treasury is Adamant Regarding No ADB Membership Now for North Korea', KEI Executive Summary, no. 9606-12.

KIEP (ed.) (1994), *Studies in Support of TRADP (Tumen River Area Development Program)*, Seoul: KIEP for UNDP, July 1994.

Kim, Icksoo (1994a), 'Introduction', in KIEP (ed.), *Studies in Support of TRADP (Tumen River Area Development Program)*, 21–8.

Kim, Icksoo (1994b), 'TRADP: A Mini-Model for Northeast Asian Economic Cooperation', in Yoo, Jang-Hee and Lee, Chang-Jae, *Northeast Asian Economic Cooperation: Progress in Conceptualization and in Practice*, Seoul: KIEP, 122–52.

Kim, Icksoo (1994c), *TRADP and the Korean Peninsula*, Seoul: KIEP (in Korean)

Kim, Icksoo (1994d), 'TRADP: Strategic Frameworks of PRC, Japan, Russia, DPRK and ROK in Comparative Perspectives', Intra-Korean Exchanges and Investment Prospects (Nam-Bukhan Kyoryu wa Tuja Jonmang), Seoul: Hansei Research Institute, 82–116 (in Korean).

Kim, Icksoo (1995a), 'Current Status of the TRADP and the Respective Positions and Strategies of Each Country', *Bukhan-yonku (Journal of North Korea Studies)*, Seoul, **6** (**1**), pp. 26–55 (in Korean).

Kim, Icksoo (1995b), 'TRADP: Current Status and Future Prospects', in JETRO, *The Chinese Economy (Chukoku Keizai)*, no. 351, 48–91 (in Japanese).

Kim, Icksoo (1995c), 'TRADP and the Prospects of Northeast Asian Economic Cooperation', *Asian Perspective* (jointly published by Portland State University and Kyungnam University), **19** (2), 75–102.

Kim, Icksoo (1995d), 'Promotion of Cross-border Trade and Progressive Harmonization of Investment Mechanism in Lew Seokjin (ed.), *Tumen River Area Development Project: The Political Economy of Cooperation in Northeast Asia: The Political Economy of Cooperation in Northeast Asia*', Ch.12, 217–56.

Kim, Won Bae, Campbell, B. O., Valencia, M. and Cho Lee-Jay (eds) (1992), *Regional Economic Cooperation in Northeast Asia* (Proceedings of the Vladivostok Conference), Hawaii: East–West Center.

Korea Chamber of Commerce (1996), Materials for Rajin-Sonbong Investment Promotion Forum (in Korean).

Korea Investment and Trade Promotion Corporation (1996), 'Rajin–Sonbong Economic Trade Zone: Investment Environment and Related Laws and Regulations' (in Korean).

Korea Investment and Trade Promotion Corporation (1998), 'Current Status of FDI into the RSETZ of North Korea', North Korea Newsletter, 18–22.

Kornai, J. (1979), 'Resource-Constrained vs. Demand-Constrained Systems', *Econometrica*, **47** (4), 801–19.

Lavallee, Michael P. (1997), 'The Tumen River Development Area: A Future Trade and Transportation Hub in Northeast Asia', *Far Eastern Economic Review*, July.

Lee Kyong-il (1998), 'General Introduction of the RSETZ', paper presented at the First Rajin-Sonbong Investment Forum held at Rajin during September 24–6, 1998.

Lew Seokjin (ed.) (1995), *Tumen River Area Development Project: The Political Economy of Cooperation in Northeast Asia*, Seoul: The Sejong Institute.

Manguno, Joseph, P. (1993), 'A New Regional Trade Bloc in Northeast Asia?' *The China Business Review*, **20**, March/April, 6–11.

Noland, Marcus and Flake, L.Gordon (1997), 'North Korea and the Rajin–Sonbong Economic and Trade Zone', *Journal of Asian Business*, **13** (2), 99–116.

Park, Sung Sang (1992), 'The Korean Experience and the Potential Role of Financial Policy in Northeast Asian Regional Cooperation', in Kim, Won Bae et al. (eds), *Regional Economic Cooperation in Northeast Asian*, (Proceedings of the Vladivostok Conference), Ch.23, 331–9.

Tumen Secretariat (1999), 'Tumen River Area Development Program' Briefing Notes.

UNDP (1997a), 'Tumen Secretariat Analysis: Overview of Recent Foreign Investment Trends and Major Achievements in the Tumen River Economic Development Area, 1996–97', mimeo.

UNDP (1997b), 'UNDP/Tumen River Area Development Program: The Tumen Region's Major Economic and Developmental Achievements in 1996–97' mimeo.

Valencia M. J. (1994), 'North Korean Infrastructure: Status, Problems, Plans and Implications', mimeo.

Valencia. M. J. (1996), 'Tumen River Project', *East Asian Executive Reports* (published by East Asian Executive Reports), **14** (2), p. 9.

Xinhua News Agency, 'Investors See Promise in Northeast Asia Development', August 18, 1993.

Xinhua News Agency, 'Tumen River Delta: Promising Land of Northeast Asia', May 13, 1993.

Yanbian Tongji Nianjian (1998), Yanbian Pretecture Statistical Yearbook.

Yang Un-chul (1995), 'North Korea's Choice for Survival: Rajin Sonbong Trade and Economic Zone Scheme', in Lew Seokjin (ed.), *Tumen River Area Development Project: The Political Economy of Cooperation in Northeast Asia: The Political Economy of Cooperation in Northeast Asia*, Ch. 6, 117–135.

Yanbian Ribao, August 25, 1997

Yuan, Shuren, Song, Deqing and Tuan, Chi Hsien (1994), 'Geographical Position and Resource Combination of the Tumen River Economic Growth Triangle', paper presented at the Sejong Institute, August 4–5, 1–19.

Zhu, Yuchao (1995), 'Northeast Asian Regional Economic Cooperation: Tumen River Area Development Project', International Studies Association Conference, February.

Index

acid rain 248
agglomeration effects 274–75
agglomeration type 271
Agreed Framework 6, 20
agricultural reform 131
air pollution 248
Asian Development Bank 22
asymmetric information 144
autarkic development 95
automobile industry 285
aviation transport 224
backbone networks 201
Bank of Korea 72, 237
big-bang reforms 120
big-bang strategy 128
bourgeois capitalism 318
brinkmanship 19, 89
  strategy 7
build–operate–transfer (BOT) 233, 251
Cabinet system 25
capital goods imports 53, 55
capitalist contamination 318
capital stock 73, 80, 100
catching up 100, 112
China's prominence 76
Chinese assistance 20
Chinese Communist Party 139
Chinese economic reforms 122
Chinese industrial reform 132
coal-dependency 260
coal production 241
communication systems 223
comparative advantage 60, 69, 79, 297
competition-oriented restructuring 209
competitiveness 297
complementary effects 250
Constitutional amendments 25
contract responsibility system 123, 131
coordination costs 144
cost-based tariffs 186
credible commitment 186
cross-border trade 303–4, 306–7, 320
cross-financing 203, 210
crude oil 242
double-tracking 223
DPRK export 57–8
DPRK import 58–9
dual-track approach 137
dual-track credit market 136
dual-track price system 133, 136
dual-track strategy 128
duty-free 305
East Asia economies 112
East German economy 147
East German restructuring process 145
East Siberia 250
economic cooperation 239, 252, 295

economic crisis 54
economic development 33, 216
economic engagement 28
economic growth 99, 186, 215
economic incentives 324
economic infrastructure 52
economic reform 6, 88, 108, 127, 327
economies of scale 211
economy-wide transition 145
educational attainment 105
education stock 101
efficiency 128
electrical and electronics industry 284
electricity trade 251–52
electric networks 239
electric power demand 244
electric power import 245
embargo 87
energy consumption 237
energy cooperation 249, 251, 254, 259
energy efficiency 244, 246
energy shortage 250, 261
energy supply 240
engagements 22
entrepôt 306, 315
  trade 303
environmental cooperation 248
export markets 314
export-processing base 303, 312
export-processing zone 304
expressways network 223
extensive development 47
fiber-optic cables 208
finance center 308
food crisis 20
foreign capital 14, 184, 210
foreign direct investment 87, 209, 301–302
foreign exchange reform 133
foreign investments 235
foreign investment law 97
foreign investors 208, 303, 319
foreign trade 48
Four Party Peace Talks 22
fundamental reforms 109, 113
gas pipelines 251, 257
general equilibrium model 79
geo-economic rationality 319
geographical proximity 314
geography 100
geo-political logic 319
German privatization strategy 172
government revenues 74
gradualist 131
growth strategy 97
hierarchy 144
historical diversity 275
horizontal mergers 172
humanitarian assistance 20
human capital 101
human resources 94, 101, 105, 295
hydroelectric power plant 242, 250
idiosyncratic knowledge 173
industrial development 273, 295
industrial zones 277, 282
information infrastructure 186
institutional quality 104
interconnection 247
interconnection of electric power system 249, 253
international community 27
international financial institutions 326
International Monetary Fund (IMF) 22, 72
international trade 81, 85
investment protection 327
investment security 324
iron and steel industry 284

Japan 87
joint ventures 311
juche 70, 86, 97, 301
jurisdictional conflicts 325
Kim Dae Jung 22, 28
Kim Il Sung 21, 70
Kim Jong Il 24–6
Kombinate 148, 150–52, 154, 169
Korea Energy Development Organization (KEDO) 19, 238
Korean Peninsula 278, 298
Korean War 3, 22, 34
Korea's economic planning 232
Labor Force 46
  distribution of 46
  participation rates 47
labor-intensive industries 298
liberalization policy 208
life expectancy 107
Light Water Reactor Nuclear Power Plant (LWRNL) 238
liquidation 166
localization effect 275
locational factors 290
locational plans 270, 282
long-term growth 101
long-run economic growth 105
machinery industry 284
malnutrition 62
management buy-outs (MBOs) 158, 163
market economy 97, 143
marketization 123, 137
market liberalization 121, 128
market-oriented pricing reform 231
market-oriented reforms 113
market structure 150, 209
mergers 150, 161
military conflict 113
military manpower 40
mirror statistics 39, 60
modernization project 207
monetary union 84
monopoly structure 211
motorization 223
muddling through 4, 108, 110
multiple equilibria 130
National Unification Board (NUB) 72
natural resources 100
negative externalities 275
network externalities 183
non-ferrous metals 284
non-metallic mineral industry 283
non-state Sector 242
North Korean economy 3, 51, 70, 84, 97, 139
North Korean government 73
North Korean leadership 327
North Korean per capita GDP 112
North Korean regime 21, 97, 113
North Korea's diplomatic environment 89
North Korea's energy policy 240
North Korea's fertility 35
North Korea's industrial location 295
North Korea's international trade 48
North Korea's labor force 44
North Korea's level of urbanization 37
North Korea's life expectancy 36
North Korea's military burden 41
North Korea's population 34, 193
North Korea's telecommunications 199
North Korea's transport infrastructure 218
nuclear power generation 243
nutrition survey 24
oil refineries 242

open door policy 4, 123
openness 103, 129
overseas loans 232
ownership 144
ownership concentration 146
Pareto-improvement 121
Pareto-improving transition 119
petrochemical industry 283
potential losers 120
private ownership 144
private sector participation 233
privatization 144, 152, 156, 169, 172, 208, 211
  of the electricity sector 250
product differentiation 297
production factors 272
production-specific factors 271
productivity 297
public ownership 144
rail-oriented transport system 222
railway electrification 219
railway network 219
Rajin–Sonbong Economic and Trade Zone (RSETZ) 184, 301–305
rapid privatization 157, 166
rationing system 323
reform without losers 120, 139
regional imbalances 295
relationship-based investments 313
remittances 76
restitution 158, 164
restructuring 152, 154–7, 166, 168, 209
restructuring policy 171, 173
reunification 21
road networks 223
road transport 220
Russian collapse 20
Russian gas 254, 256
Russian law 260
saving rate 122, 127
seaport 220
second economy 21
self-sufficiency 5, 60, 69, 97
self-sufficient energy policy 245
shipbuilding industry 285
Siberian gas production 255
social infrastructure 11, 216
social stability 139
South Korea 3, 70, 87, 108
South Korean electric power system 247
South Korean gas industry 260
South Korean per capita GDP 112
South Korea's industrial structure 295
South Korea's transport investments 226, 229
South Korea's work force 45
Soviet 42
  break-up 55
  collapse 4, 20, 63
  economy 323
Soviet–DPRK commerce 49
Soviet-type economy 32
Soviet Union 256
Stalinist accounting 323
state-owned enterprises 85, 136
state power 130
steel industry 241
sulfur dioxide emissions 248
Sunshine policy 22, 313
Supreme People's Assembly 25
systemic collapse 88
tax reforms 135
tax revenues 233
technical efficiency 100
technological gaps 297
telecommunications equipment 198
telecommunications infrastructure 186, 207

telecommunications network 190, 198
textile industry 283
thermal power plants 242
total factor productivity 79
tourism agreement 24
tourist center 304
township and village enterprises (TVEs) 123–24
trade deficits 76
trade distortions 79
trade performance 50–51
trade shock 71
train control 223
Trans-China Railway (TCR) 278
transitional economies 85
transition economies 196, 207
transport and logistical infrastructure 319
transportation costs 273
transportation factors 271
transportation infrastructure 311
transportation technologies 272
transport demand 224
transport infrastructure 215, 233, 320, 328
transport infrastructure investment 231, 235
Trans-Siberia Railway (TSR) 278
Treuhandanstalt (THA) 142, 158
Tumen River Economic Development Area (TREDA) 301
United Nations Development Program (UNDP) 23, 81, 259
universal connectivity 211
urbanization effect 275
underinvestment 313
wireless local loop (WLL) 197
wood industry 283
working-age population 102, 107
World Bank 22, 233
World Food Program 23, 81